KEATS AND THE DAEMON KING

KEATS
and the Daemon King

WERNER W. BEYER

NEW YORK

OXFORD UNIVERSITY PRESS

1947

PRINTED IN THE UNITED STATES OF AMERICA

TO

My Mother and Father

❧ PREFACE ❦

As THE one-hundred-fiftieth anniversary of the birth of John Keats passes, his stature as man, poet, and thinker continues to grow. Deeper and more widespread study of his life and writings has led to the realization of his enduring greatness. That his poems and letters have depth beneath their beauty and reflect the thorniness of life is the discovery virtually of our time. From one whose 'name was writ in water' has risen the spirit of a man heroic in strength of character and mind: the poet who 'is with Shakespeare.'

His character has long since been vindicated. His aim, in poetry and the drama, and the incomparable achievement in the four short years of his poetical life have been pointed out. Some of the profundities in his thought about life and his art have been laid bare. Painfully and laboriously particles of truth have been found by many critics and scholars and have been fitted into the likeness of the real Keats. Only gradually have the conflicts, both spiritual and poetical, and the sharply focused aspiration in which he lived and wrote been discerned. The ageless worth of his work has been perceived, and gradually the events and influences, personal and literary, that molded his career have been realized. We know that he was nourished first by Spenser and then by the eighteenth-century poets, Hunt, and the Elizabethans, by Greek myth, Wordsworth, Shakespeare, and Milton. Yet in some quarters understanding has not progressed beyond that of Matthew Arnold's day.

Arnold was impelled to say: 'Keats as a poet is abundantly and enchantingly sensuous; the question with some people will be whether he is anything else.' That doubt still blinds many people. Intellectually and spiritually, they still say, Keats was insignificant;

sensory delight was the cardinal fact of his life. Did he not exclaim, 'O for a life of Sensations'? Since what he meant quite escapes them, in their eyes he lacked the higher vision of the greatest poets. His poetry was not a criticism of life. He was indifferent even to the problems of his time. All this is still said by many.

Why is it? 'We read fine things but never feel them to the full until we have gone the same steps as the author.' Impressionistic criticism, confined to what is expressed in the art work itself and circumscribed by the critic's temper and competence, is beset with pitfalls—even as the history of Shakespeare criticism attests. All the influences are not yet known. And Keats' language and thought 'swayed in the winds of self-discovered doctrine.' Thus there is no question that he used such words as 'sensations' with various mean- ings, which were sometimes different from everyday usage, and that he has not yet been fully understood. The meaning of *Endym- ion* and parts of the great Odes, the intention in *Lamia,* Keats' very philosophy of life and art are still moot matters. Despite his ever-increasing popularity and the study and penetration of such critics as Colvin, Robert Bridges, De Sélincourt, Garrod, Murry, and Thorpe, a large portion of the picture has remained utterly blank. Not only is a good deal of Keats' thought still unclear; in his best-loved poetry many allusions and symbols are still unidenti- fied. Without an understanding of these, our grasp of his thought must at best remain partial—and of questionable authenticity.

While it is often overlooked, the setting a work of art or thought had in its creator's mind is obviously of great moment in any attempt to understand that work of art or thought. This is particu- larly true of works whose mode of communication is elliptical: that is, in which thought is conveyed by symbols, as is so often the case in poetry. Now allusions and symbols are clues to the 'setting.' And symbols, of which Keats was peculiarly fond, are somewhere de- rived. If their source can be found and the background can be re- constructed, we can much more readily see the values the symbols had in the poet's mind. His thought, contained in those symbols, can be disclosed; and a whole work, often revolving upon a key passage, can be clarified. This is the peculiar value of the study of a poet's reading, for allusions and symbols are, more often than not, literary in origin.

This book is concerned with the literary and biographical background, the genesis, and the meaning of *Endymion, The Eve of St. Agnes, Lamia,* and various other poems. It explores an overlooked portion of Keats' experience: the demonstrable source of some of his most vital symbols. By throwing light upon their source it clarifies and, I believe, greatly enriches the meaning of a host of lines and passages, indeed the meaning of whole poems in the canon, and illuminates entire areas of Keats' art and thought. Till now, at least one region in which Keats spent many hours rich in emotional and imaginative experience has been all but completely overlooked. While the inspiration he drew from Shakespeare and Greek myth has been fruitfully studied, his use of daemonology, which stimulated his imagination no less persistently and which provided a considerable number of themes and images, has heretofore been ignored. Yet this daemonology played a key part in his characteristic mode of expression and in his conception of *Sleep and Poetry,* and *The Poet, Endymion, The Eve of St. Agnes,* and *Lamia.* The neglect of this portion of his background has led to frequent misunderstanding of his symbolism and his imagery, his architecture, intention, and thought. This study will touch upon all these elements in uncovering an extraordinarily rich mine in which Keats found inspiration and much ore. Among other things, it will also help us, I think, to understand far more clearly the conception and development of three of his best-known works, the creative process underlying them, and their meaning.

We shall be concerned with an enchanted isle, which has evidently remained obscure because of its location in the shadow of Shakespeare. For Keats knew also C. M. Wieland's *Oberon.* As we shall see, he traversed its fairyland again and again, with increasingly momentous results. He did not in the least attempt to efface his tracks or conceal the fact that it repeatedly guided the imaginative processes of his mind. Instead, he left plentiful clues to the identity of the 'tale from faery land,' the tale of the 'liege-lord of all the Elves and Fays.' Our initial purpose will be to trace those clues and to point out the phenomenal riches to which they led.

It is more and more clear that Keats' book, like Milton's, is the 'precious life-blood of a master-spirit': that his writings reflect the aspirations, events, and conflicts of his own life. Yet Keats, like Shakespeare, invented none of his plots. And it has been said that 'of all the romantic poets Keats was the most "literary" in the sense that almost all his work bears the impress of his really wide reading.' Since John Livingston Lowes' *Road to Xanadu,* it has been widely realized that no creating mind works in a vacuum, and that his reading is a crucial part of a poet's experience. It has become clear that the imagination is a shaping power which 'dissolves, diffuses, dissipates' the stuff of experience, in its broadest sense, 'in order to re-create.' We shall repeatedly observe this process, and the truth of Coleridge's dictum, in tracing some of Keats' symbols and in studying his use of Wieland's romance.

Such a study bids fair to increase greatly our understanding of the ways of the creative imagination and also of the achievement in the four years allotted to Keats: 'the most prodigious four years in the life of a genius,' thinks Mr. Murry, 'of which we have record.' The substance in *Oberon* not only illumines many of Keats' finished art forms, their impelling spirit, and their curious inter-relations; it also reflects the process of their fashioning. It enables us to observe whole clumps of his ore in the very act of mutation or creation. What is more, in his use of *Oberon* is preserved for all to see a record of his evolving thought, maturing judgment, and sense of artistic fitness. Finally in this restorable portion of the background-of-the-unexpressed lies a new answer to Arnold's 'question.'

•   •   •

This book is the first of two concerned with the effect in England of Wieland's *Oberon*. Some years ago, spurred by the realization of an error of omission of considerable consequence in literary history, the author published preliminary drafts of some chapters in the *Review of English Studies* and then temporarily laid them aside. In this book he confines himself to Wieland's relation to Keats.

Since to most English readers of today Wieland is little more than a name, it was found advisable to sketch his contributions to German and world literature. The remaining sections of the Introduction are vitally concerned with the daemon king and the romance that played so unsuspected a part in the English romantic movement. And since familiarity with *Oberon* is essential for understanding this book, a synopsis of the romance also appears in the Introduction.

In connection with the Keats chapters, I must first of all acknowledge the impetus given my curiosity by a passage in Colvin's great biography of the poet. Secondly, I wish to remember the late John Livingston Lowes for his inspiring interest and early encouragement. To the following four members of the Department of English and Comparative Literature of Columbia University I shall always be deeply indebted: To Ernest Hunter Wright and Oscar James Campbell I owe much for faith, guidance, and invaluable criticism. To Emery Edward Neff I owe many stimulating suggestions. And to Susanne Howe Nobbe I extend my grateful thanks for editorial help. In addition, my wife has contributed to almost every page. And since much of the research and writing was done while I was the incumbent first of the Lydig and then of a William Bayard Cutting Fellowship, I should like to express here my gratitude to the generous donors and Dean George B. Pegram of Columbia University. Finally, I want to thank the Louise Foote Foundation for help at a critical hour.

To earlier students of Keats my indebtedness is incalculable. Particular acknowledgment must be made to the work of Mr. John

Middleton Murry, Professors H. W. Garrod, C. D. Thorpe, Douglas Bush, and C. L. Finney; and to Mr. M. R. Ridley and Mr. M.
Buxton Forman. The latter I wish to thank too for some information communicated by letter.

New York, N. Y.   WERNER W. BEYER

❧ CONTENTS ❧

KEATS AND THE DAEMON KING

> . . . its music long,
> Like woven sounds of streams and breezes, held
> His inmost sense suspended in its web
> Of many-coloured woof and shifting hues.
>
> —P. B. Shelley

The mighty abstract Idea I have of Beauty in all things . . . Then I should be most enviable—with the yearning Passion I have for the beautiful, connected and made one with the ambition of my intellect.

> —Keats, letter to his brother George: October 1818.

❧ INTRODUCTION ❧

i: *C. M. Wieland: His Achievements and Fame*

THE EIGHTEENTH CENTURY was peculiarly an age of revolutions. Along with political upheavals in America and France, that century produced a less sanguinary but far-reaching revolt in Germany. Of that revolt, against the domination of German life and thought by the fashionable language and culture, literary tastes, and conventions of pre-revolutionary France, was born a golden age that left its marks upon all the western world. The greatest figures of that age—which transformed philosophy, science, and history, literature and man's faith—were Klopstock and Lessing, Winckelmann, Herder and Kant, Wieland, Schiller, and Goethe. In the last the world long ago recognized one of its greatest poets. Those writers, however, who prepared the way inevitably have been over-shadowed. This was especially true in the case of Wieland.

As late as the mid-eighteenth century, it will be recalled, German letters were insignificant beside those of England and France. The exhausting religious wars, for which Germany had been chief battleground, and the poverty, misery, and depopulation of the previous century; the lack of political unity and any national tradition; the ascendancy of France internationally and the contempt in which the German language was held by the Francophile aristocracy and, indeed, by Frederick the Great: all this had retarded German development. It was not until a newly prosperous middle class became self-conscious that the need for a literature began to be felt.[1] * Closer commercial bonds with mercantile England spurred the German peoples in their groping, and the first glimmerings of renewed literary activity came to owe much to English examples.[2]

* Numbered notes, corresponding to this reference and later ones, will be found in the Appendix, p. 299 f.

3

In 1750, German literature, with some striking exceptions, consisted chiefly in sundry imitations of foreign models. Gottsched had tried to give the language and drama a more elegant French form, while Bodmer and Breitinger, his bitter foes, had championed Milton and other English writers. Various lyrists had sung more or less feebly, and Gellert had produced his rather insipid *Fables*. Seeds of Pope and Swift had borne green fruit in some satires; while novels of Defoe and Richardson had been for the most part dully imitated, as had the nature poetry of Thomson. But at best this was light before dawn.

With Klopstock day broke. In the first cantos of his *Messiah* (1748), German poetry quickened with a new idealism, ponderously and diffusely voiced, to be sure, but in bolder flights than before. The 'German Milton' went on to themes of liberty and the national past, and with lofty if vague emotion pointed the way. But his own promise as poet was never really fulfilled.

What Klopstock only partly succeeded in doing for poetry, Lessing achieved in criticism and the drama. His critical writings, in the most powerful German prose since the Reformation, redefined the spheres of plastic and poetic art, challenged the basic tenets of French poetics, and destroyed the clogging French dramaturgy. In its place Lessing set the Greeks and pointed out Shakespeare as the essence of the dramatic. And he virtually founded the German drama. In *Minna von Barnhelm* (1767) he wrote the best German comedy for many a decade, and in *Emilia Galotti* (1772) he set younger writers like Schiller the example of urging freedom.

Christoph Martin Wieland (1733-1813), a gifted and prolific writer, was the original 'sage of Weimar.'[3] For long he was more popular than Goethe, and he 'probably maintained a popularity more unbroken than any of his contemporaries.'[4] Poet, novelist, and editor, essayist, translator, and scholar, he was read as eagerly by his rivals as by that growing reading public which, more than any other, he attracted at home and abroad to German letters. He was an influential and versatile writer whose works appeared in many editions and more than 375 translations into 14 languages.[5] In the English-speaking world of our time, the extent of his fame and great success is as often overlooked as his remarkable achievements are minimized. To understand him, the worldly wise son of the eighteenth century, we must try to see him with the eyes of his contemporaries.

Starting his career with pious effusions amid the dearth of German literature about 1750, young Wieland, characteristically groping for a balance between the rational and sensuous sides of his nature, soon discovered Shakespeare and other English authors, the writers of the Enlightenment, and Tasso and Ariosto. Attracted to humor and realism, he began to write in a lighter, more worldly vein than before. About 1760 he met the cultivated Count von Stadion and began acutely to feel the lack of reason and of a cosmopolitan attitude in German life and thought. From his own experience he realized the want of self-knowledge and harmonious self-culture in the German people. And he sensed, too, the lack of urbanity, grace, and sensuousness in their language. With considerable judgment, he set out to remedy all these shortcomings. Sensitive to lightness of style in the French and Italian, he began to cultivate the neglected art of amusing. But he learned much more from Greece and England. He absorbed not a little of their spirit and soon set about infusing it into the German, in translations and creations in prose and verse which became ever more considerable.

The first in point of time of his four outstanding achievements was his translation (1762-6) of twenty-two plays of Shakespeare.* Undiscouraged by the poverty of his native tongue and the lack of

---

*He began the study of English about 1752 and was introduced to the plays by Bodmer in 1755. By 1758, before Shakespeare had become a cult among pioneers like Lessing and Mendelssohn, Wieland was censuring Voltaire for his notorious vilification. In 1761 he translated and successfully staged an ungarbled version of *The Tempest,* apparently the first Shakespeare production in Germany since the English comedians. (See F. W. Meisnest's 'Wieland's Translation of Shakespeare' in *MLR,* x, 12; also Ernst Stadler, 'Wielands Shakespeare' in *Quellen und Forschungen* . . . No. 107, Strasburg, 1910; and, of course, Friedrich Gundolf's *Shakespeare und der deutsche Geist.*)

adequate dictionaries, with an English text (Warburton's) in a deplorable state of emendation, he produced the first version of Shakespeare in German. Through Wieland's prose the young Goethe, Schiller, and a host of others first met that mighty spirit whose influence in Germany can hardly be exaggerated. For many years that influence was felt primarily through Wieland's translation, among the many fruits of which were *Götz von Berlichingen* and *Die Räuber.*

While working on Shakespeare, he also turned to the novel. In quick succession he produced novels extraordinary for psychologic insight, learning, knowledge of the world, and felicity of style. To German prose fiction, which had been dull or lurid or else shallow and insipid, he brought much of enduring value. He lifted it out of the sphere of idle *divertissement* and gave it depth, made of it an artistic medium for broaching the problems of civilized living. In *Agathon* (1766), he was the first German writer to attempt, on the strength of personal observation and experience, to depict with truth and conviction the inner development of an eminent man.[6] As in his other Hellenizing novels, designed to broaden the mind as well as entertain, Wieland did not try to reconstruct antiquity yet succeeded in bringing the antiquarian novel a step nearer to verisimilitude. Lessing's comment is pointed: the great critic called *Agathon* 'the first and only novel for the thoughtful reader of classical taste.' In it, moreover, Wieland anticipated important elements of later Weimar thought, by his interest in the problems of inner experience and the harmonious cultivation of all the faculties of man.[7] Of his later novels two at least have greater artistic finish.* *Die Abderiten* (*The Republic of Fools*) is still thought one of the best German comic novels for its good-humored satire on contemporary life; and *Aristippus* is a better antiquarian study of Greece. But *Agathon* remains the forerunner of *Wilhelm Meister.*[8]

Wieland found time to edit his famous journal, *Der Teutsche*

---

* Shelley read at least four and found them 'delightful.'

Merkur. During crucial years (1773-95) it did much to arouse and foster the literary, cultural, and political interests of the German peoples. To this Goethe attested.* G. P. Gooch adds that Wieland's 'cool and observant mind' and vast literary output made his readers look to him for guidance not only in literature and taste but in practical problems of life and politics. 'The only political head among the classic writers of Germany . . . unlike Goethe and Schiller, he worked steadily at the formation of opinion.'⁹ He sympathized with the American cause. And while he shared the early enthusiasm for the revolution in France, like many another, he became increasingly skeptical of its ultraradical manifestations. Yet he sketched the good and evil of the troubled period with rare insight.

Our chief interest in connection with Keats, however, is Wieland's poetry, his greatest single achievement. His Latin ease and grace and his power over diction were particularly revolutionary in German verse. Both innovator and master in poetical forms and style, he was much more than a stylist. And he was far more than a genial and witty worldling. In Klinger's phrase, 'he conjured the delicate romantic hues about [the German] Parnassus and relieved the sombre heavy colors.'¹⁰ He not only restored rhyme to favor and adapted freer forms like ottava rima to the language; he revived poetic narration. He wrote many poems on classical themes: his *Musarion,* in the spirit of the day, is still one of the most graceful didactic poems in German. He ushered into German literature the gorgeous tales of the Orient. And, significantly, he wrote on long untried themes of chivalry and faëry. With *Das Wintermärchen* (1776) he opened the mine of the *Arabian Nights. Geron der Adlige* (1777), perhaps the best of his serious romances, is the first modern German poem on Arthurian legend. In *Alceste* Wie-

---

* Goethe said: 'Wieland's influence upon the public was uninterrupted and lasting. He molded his age, gave direction to the taste as to the judgment of his contemporaries.' ('Zu brüderlichem Andenken Wielands.') In the 1825 Conversations Goethe said, 'To Wieland all upper Germany owes its style. It learned much from him.' (J. P. Eckermann, *Gespräche* . . . Leipzig, 1883, I, 136.)

land wrote 'the first German opera libretto of thoughtful content and worthy form.'[11] Finally he wrote his greatest poem.

In *Oberon,* says C. E. Vaughan, Wieland 'produced what probably still remains *the best narrative poem of any length in the language.'* (Italics mine.)[12] More than one reader has thought that 'in all later [German] romanticism there is no work which in brilliancy of imagination, in lightness of movement, and in golden worth of sentiment, surpasses the ever-youthful romance.'[13] Both in Germany and in England these qualities were appreciated far more intensely than has been realized. Internationally famous, *Oberon* was Wieland's masterpiece and most enduringly popular work.

Its reception in Germany is significant. As early as 26 July 1779, after hearing the opening cantos, Goethe wrote in his Journal:

It is great art in the whole, as far as I've heard it, and in detail. It . . . is woven together with a great poetical understanding, truth of characters, sensations, descriptions . . . so that it will not be his fault if it does not entertain and delight.[14]

On 3 July 1780, in a famous letter, Goethe wrote: 'So long as poetry remains poetry . . . *Oberon* will be loved and admired as a *masterpiece of poetical art.'* Herder thought it 'an excellent poem in matter and form, perhaps the best of its kind.' Lessing spoke of it 'with the greatest applause.' And Klopstock's delight was even conveyed to Wordsworth in the fall of 1798. The passage in *Biographia Literaria* is well known:

[Klopstock] said Wieland was a charming author, and a sovereign master of his own language: that in this respect Goethe could not be compared to him, nor indeed could any body else. He said that his fault was to be fertile to exuberance. I [Wordsworth] told him the OBERON had just been translated into English. He asked me if I was not delighted with the poem.[15]

Schiller admired it yet more. He alluded to it,[16] borrowed from it, for years wanted to adapt the romance to the operatic stage, and as late as 1795, in *Naive and Sentimental Poetry*, called Wieland 'our cleverest and most charming poet.'[17]

First published in 1780, *Oberon* had been reissued five times by 1792 in editions whose perfected verse reveals Wieland's craftsmanship. The definitive version appeared in 1796 in four simultaneous editions of his *Works,* and has continued to be reprinted as a favorite classic in school, popular, and illustrated de luxe editions. Such was its appeal about 1800 that John Quincy Adams said of his years in Germany (1798-1801), *'Wieland was there I think decidedly the most popular of the German poets.'* (Italics mine.) [18] Adams himself felt Wieland's spell so profoundly that he translated the lengthy *Oberon* in three complete versions and part of a fourth, all of which have recently been recovered. Another distinguished visitor to Germany, the poet Thomas Campbell, wrote in 1800: *'I cannot conceive of a more perfect poet than their favorite Wieland.'* (Italics mine.) [19]

Regarded as one of the greatest writers in Germany, Wieland was also among the very first known in England. Miss Stockley has said that 'after Gessner Wieland was probably the most popular' German author in England in the second half of the eighteenth century.[20] By 1800 at least eleven of his works had been translated, while fourteen further excerpts had appeared. And his prestige, unusual both as to quality and quantity, lasted long.* Especially *Oberon* was widely known to several generations. Sir Sidney Colvin said that it played a part in the English romantic movement; yet how vital that part was has not heretofore been suspected.

Of Wieland's after-fame in Germany little need be said here.[21] Because of his great prestige and manifold activities in the forefront

---

* It is significant that no less than five of the best earlier translators (John Richardson, William Taylor of Norwich, Coleridge, William Sotheby, and Henry Crabb Robinson) undertook or published one or more translations from his works. Three great publishers (John Murray, Bell, and Longman) issued translations, while J. Johnson and Robert Burns' publisher Cadell speculated with several in quick succession. Between 1764 and 1861 at least 38 of his works were translated entirely or in part, and of his most important ones only *Aristippus* and *Musarion* were not published entire, yet even they had been translated in manuscript.

of a turbulent and shifting age, he was often violently attacked by partisan groups. Although he was never gross, the pietists early burned and railed at his books as licentious. Political extremists termed him a renegade, although he was always a clear-sighted liberal. The doctrinaire romantics abused his rationalistic prose writings. And the zealous nationalists berated the aging dean of letters more and more acrimoniously for his cosmopolitanism. In some quarters this animus perpetuated itself. But though his fame was dimmed in time by that of his friend Goethe, his eclipse was neither so complete nor so sudden as some historians still assume. His *Collected Works,* in forty-two volumes, were reissued four times between 1813 and 1853, while many editions of individual and selected writings have appeared steadily into the present century.

It is particularly unsound, however, to forget his great contemporary fame, and that 'both the Hellenic and the romantic revival stood deeply in his debt' [22]—far more deeply, indeed, than has been realized. For Wieland, while of the eighteenth century, lived on into the nineteenth as a popular romantic poet. Coleridge, Wordsworth, and Southey knew *Oberon* early. And in 1813, when their prestige was increasing, when Scott had turned to the novel and Byron's star was in the ascendant, many English readers shared the opinion of the anonymous critic who wrote that Wieland 'was the most distinguished of that galaxy of learned men who during the last thirty years have raised the literary fame of Germany.' [23] In this study it is important to remember that when Keats' career was beginning, Wieland was widely known, especially for his *Oberon.*

ii: *The Antecedents and Revolutionary Nature of 'Oberon'*

The fairy king Oberon first became familiar in England through Sir John Bourchier's (Lord Berners') version (1534) of *Huon of Burdeux.*[1] In that thirteenth- or fourteenth-century romance, based on a lost *chanson de geste* of the late Charlemagne cycle, the Teutonic dwarf Alberich (of the *Nibelungenlied* and the *Heldenbuch*) had become Auberon, 'dwarfe kynge of the fayrey.' His antecedents lost in the mists of time and medieval geography, this Auberon springs ostensibly of a typical fay of romance.

'Dwarf of the fairy' is he, child of a fairy mother, 'the lady of the [Secret] isle,' and a mortal father, Julius Caesar . . . *Auberon . . . is mortal*, he can weep, he falls sick; but he is never of more stature than a child of three . . . and his magical powers are so absolute that he has only to wish, and his will accomplishes itself . . . He is a much better Christian than Huon . . . is buried in an abbey, and his soul is carried to heaven by . . . innumerable . . . angels. (Italics mine.) ²

His powers of prophecy and enchantment are the gifts of his mother; his dwarfed stature (wherein he differs from his taller retainers) derives from the enchantment of a wicked fairy. Thus he has not a few connections with the fays of romance.*

This Auberon left his marks on Spenser's *Faerie Queene*, Greene's *James the Fourth*, and Middleton's *Chinon of England*. But also his name and some features were adopted and made famous by Shakespeare in *A Midsummer Night's Dream*, in which he wrought a new fairy mythology of three distinct elements: the folklore fairies of England, the fays of romance, and classical prototypes.

---

* The confusing fairy problem has been clarified and painstakingly documented by Professor M. W. Latham in *The Elizabethan Fairies: The Fairies of Folklore and the Fairies of Shakespeare* (N. Y., Columbia Univ. Press, 1930), which incorporates all earlier conclusions. The fays of romance, Miss Latham cites by way of contrast, 'were mysterious ladies, "primarily enchantresses" and "often regarded as mortal" with "no limitations of beauty, age, or resources." They dwelt in some inaccessible country concealed from human eyes by glamour, or in some mysterious islands of the ocean, or in the far-off island paradise of Avalon, usually unapproachable save through their guidance or that of one of their messengers. They came into the world to gain a knight's love . . . concerned themselves with pleasure and the joys of love, and used their power to shift their shapes, to build enchanted dwellings, to fashion magic objects, to take dire revenge on mortals who had offended them, and to insure for their mortal lovers youth and never-ending bliss as long as they remained in fairyland. As may be seen, they were not the fairies of sixpences and shoes.' (See ibid. pp. 27-8 and references.)

Allusions and incidents in more than a dozen plays show that Shakespeare was deeply versed in the folk-fairies, those 'real and fearful spirits' that long consorted, in English life and law, with the devil, witches, and other 'tempters of the night.' He depicted their traditional human stature, dairy activities, moonlight sports, their knowledge of herbs and influence on disease, their fondness for cleanliness and chastity, their gifts and pinchings, misleading of nocturnal wayfarers, and penchant for changelings and the abduction of grownfolk. Yet his knowledge and representation of these fairies of popular tradition were eventually ignored because of the charm of his 'poetic and imaginary fairyland' in the one play wherein he modified the dreadful folk-fairies.

While the fairies of *A Midsummer Night's Dream* retain many folk characteristics, they have been made consistently good:

No longer do they function as the mischievous and dangerous beings they were believed to be, with occasional erratic lapses into beneficence and the bestowal of good fortune . . . Every aspect of their wickedness . . . and devilish connection is omitted . . . and the period of their earthly materialization is devoted to making the world happier and more beautiful . . .

All their sinister traits have disappeared, and

only their rulers are still invested with formidable powers and uncertain tempers. *Diminutive, pleasing and picturesque sprites, with small garden names and small garden affairs, associated with moonbeams and butterflies, they present themselves as a new race of fairies,* as different from the popular fairies of tradition as are those fairies from the fays of the medieval romances. (Italics mine.)

In effecting this change, by which eventually the superstitious fear of their predecessors was destroyed, Shakespeare made the fairies tiny, 'innocuous, and almost negligible attendants upon two literary or mythological sovereigns, Oberon and Titania.'[3]

The latter name he derived from the tale of Actæon in Ovid's *Metamorphoses,* where 'Titania' is a synonym for the chaste Diana, long regarded as the fearsome sovereign of fairies. Shakespeare's Titania, however, is no longer sinister nor strictly chaste, and her concerns are quite different. Oberon came directly from Berners' *Huon of Burdeux*.[4] Shakespeare modified its Auberon and made him a permanent medieval monarch, complete with jester and attendants, of his new race of fairies. His Oberon, while jealous, unfaithful, and irascible toward Titania, is otherwise beneficent and tender-hearted. He retains traits of the nocturnal folk-fairies, such as knowledge of herbs and fondness for moonlight dancing. He also has some physical traits of his namesake in *Huon of Burdeux*. His new and characteristic action, however, is to assist true love.*

Now Wieland's Oberon resembles both the Auberon of Shakespeare's source and the monarch of his fairy play. Yet Wieland's is essentially a spirit of quite another sort, with far greater powers than either.

·   ·   ·

Wieland began his tale toward the end of 1778, little more than a decade after completing his version of Shakespeare.[5] In a preface to *Oberon,* he acknowledged as his sources *Huon de Bordeaux* (as summarized, however, by Count de Tressan in the *Bibliothèque Universelle des Romans*), Chaucer's 'Merchant's Tale,' and *A Midsummer Night's Dream*. He said his Oberon was the same person as the 'King of Fayries' in the two English works, and added that the manner of interweaving the fairy rulers' discord with the story of Huon and Rezia was the characteristic feature of his poem. Others, however, have discerned an achievement far greater.[6]

After the manner of its kind, the prose romance *Huon de Bordeaux* deals with an interminable series of heroic, comical, and mock-heroic exploits—mostly at the expense of the Saracens—of a knight sent on a fantastic quest by an aged, choleric, and debased

---

* In later English literature, owing to Shakespeare's influence, Oberon appears chiefly, as in Drayton's *Nymphidia* or Herrick's *Hesperides,* as a frustrated and diminutive ruler of garden fairies. Particularly in Drayton, he is a Lilliputian cuckold, ridiculous in his jealousy.

Charlemagne. It piles incident upon episode, involves Huon in all manner of meaningless adventures, and with the aid of the (mortal) fairy Auberon finally extricates him from a third and fourth anti-climax. While it has a charm of its own, it is an involved and rather amorphous tale. Though Wieland followed its plot closely at the outset and heightened some of the comic features, he omitted more and more, and invented the greater part of the last two-thirds of his action.[7] The quest, meeting with the fairy, passion for a princess, and Oberon's wrath derive from *Huon de Bordeaux*. But the intensification and motivation, the machinery, characterization, and poetry are Wieland's own.

In the old romance Auberon's interest in Huon (incongruously an ignoble and 'perjured simpleton'[8]) had no real foundation. In Wieland's poem the characters have been humanized, motivation has been provided, and the lives of the mortal and preternatural actors have been intertwined with exceptional skill. Thus *Oberon* is composed of three related actions: Huon's quest, the love and trials of Huon and Rezia, and the discord and reconciliation of Oberon and Titania. While Shakespeare's fairies bicker comically over a changeling and marital infidelity, Wieland's king and queen become deeply estranged by a difference in moral outlook. Somewhat like Chaucer's Proserpyna and Pluto (in the 'Merchant's Tale'), they take opposite sides while observing the aged Januarie deceived by the unchaste May.[9] But Oberon's insistence upon truth, constancy, and chastity leads to Titania's banishment until a mortal pair by unswerving love redeem his impassioned oath. Thus the motivation of Oberon's interest in Huon and Rezia is established, while the terms of Titania's banishment govern the whole latter and more serious half of the action. The gain is not only architectural; an impelling ideal of spirituality underlies the best portions of the poem.

But there is another feature, which, to my knowledge, has not been realized clearly. Wieland's Oberon emphatically is *not* the

Oberon of Shakespeare.* Wieland's Oberon is *not* a modified English folk-fairy. Nor is he the male equivalent, if that were possible, of a fay of romance. Indeed, though he possesses some attributes of Chaucer's king of fayerye, some of those of Shakespeare's Oberon and Puck, and some of those of Auberon of the old romance, he is hardly a fairy at all. Wieland's Oberon is a more potent and lofty being, who ranks above any of these in the hierarchy of the supernatural. He represents, I think, a fusion of all these elements with others more cabalistic. For he has almost all of Prospero's powers— which originally were those of Ovid's Medea.† And he has other powers yet more mysterious. He is a creation, in large measure, of occult science: the omniscient, ubiquitous, and all but omnipotent *king of the daemons of the elements.*

We must not confuse the unclean and diabolic demons of Judaeo-Christian lore equipped with hoof and horn with these good

* The fairy king of *MND* is (cf. ii, i) 'jealous,' *'fell and wrath'* toward Titania; is accused of 'versing love To amorous Phillida' and also of coming to the wood a league outside Athens because of Hippolyta 'the bouncing Amazon, Your buskin'd mistress and your warrior love.' (Titania's love for Theseus is likewise known to Oberon.) His 'brawls' have disturbed the fairy sports so that Nature is sympathetically distraught: all this primarily because 'I do but beg a little changeling boy.' He plots to 'torment thee for this injury' and makes use of his knowledge of herbs on two occasions. *'I am invisible'* he says; but he is not omniscient nor even very potent, since, owing to ignorance of the presence of two sets of lovers in the wood, he gives faulty directions to Puck, upon which hinges the main plot of the comedy. Also he must depart 'ere the first cock crow' or shortly thereafter. Again, he says 'I wonder if Titania be awaked, Then what it was that next came in her eye'; and again, 'this falls out better than I could devise.' He would *foster 'true love'* and urges Puck to *'overcast the night'* with fog to prevent a duel. He disowns any connection with 'damned spirits' (iii, ii). And he begins 'to pity' only after Titania 'her fairy sent To bear [the changeling] *to my bower in fairyland';* he then promises that all will be forgotten as 'of a dream.' Upon being reconciled with his queen, he dances with her ('rock the ground whereon these sleepers lie'). On being warned of coming day, he says: 'in silence sad, Trip we after night's shade: We the globe can compass soon, *Swifter* than the wandering moon'; while Titania speaks of 'our *flight'* (iv, i). At the end he blesses the bridal bed to keep Nature's blots from marking its offspring (v, i). The italicized traits are shared by Wieland's Oberon, who also has powers exercised only by Puck: shape-shifting, overcasting the sky, and a certain delight in 'things . . . that befal preposterously.'

† Cf. *The Tempest,* v, i: [Cont. on p. 16.]

daemons, these beings of the vast and mysterious invisible world who since hoary antiquity had been worshiped as the potent spirits animating and controlling nature's four elements of earth and air, fire and water. Wieland's Oberon is king of daemons, as in Platonic myth. Like Diotima's Love in the *Symposium,* 'He is a great spirit [daimon], and like all spirits he is intermediate between the divine and the mortal.' Thus Oberon is the 'guardian god,' a 'kind genius whose protecting grace' is felt like that of a tutelary angel. The awful ruler of all nature, he is 'a spirit,' a 'wood god' whose minions (no mere diminutive fairies, they!) are 'angelic.' The distinction between this conception and the garden fairies of Shakespeare is of vital significance for this book.

Though he is attended by aerial spirits or sylphs and his favorite realm is air, all daemons of all four elements are subject to Oberon's sway. He has strange punitive power over sinners; and like his angelic kindred is the stern and fearsome guardian spirit of righteousness. His preternatural senses and understanding transcend space and time: he appears by day as well as night (unlike nocturnal folk-fairies); he traverses immeasurable distances instantaneously, controls mortal dreams, and reads the hearts of mortals. Yet he acknowledges God and is subject to Fate. This new Oberon is a composite figure to which Wieland, an eminent classical scholar, added at least some of the arcana of daemonology. Wieland knew the fountainhead in Plato's *Symposium* as deeply as the

> 'I have bedimm'd
> The noontide sun, call'd forth the mutinous winds,
> And 'twixt the green sea and the azured vault
> Set roaring war: to the dread-rattling thunder
> Have I given fire . . .
> . . . the strong-based promontory
> Have I made shake . . .
> . . . graves at my command
> Have waked their sleepers, oped, and let 'em forth
> By my so potent art.'

These, essentially the daemonic powers of antiquity and the cabalists, Oberon possesses and exercises in the course of Wieland's romance.

several Platonizing schools of the Greek decadence.[10] He may have taken an initial hint of the daemonic from Shakespeare.[11] But in developing it harmoniously before our eyes he had to be well versed in the occult, for he created an essentially new figure, at once more unearthly, sublime, and potent than Shakespeare's. Master of the fabulous seal of Solomon whose powers repeatedly appear in the *Arabian Nights,* the prime mover of Wieland's tale is clearly a composite figure who has marked affinities with the daemons and angels of antiquity.[12] In this daemonic strain, moreover, lay the reason for some of the profound interest manifested in *Oberon* by certain of the English romanticists—pre-eminently by John Keats.

Wieland conceived his poetical romance at a time in the history of European poetry when the gods of the Pantheon were moribund; when the mythology of Greece, long become conventional, had lost its power to move the imagination. In his preface, Wieland pointed out that the romances and books of chivalry of the twelfth to fourteenth centuries were 'just as much a mine of poetic stuff as the fabulous tales of gods and heroes of the Orient and the Greeks.' And in *Oberon,* for all its initial banter, and all his courtly sophistication, Wieland was a conscious revolutionary, not in medievalism only. For the romantic conception of nature was crystallizing. The eighteenth-century interpretation of nature as mechanical, as the Newtonian world-machine, was giving way. And the romantic view of the universe as metamorphic and organic, as the embodiment and manifestation of that living spirit which is ultimately divine, was crystallizing in the minds of Wieland, his friends Herder and Goethe, and many others. That romantic view (which contained the germ of the later biological approach) needed a new mythology. In creating his daemonology of Shakespearean fairy lore and Platonic myth as machinery for a medieval plot, Wieland anticipated this need. In *Oberon* he created a new world, of youthful freshness, whose every element has its genius or guardian spirit. It is a living world governed by spirits that animate and control its winds and clouds, that are immanent in earth and air, fire and water, and yet through their ruler obey the Creator. In this respect, too, in its new mythology, *Oberon* was revolutionary.

But it was something more. Exuberantly imaginative, it is a charming and sprightly tale rich in marvels, highly colored incidents, and kindling visions. In a style spirited and genial and remarkable for its range, Wieland produced a romance blending banter and sentiment, comic and serious, erotic, heroic, and mystical moods. While he began gracefully with humorous detachment in a light-hearted vein, insensibly he was carried away by a love for the rich diversity of life. He caught not a little of the Shakespearean spirit. ('The mastering of the German tongue . . . for sensuousness and the imagination: that is the influence of Shakespeare' in *Oberon,* said Gundolf.[18]) And with the elfin and iridescent he succeeded in blending some of the color of chivalry and the contagious joy in the fabulous which marked the Middle Ages. In the best portion, finally, he created a provocative tale of sin and penance.

In it some readers may have seen chiefly 'sex and sentiment.' But others, less jaded, saw a meaning implicit in Oberon's nature and oath; a meaning true to life itself, where a moment's forgetfulness leads to long suffering and where the conflict of spirit and flesh is eternal. The resolution of that conflict in *Oberon,* with the help of the daemon king and the hermit, lent the romance poetic vitality and truth, for those who had eyes to see. There is no denying that in *Oberon* Wieland, the courtier and sprightly raconteur, did not maintain or elicit consistently that 'suspension of disbelief which constitutes poetic faith.' The naive style befitting his theme and allegory was occasionally marred by a note of raillery or dry sophistication or sly eroticism. But such lapses were momentary and more than counterbalanced by the pervasive idealism best exemplified in the hermit. It is in this and the manifold nature of his achievement in creating an organic art form, a new mythology, and passages of sheer poetry that Wieland's claim to being a creative poet lies.

Written in a rapid unconstrained manner in loosely rhymed
ottava rima, *Oberon*, while harking back to the ornate rococo spirit,
anticipated the most characteristic interests, internationally considered, of later romanticism. Not only is it marked by the typical
rebellion against formal restraints, but it also moves upon the inner
springs of an exceptionally broad romanticism. Daemonology and
medievalism aside, it radiates that sense of wonder which, in
Shelley's phrase, 'lifts the veil from the hidden beauty of the world.'
It conveys the wonder and beauty in the visible world and in that
realm beyond—that other realm by which the familiar is made
meaningful and is spiritually enhanced, in the mysterious sense of
'something far more deeply interfused,' the transcendental sense of
the ideal within and beyond the real. That sense is manifested in
Oberon not only by a modified Platonic daemonology; Wieland's
basic idealism is also evident in his characterization, and allegory,
and in the theme of the island episode. From the poetic fusion of
all three of these derive the innermost nature of the hermit and
more than one scene in the dense romantic poem. For romantic
it was, and revolutionary while widely popular, as early as 1780.

iii: *William Sotheby's Translation*

In England *Oberon* was first noticed by a reviewer for *The
Gentleman's Magazine* in November 1784. In a review of De
Boaton's French version, the anonymous writer twice urged that
it be rendered into English.[1] Unknown to him, an English transla-
tion, begun two years earlier, had been completed in May 1784 by
James Six; but owing to Wieland's diffidence it was never pub-
lished, except for some sample stanzas in the periodical *Deutsches
Museum*.[2]

The romance was actually introduced into England by the
acknowledged pioneer of German studies, William Taylor of Norwich, to whom Hazlitt paid tribute as the initiator of philosophical
criticism in England.[3] In the August 1797 issue of *The Monthly*

Review, as fifth of a series of articles on Wieland, his favorite German author, Taylor reviewed *Oberon* in great detail, analyzed it canto by canto, and among other things hailed it as 'popular beyond example,' as having attained 'in its native country all the honors of a sacred book.'[4] As a result, shortly thereafter, Coleridge undertook a translation, with results I have partly discussed elsewhere.[5] And in June 1798 William Sotheby (1757-1833) published his version.

Already known as a minor poet, in his translation of *Oberon* Sotheby surpassed himself. This translation was his masterpiece and conveyed more than enough of Wieland's poetic power to do him justice in English eyes. It revealed a mastery of two languages and transcended contemporary standards of translating.* Despite uneven quality, it was an outstanding achievement in poetry, at a time before the romantic style of concreteness, simplicity, and intensity of utterance had been established in England. It was by far the best poetical translation of the time, and it remains one of the best to this day. As a translation of Wieland's *Oberon,* however, it had unmistakable shortcomings which some critics were not slow to perceive. In general it was faithful to the original, but in some respects it was not. It failed to render the form, omitted some of the matter, and infused an alien spirit of stilted artificiality remote from Wieland's manner. Thus Coleridge said in 1811, 'Sotheby's translation had not at all caught the manner of the original.'[6] But if he was right, he still failed to do Sotheby justice.

Wieland had written in loose ottava rima, in lines of from four to six feet, preponderantly in iambic rhythm. He had used feminine rhymes for further stylistic freedom. Poetic diction of the kind current in England was not found in his writing. Sotheby chose a modified Spenserian (nine-line) stanza and consequently had often to expand Wieland's thought or to add something of his own. But he did this without destroying the sense and generally 'in the spirit

* Only William Taylor's translation of *Lenore* (1796) and possibly Coleridge's version of *Wallenstein* (1800) surpassed it.

of the original.'[7] A worse fault was his proneness to embellish Wieland's more natural style; to introduce Augustan devices; and to obscure, often completely, both Wieland's daemonology and imagery. For the storm (VII, 18):

Inzwischen bricht mit fürchterlichstem Sausen
Ein unerhörter Sturm von allen Seiten los;
Des Erdballs Axe kracht, der Wolken schwarzer Schooss
Giesst Feuerströme aus, das Meer beginnt zu brausen,
Die Wogen thürmen sich wie Berge schäumend auf,
Die Pinke schwankt und treibt in ungewissem Lauf,
Der Bootsmann schreit umsonst in sturmbetäubte Ohren,
Laut heults durchs ganze Schiff: 'Weh uns! wir sind verloren.'

Sotheby wrote, characteristically:

Meanwhile the tumult maddens more and more;
Fierce from all sides at once a whirlwind breaks;
Rock'd by rude gusts the earth confus'dly shakes,
The welkin flames, with lightning vaulted o'er:
High in the air by surging tempests cast,
The world of waters bellows to the blast:
The vessel reels at random to and fro,
The boatswain calls in vain, while shrieks of woe
Ring thro' the staggering ship, all hope of safety past![8]

Here he completely disguised the romantic imagery and wrote a stanza resembling a contemporary *Georgics* much more closely than Wieland. But Sotheby did not always write thus.

To a certain extent he wrote in terms of accepted English style. Consciously or not he was subject to the taste of his time. Thus in the opening stanzas particularly, there are insipid clichés and abstractions, obtrusive 'swains,' 'the fair,' and 'sulphureous tides.' At first echoes of the stilted heroic style repeatedly chill the modern reader by a cold and specious artificiality that catches little of the intimacy, sensuousness, and concreteness of Wieland's vigorous verse. Sotheby seems feeble at first, seems quite to miss the pithy familiarity of dialogue, the vivid detail and lightness of Wieland's poem. But he warmed to his task, and before long he was writing poetry that repeatedly sings in the mind. By occasional concessions to current taste, whether or not deliberate, he doubtless helped make *Oberon* more generally palatable to contemporary readers.

Moreover, Wieland's romanticism did not fail to infect Sotheby. Gradually his lines became sprightly and his style less cool and constrained. As increasingly he caught the spirit, time and again he achieved a certain felicity that was to leave its marks on some of the greatest English poetry of the dawning era. The wonder in Wieland's scenes was reflected in smooth, at times haunting, verse.

At random, this is in his more successful manner:

> Sport of rude blasts, the desolated trees
> Strew with sear leaf the melancholy shore;
> Thro' naked boughs the wintry tempests roar,
> And hoary mists that sweep along the seas
> Veil in dark clouds the sun's meridian light;
> In sad confusion air and sea unite:
> High o'er the strand tempestuous ocean breaks,
> The furious tide its rocky boundary shakes,
> Spangling with silver foam the cliff's aerial height.
>
> (CANTO VII, st. 86)

Here and even more distinctly elsewhere Sotheby caught the romantic spirit. This is more than 'harmonious' and 'poetical': it is essentially different from the school of Pope. Sotheby, as we shall see, rose more than once to the level of imaginative poetry with a contagious appeal of its own. And that was most fortunate.

As for the public career of his version, it was generally well received.[9] Two different issues had appeared in 1798.[10] In 1802 at the height of the 'Anti-Jacobin' reaction against all literary things German, Sotheby adapted it in a masque [11] which he dedicated to none other than George Ellis, one of the leading 'Anti-Jacobin' satirists. A second edition of the translation, illustrated by Fuseli, appeared in 1805; and a third, with curious expurgations,[12] in 1806.[13] The first American edition appeared in 1810; and the fourth and fifth English (the former from the press of John Murray) in 1826 and 1844. In these years, moreover, it was thrice adapted to the professional stage. On 21 May 1816, Benjamin Thompson's *Oberon's Oath, or the Paladin and the Princess* 'was acted five times at Drury Lane . . . founded on *the celebrated poem by Wieland as translated by Sotheby . . .*' (Italics mine.) [14] A decade later another adaptation was performed with far greater success, for on 27 March 1826, at Drury Lane (Thomas Simpson Cooke's) *Oberon or the Charmed Horn,* 'Romantic Fairy Tale in two acts, was acted twenty-eight times.' [15] It preceded the first performance, personally conducted at Covent Garden by the composer on 12 April 1826, of Carl Maria von Weber's opera, for which James Robinson Planché had written the libretto.[16]

The year before that, Carlyle had judged Sotheby's version thus: 'We should pronounce [Coleridge's *Wallenstein*], excepting Sotheby's *Oberon,* as the best, indeed the only sufferable translation from the German with which our literature has as yet been enriched.' [17] But just how Sotheby enriched English literature still remains to be told. His translation was widely known for many years. It was read and admired by many English poets, among them Southey, Campbell, and Byron. But most important of all, it haunted John Keats. /

iv: *The Story of 'Oberon'*

[Familiarity with Wieland's tale is essential for understanding Keats' symbols and allusions to it. In prose summary, many of the qualities of the romance as pointed out in Section ii, above, must be lost. Yet a summary is indispensable here for two reasons: to convey at least some idea, to those unfamiliar with it, of the seminal nature of its spirit, style, allegory, and mythology; and to facilitate an understanding of the relation of particular parts to the whole of Wieland's design— parts to which John Keats was amazingly susceptible. Some of those parts are therefore summarized in greater detail. But the imagery, melody, and actual phraseology— in Sotheby's imperfect translation, which has been long out of print—must appear in later chapters.]

Canto i

After an invocation hinting the natural and supernatural in the action, the poet turns to his hero, Huon of Bordeaux.

While on his way to Bagdad by command of his liege-lord Charlemagne, Sir Huon receives the Pope's blessing and promises to visit the Holy Sepulchre. This done, with new faith he resumes his perilous pilgrimage. (st. i-xi)

Over hill and dale he rides until one stormy day, overtaken by fearful darkness in a mountain-forest, he stumbles upon a cavern on Mount Lebanon. Its wild-looking occupant proves to be Sherasmin, who sixteen years earlier had accompanied Duke Siegewin of Guyenne to the Holy Land, where, his beloved master dying, the loyal liege-man had remained. Huon, as Siegewin's son, is welcomed beside the fire and soon relates what has brought him there. (st. xii-xxviii)

Reared by his widowed mother, he had at length been proclaimed lawful Duke of Guyenne. Two years later, Charlemagne, incited by Amory Baron of Hautefeuille, ancient foe of Huon's race, had summoned the youth to do homage for his fief. On the journey to Paris, however, Huon and his younger brother Gerard were waylaid by Amory and the disguised Charlot, base second son of the emperor. Gerard having been treacherously wounded and Huon himself attacked, the latter had defended himself so vigorously that Charlot was slain. (st. xxix-xxxvii)

Hardly had Huon completed his journey than twelve mute servitors bore the dead Charlot into the emperor's presence, where Amory accused Huon of murder. In grief and vengeful rage the aged Charlemagne had refused to hear Huon's plea and had ordered him put to death. But the peers had sided with him; and the youth having denounced Amory and challenged that veteran to trial by single combat, the emperor had been constrained to consent. (st. xxxviii-liii)

The court and populace having assembled in feudal pomp, Huon, with faith in God's justice, had at length overcome his proud accuser, who, however, refused even in the throes of death to confess his treachery. Charlemagne, his thirst for vengeance unquenched, had thereupon banished Huon with a promise of pardon only if he succeeded in a desperate quest. He was to journey to Bagdad and gain admittance to the royal palace; he was to enter the caliph's presence and amid the assembled emirs was to cut off the head of him seated at the caliph's left; with a kiss thrice repeated he was to claim the heiress to the throne for his bride. Then, prostrating himself before the caliph, Huon was to request four of his teeth and a handful of his beard as a token of friendship for Charlemagne. Despite the angry murmur of the peers and his own realization of the emperor's bloody purpose, Sir Huon had proudly undertaken the quest and had proceeded thus far to perform it.

Desperate though his fate seems, Huon is joined by Sherasmin, who promises to follow him in life or death. (st. liv-lxxiii)

Canto ii

After journeying three days down Lebanon, Huon and his squire, attacked by a band of Arabs whom they put to flight, equip Sherasmin with a sword and steed and hasten on toward the endless plain at their feet. They rest at a village; then ride on until at twilight they come to the edge of a great forest. Since Huon is impatient to reach Bagdad, and the shortest route is through this ominous wood, the knight determines to traverse it, despite the entreaties of his squire. 'One speaks no good of it,' the latter warns: none who entered it has ever emerged, for it is the haunt of a malicious spirit and teems with transformed beasts of chase who once were men. But Huon, though he turns pale, will not be swayed from his purpose and rides into the forest followed by his shuddering companion. (st. i-xiii)

Hardly have they entered than their passage is opposed by herds of deer who, Sherasmin says, would warn them away with tear-filled eyes. Again he begs his master to turn back, but in vain. Spurring his horse, Huon disperses the beasts, who vanish instantly. Night now descends upon the silent wood, and as they cautiously pick their way on, the squire discourses knowingly of spirits. Mortal foes he does not fear, but he admits to a healthy respect for the invisible world; pointedly he says that while all ghosts and elves and such vanish at cockcrow, the spirit who here abides is of quite another sort, who appears by night and day and eats and drinks like ordinary mortals. (st. xiv-xxiv)

Gradually while they talk the wanderers ride deeper into the wood and at last are bewildered by a maze of paths. Suddenly through the trees they espy a resplendent crimson castle that seems to hover in the air. As they stare in awe and delight, the golden portals fly open and a silver chariot drawn by leopards appears, in which sits a boy beautiful as the god of love. Terrified, Sherasmin bids his master flee the dwarf, seizes the bridle of Huon's steed, spurs his own mount, and gallops madly toward the edge of the wood. Forthwith they are overtaken by a raging tempest. Rain and lightning pour out of the night, yet from amid the crashing and roaring of all the embattled elements Huon hears the spirit's gentle voice bidding him turn back. But Sherasmin's terror increasing, they ride on madly through the howling storm until the sheltering walls of a cloister offer a sanctuary. It so chanced that the nuns had just returned from a procession in which the monks of a neighboring monastery had also taken part. Among all these, on holy ground, the squire seeks refuge. But the pursuing tempest engulfs them all, the procession is weirdly dispersed, and suddenly the dwarf appears before them. (st. xxv-xxxv)

Although the sky is clear at once, and for all his angelic beauty, a strange horror possesses all as they see him, an ivory horn at his shoulders, leaning upon a lily stalk, anger darkening his eyes. Before they can recover from their astonishment, he puts the horn to his lips and blows a witching tone. Irresistibly the crowd whirls in pairs in a mad consuming dance, dignity and devotion forgotten. The knight alone stands to one side, convulsed at their ridiculous antics. The dwarf approaches him and in the Frankish tongue asks why he had fled; and in the name of God, whom the sprite acknowledges, requires an answer. He has always been Huon's friend, he says, for the knight is forthright, brave, and pure of heart, and 'on spotted souls alone my vengeful torments fall.' These monks and nuns are hypocrites, while Sherasmin had been too free of his tongue. Huon, thereupon pitying the gasping dancers, prevails upon the dwarf to break the spell. Waving his lily wand, Oberon dismisses the cloister-folk with a rebuke, while he urges Sherasmin, half dead with fatigue, to drink from a proffered goblet of gold. No sooner has he put it to his lips than the goblet fills itself with a wine which sends new life through his every member. (st. xxxvi-xlvii)

Thereupon Oberon reveals his knowledge of Charlemagne's decree, promises to help Huon, and presents the horn and magic cup to him, warning him not to abuse the gifts. A gentle breath on the elf-horn will compel even a thousand armed men to whirl until exhausted; a blast in a moment of extremity will cause Oberon himself to appear from near or afar. And the goblet will always fill itself for an honest man. Urging the knight to remain virtuous and loyal to his oath, as tears form in his eyes the strange woodland spirit dissolves into air, leaving only a fragrance of lilies behind. Sir Huon and his squire, marveling at the encounter and delighted with their gifts, at length resume their journey. (st. xlviii-lv)

CANTO III

Four days later the wanderers come upon the courteous Prince of Lebanon and his retinue of armed knights. Requested either to break a lance with the Prince or else do his bidding, Huon learns that near at hand is the impregnable castle of the giant Angulaffer, who for seven months has held the Lady Angela, Lebanon's bride, in his possession. What is more, the giant is invincible by virtue of a ring that he had stolen from the dwarf of the adjacent forest. Lebanon has overcome every passing knight errant in order to recruit a force to deliver the sorely beset lady from the hated werewolf. Sir Huon, however, challenges the entire retinue, unhorses the Prince and his knights successively, and sets out the next morning to undertake the perilous quest alone. (st. i-xiii)

Approaching the castle and finding it guarded by two enchanted warders, Huon draws his dagger and, commending himself to God, rushes forward, to find that the warders become motionless when touched. Entering the castle he meets the damsel, who implores his aid. She tells him of her kidnaping, and how in answer to her prayer the giant has been afflicted with a strange sleep that overcomes him whenever he offers any violence. She urges Huon to remove the magic ring from the finger of her sleeping captor and then to slay him. (st. xiv-xxvi)

Huon puts the ring on his own hand and unwittingly makes himself master of the daemons of the elements. But scorning to slay a sleeping foe, he wakes the infuriated giant, who, finding himself despoiled of the potent talisman, reluctantly arms himself. Overcoming him in a fearful battle, Huon releases all the captives, courteously but coolly accepts the thanks of the coquettish Angela, and gives her into the keeping of the Prince. Without further ado he and Sherasmin proceed on their way. (st. xxvii-li)

At nightfall, as the moon steals up the horizon, the weary wanderers decide to halt. Seeking a place to rest, they suddenly see a magnificent canopy in which are rich carpets and cushions and a table of jasper and gold, laden with delectable food. Thanking the friendly spirit, they feast, drink of the magic goblet, and soon fall asleep, lulled by the loveliest aerial music, which seems to issue from a thousand fairy throats. At length a wondrous dream possesses Huon. As he seems to wander along a stream through shadowy fields, a damsel of supernatural beauty stands before him, with whom he falls instantly in love. She vanishes and he lies as if dead beside the stream. She reappears, bends over, pities and embraces him. Then all at once a frightful tempest engulfs them and tears her from his arms into the stream. As he struggles violently to leap to her rescue, Sherasmin wakes him. Deeply shaken Huon and he discuss dreams, their cause and significance. (st. lii-lxviii)

CANTO IV

Huon, relating his vision, is advised to discredit what had so terrified him and to regard the rest as prophetic. Perhaps one day he will find the lady of his dream. Sherasmin has had his share of indigestion and nightmares; but dreams, he says, are strange things and the damsel may really exist, perhaps even in Bagdad. At this, Huon's spirits soar; and the fairy canopy vanishing as mysteriously as it appeared, eagerly they resume their wandering. (st. i-xviii)

Riding along the banks of the Euphrates that balmy sunlit day, each daydreams silently, the one of heroic rescues and the other of his own country. Resting at noon, they hear the roar of a lion and then a terrified scream. In the nick of time they save the life of a Saracen lord, who, offered the magic goblet which scorches his hand, blasphemes and flees on Huon's steed. At the next village, therefore, they mount the jovial Sherasmin on a superannuated mule and, no whit discouraged, ride on. At last toward sundown they see beneath them in a spreading vale, the queen of cities crowned with towers numberless, and the rapid Tigris flowing through a paradise of green. The golden minarets, the spectacle of the emirs' mighty castle gleaming, fill Huon with awe. But as death seems imminent, a disembodied voice breathes in his ear that he will find her he loves within those mighty walls. Therewith his doubts disperse, and descending rapidly they are soon in the city. (st. xix-xxxv)

Inquiring of an old woman for an inn, they are invited to spend the night at her hut. Later that evening she tells them she is mother to the nurse of the sultan's daughter, who is to be married next day to Prince Babekan. The Princess Rezia, however, does not love him and has loathed the thought of marriage ever since, a few weeks past, she dreamed a wondrous dream. In a vision she had seen herself in the guise of a deer pursued by the hounds of her suitor. Just as she was to be torn limb from limb, a chariot drawn by leopards had appeared in which sat a beautiful dwarf and a strange young knight with golden hair and blue eyes. Handsome as an angel, to him at first sight her heart had succumbed. Suddenly the chariot had stopped. The dwarf had touched her with his lily wand; her human shape had been restored; and swiftly she had found herself seated in the chariot between the dwarf and her lover. In fear and delight she had awakened, and ever since this dream her suitor had been as hateful to her as a serpent. (st. xxxvi-l)

Nonetheless, Babekan had sought to win her love by slaying a monster that had terrified the countryside, and only today had returned on another steed. Meantime, preparations for the feast had proceeded, and the very next night Rezia was to see herself in hated arms. Huon vehemently doubting this, the old crone looks at the stranger closely, wonders at his golden hair and blue eyes. Later, consumed with curiosity, she overhears her guests' foreign speech, of which she recognizes only the name of Rezia. All the while Huon and Sherasmin, marveling at the Princess' dream, try to resolve upon a course of action. His anxiety does not permit Huon to sleep that night. (st. li-lxv)

Canto v

That night the Princess Rezia also lies awake, in dread of the hated festival. Not till dawn does she slumber, when Oberon grants her a second dream-vision. She seems to be in the moonlit palace gardens, desperately seeking her lover. Her restlessness makes her rise, and she hurries into every shadowy nook, her eyes tearful as she listens fearfully to the slightest rustling. At last where the moonlight breaks through the shrubbery, half in shadow she sees him. He flies toward her with open arms. But she hesitates, at last hides behind a tree, and in agitation awakes. Vainly she tries to fall asleep again that the dream might continue. A third of the day is already over and still she lies abed dreaming awake when the nurse undraws her curtains. (st. i-vi)

As Rezia rapturously tells Fatme that she has seen her lover again, the nurse slyly looks around the chamber. Laughing, Rezia expresses her belief that he is not far off. Then she recollects that the fateful hour draws near which will prove her undoing. Fiercely she vows that before her hated wooer shall have her, a serpent shall sink its sharp teeth in her breast; if her lover does not come in time, at least a dagger shall save her. At that moment the terrified nurse hurries to the door and returns with her mother's news of her guests. Delirious with joy, Rezia leaps from her bed in all her loveliness and has the old crone ushered into the chamber. As her maidens robe her and arrange her gems, the radiant bride, flushed and oblivious of all save him of her dream, listens as the grandam tells her story again and again. (st. vii-xviii)

Meanwhile, the emirs and vizirs, magnificently garbed for the revelry, are gathering. The feast is set, and at last trumpets herald the sultan, the gorgeous Prince Babekan, and numerous attendant slaves through a golden door of the sacred palace. Opposite, an ivory door unfolds to admit the gleaming bride, who seems to fill the hall with unearthly radiance. With Babekan's eyes devouring her features, she bestows but one freezing glance upon him and takes her place beside the sultan her father. As the imam speaks a prayer, the music and feasting begin. (st. xix-xxii)

Huon had also fallen asleep at dawn and slept till noon. Awaking at last, he is startled to find a suit beside him, befitting an emir of highest rank. This jeweled magnificence the spirit had provided that he might gain access to the palace. The old crone having helped him with his disguise, Huon takes his leave and finds awaiting him a richly caparisoned steed and two pages magnificently attired. Soon they have passed into the forecourt of the palace. In an inner court Huon dismounts and is admitted reverently by the gigantic guards. His heart beating high as he hears the gates close behind him, he advances along the pillared walk until he hears the sounds of revelry within. (st. xxiii-xxxiii)

Already the music and song have become noisy in the great hall; already the sultan nods and the bridegroom's eyes gleam expectantly. But Rezia still looks fixedly at her plate, lost in dreams of her love, as Huon strides forward, his magnificent attire amazing all the guests. Babekan at the sultan's left is the blasphemous Saracen of the day before. Instantly the jeweled scimitar leaps out, the hated wooer's head flies, and spurting blood gushes over the table. Paralyzed with dread, every guest draws back at so quick and bold a deed, while the sultan sinks back utterly bereft of speech. The uproar ceasing so suddenly, Rezia awakes from her reverie, turns, and is recognized by Huon as the damsel of his vision. As he leaps to her side, scimitar and gem-studded turban drop to the floor and his golden hair floats down. ' 'Tis he!' she cries and finds herself in his arms, kissed once and twice and again. Slipping the talisman onto her finger, he proclaims her his bride. (st. xxxiv-xlii)

At this crowning affront the sultan shrieks imprecations upon the Christian dog. Raving in titanic fury, he bids the intruder be seized, that his blood be drawn drop by drop. Huon barely has time to snatch up his scimitar before a thousand swords flash toward him. Rezia, flinging herself before him, shields her lover with her body and for a moment checks the onslaught with a wild cry to her father. But the sultan urges them on; Rezia is pulled aside and Huon fights for his life until he can put the elf-horn to his mouth. At once every sword falls; all save Huon and Rezia take hands and more and more rapidly whirl about them in dance. Sultan and emirs, slaves, eunuchs and concubines, all in the sacred palace must dance, rank and age forgotten. Sherasmin enters the unguarded hall and urges Huon to fly with his bride. But the knight waits till the dancers fall exhausted. Then giving the horn and Rezia into his squire's keeping, he approaches the panting, incredulous sultan, does obeisance before him, and repeats Charlemagne's request. (st. xliii-lvi)

The sultan, veins distended with rage, bids his slaves lop Huon's limbs, draw his blood with awls, cast him into the flames; and shrieks the fervent wish that Charlemagne be eternally damned. Huon, proudly bidding him reflect how mighty the emperor must be if his vassal can perform such wonders, asks the sultan to embrace the Christian faith in lieu of remitting the gifts. At this the sultan is as one possessed. Screaming with impotent frenzy, he arouses the still gasping guests who leap at Huon as one man. Although the latter lays about him with deadly effect, his last hour seems at hand. Sherasmin watches his prowess with awed delight, and only at the very last moment remembers the horn. Then, putting it to his lips, he blows as if to awake the dead. (st. lvii-lxvi)

Forthwith the whole castle resounds and cracks. Fearsome night engulfs the hall. Ghosts flit about like lightning flashes, and amid steady thunder the earth's foundation heaves. Their courage gone, the tottering paynim fall insensible and lie about in heaps. The sultan seems to strive with death itself, and finally he too lies silent as in death. Suddenly the storm is hushed; a breath of lily-fragrance fills the hall, and Oberon appears out of the air. Uttering a cry of terror and delight, Rezia stands beside Huon and listens as the daemon king praises her lover. Then the potent spirit turns to her, bids her consider carefully before leaving regal luxury to share the world's perils with Huon. Those in the hall who lie about her, seeming dead, merely slumber. They will awake at Oberon's bidding and will pardon her. Ashen but proudly silent, Huon awaits Rezia's decision. Hiding her face against him, she embraces her lover, while Oberon blesses them with his wand and bids them hasten to Rome and be wed. The spirit having melted into air, Huon urges his bride to hurry; and casting a last look of pity upon her father, they leave the deathlike sleepers in the ghostly hall, and Huon bears the lovely lady down the marble steps to Oberon's waiting chariot. (st. lxvii-lxxviii)

While the castle remains silent as a tomb, the aerial car drawn by four swans departs, bearing the ecstatic lovers and the squire and nurse away. (st. lxxix-lxxxvi)

Canto VI

At dawn the car descends near Ascalon. Rezia, awaking, with awe espies the illimitable sea. Oberon appears out of the air and hands Huon a richly gemmed casket containing the gifts Charlemagne had demanded. Then he urges them to board their ship for Rome to receive the Pope's nuptial blessing. With great earnestness he impresses upon Huon that till then Rezia is to be a sister to him: the moment they taste unhallowed love, Oberon must depart from them forever. With a sorrowful sigh he kisses them both and vanishes. (st. i-x)

Dejected and deeply oppressed, they soon embark on the ship furnished by their protector. Although the sea is calm and unruffled, the ship sails swiftly. The lovers stay on deck and stare out at the immeasurable sea and request their attendants never to leave them alone. Soon Huon undertakes to instruct his bride in the Christian faith, and she is baptized Amanda by a monk on board. But though he represses his passion to the utmost, Huon is drawn to her as she to him, and such is their tenderness that Sherasmin intervenes with a tale to distract them and cool their dangerous ardor. (st. xi-xxxiv)

[In his translation Sotheby omitted st. xxxv-lxxxiv with the following note:

Sherasmin's tale is sufficiently known to the English reader by the January and May of Pope: yet, though I have omitted nearly the whole of it, I trust that the part which I have inserted will clearly point out the art and contrivance with which Wieland has interwoven into the texture, and rendered essential to the completion of the main object of his poem, the only incident in the story which could have induced him to revive the subject.—The incident to which I allude is the presence of Oberon and Titania in the garden scene: and with this I begin the narrative. (1798 ed., vol. 1, p. 198.)

Although this omission did not destroy the central motivation of the entire romance, I have summarized the missing stanzas:

The aged Gandolf, a reformed rake of sixty-five winters, marries the beautiful young Rosetta. He buys her all manner of gifts and gewgaws and in return is petted and flattered. Grown blind, jealous, and moral, he preaches virtue incessantly and keeps her a languishing prisoner in his castle, her only pleasure being the garden with its pear tree, tended by the youthful squire Walter. With him finally, in sheer desperation, Rosetta comes to an understanding. One summer's day on which Gandolf had been particularly relentless, as the crotchety husband walks in the garden supported by his wife, she begs him to let her climb up into the pear tree to pick some of the fruit. Reluctantly he lets her climb from his shoulder into the tree—in which Walter sits concealed. (st. xxxv-lxxxiv.) Sotheby continues from here:]

Now it so happened that all this was observed by Oberon and Titania, who, with their attendant fays, were resting invisible in Gandolf's garden. Angered by the treachery practiced against the blind old man, Oberon swears by his throne that nothing shall help the wife's cunning, that he will remove the veil from the husband's eyes. Hastily Titania takes Rosetta's part and swears to help her to an explanation. But Oberon, disregarding his consort's impatience of female oppression, touches the old man's eyes with his wand and makes him see—his wife in another man's arms. Hardly has Gandolf cried out in rage than by Titania's power the lover becomes invisible, and indignantly Rosetta proclaims her innocence: she had been struggling with an evil spirit that her husband's sight might be restored. Gandolf, readily convinced, is reconciled with his weeping wife. But Oberon, infuriated by this double breach of virtue, exclaims against woman's deceit and Titania's defense of it. Forthwith he *swears a fearful oath*. (st. lxxxv-xcviii)

Never shall they meet again in any element! He hates the air in which she breathes. He bids Titania flee, and inveighs against the treacherous sex and the subdued slave of love. He curses deceived sensualists who suck the poison from voluptuous woman's glances, who think love the envenomed passions of her serpent bosom, and believe her vows and treacherous tears. By his lily wand and sceptre and by the awful name ineffable even to spirits, he bids naught revoke his curse and sacred vow until a constant pair, chosen by fate itself, shall be drawn to one another; and, tried by bliss and suffering alike, remain unchanged in their love! Not till such be found and tried by death itself in several elements, by death and by possession even of a throne, will he see Titania again. (st. xcix-cii)

Therewith, Sherasmin concludes, Oberon had vanished and had never again been seen in his natural guise. His habitation now a mountain-top and now a wood, his sole pleasure was to plague plighted lovers. That he had aided Huon and Rezia was wondrous indeed. They, suspecting their lot, are eager to undergo trial if thereby they can help him who had brought them together. But such is their heightened ardour that the squire doubts he has accomplished anything by his tale. (st. ciii-cvii)

CANTO VII

After a voyage during which every element had been favorable through Oberon's sway, the lovers reach Lepanto. Huon, tired of his vigilance, sends the reluctant Sherasmin on ahead to Paris with the casket for Charlemagne; while Rezia, himself, and the nurse embark for Rome. But no sooner has Sherasmin departed than Huon is most uneasy. Feeling the disembodied presence of his guardian spirit, he vows to abide by his promise at whatever cost. And so he avoids the presence of the mystified Rezia; by night stares moodily up at the polar star and by day upon the desolate sea. Though distressed by this altered conduct, Rezia responds with nothing but patient tenderness.

Late one starry night when even the steersman nods, only the lovers toss sleepless, in adjoining chambers. At last Huon sighs with such anguish that Rezia, thinking him ill, enters his chamber with tender pity. Struggling against a flood of passion, he tears himself from her gentle embrace and wildly draws back. Innocently she sinks down in bitter tears, until Huon, overcome with emotion, takes her in his arms, and as if unconsciously their love is consummated. (st. i-xvii)

In a flash the heavens blacken and each star is quenched, the lovers unheeding. The winds roar from afar, but are unnoticed. For the third time the rolling thunder threatens, all in vain. At last an awful tempest bursts upon the ship. The waves rise to savage fury and momently threaten to engulf the foundering vessel and its terrified crew. At last the lovers awaken conscience-stricken to a sense of their sin. Only too soon they realize that the daemon king, no longer their gentle guardian spirit, is now the fearsome ruler of the elements and stern avenger.

The captain, suspecting that one evil-doer's presence is the cause of their common peril, resolves upon the choosing of sacrificial lots to appease Heaven's wrath. All consenting, Huon draws the lot of death. Conscious of Oberon's hand, he delays amidst his mute shipmates only to implore pity for Rezia. Then, the storm returning in full fury, he prepares to leap into the boiling seas. But the livid Rezia, her hair blowing fiercely in the gale, leaps toward him madly, clasps him in her arms, and hurls him with her into the waves. At once the storm abates, and the ship proceeds without them. (st. xviii-xxxi)

Meanwhile, tightly embraced, the unconscious lovers float on the waves, Oberon's favor and gifts withdrawn. The potent talisman, however, still on Rezia's finger, prevents their sinking to a watery death. For whoever possesses this ring, the awful seal of Solomon, must remain unharmed by every element. In earth and air, in water and in fire the daemons all are subject to its power. And by its wondrous virtue the lovers are cast up by the sea upon an island, whose dreary and rocky expanse seems one volcanic ruin unrelieved by anything green. Nevertheless, happy to be alive, they dry their clothes and rest under a scorching sun. At last Huon espies a cave, carries Rezia into its cooling shade, and rests beside her to whom this wild grot that love inhabits is sweeter far than the most resplendent palace. (st. xxxii-xlii)

Since she is famished and parched with thirst, Huon with tireless feet climbs the towering broken crags in search of food, but sees only a frightful mixture of rocks and clifts. In despair, he sinks to earth and cries out in bitterness of soul at the thought that the loveliest of created beings may perish because of his sinfulness. At last, in the light of the setting sun he sees the fairest golden fruit. Rezia, meanwhile, had gathered moss for their cavern until, utterly exhausted, she had sunk down on the desert shore. At last from afar she sees him returning, the golden fruit triumphantly held high. No sooner is he beside her than they cut the fruit open, only to find it an empty mockery, bitter as gall and rotten through and through. Their last hope gone, they stare at each other speechless, with bloodshot eyes and swollen tongues. In the depths of despair, feverish, starving, and parched, Rezia through charred lips faintly says she will gladly die on Huon's breast. He, seeing her sink in a faint, is beside himself with anguish, cries out madly for but one drop of water that at least her life may be saved. He alone is guilty and will gladly expiate his transgression if only she be spared. Scarcely has he prayed aloud in utmost agony of soul than he hears a distant fountain. This time his hopes are not deluded, and joyfully he quenches her thirst. (st. xliii-lxi)

The next day he resumes the search for food and at last finds some date trees upon which for a time they subsist, their love and faith undimmed. When one day Huon's spirits flag and he reproaches himself bitterly as the cause of all her woes, Rezia, renouncing the bliss of thrones for that of love, inspires him anew as she pledges never to complain or falter in her devotion and ever to toil beside him happily. Such is her womanly spirit that for him the desolate island seems transformed to a paradise, and Huon vows eternal and unswerving love. (st. lxii-lxxxiii)

Although they find berries and sea-mews' eggs, the changing season and Rezia's condition impel Huon to explore the other side of the towering cliffs. Time and time again he had ascended as far as he could, to see only the endless sea. This time, however, necessity urges him on, and at last he takes his leave and stands at the foot of the vast broken pinnacles that, wildly majestic, seem insurmountable save to despair alone. Winding up sheer rocky walls, bruised and bleeding, saved from death by only a frail handhold, he fights his way up the dizzy heights, recalling Rezia's image when exhaustion threatens death. Higher and higher he toils, and at last his path levels off, and he finds himself at the first summit. (st. lxxxiv-xcix)

CANTO VIII

Before him, in silent twilight, lies a small mountain valley, shaded by arching firs. The exhausted wanderer shudders as he enters this sanctuary of solitude, which seems a realm of shades. A gently curving path leads him to a narrow bridge, beneath which thunders a foaming mountain torrent. Suddenly he finds himself enclosed by rocky walls, the path having vanished as by magic. Fearfully he searches about and finally discovers a passage that winds perpendicularly through the rock like a winding stair. Breathless on reaching the last step, he sees a paradise before him. And all at once a man of noble features, with a rosary, confronts him. Startled and spectrelike with suffering, the wanderer, believing the hermit is a ghost, is himself mistaken for one. Both are taken aback, until Huon satisfies the hermit's inquiries and is welcomed with water and fruit. The venerable father at last shows him a much shorter path to the desert shore, and in a few hours

Rezia enters the rock-girt valley, an enchanted fairy paradise of fruit trees, grass, and flowers, where figs still ripen and orange trees yet bloom. (st. i-xii)

Falling at the feet of the ancient man as if he were the genius of the sacred spot, Rezia regards him with pious awe and soon looks upon him as their father. His inborn worth and open countenance distinguish the noble Alfonso, who after fearful suffering had been freed of the world's slow stain and now, inwardly at peace, is every creature's friend. Unmoved by worldly passions, his soul is attuned to nature's truth alone. From lonely agonies that followed upon the loss of all he loved, the beauty, purity, and consoling power of nature, first manifested in a radiant sunbeam, by degrees had raised him to highest bliss. And now, awakened to the higher life, his days are consecrated to God, and in the night he feels the disembodied touch of spirits on his cheek. With shuddering delight his half-slumbering ear hears angelic voices from the grove. The thin wall seeming to fall that separates him from his loved ones, in the pure light of the invisible world his spirit sees celestial faces; and at sunrise blissful he stands in the radiant presence of the Uncreated, whose beauty he sees in all things of earth. (st. xiii-xxix)

This, then, is the sage who had transcended earthly woes. And now he welcomes the lovers to his paradise and bids them live and toil beside him. At first they think him a guardian spirit, perhaps even the daemon king himself, who, since they have done heavy penance, has now determined to make them happy once again. But this delusion vanishing, Huon feels himself drawn to this saintly man, and before very long tells all his story and confesses how one moment's sweet forgetfulness had brought their guardian spirit's vengeance, and how all nature had turned against them. Alfonso reminds him that that man is blest whose fate rebukes him so swiftly and sternly. The guardian spirit's eye still hovers invisibly over Huon, who should deserve his favor to have it restored. When the sage counsels him to give up of his free will that in which

he had sinned, at once Huon pledges his word and vows his love
will be chaste. And when Alfonso urges him to toil that the spirit
may chasten the senses, Huon joyfully assents. (st. xxx-xl)

First he builds a hut for his beloved. Then he labors in the
forest, sword exchanged for the woodman's ax. And while the aged
hermit cultivates their garden, the spirited Princess Rezia, radiantly
happy and with increasing skill, performs the domestic duties of the
little household. To Huon she seems a supernatural being sent to
console him, and he comes to adore her with purer devotion. As
winter comes, they sit before their fire, the hermit telling of his
days in the world and at court, or Rezia sings; or they walk beneath the snow-clad peaks empurpled by the setting sun. (st. xli-l)

Thus insensibly winter slips by and at last nature is reborn. Rezia,
whose fateful hour approaches, secretly rejoices in dreams of her
child and seeks out shadowy paths beneath the blossoming boughs.
Only as her travail seems at hand does she become tearful and wish
for her nurse Fatme. But a higher power had provided. The elfin
queen Titania, since separated from her beloved lord, had found a
sanctuary here in the gloomy caves, where for many a season she
had lamented her sorrows alone, hating the fairy sports and the
enchanting light of the moon. Reconciled at last to her own and
Oberon's lot, and surfeited with grief and her gloomy cavern, she
had transformed a part of the forbidding island into a paradise and
called three aerial spirits to attend her. It was from out her sacred
grot that there issued the angelic music and the invisible spirits
sensed by the saintly hermit. (st. li-lxvi)

From the day of their arrival Titania had observed the devoted
lovers. And, as invisible she continued near them, she had come to
believe that they might be the couple fated to restore her happiness.
Thus, when Rezia's hour drew near, Titania determined to assist
her. Drawn as by a magnet, Rezia wanders on beneath the fragrant
shrubs and finally reaches the ivy-mantled entrance to a cavern.
Although the hermit and Huon had often sought to enter it, their
curiosity had been thwarted as by an invisible door. But Rezia

pushes the ivy aside easily, enters, and sinking down on a soft seat of roses and moss feels pain after pain shoot through all her being. A pleasant faintness overtakes her. Her eyes perceive increasingly shadowy moonlight, and losing consciousness she falls asleep. Confused shapes dawn on her mind: three angels seems to kneel before her mysteriously; and a damsel veiled in a rosy glow stands beside her, holding a sprig of roses to her mouth. One last muted pain, and the images vanish and again she slumbers. Awaking to the echo of sweet songs, she seems to dream awake: sees the angels no more, only the queen of fays softly smiling, a new-born child upon her arm. Handing him to Rezia, Titania disappears, leaving the radiant mother alone with her lovely child. A few moments later, the frantic Huon enters as if spellbound upon the scene. (st. lxvii-lxxx)

CANTO IX

In the meantime, the ship on which Fatme had sailed on alone, had been driven hither and yon and was finally wrecked on the shore of Tunis, where Fatme was sold as a slave to the gardener of the royal palace. Sherasmin, on the other hand, more and more dissuaded from his purpose, had determined when almost in Paris to turn back; had hastened to Rome in search of his master; and, after waiting several weeks, had adopted the garb of a pilgrim and for two years had inquired everywhere fruitlessly. One day he had wandered into Tunis, where in the royal gardens he encountered Fatme with joy and tears. Having heard her story he had decided to stay by her side, had found work in the gardens, married Fatme, and all but become convinced of the death of his beloved lord and lady. Yet dimly he had felt that Oberon could not have abandoned them utterly. (st. i-xxiii)

In the Elysian hermitage, to which trying fate had banished him, Huon not without secret grief sees the third spring bloom. The little Huonnet seems formed for a higher station than that of woodman. Rezia too is often overheard weeping by her guardian spirit, while the kindly hermit is not deceived by their cheerfulness. One night as thoughtfully they sit beneath the brilliant star-studded sky, the aged man begins to speak of this life as but a dream and of departing into the real existence. Love, truth, and inner peace in the consciousness of duty faithfully performed—these are all that man can take with him. At last with a tear in his gentle eye he quickly goes within. That same night Titania, oppressed by forebodings, looks aloft and reads the mysterious stars. Quickly she flies to the hut where the infant slumbers beside the sultan's daughter, touches the mother's breast with her rose-wand, and steals the child away, bidding her aerial attendants to care for him as if he were her own son. (st. xxiv-xxxv)

Hardly has day dawned than Rezia and Huon fearfully enter the hermit's hut, where they find their mentor dead, his saintly features at peace. His blessing still seems to hover above them as rapturously they feel themselves close to God. Turning at last to leave the cell, they raise their eyes upon ruin. For as if with the hermit's passing, their paradise has vanished, and all once again is a frightful mixture of black misshapen rocks. Recollecting her son, Rezia rushes into her hut only to find him gone. Frantically then the anguished parents call and seek him everywhere in vain, until at last Rezia becomes separated from her husband. (st. xxxvi-li)

All at once she hears an unaccustomed sound of voices, drowned out again by a waterfall that cascades over a high rocky arch. Descending rapidly and thinking only of her child, she finds herself suddenly surrounded by a band of yellow-black men whose ship rides at anchor off shore. Seeking water, they had landed and now stand stunned at the apparition in this desert spot of a woman who hardly seems mortal. Though beauty often makes rough souls gentler, these men feel naught but greed. As Rezia is about to plead with them to rescue her family, the pirate chieftain bids that she be captured and sold to their sultan, whose queen she far surpasses in loveliness. Advancing without suspicion, Rezia finds herself seized and borne toward the boats. Huon, still seeking his son in the rocks above, hears her pitiful cries, rushes down through the forest, snatches an oaken club in his stride, and falls upon the robbers like a thunderbolt. Seeing his lovely wife in brutal claws, he lays about him with titanic rage. Already seven moors lie at his feet as their fellows rush upon him together. Sheer weight of numbers fells him, but still he bites and strikes. Rezia, thinking him choked to death, faints and is borne to the ship. The rest of the pirates bear Huon into the forest, where bleeding from a dozen wounds he is bound to a tree. While he stands thus, crushed in his misery, the exulting pirates depart for their home port of Tunis with their beautiful prey. (st. lii-lxiii)

Canto x

As night sinks over the desolate isle, Titania, hovering invisible high in the air, hears Huon moaning in the forest. Although she sees his anguish and pities him with all her heart, some stronger power bars her from the side of the sufferer. But as sadly she flies on, she suddenly spies the talisman, which had dropped from Rezia's hand. Joyously Titania cries out that soon the stars will restore her to Oberon, and swiftly she flies after the ship. Rezia meanwhile has been brought back to consciousness and to a sense of her loss. The pirate chief humbly assures her she will soon be their happy queen. But Rezia, her spirit broken by the loss of all she had loved, languishes silently and suffers without complaint. In the night, however, as mutely she waits for death, her guardian spirit draws near and gently puts her to sleep. In her dream-vision she sees Titania, who bids her take courage, for her son and husband still live. When Rezia sees her for the third time, Titania says, then Oberon's vow will have been redeemed; and with the termination of Titania's penance the lovers will be happy. Therewith the goddess vanishes and Rezia awakes with new life. (st. i-xii)

Meanwhile, Huon had spent the long night bound to the oak tree; and the daemon king, before the light of whose eyes nothing is dark, still tarries. He stands at the source of the Nile on a mountain-peak eternally cloud-capped. Turned toward the distant isle, he hears Huon's every moan from afar. Glancing at the morning star, he sighs deeply, and from out the troop of spirits that everywhere attend him, one draws near who was his special confidant. Paling with awe, the aerial spirit mutely inquires the cause of his lord's sorrow, and silently Oberon bids him look up. In a passing cloud, as in a gigantic mirror, the gentle spirit sees Huon awaiting slow death. In his despair Huon asks of Heaven: 'Deserved I this? did Rezia? is our misery mere sport of higher powers?' And hearing the silence about him, he laments that nothing feels with him, no particle of sand nor single leaf stirs to his aid. Yet if it were the will of the daemon king, forthwith every twig would be transformed into a hand. The instant of his plea, a shudder flashes through his bones, the ropes fall, and he totters into an invisible arm. Unable to bear the sight of suffering, the gentle son of light had pleaded with his master. And at last Oberon had commanded him to fly to Huon's side and, without revealing himself, to bear him swiftly to the hut of the royal gardener of Tunis, and there to leave him and return. This the spirit had done, while Huon, borne aloft over sea and land, thinks he is merely dreaming. (st. xiii-xxii)

As day breaks, a tall man with a spade emerges from the hut, and Sherasmin recognizes his master with incredulous joy. The squire swiftly brings him food, tells Huon his story, and hears how Rezia had been kidnaped twelve hours before. The location of the island is unknown to Huon, such was the infinite speed with which he had been borne away, but in this very speed the squire sees Oberon's favor restored. Huon urges him to provide a steed and armor with a jewel from the casket. But collapsing from his sufferings, he lies in a high fever for several days, during which he is nursed by Sherasmin. (st. xxiii-xliii)

While he is convalescing, news is brought by Fatme. The night before, a vessel off the coast had suddenly been struck by a bolt of lightning and had foundered, one beautiful woman alone being saved from the sea. Welcomed by the sultan and sultana in person, such was her beauty that the sultan's heart had succumbed to her instantly, while the lovely queen had dissembled her jealousy with feigned cordiality. Huon, hearing that the stranger is lodged in the queen's summer palace, is torn by contending emotions. Confident that Oberon again guides their destiny, he realizes that he cannot rescue Rezia by force but must await a propitious hour and must meanwhile adopt the disguise of a gardener. (st. xliv-liv)

Canto xi

Huon, restored to health and hoping to encounter Rezia, labors in the gardens of the seraglio. After sundown, when they are closed to all save the women, he haunts the forbidden precincts stealthily. For three perilous nights he has lain concealed in a bush without seeing her. The fourth evening, however, as he rounds a hedge, he is suddenly confronted by the lovely sultana Almansaris, whose voluptuous being is revealed by her every feature. Huon, doing obeisance instead of fleeing, is questioned imperiously in an entrancing voice. His beauty and grace not lost upon her, she accepts his ready apology and basket of flowers, pardons his temerity, and dismisses him reluctantly with a meaningful glance. (st. i-xiv)

This, the handsomest youth she has ever beheld, fills her with wonder. She strides along silently, even turns her exquisite neck to look after him, and is angry that he had obeyed so swiftly. Restlessly she wanders all night long through the wooded paths, listening to every breeze expectantly, in hopes of seeing the youth again. Her sighs and disappointment betray her state. For three days her passion silently grows, nourished by resistance. Each evening, as soon as the sun has set, she wanders nymphlike through the groves, her hair half unbound, in hope of meeting the youth. Finally her regal pride succumbs and she confides in her attendant Nadina, a past mistress of intrigue. Nadina urges her voluptuous mistress to lure him she desires into her net. To smuggle him at midnight into that part of the palace where Almansaris alone commands, would be simple now that the sultan is consumed with a passion for the beautiful stranger. (st. xv-xxiv)

As to the latter's identity, Fatme had not been misinformed. It was Rezia who had been rescued by Titania's power. And her noble bearing and cool dignity, added to transcendent beauty, had impressed the watchful Almansaris as a masterpiece of art. Seeing her rival's immediate success, the queen had treated her with feigned tenderness but with secretly jealous concern for her own unlimited power. Now that her own heart had succumbed to the handsome youth, however, all the world might lie at her rival's feet if only she might hold him in her arms. Accordingly she encourages the sultan to install Rezia in another apartment, that she may be free to hatch her cherished plot. (st. xxv-xxxi)

Outside the walls of the palace, meanwhile, Huon, or Hassan as he is known, who for seven days had furtively sought a glimpse of his beloved through some barred window, is nearing the end of his patience. Desperately he appeals to his friends to find some means of letting Rezia know of his presence. At last Fatme conceives a stratagem: they will send a message in the language of flowers into the palace. The bouquet contains a laurel leaf bearing the initials A (for Amanda, Rezia's baptismal name) and H. Swiftly the nurse hands it into the seraglio, where it is passed on from hand to hand until it is intercepted by the sultana's watchful confidante. Since the flowers were brought by the slave of the gardener, she concludes they must have come from Hassan for Almansaris, as the letters A and H indicate. And so Fatme returns triumphantly with the answer that at midnight a little door leading into the palace would stand open. (st. xxxii-xl)

While Huon impatiently awaits the fateful hour, the queen is no less anxious. A feast in honor of her rival affords Almansaris greater freedom and clears the way for her design. At midnight with beating heart Huon approaches the little door. A soft hand draws him within. Mutely and with silent step he stops by a door. His whispered inquiry unanswered, he no sooner touches the door than it opens and a faint glow discovers an endless suite of chambers. As he proceeds, the faint light increases to brilliance, and confused and blinded by an incomparable splendor, he stops. Gold and lapis lazuli, the riches of Golconda and Siam, are everywhere revealed, but Rezia is not to be seen. Suddenly a curtain of rich gold-stuff rustles aside and before his fixed eyes a golden throne appears on which is a damsel of brilliant beauty with twelve attendants grouped at her feet. In richest array and gleaming with jewels, all her glittering splendor cannot extinguish her native beauty. But Huon, raising his eyes, recognizes Almansaris and is startled and confused. The queen, thinking him stunned by her awful magnificence, descends from her throne, comes toward him smiling, and taking his hand seems ready to lay all pomp aside. Her actions momently less constrained, a soft flame rising in her eyes, she presses his hand and bids him be merry. (st. xli-li)

When she dismisses her attendants, the youth appears even more constrained, and she leads him into another chamber where stands a table decked with delicacies and where song and string music greet him, as he is seated opposite the soft-eyed queen. Her voluptuous and impatient glances betray his conquest. Yet his expression makes her uneasy, for although he looks upon her beauty, his eyes are cool and critical. She hands him a gleaming beaker which her lips have barely touched and whose contents he drinks as one drinks poison. At a nod the lithesome damsels reappear in a dance. But their soft charms and sensual swoonings like all else are plainly designed to arouse his passions. Closing his eyes, he calls upon Rezia's image to protect him; in thought, he falls on his knees before her sacred image; and suddenly he feels as if an angel's shield protected him. The voluptuous dancers dismissed by the watchful queen, she determines to melt her stony prey in her arms and seizes her lute. Playing softly, her graceful arms and exquisite bosom revealed by her robe, she sings a song of love until, overcome by her passion, she lets the lute fall and opens her arms to the youth. But Huon, quickly catching the lute, intones a reply and firmly tells her his heart is another's. Against her will the lovely enchantress feels his superior power and pales, as tears fill her angry eyes. Desire conflicting with pride, she arises to veil her features, and with an icy glance waves her intended prey away. Soon, in the first light of dawn, Huon, bitterly reproachful, rejoins his friends. (st. lii-lxix)

CANTO XII

Meanwhile, 'love's wildest fire raging in her breast,' Almansaris vainly seeks an hour's rest. Unable to believe herself spurned, she writhes in loathing and rage. One moment she vows boundless vengeance, and in two minutes has forgotten her oath. Now he is to bleed drop by drop in the dust before her, now ecstatically she presses him to her breast. Again she sees him before her, a figure heroic: none but him will she have. Through the mouth of her confidante whispers the demon of lust, that she should tempt the youth once more with every art that beauty commands. If still he resists, then let pride taste the sweetness of vengeance. (st. i-viii)

And so, the second dawn, when full-throated birdsong resounds from the gardens, a slave bids Huon fill the shadowy grot with flowers since a lady would bathe therein. Heaping his baskets full, he approaches beneath the fragrant boughs until an invisible arm seems to bar the way. Smiling at his fears, he enters through the gloom. Within, he first perceives a twilight as of moonlight filtered through rose trees, and then a partly veiled figure, whose every beauty is revealed. For a moment he thinks it is Rezia; then he turns to flee and is caught by two milkwhite arms. Struggling against the lovely seducer's impassioned kisses and ardent pleading, he is almost overcome by her frenzy when suddenly the sultan approaches. (st. ix-xxi)

Apprised of the royal step at a distance, the temptress cries out wildly for help, and, dissembling with the look of innocence itself, accuses her prey of attempting to ravish her. Huon, disdaining any defence, casts one scornful glance at the enchantress before he is dragged to prison to be burned alive. All day he remains in darkness, praying only that Rezia may be saved and his honor be untarnished. (st. xxii-xxxi)

Late that night he hears a key in the door of his prison. The iron door opens and he hears a soft step. Getting to his feet he suddenly sees in a gleaming robe, with a crown on her head and a lamp in her hand, Almansaris standing beside him. Holding out her white hand and smiling bewitchingly, she begs his forgiveness for her untruth, calls him beloved, and says she has come to free him from death and to set him upon the throne he deserves. Ardently she offers him fame and glory, her hand and all beneath its sway, but Huon remains steadfast in the face of her every entreaty. In anguish and despair she throws herself on her knees, pleading, imploring, threatening in a frenzy of love and pain. But he remains firm. At last breathless with savage fury, she curses herself and him and storms away in a passion. (st. xxxii-xxxviii)

In the meantime rumor finally reaches Fatme and Sherasmin. In desperation the nurse gains entrance to the palace and awakens Rezia with the news of Huon's presence and danger. Waiting to hear no more, Rezia springs from her bed, throws a mantle over her shoulders, and, hurrying past the startled slaves, enters the sultan's chamber to fling herself at his feet. Astonished but pleased, the sultan offers her anything she desires, his treasure, throne, empire—if only she will be his. When she asks but the life of Hassan the gardener, the sultan, thunderstruck and suspicious, discovers their love. He tells her of Huon's infidelity, but in vain; promises to send him back to his people with regal gifts if she will become a queen. But proudly Rezia replies that the man she loves would scorn life itself at such a price, and she remains adamant as the sultan, writhing like a snake, grovels before her. At last in a frenzy of wounded pride and disappointed passion, he condemns her to the flames with her lover and bids them quickly be burned at the stake. (st. xxxix-lv)

Soon the fuel is piled high in the courtyard and the thronging populace have flocked around the lovers, who, bound to the same stake, devotedly await death. At last twelve blacks apply the torches. Quickly the flames mount, when suddenly in a deafening crash of thunder the earth quivers. Instantly the fire is quenched and the singed ropes fall and Huon sees the elf-horn once again slung from his neck. At the same moment the sultan and sultana appear from different directions, loudly bidding the auto-da-fé be stayed, while a black knight with flashing sword leaps through the startled spectators. But Huon anticipates all their efforts: a gentle breath on the elf-horn and all the paynim in the city must dance, water-carriers and sultan, sultana, slaves and rabble. In their midst, speechlessly embraced, Huon and Rezia stand ecstatic in the knowledge that their guilt is redeemed and fate reconciled, that at last their long bitter trial is over. As Sherasmin and Fatme come to help them down, the aerial car of the daemon king appears out of the air, and quickly they embark. (st. lvi-lxvi)

Swiftly as thought, and softly as sleep, they are borne through the air over land and sea, silvery clouds floating by them. Already fragrant dusk sinks upon mountains and hills. Already they see the moon mirrored in many a lake, as the realm of air becomes ever more silent. Imperceptibly the aerial car descends, and suddenly as if woven of crimson twilight a shimmering palace hovers before their startled eyes. In a wooded park amid high-blooming rose trees the palace stands, irradiating all the grove in its wondrous glow. Hardly has the awed Huon turned to ask Sherasmin, 'was not this the place?' than a golden portal opens and twenty immortal damsels emerge from the enchanted palace. Perpetually lovely as May, they come clad in gleaming white to welcome the children of earth with elfin music and song. The daemon king himself appears, and by his side, shimmering in pale moonlight, they see Titania restored to her beloved. Amid songs of jubilation the lovers are welcomed to the home of their grateful guardians, and Huonnet is restored to his mother. Then as in a dream, blissfully they are ushered into the palace of spirits. (st. lxvii-lxxiv)

At daybreak they find themselves on the bank of a river, with four steeds and a gleaming heap of fairy gifts by their side. The squire, marveling, points out the distant towers of Paris, and soon they hear the blare of trumpets. When Sherasmin returns, they learn that it is the third day of a tournament, the winner of which is to receive Huon's lands in fief. In the armor Oberon had provided, Huon unrecognized enters the lists and vanquishes the champion of the previous days; then he presents himself and his radiant bride to the startled emperor, with the jeweled casket as proof of his achievements. Charlemagne, now mollified, bids his valiant paladin and the sultan's daughter welcome, and at last all are reconciled. (st. lxxv-xciv)

ᘔ I ᕽ

1815: Strange Tales of the Elf and the Fay

ACCORDING TO Sir Sidney Colvin, who was the first to suggest the poet's familiarity with *Oberon*, Keats knew the poem as early as 1815. Of the second set of 'Shell Stanzas,' which were addressed to the Mathews in that year, Colvin remarked:

They seem to suggest an acquaintance with Oberon and Titania not only through the *Midsummer Night's Dream* but through Wieland's *Oberon*, a romance poem which Sotheby's translation had made well known in England and in which the fairy king and queen are divided by a quarrel far deeper and more durable than in Shakespeare's play.

After citing four lines from the 'Stanzas,' he added: 'There are several [other] passages in Keats, notably in the "Cap and Bells," where I seem to catch a strain reminiscent of this "Oberon." ' And he also pointed out a verbal echo in *The Eve of St. Agnes*.* But just how and when Keats discovered the popular romance, the impact of which upon his imagination was much more powerful than Colvin could have surmised, it seems at first impossible to establish. Yet the obstacles are not insurmountable.

The letters of Keats, while of exceptional charm and affording us insight into the evolution of his thought, throw little or no light on the early years. Indeed, the letters have admittedly been far from completely collected. Maurice Buxton Forman, their most recent

---

* Sidney Colvin, *John Keats*, 3rd ed., 1920, pp. 86-7 and 445. It is noteworthy that his findings have been accepted by De Sélincourt in his valuable notes (*Poems . . .* 6th ed., 1935, p. 577); by C. L. Finney (*Evolution of Keats's Poetry*, I, 67); and by Amy Lowell (*John Keats*, 1929, II, 369). Ridley went a step farther and, as we shall see in a later chapter, supplemented Colvin's discovery in *St. Agnes* with another of his own.

53

editor, in the preface to his collection lists more than thirty letters known to be missing. He says, for example, 'To Keats's earlier friend Cowden Clarke we have five letters.'[1] This despite the fact that the momentous friendship began in the poet's childhood at Enfield and lasted almost until his death. Mr. Forman adds: 'I have been able to print only four letters to Severn and it is probable that the painter distributed a good many among autograph collectors.' Moreover, 'Of letters to Leigh Hunt I know of only two.'[2] And, let us note especially, 'We have no correspondence with George Felton Mathew, with Cripps . . . Charles Ollier, with Hazlitt . . .'[3]—while the name of many another friend might have been added. Because of this lack, particularly of early letters, there have been gaps in our knowledge. Here it is significant that the earliest extant letter, tentatively dated as of October 1815, but actually written a year later (it belongs not 'to 1815 . . . but to 1816'[4]) was in any case written after the 'Shell Stanzas,' verses in which appears the earliest evidence of Keats' knowledge of Wieland's romance.

What, then, of other potential channels of information?[5] 'If one of Woodhouse's note books of Keatsiana had not been destroyed in a fire,' Dorothy Hewlett, the poet's most recent biographer, laments, 'we might know considerably more about Keats's early life.'[6] As it is, our knowledge of the early years and apprenticeship days is no more than fragmentary. His publisher and friend John Taylor obtained some dubious data from the poet's guardian, Richard Abbey. In the 1840's his biographer Lord Houghton gathered various reminiscences from a few schoolmates, contemporaries at medical school, and other friends. But while we owe these men a good deal, our chief source of information, aside from the poems themselves, remains the belated 'Recollections' of Charles Cowden Clarke, the son of Keats' headmaster at Enfield, and his first guide into the world of poetry.

In his *Recollections of Writers,* however, in the famous chapter on Keats (first published in 1874 in the *Gentleman's Magazine*), Clarke warns: 'It will readily be conceived that it is difficult to recall from "the dark backward and abysm" of seventy odd years the general acts' of Keats as a child. Clarke says: 'He had a tolerably retentive memory, and the quantity that he read was surprising. He must in those last months [at Enfield] have exhausted the school library.'[7] Clarke goes on to mention the books often cited since: abridgments of voyages and travels, the various histories of Robertson, that of Burnet, the works on mythology of Tooke, Lemprière, and Spence, along with the novels of Miss Edgeworth and Leigh Hunt's periodical, *The Examiner*. To this list he adds Edward Holmes' testimony that Keats read *Robinson Crusoe* and was sensitive to the horrors of *Macbeth;* but that 'he was not literary—his love of books and poetry manifested itself chiefly about a year before he left school'—till which time 'in all active exercises he excelled.'[8] From yet another source we know that he won Bonnycastle's *Astronomy* as a prize at the end of his school career in 1811; and that the next year he received an Ovid as a gift, either from the school or from his friend and master.[9] That is virtually all that we know about his earliest reading.

While Keats was apprenticed to Mr. Hammond, the surgeon, at near-by Edmonton (1811-15), Clarke tells us further, 'his whole leisure hours were employed in indulging his passion for reading and translating.'[10] But just what he read and translated, besides the *Aeneid* and presumably Ovid, Clarke does not say. He does mention, however, that Keats visited him regularly, and almost always with a book 'to read . . . or to be exchanged'; and that it was in the school garden one momentous day that under his tutelage Keats discovered Spenser and the *Faerie Queene*. Thus, unknown to Clarke, Keats first came to write verses, the 1814 *Imitation of Spenser*. Clarke also tells us he read *Cymbeline* aloud one day and that, while Keats was susceptible to some of its imagery, he did not know much of Shakespeare till later.* Clarke himself

---

* With the 'Shell Stanzas' in mind, it is noteworthy that Clarke says of Keats: 'His own intensity of thought and expression visibly strengthened with the study of his idol; and *he knew but little of him till he had himself become an author*'

is not very specific; but his emphasis upon the late but increasing passion for reading and upon its quantity is significant here, as is one thing more. He quotes a revealing remark of Keats the medical student of 1815-16, a remark made in the Borough period in London after the 'Shell Stanzas' had already been written. At that time Keats told him: 'The other day . . . during the [Anatomy] lecture there came a sunbeam into the room, and with it a whole troop of creatures floating in the rays, and I was off with them to Oberon and fairy land.' [11] What association it could have been that linked floating motes with Oberon, Clarke did not venture to suggest.

We know little more of the Edmonton period save from internal evidence in the earliest poems, from a later letter or two, and from the 1816 *Epistle to . . . Clarke*. In that poem Keats acknowledged that Clarke had introduced him to 'all the sweets of song' and the various poetic forms such as sonnet, ode, and epic; to Spenser and Milton, Ovid and Tasso (evidently in Fairfax's translation), and also to 'the patriot's stern duty' and political liberalism and the delights of music. From this Epistle it is also clear that Keats enjoyed the rural world around him and observed and absorbed much. But his earliest poems show that their imagery and diction were drawn largely from Spenser and Milton and their eighteenth century imitators, and that 'he learned the art of poetic composition from the imitative poets of the eighteenth century.' [12] Among others he seems to have known Thomson and Beattie and Mary Tighe early, and in his turn to have learned by imitation of their works.

There is also little question that well before his indenture to Hammond was terminated, and well before he removed to the Borough late in September 1815 to study at the joint hospitals, he frequently went up to London to see his brothers at Mr. Abbey's.

(ibid. p. 136)—a 'till' which would seem to refer to the publication of his first volume in 1817 when, the *Letters* show, Keats began studying Shakespeare intensively. Italics mine.

It was evidently through George that he met the Wylies and the Mathews, Ann and Caroline, and their cousin George Felton, who 'became for a time an intimate friend . . . and next to his brothers and Cowden Clarke the closest confidant of his studies and ambitions.'[13] With him, Mr. Finney has made clear, Keats 'read and imitated more contemporary poets of the eighteenth century schools.'[14] In the social and versifying Mathew coterie, Keats seems to have gone farther afield and to have discovered various contemporary poets.

. . .

Now it is well known that after the wholesale importation chiefly of sentimental and horrific German works in the last decade of the eighteenth century, the combination of 'Anti-Jacobin' ridicule and the reaction of the war years had brought about a marked decrease of interest in German literature. But in November 1813, the translation of Mme. de Staël's *De l'Allemagne* appeared, and that famous book was very widely read and discussed.[15] Its appearance and the approaching end of the war brought about a revival of interest in German literature. And that revival led to widespread curiosity, serious study, and knowledge. It is significant that two of Keats' later letters reveal the fact that he was familiar with some of the most celebrated and most romantic of German works.[16] With that knowledge Mme. de Staël's book, or the lengthy reviews it received in all the chief periodicals, may well have had something to do.

De l'Allemagne was a popular romantic manifesto written with the help of A. W. Schlegel himself, and a certain doctrinary bias was discernible in some of the remarks on Wieland. But Mme. de Staël devoted pages to him and went to some lengths to pay tribute to his fame as a Greek scholar, to his erudition as greater than that of Voltaire, and to his numerous contributions to German letters.[17] Moreover, she gave an enthusiastic account of *Oberon,* as being 'charming and full of imagination'; thought 'we cannot too much admire the poetry'; and gave a summary of part of its action, which, she said, 'is full of sentiment and truth.'[18] What is more, such was Wieland's contemporary fame that various reviewers of Mme. de Staël repeated some of her remarks about him, and ranked Sotheby's *Oberon* conspicuously as one of the few notable translations from the German.[19]

The stir that greeted Mme. de Staël's influential book may well have penetrated among the ambitious young versifiers of the Mathew set, of whom John Keats was one during just this time. For his and Mathew's knowledge of *Oberon* dates, as we shall see, from about 1815, when the revival of interest in German writings had barely begun and when Wieland's fame was considerable.

. . .

In Keats' biography, because of the lack of letters, the later Edmonton period and the early London days that followed long remained obscure. In fact not until recently was the 'Mathew chapter' studied. That period of intimacy between the groping Keats and the Cockney versifier Mathew, the first of his 'poetical' friends, evidently lasted from the autumn of 1814, or earlier, at least to February 1816.[20] In Keats' brief span that period was not insignificant. Yet 'we have no correspondence with . . . Mathew.' As a matter of fact, we have no prose correspondence, but we do have two curious Epistles in verse and various other poems connected with Mathew, which throw considerable light upon their intercourse. The 'Epistles' and verses that concern us, moreover, are closely interrelated, as John Middleton Murry has proved. He showed that even

the sequence of the whole series of poems seems clear. First, the two poems ['Shell Stanzas' and *To Some Ladies*] addressed and sent to Mathew's cousins [by Keats]; then, *O Solitude* addressed and sent to Mathew; then, Mathew's elegantly allusive invocation to his 'poetical friend'; and, finally, Keats' *Epistle* [*to George Felton Mathew*], dated November 1815.[21]

Let us now examine this series of poems in their demonstrably correct order.

The first of them, *To Some Ladies* and *On Receiving a Curious Shell, and a Copy of Verses, from the Same Ladies,* were composed in Tom Moore's manner in the late summer of 1815 while or shortly after Ann and Caroline Mathew with their cousin George were at Hastings, by 'the verge of the sea.' In the former piece Keats described the finding of the shell that his friends had sent him. In the latter, he addressed George as 'courteous Sir Knight' and 'warrior' in the fashion evidently popular in the Mathew circle. Keats asked whether he had a gem from the caves of Golconda; whether he had a goblet of gold engraved with the story of Armida the fair and Rinaldo the bold; whether he had a steed, sword, and trumpet, and the shield of the famed Britomartis, and other trappings. In these questions, the allusions show, Keats was referring to Tasso and Spenser, whose great metrical romances he had read with Clarke.[22] But if Sir Sidney Colvin was right, then Keats in what followed was alluding quite logically to a third metrical romance. In those lines Keats listed his 'blisses,' the two gifts he had just received from the Mathews: Tom Moore's tale of *The Wreath and the Chain* and that dome-shaped shell which he now likened to the work of a fay, thus: *

> *This canopy* mark: 'tis *the work of a fay;*
> *Beneath* its *rich shade* did King Oberon languish,
> When lovely *Titania was far, far away,*
> And cruelly left him to *sorrow, and anguish.*

> There, oft would he bring from *his soft sighing* lute
> *Wild strains* to which, *spell-bound,* the nightingales listened;
> The wondering *spirits of heaven* were mute,
> And *tears* 'mong the dewdrops of morning oft glistened.

* Italics are used, as sparingly as possible, to help the reader grasp the various parallels, whether verbal or conceptual.

In this little dome, all those *melodies strange,*
Soft, plaintive, and melting, for ever will sigh;
Nor e'er will the notes from *their tenderness* change;
Nor e'er will *the music of Oberon* die.

So, when I am in a voluptuous vein,
I pillow my head on the sweets of the rose . . .
(ON RECEIVING A . . . SHELL, 25-38) [23]

It was Colvin, we have seen, who first suggested that Keats in the first of these stanzas was alluding not only to the *Midsummer Night's Dream* but to Wieland's celebrated romance.* And Colvin might well have gone farther, for in the play Oberon does not languish under a canopy; nor is there any canopy with rich shade, made by a fay. Titania there is never 'far, far away.' Nor is Oberon in sorrow, let alone anguish, because of her abandoning him. In the play, what is more, Oberon does not possess a lute or any other musical instrument. Finally, in the comedy the fairies are diminutive garden creatures, certainly no 'spirits of heaven.' And they are not 'spell-bound,' together with the nightingales, by the 'wild strains' of a fairy instrument.[24] All these allusions in Keats' lines, all these elements concerning Oberon and Titania for which warrant is totally wanting in Shakespeare's play, do appear, however, and with but slight modification, in Wieland's poetical romance.

In the third canto of *Oberon* (a canto replete with the deeds of courteous knights and a *'brave warrior'* and with conventional steeds, trumpets, and swords—to which Keats also alluded), Sir Huon and his squire, having rescued the lady Angela from the giant, find themselves on a wooded plain. Weary and hungry, and even while Huon 'seeks *beneath* the *shade* repose,' they suddenly discover a *rich tent* that had appeared from nowhere, *the work of the fairy* king's enchantment (cf. Keats' 'canopy,' with its 'rich

---

* Cf. p. 53 above. Because of the play diminutive fairies are conventional. Keats' second line ('Beneath' and the word 'languish') might suggest the play. But there is no external evidence until April 1817 of his having read it.

shade,' 'the work of a fay').[25] After they have regaled themselves, they fall asleep; while from

> . . . the *heavenly* sphere,
> Along the silent air *soft voices* sweep;
> From every tree a sound melodious floats,
> As if the leaves were chang'd to *fairy* throats . . .
>   (OBERON III, 56)

an aerial music that gradually becomes *mute* (as Keats' 'wondering spirits of heaven were mute'). Again, shortly before that adventure, when during the fearful storm in the enchanted forest Huon is first confronted by Oberon, 'the gentle whisper of th' aërial form' is heard (II, 30). And since the squire in his terror won't let Huon stop, Oberon puts *his elf-horn* to his lips, literally 'breathes enchanting tones of fairy sound' (II, 37), and all are at once *spellbound by his music,* as Keats says. In both instances, in short, there is a canopy, a spellbinding fairy instrument, Oberon's soft music and wild strains, and a suggestion of heavenly or aerial spirits, as well as verbal echoes.

Moreover, with his lily wand Oberon breaks the horn's spell, and gives Huon the instrument and *a goblet of* finest *gold* (II, 46) that fills itself with *sparkling* fairy *wine* when held by a virtuous man. (Keats alluded in his lines 5 and 6 to 'a goblet for dark sparkling wine . . . heavy, and massy, and gold.') Then, promising to come to his aid if he were *'far* as the world' *away,* Oberon vanishes as two large tears roll from his azure eyes (II, 50-2). This, again, recalls Keats' 'and tears . . . glistened.'

All this Oberon imagery, which is not found in Shakespeare or anywhere else,[26] but which minutely resembles that in Keats' stanzas, is closely concentrated within a few pages in Wieland's romance. In that romance too, Titania, even as Keats said, is 'far, far away,' and it is she who dramatically *languishes in* deeper *sorrow and anguish* than the sad Oberon. Over her craggy enchanted isle, from a deep forest in which the melodies of nightingales and unearthly singing are heard in the moonlight, the lonely Titania flutters about tempest-tossed and unresting, 'sunk in deep despair' as she seeks 'some lonely spot, grief's consecrated ground' (VIII, 59). It is even for *Oberon* an unusually vivid passage, the highly visualized description of the ruinous daemon-haunted isle, of Titania's sequestered haunts, and of her sorrow because of the vow that has compelled her lord's absence of many years. Keats could have derived all this, his peculiarly un-Shakespearean knowledge of Oberon and Titania, from no other source than Wieland's romance. This will become more and more evident.*

The third poem of Murry's demonstrated sequence is the sonnet *O Solitude,* written in October or November 1815, in which Keats addressed Mathew, in a state of deep personal dissatisfaction with his surroundings in the 'jumbled' city. This sonnet contains Keats' first echo from a poem of Wordsworth, but it need not concern us farther.

The fourth poem, written in October or November 1815 but after Keats' sonnet (to which it alludes), is George Felton Mathew's 'Lines' *To a Poetical Friend,* a piece found in the Woodhouse Book by Miss Lowell and yet more recently discovered in a somewhat revised version in the *European Magazine* for October 1816.[27] Only

---

* In connection with the daemonic features of Titania's island, where she abides while 'far, far away,' it is suggestive that in the synchronous companion-piece of the 'Shell Stanzas,' the lines *To Some Ladies,* Keats again alluded to aerial spirits and nightingales:

'Ah! you list to the *nightingale's* tender condoling,
Responsive to *sylphs,* in the *moon* beamy air.'

And just before that he wrote of the '*steep,* whence the *mountain stream* rushes' and its spray that bedews 'the wild *flower.'* Keats' ultra-fanciful vision of Hastings, where his friends the Mathews were, may well have been modified, I think, by reminiscences of Titania's mountainous retreat where streams descend their steep mossy and flowering beds; and where the nightingale 'amid the thickening wood Trills to the silent moon her melancholy lay' (VIII, 51). For there too 'by whispering night-winds blown, Soft notes seraphic flow'd' (VIII, 65), the music of Titania's fairy folk and 'lovely sylphs' (VIII, 64). The closely similar and by no means conventional configuration, comprising no less than seven parts, is particularly noteworthy because of Keats' and Mathew's intense interest in just these stanzas.

in the last few years has it been realized that between these verses and the three early poems of Keats there was an intimate connection. For Mathew's 'Lines' reveal that both the 'Shell Stanzas' and *O Solitude* were 'before Mathew's eyes or in his memory' when he composed them.[28] Murry has conclusively demonstrated that Mathew's verses were of the nature of a poetic epistle, a reply to Keats, and that he quoted freely from the poems that Keats had addressed to him. But the 'Lines' also have another, far greater and hitherto unsuspected interest. This is what Mathew, replying to and echoing Keats, now wrote in the first of them:[29]

> Oh thou, who delightest in fanciful song,
>   And tellest *strange tales of the elf, & the fay;*
> Of *Giants tyrannic, whose talismans strong*
>   *Have power* to *charm* the *fair ladies astray;*
>
> Of *courteous knights,* & of high mettled *steeds,*
>   Of *forests enchanted,* and *marvelous streams,*
> Of *bridges,* & *castles,* & *desperate deeds,*
>   Of *magical curses,* & *fair ladies' screams,*
>
> Of *captures,* & *rescues,* & *mutual loves,*
>   Of *blisses* abounding *in* fair *ladies' bowers.*
> Of *murmuring Music, melodious groves,*
>   And beauty reclined on a pillow of flowers . . .

On the face of it this seems a compact and conventional catalog of a few romances. And concerning the bizarre and formidable schedule, Miss Lowell duly said: 'What the fairy tales were of which Mathew speaks we can have no idea. Either they have perished, or they existed merely in conversation, or they are a heightened allusion to the Shell poem.'[30] This last surmise was quite accurate. It is now known that 'Keats did not compose romantic tales at this period, but he did read them with Mathew and we suspect reacted to them very much as Mathew did.' In Mathew's own words, Keats 'used to spend many evenings in reading to me.'[31] It was this habit which underlies Mathew's 'Lines.'

His reply to Keats, his pointed allusion to 'strange tales of the elf and the fay,' is indeed a heightened allusion—not to, but through, the 'Shell Stanzas'—to Keats' source, a portion of Wieland's romance. Not only did Mathew unerringly recognize the source of Keats' strange fairy lore; every element italicized in his 'Lines' (and I count at least 23 in the first ii verses) occurs in parallel sequence in the self-same Canto iii of *Oberon* from which Keats had derived the fairy canopy, suggestions for the peculiar fairy music, and some at least of his chivalric trappings. That canto, again, follows immediately (within three stanzas) upon the episode of the golden goblet, the spellbinding elf-horn, and Oberon's tears, which we also saw in connection with Keats' 'Shell Stanzas.' But what was the tale to which Keats' Oberon allusions had drawn Mathew? It was this.

After taking leave of the sorrowful Oberon in the *enchanted forest,** Sir Huon sees in a grove a number of 'rich tents' in whose shade (cf. 'Shell Stanzas') the Prince of Lebanon and a score of *courteous knights* are resting (iii, 1-3). The Prince tells Huon that the fierce *giant* Angulaffer had *captured* the *lovely lady* Angela, Lebanon's bride; that the giant is invincible by virtue of a *powerful talisman* which he had stolen from a dwarf (iii, 5). Huon resolves single-handed to undertake the *desperate deed,* the *rescue* of the immured damsel (iii, 13). Mounting his *steed,* he rides to the giant's *castle,* crosses the draw-*bridge* guarded by enchanted warders, and is seen by the lady. She tells Huon how a miraculous, *magic* spell or *curse* caused the giant to sleep whenever he offered violence, and urges Huon to seize the ring and slay the giant (iii, 19-26). Huon retrieves the talisman but awakes Angulaffer, while Angela flees with piercing *screams* (iii, 32). By virtue of the ring, Huon slays the monster and is welcomed into her *bower* by the amorous damsel (iii, 38-42). But the chaste knight merely releases her and the other captured *ladies,* takes his leave, and soon dis-

---

* Here, as elsewhere, the italics are used to help the reader grasp the verbal and conceptual parallels.

covers Oberon's canopy in the musical grove (III, 56). After the music of the heavenly spirits has become mute, Huon in a dream perceives himself beside a most *marvelous stream* (III, 60). He sees and falls in love with a goddess-like maiden who is torn from his arms in a fearful storm and sinks *shrieking* into the waves (III, 63). Huon, agonized, at length awakes.

Now reread the first eleven of Mathew's 'Lines.' That epistle, we know, was a reply to two, probably three, poems by Keats and echoes phrases from them. And Keats' allusions to Oberon and Titania (which we traced chiefly to this Canto III of Wieland's romance) elicited from Mathew, to whom Keats 'used to spend many evenings reading,' the lines containing a lengthy, almost precisely parallel sequence of exact and circumstantial allusions. Every one of them occurs in the identical canto previously alluded to by Keats. And of the lengthy sequence, comprising twenty-odd concepts or elements, explicitly drawn from 'strange tales of the elf and the fay' and listed and described by Mathew, every one (though by no means of necessity so related) occurs in identical correlation, tone, color, and fashion in *Oberon*. Every single element is precise, even the fairy music that 'melodious floats' (*Oberon* III, 56): Wieland had likened it to the soughing of the wind in the leaves of the grove and to the murmur of a brook; Mathew duly speaks of 'melodious groves' and 'murmuring music.'

The exact verbal echoes and long parallel pattern, which is nothing less than a summary of Canto III of *Oberon,* are not idle chance. And in his sequel, throughout all the rest of his 'Lines' *To a Poetical Friend,* Mathew, still replying to Keats' allusions, followed him faithfully to Cantos VIII and IX of *Oberon.* For the first of these cantos had already left echoes in Keats' 'Shell Stanzas' and very likely in *To Some Ladies.*

But this is how Mathew's 'Lines' continue:

12   And *beauty reclined on a pillow of flowers;* *

* Cf. Rezia.

Oh *where* did thine *infancy open its eyes,*

14   And *who was the Nurse that attended thy spring?*

For sure thou art exotic to these frigid skies;

16   So splendid the song that thou lovest to sing.

That assertion, in the light of this study, is most significant.

Perhaps thou hast *traversed the glorious East,**

18   And, like the warm breath of luxurious gales

That *wander, mid gardens of flowers,* to feast,

20   Art tinctured with every sweet that prevails.

It is not the climate, nor Nature around,

22   It is *not thy nurse* that attended thy youth,

That give thee those blisses that sweetly abound

24   In *magical powers* to bless, and to soothe;

Oh! no, *'tis the Queen of those regions of air,* †

26   The gay fields of fancy, thy spirit has bless'd;

She cherish'd thy childhood with fostering care,

28   And *nurtured her Boy with the milk of her breast—*

She gave thee them, ere *thou couldst wander alone,*

30   And cheer'd in thy walks *amid terror and dread,* ,

She sung thee to sleep with a song of her own,

32   *And laid thy young limbs on her flowery bed.*

She gave thee those pinions, with which *thou delightest*

34   Sublime o'er *her boundless dominions* to rove,

The tongue too she gave thee, with which thou invitest

36   The ear to the *stories of wonder and love.*

When evening shall free thee from Nature's decays,[1] ‡

38   And free thee from study's severest controul,

Oh! warm thee in Fancy's enlivening rays,

40   And wash the dark spots of disease [2] from thy soul.

* Cf. Huon.
† Cf. Titania.
‡ For Woodhouse's notes, at the points indicated by [1] and [2] and [3], see Appendix 1, p. 317 f. I have also given there his prefatory remarks, as well as the text of the slightly revised version of *To a Poetical Friend* which Mathew published in 1816 in the *European Magazine.* Into that version Mathew interpolated an additional stanza containing at least one interesting feature.

Oh! let not *the spirit* of poesy sleep;
42   *Of fairies and Genii continue to tell;*
Nor suffer the innocent deer's timid leap [3]
44   The wild bee to fright from her flowery bell.—
G. F. M.

Even the most cursory reading of *Oberon* viii, 67-79 and ix, 34-6, shows that in these lines Mathew was alluding pervasively to the scene of the birth of the infant Huonnet in Titania's enchanted grot, where Rezia sinks as in a dream upon *a pillow of roses.* It was to this scene of *Oberon* that Keats had first alluded in 'Shell Stanzas' thus:

So, when I am in a voluptuous vein,
I pillow my head on the sweets of the rose.*

Evidently reminded by this allusion, Mathew had simply recalled its source and elaborated. (Cf. Mathew: 12-13, 22, 28, 32.) Indeed, excepting only Mathew's two last lines, which echo two lines in Keats' sonnet *O Solitude,* and excepting the plea for poetry in lines 37 ff., Mathew's entire piece is an exact and unequivocal series of allusions to Cantos iii, viii, and ix of Wieland's tale of wonder and love, the greater part of which has its setting in 'the glorious East,' and to which Keats had previously alluded. It is obvious that Mathew in a fanciful tribute † identified Keats with Rezia's infant, who is attended at birth not by the nurse but by Titania, and who is later abducted by her in the night of the hermit's death. (Cf. Mathew's 'thy': 14, 22, 26, 27-32.) And by her, by Wieland's Titania, who is the 'Queen of those regions of air,' the infant was given to her three aerial spirits with the command:

'Haste! to my fav'rite bow'r this babe convey:
There *tend* him as *my* new-born only *son:*
So may this child the threaten'd *danger* shun.'
(OBERON IX, 34)

* Cf. p. 60.
† Cf. Keats' earlier tribute, 'courteous Sir Knight' in 'Shell Stanzas.'

The precise verbal echoes are significant. And in line 30 Mathew was clearly recalling Huon and Rezia's terror and dread on discovering the infant's absence after the hermit's death.

Moreover, Mathew's line 42, 'fairies and Genii,' is peculiarly revealing, for the hermit at first seems to the lovers

> . . . some kind genius whose protecting grace
> Consoles their sorrow in this lonely place:
> Perchance 'tis Oberon . . .
>
> (OBERON VIII, 32)

The 'genius' of a 'place' is a guardian spirit or benevolent daemon. And it is just that which distinguishes Wieland's Oberon and Titania from all others. Keats and Mathew had realized this quickly in their reading of the 'strange tales of the elf and the fay' and of 'wonder and love' and 'the glorious East.' And with those tales, Mathew attests, Keats was delighted, even as he was with the pinions and 'tongue' which Titania had given him. In that testimony there lay a wide meaning.

Thus Keats' intense interest in Canto VIII, with its hermitage and enchanted flowery grot in a dreamlike mountainous setting, began early. Mathew's comment, 'So splendid the song that thou lovest to sing,' is significant. It leads one to believe that elements in the setting of To Some Ladies derived from the stanzas that immediately precede the childbirth scene.* Furthermore, it is noteworthy that the abducted infant is restored to Rezia in Canto XII, near the end of the romance, in that other visionary setting in the enchanted forest. For that triumphant fairy jubilee seems to have left some echoes in Keats' mind when he replied to the 'Lines' in his own 'Epistle' To George Felton Mathew.

But first, this much is clear: In the light of Mathew's lines 12-44, comprising an exact replica of highly exceptional features, yet in

---

* Cf. p. 62, note.

identical correlation, found in Canto VIII; and in the light too of the circumstantial summary of Canto III of *Oberon* in the first eleven of his verses, Mathew's 'Lines' *To a Poetical Friend* are unimpeachable evidence of what had happened. He and Keats had recently been reading Wieland's celebrated romance together. They had been attracted by the chivalric and fairy features of Canto III and the childbirth scene of Canto VIII. Keats' allusions to these scenes, in the poems addressed to Mathew and his cousins, were recognized immediately by Mathew, and led him to reply to Keats in heightened allusions to precisely the same episodes in *Oberon*. Now Mathew's 'Lines' are *a letter in verse* from Keats' most intimate friend of this period. That letter corroborates the internal evidence in Keats' poems, which are connected with Mathew's letter. That letter constitutes *external evidence* of Keats' knowledge of *Oberon* at this early time. And that, as we shall see, lends Mathew's verses their greatest significance.

. . .

It has also been shown by Murry that Keats' 'Epistle' *To George Felton Mathew,* dated November 1815, in which Keats continued to write of the conflict of medical studies and poetry, was in its turn a reply to Mathew's 'Lines.' 'Too partial friend . . . Fain would I echo back each pleasant note,' Keats replied. Addressing Mathew as his brother in song, he alluded, if not too aptly, to the 'brother Poets' Beaumont and Fletcher, and later also to Chatterton, Shakespeare,* Milton,* Burns, and the political heroes of Hunt's *Examiner.* In writing this, his first verse Epistle, Keats seems to have been imitating such seventeenth-century poets as William Browne. But also in his turn he alluded in some detail to Mathew's 'strange tales of the elf and the fay' as if in compliance with the latter's request 'of fairies and Genii *continue* to tell.' Along with Keats'

---

* To both of whom, together with *Oberon,* Mathew had been alluding.

own earlier allusions to the childbirth scene, and along with Mathew's extended allusions to Canto VIII with its enchanted setting on Titania's sequestered isle, it is important now to bear that request in mind.

For now Keats writes: 'Fain would I follow thee Past each horizon of fine poesy.' And after alluding to three mythological figures, he adds:

> Or *again witness what with thee I've seen,*
> K 26   The dew by fairy feet swept from the green,
> After a night of some quaint *jubilee*
> 28   Which *every elf and fay* had come to see:
> *When bright processions took their airy march*
> 30   *Beneath the* curved *moon's triumphal* arch.
> (TO GEORGE FELTON MATHEW, 25-30)

There the streaming imagery pauses momentarily while Keats interpolates his lament that he cannot 'each passing moment give To the coy muse,' who, he says (much as in *O Solitude*), would not live with him 'in this dark city.' If ever she 'be kind' again, he adds, it must be

> whene'er I find
> 37   Some *flowery spot, sequester'd, wild, romantic,*
> That often must have seen a poet frantic.

He goes on to describe this suggestive spot, as one where oaks and sundry flowers grow, where there is a stream, and a covert inhabited by nightingales, and a *'sylvan roof'*—natural imagery evidently recollected in part at least from personal experience of the familiar countryside—to which is suddenly added what seems a typical romantic *'ruin, dark and gloomy.'*

Was there any connection in his mind between that 'flowery spot, sequester'd, wild, romantic,' this 'ruin dark and gloomy,' and the interrupted train of thought of the 'elf and fay'—to which Mathew had just been alluding in terms of Canto VIII of *Oberon?* I think there was: that the train of thought was merely interrupted but not broken. In view of Keats' rose pillow in the 'Shell Stanzas,' of Mathew's allusions to the 'Queen of those regions of air,' and particularly of his request 'Of fairies and Genii continue to tell,' I suspect that the fairies and setting in Keats' obliging reply were not from Shakespeare's play.* For it is significant that the pictures in Keats' reply to Mathew do not correspond to those in the comedy, whereas his entire sequence reappears in Cantos VIII and XII of Oberon, in close connection with the childbirth scene and 'forests enchanted.' In view of Keats' explicit desire to 'echo back each pleasant note' from Mathew's 'Lines,' more narrow scrutiny here may prove fruitful.

In September 1816, in the verse Epistle To . . . Clarke, Keats mentioned the 'sequester'd haunts of gay Titania.' It is noteworthy that that very phrase (nowhere occurring in the play) appears in Oberon (III, 4): 'sequester'd haunts' describes the grove of the rich tents, which we saw in conjunction with the 'Shell Stanzas.' But now, in Keats' reply to Mathew's letter, he saw a 'flowery spot, sequester'd, wild, romantic,' and I think Titania was still hovering invisible in the offing. For the childbirth takes place in her *flowery* elfin grot with its 'sequester'd throne.' And that grot is located in just such a spot as Keats described.

The setting, it will be remembered, is an Elysian garden so beautiful in its shadowy silence that it leads the lovers to think their sorrow is being consoled by 'some kind genius . . . in this lonely place.' It is not merely shadowy because of the *sylvan roof*.† It is not merely full of streams and flowers, oaks and firs and exotic fruit trees, and nightingales and sylphs. Its setting is like the

---

* Because of the bickering of the fairy rulers in MND, who 'never meet . . . But they do square; that all their elves, for fear' creep into acorn cups and hide, there is no fairy jubilee attended by every elf and fay. Nor are there any bright processions in triumphant march beneath the moon during or after such jubilee. At best there is but one implicit suggestion for such a scene: after the play is over.[32] Again, if there are flowery spots in the play, they are 'a league without the town' and frequented by 'a crew of patches, rude mechanicals' who disturb Titania's slumber—surely in no setting 'sequester'd, wild, romantic.'

† Cf. Oberon VIII, 50: the forest trees, like 'arch'd embow'ring roofs.'

imagery of *To Some Ladies,* and also like the sequel to line 36 of Keats' 'Epistle' *To . . . Mathew:* the 'flowery spot, sequester'd, wild, romantic' that leads deviously to the 'ruin, dark and gloomy.' For Titania's mountain-girt paradise lies high up amid the *dark gloomy ruins* of shattered cliffs, in a visibly *wild and romantic* spot, haunted by daemons and inaccessible.* In its midst,

> . . . the shelt'ring cliffs between,
> Stood the lov'd grotto, her *sequester'd* throne . . .
>
> (VIII, 65)

and the *'flowery* bed' where the infant is born. And the similar correlation of features in Keats' *Epistle* is revealing.

The lonely paradise that is 'far, far away' had been created by the enchantment of Titania (who is both fairy and genius) when the penanced elfin queen had become surfeited with grief. But while the sorrow of banishment by her beloved lord grips her,

> Loath'd are the fairy sports—she turns in scorn
> From dances glittering to the moonlight ray.

And that picture, recalling the traditional folk-fairy sports, appears side by side in Canto VIII with the other italicized imagery. Thus the whole complex appears on adjoining pages, even as in Keats' 'Epistle.' That circumstance, the reappearance of much the same imagery in similar configuration, leads one to believe that Keats had heeded Mathew's request, 'Of fairies and Genii continue to tell,' and that he did so in terms of Wieland's Titania, who is both of these. In the light of Keats' explicit 'fain would I follow thee Past each horizon of fine poesy; Fain would I echo back each pleasant note' it is not surprising.

---

* Amid 'the *wild* unknown' of a 'lonely-tow'ring island . . . Pil'd up with monstrous *ruins* height on height,' and beneath the *'gloomy* clouds' that make it more forbidding, the penanced Titania lies grief-stricken and 'loathes the cliffs and *dark* o'ershadowing height' (VIII, 60 and 64). The compactness of this imagery is noteworthy. And it appears just before the childbirth scene of Mathew's 'Lines,' to which Keats was replying.

Evidently, too, Mathew's request and his allusion to 'forests enchanted' led Keats' thought to Oberon's enchanted forest. There, when Titania's sorrow is ended by her reunion with the daemon king, the lovers who had brought this about are welcomed with a most quaint nocturnal *jubilee* 'which *every elf and fay*' and aerial spirit, too, had reason to come to see. That iridescent scene, visibly enacted in Canto xii of *Oberon,* seems to have suggested Keats' lines 28-30. The *airy march* of aerial spirits and others, the *gleaming* bridal *procession beneath the moon,* celebrates the lovers' *triumph* and enters the diaphanous palace of the daemon rulers amid the dancing and jubilation and angelic songs of all their attendants. That picture seems to have been evoked in Keats' memory by Mathew's allusions to the 'infant' and 'pinions' and 'forests enchanted.' For the child born in Titania's grot is restored to its mother by aerial spirits who descend from the sky in that jubilee in the forest. Thus evidently the enchanted forest came to telescope with the scene in Titania's sequestered paradise: the child was the link between them. Such fusing of recollections from the romance is evident for only the first time here. One or another of the same scenes reappear visibly in Keats' later poems.*

•   •   •

'Nor e'er will the music of Oberon die,' Keats had said early. Mathew spoke of it, among the revealing allusions to Wieland's romance which constitute his 'Lines,' as 'So splendid the song that thou lovest to sing.' These phrases are as telling as 'Queen of those regions of air' and 'Of fairies and Genii continue to tell.' The daemonic overtones in these latter concepts distinguish Wieland's Oberon and Titania from Shakespeare's and indicate Keats' early awareness of the difference. The series of poetical exchanges that culminated in Keats' 'Epistle' *To George Felton Mathew,* had from

---

* For some further echoes from Mathew's 'Lines' in Keats' 'Epistle' *To George Felton Mathew,* see Appendix i, p. 319.

the first been marked by allusions to Wieland's 'tales of wonder and love.' In Keats' phrase 'What with thee I've seen,' together with the ingredients in Mathew's verse epistle to him, lies the two-fold testimony, the extensive internal and external evidence, that Keats had read *Oberon* with Mathew, probably during or not long before the summer of 1815.*

*For further discussion of this point and the connection with Charles Cowden Clarke, see Appendix II, p. 321.

ᕗ II ᕕ

1816: More Full of Visions Than a High Romance

DURING 1816 Keats gradually grew away from Mathew and the sentimentalism of his circle. But although he formed new friendships which helped the 'horizon of fine poesy' to expand rapidly, he did not free himself from the spell of Wieland's romance. Instead, upon his release in July from medical studies, that spell became much more powerful as the poet in him became self-conscious and at length dominant.

For a time, as his poems show, he remained sensitive to the more obvious chivalric and fairy features of *Oberon*. Little by little, however, he began to realize its deeper suggestiveness. He had early differentiated the Shakespearean garden fairies from Wieland's subtler creatures: aerial spirits or sylphs ruled visibly by an Oberon who reigns over the daemons in all nature's elements, earth and air, fire and water.* And as Keats' mind repeatedly reverted to the sources of poetic inspiration and the nature and function of the poetic art, it was drawn as though irresistibly to Titania's mountainous isle, instinct with spirits, natural imagery, and mysticism. Poem after poem reveals this preoccupation.

In the first of the pertinent pieces of 1816 some faint echoes from Titania's forest hermitage can be heard. In *Calidore,* the fragmentary 'tale of chivalry' written in April or May in the manner of Leigh Hunt, reminiscences from Wieland's tale of chivalry seem to have begun to stream in the wake of a suggestive simile. 'Sweet

---

*It was not by chance that in *To Some Ladies* Keats wrote of 'sylphs' and nightingales and thereby reminded Mathew of *Oberon;* that in the 'Shell Stanzas' in alluding to the romance, Keats spoke of 'spirits of heaven'; or that to Clarke he mentioned 'Oberon' and 'fairy land' and 'creatures floating.'

as *blue heavens o'er enchanted isles'* Keats wrote. And without pause he continued as in a reverie:

> K 152   Softly the *breezes from the forest* came,
> Sof*t*ly they *blew* aside the taper's flame;
> 154   Clear was the *song from* Philomel's *far bower;*
> Grateful the incense from the lime-tree flower;
> 156   *Mysterious, wild,* the *far heard* trumpet's *tone;*
> Lovely the moon in ether, all alone:
> 158   *Sweet* too *the converse* of these happy mortals,
> *As* that *of busy spirits* . . .
>
> (CALIDORE, 151-9)

This cluster, with its curious configuration, daemonic undertones, and verbal echoes in a tale of chivalry, is not, I think, mere chance. It is explained by the concept 'blue heavens o'er enchanted isles.' And it resembles echoes we heard as early as *To Some Ladies.** For Keats' mind seems once again to have wandered to Titania's haunts when the phrase 'enchanted isles' flashed on his inner eye. Titania's is an *enchanted isle:* a 'fairy land' that makes Rezia think she had never seen 'the *heaven so blue'!* (*Oberon* VIII, 12.) On that isle is the grot of the childbirth scene of Mathew's 'Lines,' Titania's *far bower* and

> . . . her sequester'd throne:
> *Whence, from the grove,* by whispering night-*winds blown,* †
> *Soft* notes seraphic flow'd . . .
>
> (OBERON VIII, 65)

These notes are the 'converse' and *sweet songs,* heard afar from this bower by the mortal lovers. It is the music of Titania's *busy spirits,* into whose cavern, that '*mysterious* spot' with its pillow of roses, Rezia wanders through 'opening *flow'rs'* that 'breathe fresh *incense'* on the morning her infant is born.‡ The verbal echoes

---

* See p. 62, note.
† Cf. K 152.
‡ Cf. *Oberon* VIII, 68-9. To the very next stanzas Mathew had alluded in his 'Lines,' as Keats had in the 'Shell Stanzas.'

hint that Keats' closely similar imagery was not coincidence. The similar correlation, in a compact cluster which he and Mathew had recently read in a tale of chivalry, reveals, I think, the reminiscence.

In that same month, beginning on 21 May 1816, while Keats was still walking the hospitals, the fairy tale, or 'song that thou lovest to sing,' came to life for five nights in Benjamin Thompson's adaptation: *Oberon's Oath, or the Paladin and the Princess.* This was at Drury Lane Theater, not far from the medical school. One wonders whether Keats was in the audience, attracted by what for him must already have been a magnetic title.[1]

The next month, June 1816, in the fifth sonnet, *To a Friend Who Sent Me Some Roses,* he alluded to a clear feature in the same portion of *Oberon* as that above. In this sonnet Keats told Charles Wells of having rambled in the fields; and that personal experience he interwove characteristically with literary recollections. For he wrote that he had walked at dawn, the hour when

> Adventurous knights take up their dinted shields:
> I saw the sweetest flower wild nature yields,
> A fresh-blown *musk-rose;* 'twas the first that threw
> Its sweets upon the summer: graceful it grew
> As is *the wand that queen Titania wields* . . .

But one may well ask: Where does Titania wield a floral wand? In Shakespeare's play the musk-rose appears on the flowery bank and in the scene where Titania sticks that flower in Bottom's ass' head. Yet Shakespeare's Titania does *not* boast a wand. What, then, could have led Keats to link a bouquet of roses with a fairy wand? The flowers he had received evidently reminded him of the musk-rose he had seen, which promptly recalled Shakespeare's queen. She evoked Wieland's Titania who, quite unlike Shakespeare's, is always attended by the fragrance and vision of but one flower—

the rose: as in the enchanted grot where Rezia reclined and where she is put to sleep by a sprig of roses; particularly when with her *wand,* 'with *rosy* branch *Titania* softly swept [Rezia's] half-shut eyes' (IX, 33). Keats must have recalled this. And by a simple but eminently characteristic train of associations, a bouquet of roses evoked in his weaving thought the 'wand that queen Titania wields' in the German romance.

Verbal associations and association of ideas, indeed, are apparent in many of Keats' poems. In conjunction with the 'Shell Stanzas,' we saw Oberon's *lily* wand, with which the spell of the horn is broken. But now, two months after the rose sonnet above, in the August 1816 'Epistle,' *To My Brother George,* the lily and the rose are explicitly linked. 'For there *the lily, and the* musk-*rose,* sighing, *Are emblems true of* hapless *lovers* dying,' Keats now says (lines 89-90). If there is a slight variation in key, in *Oberon* the flowers are emblems of the guardian spirits of the true lovers.*

Moreover, this 'Epistle' contains other reminiscences of Wieland's romance. Written at Margate, where he had gone shortly after he had been liberated from medical school, the 'Epistle' to his brother reveals Keats' driving poetical aspirations and his intense self-questioning as to his future. It is one of his earliest attempts to express his conception of the nature, functions, and inspiration of the Poet.

At the outset Keats reverts to experiences of the recent past: 'Full many a dreary hour have I past . . .' And, as in two of the Mathew poems, he regrets the 'seasons when I've thought No *spherey strains* by me could e'er be caught,' and that, though amid nature, he would never write greatly, or see visions, or tell 'Some tale of love and arms in time of old' (lines 1-18). But then associations begin to stream. For immediately he says:

> But there are times, when those that love the bay,
> *Fly from all sorrowing far, far away;*

* Cf. also: 'From [Titania's] pale cheek the *withering* roses fell' (IX, 32) in the stanza just before she wields her wand over Rezia.

> A sudden glow comes on them, naught they see
> *In water, earth, or air,* but poesy.
>
> (lines 19-22)

This, his earliest allusion to the elements, is yet more telling in the light of Titania's penance. For Oberon swore

> Never in water, or in air, again,
> Or flow'ry groves . . .

to meet his queen. Those lines occur in Canto VIII, 57, in the rocky isle towering above the sea, the isle to which Titania, sorrowing, had flown 'far, far away,' as in the 'Shell Stanzas.' Led by memories of the Mathew period evidently, and possibly by the suggestively similar scenery at Margate, Keats' mind was still hovering about the German poem.*

In his next lines he explains that Spenser had taught Leigh Hunt that 'when a Poet is in such a trance, In air he sees white coursers paw, and prance, Bestridden of gay knights.' That what other mortals think lightning is but the opening of 'their wide portal' by the warder, whose trumpet reaches 'naught on earth but Poet's ear' (lines 23-32). Keats' early interest in, and the source of this mythopoetic naturalism are noteworthy. But now his embroidering imagination adds other features, as he says:

> When these *enchanted portals open* wide,
> And through the light the horsemen swiftly glide,
> The Poet's eye can reach *those golden halls,*
> And view the *glory of their festivals:*
> Their *ladies fair,* that in the distance *seem*
> Fit for the silv'ring of *a seraph's dream;*
> *Their rich brimm'd goblets, that incessant run*
> Like the bright spots that move about the sun;

---

* Cf. the sonnet to his brother, also written at Margate, with its allusions to Cynthia [in Ovid, Titania], the 'wonders of the sky and sea,' and its suggestive 'rocks' and 'caves,' all links, these.

And, when upheld, *the wine* from each bright jar
Pours with the lustre of a falling star . . .

(lines 33-42)

We saw in connection with the 'Shell Stanzas' that Oberon gives
Sir Huon his rich goblet that fills itself with fairy wine. And that
'goblet never dries' (IV, 34). In the light of that goblet, and the
allusion to the elements above, and also the sorrowing of the flying
Titania, was Keats * musing upon the *dream*like *festival* at the
end of *Oberon,* where Titania and the daemon king meet again. †
In that iridescent scene the hovering fairy palace (halls) appears
beneath the *silver* moon; its *'golden gates expand'* by enchantment;
and the aerial spirits, in the guise of *fairest damsels* and ' 'mid the
songs of that *angelic* band,' emerge to welcome the true lovers to
the halls of the ruler of the sky.[2] Of this scene Keats' imagery seems
a reminiscence. And his transition from Spenser to Wieland was
natural; it appears to have occurred previously in his mind.[3]

Moreover, in the 'Epistle,' after writing of 'These wonders strange
. . . and many more, Whose head is pregnant with poetic lore,'
wonders of the sea (the daemonic element water) and the 'revelries
and mysteries of night' and sky (the element of air), Keats muses
on 'the living pleasures of the bard' and 'posterity's award' and
his influence upon human kind. Amidst this occur the lines 'For
there the lily, and the musk-rose, sighing, Are emblems true of
hapless lovers' in the manner of *Oberon* above. Then, but a dozen
lines later, the poet takes leave of earth:

'. . . Fair world, adieu!
Thy dales, and hills, are fading from my view:
Swiftly *I mount, upon wide spreading pinions,*
Far from the narrow bounds of thy dominions.
Full joy I feel, while thus I cleave the air . . .'

(lines 103-7)

---

* While recalling a phrase from Pope.
† Cf. the oath above, a link between the two scenes.

That vision of the unearthly soaring power of the poet's imagination, in the manner of the soaring king and queen of the daemons of the elements (first pointed out by Mathew: 'She gave thee those pinions'), anticipates by some months a yet more revealing conception in *The Poet*. That poem, as well as the imagery of the 'Epistle' above, establishes the close connection between Keats' interest in *Oberon,* his new animistic and mythopoetic conception of nature, and his repeated use of daemonic machinery and images. That use, distinct from but possibly sanctioned by Coleridge's example, appears in the verse letter to George for only the first time. In more ways than one, therefore, the 'Epistle,' *To My Brother George* is a milestone.

• • •

The next months were crucial and deeply exciting for Keats. Having gradually determined to devote himself to poetry, by chance he had again become intimate with Cowden Clarke. With him Keats had read various seventeenth-century poets, Chapman's Homer, the verse of Leigh Hunt, and, probably, more poetry of Wordsworth—whose greatness Hunt, the intimate of Clarke, had lately come to perceive.* Through Clarke, Keats met Hunt evidently in October or November; and through Hunt or Clarke he soon met the dynamic and self-assertive hero of the Elgin Marbles, the painter Haydon. By all these experiences and all these and other new friends, he was profoundly stirred and inspired. In October he produced his first great poem, the sonnet *On first looking into Chapman's Homer.* Shortly thereafter, his life work

---

* Keats' earliest allusion to a poem of Wordsworth's occurs, as we saw, in *O Solitude,* of Oct. 1815. In the *Specimen of an Induction* (of March or April 1816) he had written the line 'my heart with pleasure dance' in obvious recollection of Wordsworth's joy in the *Daffodils.* And on 19 Nov. 1816, Keats wrote the sonnet 'Great Spirits Now on Earth Are Sojourning,' which he sent to Haydon and in which he also paid tribute to Wordsworth's commanding genius. How much of his poetry Keats had read by this date it is impossible to say. But either from Wordsworth or Hunt, as well as from Spenser, he had earlier learned to see in nature a primary source of inspiration for poetry.

decided upon, he reverted to thoughts which he had expressed in the 'Epistle' to his brother and which he now developed further.

In November to December 1816, in that first part of *Sleep and Poetry* which envisages the nature and inspiration, the stuff and the realms of poetry, his art suddenly reached a new intensity of insight and expression. Almost at the outset he asked: *What is 'More full of visions than a high romance?'* (line 10). Then, for eight lines, with no idle fancy, he mused upon *Sleep,* which enlivens 'all the cheerful *eyes* That glance so brightly at *the new sunrise'* (line 18). Then he asks: 'But what is higher beyond thought than thee? Fresher than berries of a *mountain* tree?' (lines 19-20). Poet that he is, groping for images, he reaches higher and higher for symbols to render the very essence of Poetry. For Poetry, he says (and let us read carefully):

> K 24　. . . has a glory, and nought else can share it:
> 　　　The thought thereof is *awful, sweet,* and *holy,**
> 　26　*Chacing away all worldliness and folly;*
> 　　　Coming sometimes like fearful claps of thunder,
> 　28　Or the low rumblings earth's regions under; †
> 　　　And sometimes like *a gentle whispering*
> 　30　Of all the secrets of some wond'rous thing
> 　　　*That breathes about us in the vacant air;*
> 　32　So that we look around with prying stare,
> 　　　Perhaps to see *shapes of light, ‡ aerial* lymning,
> 　34　And *catch soft* floatings from a *faint-heard hymning;*
> 　　　To see the laurel wreath, on high suspended,
> 　36　That is to crown our name *when life is ended.* §
> 　　　Sometimes it gives a glory to the voice,
> 　38　And from the heart up-springs, 'Rejoice! rejoice!'
> 　　　Sounds which will *reach the Framer of all things,*
> 　40　And *die away* in *ardent* mutterings.
> 　　　No *one who once the glorious sun has seen,*

---

* Religion.　　　　　　　　　　　‡ Daemonic.
† Elemental.　　　　　　　　　　§ Immortality.

42   And all the clouds, *and felt his bosom clean*
For his great Maker's presence, but must know
44   What 'tis I mean, and *feel* his being *glow:*
Therefore no insult will I give *his spirit,*
46   By telling what he sees from native merit.

O Poesy! for thee I hold my pen
48   That am *not yet a glorious denizen*
Of thy wide heaven—Should I rather *kneel*
50   *Upon some mountain-top* until I *feel*
A glowing splendour round about me hung,
52   And echo back the voice of thine own tongue?
O Poesy! for thee I grasp my pen
54   That am not yet a glorious denizen
Of thy wide heaven; yet, to my ardent prayer,
56   Yield *from thy sanctuary* some *clear air,*
Smoothed for intoxication by the breath
58   Of flowering bays, *that I may die a death*
Of luxury, and *my* young *spirit follow*
60   *The morning sun-beams to* the great Apollo *
Like a fresh sacrifice; or, if I can bear
62   The o'erwhelming sweets, 'twill bring to me the fair
Visions of all places: *a bowery nook*
64   Will be *elysium*—an eternal book
Whence I may copy many a lovely saying
66   About the leaves, and flowers—about the playing
Of nymphs in woods, and fountains; and the shade
68   *Keeping a silence round a sleeping maid;*
And many a verse from so strange influence
70   That we must ever wonder how, and whence
It came. Also imaginings will hover
72   Round my fire-side, and haply there discover
Vistas of solemn beauty, where I'd *wander*
74   *In happy silence,* like the clear Meander
Through its lone vales; and where I found a spot

* The divine.

76   *Of awfuller shade,* or *an enchanted grot,*
      Or a green hill o'erspread with chequered dress
78   *Of flowers, and fearful* from its loveliness,
      Write on my tablets *all that was permitted,*
80   *All that was for our human senses fitted.*
      Then the events of this wide world I'd seize
82   Like a strong giant, and my spirit teaze
      Till at its shoulders it should proudly see
84   *Wings* to *find out an immortality.*
                                        (lines 24-84)

I have given the whole passage, as it is one of the most revealing
in all of Keats' work. It illumines *Endymion* and, as we shall see,
some of his greatest poems.

   Keats' religious attitude toward Poetry was suggested, I think, by
that of Wordsworth. In *Tintern Abbey* the latter had described his
transcendental experience thus: 'We are laid asleep In body and
become a living soul.' But the similarity of this rapt passiveness to
the experience of Wieland's hermit may well have awakened Keats
to the significance of the hermit's yearning vision of heaven and
immortality.

   Keats' excitement is revealed in the phrase 'rejoice! rejoice!' This
passage, excepting the sonnet on Chapman's Homer, was the most
vibrant poetry he had yet uttered. Still, the 'many a verse from so
strange influence' need not make us 'wonder how, and whence It
came.' The streaming of images in the creative process is transparent. We can observe the stops of his music, listen to what he had
heard, and see what came of it. In his reaching after the ineffable,
Keats, while sensing the ultimate mystery (K 70), must himself
have been conscious that *he had identified himself with Wieland's
hermit.* That he was echoing 'back the voice' of that sage's 'own
tongue'; that *Oberon* no less than nature was the 'book Whence I
may copy many a lovely saying.' The identical correlation of setting
(mountain-top), time (dawn, sunrise), and all the concepts, moods,
sensations, and imagery italicized serve to answer, chapter and

verse, Keats' initial question: 'What is more full of visions than a high romance?' Transparently that high romance was *Oberon;* the chapter, Canto VIII; the verses, chiefly stanzas 12-14, 24-8, 64-5, and 68-9. It is the self-same portion of the romance from which we caught echoes as early as *To Some Ladies,* the 'Shell Stanzas,' Mathew's 'Lines,' Keats' reply, *Calidore* and the rose sonnet *To a Friend.**

A reading of the italicized imagery reveals that the 'sanctuary' of Poesy which Keats here visioned (K 56) is Titania's *'shrine* of loneliness' (VIII, 1), her enchanted *'Elysium'* (VIII, 64). In its clear mountain air the hermit had found a refuge from worldliness and folly, 'Lost to the world, its miseries . . . A childish dream' (VIII, 24), after his loved ones had died. And in that lovely sacred spot, haunted mysteriously by Titania's aerial beings, his spirit had been gradually restored by the power of nature's beauty. Gradually purified of earth's slow stain, he had, on the mountain-top at sunrise, at last achieved mystical communion with God and his blessed loved ones in heaven and felt himself, while still on earth, a glorious denizen of their invisible world. In that same lonely vale, moreover, stood Titania's enchanted grot, into which Rezia wanders and from which the angelic music issues.

Though Keats had known its magic early, here in *Sleep and Poetry* he transformed it to his purpose for the first time. Identifying the hermit's mystical communion with God and the daemonic world, with the visionary sensations of Poesy, Keats wrought poetry before our very eyes. In this poem is visible for the first time the kindling effect upon him of the hermit's vision of the beauty of the divine in created nature, of daemonically animated nature and its consoling and spiritualizing power. Some of the ideas Keats may also have found in Wordsworth. But the long parallels both verbal and conceptual; the identical twofold imagery; the innumerable allusions; and the curious, perhaps subconscious, admission in line 65

* Canto VIII, of great importance to Keats, is summarized on p. 39 above.

of his reflected vision reveal his deep fascination for Wieland's romance. The elements in common are italicized. If they are read consecutively, it will be seen how they directed his vision. They are many and multifarious, yet in virtually identical correlation. But Keats was not plagiarizing. Steeped in *Oberon,* he absorbed and transmuted its imagery and natural and supernatural ingredients repeatedly and ever more profoundly. He re-created what he wanted in the 'ever-changing tale' and fitted the fragments into patterns of his own conceiving. We can watch him at work. The densest stanzas of *Oberon* will serve to illustrate the process here.

This is how Sotheby had rendered the hermit's dream:

Now, bow'd with years, his lov'd companion *died*—   K 58, 36 *
Alone remain'd the hermit, yet the more
His spirit turn'd to that *celestial* shore,   K 59
Where all he lov'd did with their God *reside*—   K 54, 48
There dwelt his soul—a wandering stranger here—
'Mid the still night when objects disappear,
And bodies, as external senses die,
In their first nothing seem again to lie,
Oft on his cheek *he felt a breathing spirit near.*   K 31

Then his half-*slumbering* ears *in trance perceive,*†
With shuddering rapture heard, the groves among,
Angelic harmonies at distance sung,   K 34
For him the inexpressive chorus weave:
And as he lists *he feels* earth's slender wall,   K 44
That parts him from his friends, about to fall:
His spirit swells, a *flame* celestial bright
Burns in his breast, while rob'd in heavenly *light*
Shapes of the *viewless* world his soul responsive call.   K 33

These yet remain, when softly laid in *sleep*
His *eye*lids close, and in the *morning* rays   K 18, 60

* These references are to verbal and conceptual parallels appearing in Keats' lines above.
† Sleep and Poetry and Visions.

When *the wide* world its theatre displays,
Still o'er his sense the warbled *echos* sweep;   K 34, 52
A soul-felt glance of heavenly *joy* supreme   K 38
Gilds all around, the groves and *mountains* gleam;   K 20, 50
And, over all, *he sees the form divine,*   K 39
The Uncreated in his creatures *shine,*
Bright as *in* drops of dew *the sun's* reflected *beam.*   K 41-3; 58-60

Thus imperceptibly did *heaven* and earth   K 49
United in his soul together run:
His spirit brightens like an inward sun: K 51, 44
Far from the dissonance of mortal birth,   K 26, 42
From passion's turmoil, in this *holy* gloom   K 25
Joys that await the blest his soul illume.   K 62, 44, 38
Who locks my daring lip with viewless seal,
Lest *aught ineffable* its *warmth* reveal?   K 40
Mute o'er th' abyss *I bend—man dares no more* pre-   K 79-80
sume.

(OBERON VIII, 25-8)

The faint aerial music at sunrise in an Elysium on a mountain-top; the hovering shapes of the invisible world of nature, breathing upon the half-conscious hermit who, in sleep, yearns like the poet for immortality in a dream-vision; the sunrise and immanence of God and consequent sense of spiritual exaltation, purification, supreme joy, and immortality; the glory and holiness and awful brightness that admittedly become unutterable: these components and their disposition are identical in *Oberon* and in *Sleep and Poetry.* They occur in an extensive, yet similarly compact, parallel complex. The parallels in Keats, while they are subtle, are transparent, circumstantial, minute. They indicate the reminiscent nature of the creative process and will repay sensitive study.*

And yet if time and place, spirit and matter and form and even

---

*I have indicated the verbal echoes and conceptual parallels by cross references. The reader who would see other fragments reintegrated by Keats, will find them in *Oberon* VIII, particularly 61 and 70-71.

words are closely similar to Wieland's poem, and the visionary complex is clearly derivative, still *Sleep and Poetry* is a poem of a quite different sort. It is an attempt to convey in poetical images Keats' conception of the intense or ecstatic poetical experience. And that experience—'what 'tis I mean'—resembles a dream-vision in sleep. It is to him what mystical communion with God is to the hermit. Having saturated himself in Wieland's romance, Keats expressed himself in symbols derived chiefly from a compact cluster of images depicting the hermit's experience of ultimate (dream) vision, the spirit world, and God. Keats used these same symbols, used this same passage repeatedly, alluded to it explicitly in various later works, and interwove threads of it into the very heart of *Endymion* and a half dozen other poems. It enabled him, who was groping after a mode of communicating his exalted sensations, to achieve a new intensity of perception and utterance. At the same time this, like other portions of *Oberon,* was capable of assimilation into various patterns new and strange. Keats transformed it so subtly that even Colvin overlooked his profound indebtedness to Sotheby's translation.

There are more vestiges of *Oberon* in *Sleep and Poetry.* The two most important are Titania's enchanted grot and another passage, both of which throw additional light upon the creative process and the extreme sensitivity of Keats' perception. We saw that Titania had flown far, far away to 'this sequestered scene' because the 'Monarch swore Never in water, or in air, again, Or flow'ry groves' to meet her until she had done penance. And she flew to this gloomy isle, 'pil'd up with monstrous ruins' and *crags* in a wild and 'dark O'ershadowing height,' where she lay until surfeited with grief. Then by her enchantment 'A new *Elysium*' *
arises, 'three lovely sylphs appear Swift at her call,' and the 'lov'd grotto, her sequester'd throne' appears in its midst. The enchanted grot

* viii, 64. Cf. K 64 above.

Whence, from the grove, by *whispering* night-winds blown,   K 29, 31
Soft notes seraphic flow'd: and oft by night
O'er [the hermit] at rest, she pois'd her viewless flight,
And *breath'd* upon his cheek *pure airs* to earth unknown.   K 56
(OBERON VIII, 65)

(Keats' 'sanctuary' is the enchanted grot itself, his imagery shows.) And in her hour of need it is toward this *fearful, flowery enchanted grot* that Rezia *'wanders* on forlorn' until she stops before this 'strange mysterious spot' and 'with nameless terror thrilling o'er' finally enters and sinks upon the pillow of roses and moss, as Mathew knew.* Then she falls asleep and as in a dream gives birth to her child with Titania's aid. A glance back at Keats' lines 63-78 with this imagery in mind, shows that he had wandered there once again too in musing of dreamlike poetic creation.

One of the most famous passages in the cryptically titled *Sleep and Poetry,* also reveals Keats' awareness of the supernatural features of Wieland's poem. In the lines following the long parallel sequence that we saw a few pages back, Keats wrote the well-known verses: 'Stop and consider! life is but a day.' And in a passage in which various images describe life, appears the phrase, 'the reading of an ever-changing tale.' Then, musing upon his own future, he says: 'O for ten years, that I may overwhelm Myself in poesy; so I may do the deed That my own soul has to itself decreed.' And, somewhat like Wordsworth in *Tintern Abbey,* he says he will first devote himself to beauty in the ideal world of his imagination, and then to the problems of the real world:

> And can I ever bid these joys farewell?
> Yes, I must pass them for a nobler life,
> Where I may find the agonies, the strife
> Of human hearts.

* VIII, 68-9. These stanzas adjoin both the childbirth scene and the description of the springtime song of the nightingales, etc., which we saw in conjunction with the Mathew poems and others.

In the same line he sees another vision expressed in another symbol:

> . . . for lo! I see afar,
> O'er-sailing the blue cragginess, a car
> And steeds with streamy manes—the charioteer
> Looks out upon *the winds* with glorious fear:

And Keats sees the *flying car* descend to earth, and notes how

> K 136   The charioteer with wond'rous gesture *talks*
>   To the trees and *mountains;* and there soon appear
> 138   *Shapes of delight,* of *mystery,* and *fear,*
>   Passing along before a dusky space
>   *Made by some mighty oaks:* as they would chase
>   Some ever-fleeting *music* . . .
>
> (lines 126-41)

In the light of the evidence in *Sleep and Poetry* presented above, this new symbolism is peculiarly interesting. We saw the mountainous setting of the hermitage amid the broken *crags.* (Note their reappearance here in Keats' lines.) And we heard the mysterious aerial *music* that issued from the *grove;* and saw the hermit's dream-vision, while Titania's aerial spirits, 'rob'd in heavenly *light, Shapes of* the viewless world his soul responsive call.' (The verbal echo, in Keats 138, is significant.) Until now, however, we have not seen *the flying car of the daemon king,* which repeatedly appears in the romance.[4] Nor had Keats alluded till now to his mysterious and fearful powers of mind and sense. This charioteer, nevertheless, is the symbol of the poet's divine imagination which, like the daemon king, knows the winds, communes with nature's every element, reads the souls of men, and even (K 136) 'talks to the trees and mountains' as with a living thing. The symbol was born not merely of classical mythology but of that organic, animistic, and daemonic view of nature which marks the new mythology of Wieland's romance. Since Apollo is twice mentioned in *Sleep and Poetry* the idea of his car must have occurred to Keats. But Keats' 'flying car,' like his charioteer and mountainous forest setting, suggests that his symbol for the poetic imagination was derived primarily from the daemon king. The reason for thinking this will appear in a moment.

In *Sleep and Poetry,* at any rate, Keats for the first time assimilated and transfigured Wieland's daemonology. In its visible governance of nature he found inspiration, and poetic symbols to render his thoughts. In the hermit's spiritualizing dream, which (perhaps with some help from Wordsworth's kindred example) he readily enough identified with the dreamlike poetic experience, he found a vital symbolism. Upon its wings he rose eagerly to new heights of poetic intensity. He owed this visibly to *Oberon,* in whose sensuous imagery, mystical visions, and peculiar mythology he was steeped. But he re-created the visions of the high romance boldly into a new beauty, as he was to do again and again. The imagery for a whole series of poems, of which portions of *Endymion* were but a logical culmination, derived ultimately from Titania's sanctuary and enchanted grot.

. . .

That sanctuary next left its marks upon *I Stood Tip-toe.* In those Huntian verses, significantly first called 'Endymion' and begun perhaps as early as the summer of 1816 but finished on 18 December 1816,[5] Keats wrote of 'Nature's gentle doings' with considerable sensitivity even if with excessive 'deliciousness.' Explicitly he asked (K 125-6) 'For what has made the *sage* or *poet* write But the fair *paradise of Nature's light?'* *

Soon thereafter he set out, faintly after the manner Spenser had taught Hunt, † and of Wordsworth in the *Excursion,* to write of the natural origins of various myths. Toward the end of the piece, however, some trick of association evidently lured him off once

---

* We saw above that Keats had identified himself (the poet) with the hermit (sage) who sees paradise in the light of dawn.

† See the 'Epistle' *To My Brother George,* p. 79 above.

again to Wieland's *wanderer* in Titania's paradise-sanctuary. 'Where had he been,' he asks:

> K 181   Where had he been, from whose warm head out-flew
> That sweetest of all songs, that ever new,
> That aye refreshing, pure deliciousness,
> Coming ever to bless
> 185   The *wanderer* by *moonlight?* to him bringing *
> *Shapes from the invisible world, unearthly singing*
> From out the middle air, *from flowery nests,*
> And from the *pillowy* † silkiness that rests
> 189   Full in the speculation of the stars.
> Ah! surely *he had burst our mortal bars;*
> Into some wond'rous region he had gone,
> To search for thee, divine Endymion!
>   (I STOOD TIP-TOE, 181-92)

Now as the hermit listens to the unearthly singing, the 'soft notes seraphic' that issued from Titania's flowery nest, ‡

> . . . *he feels earth's slender wall,* §
> That parts him from his friends, about to *fall:*   K 190
> His spirit swells, a flame celestial bright
> Burns in his breast, while rob'd in *heavenly light*   K 126
> *Shapes of the viewless world* his soul responsive call.   K 186
>   (OBERON VIII, 26)

To those shapes and that unearthly singing, it is clear from his imagery, Keats was still responsive.

For the second time he had identified the poet and the hermit-sage, and their dreamlike experiences. Again and again he went into the 'wond'rous region' of the hermitage. And here, in linking that region with Endymion, let us note, he was preparing the way for his own wanderer of that name. Within a few months, Canto

---

* Ideal beauty.
† Cf. Mathew's 'Lines.'
‡ Cf. K 186-7. Also *Oberon* VIII, 65 (p. 89 above).
§ i.e. his mortality: 'our mortal bars' (K 190).

VIII of *Oberon* with its daemonology and mysticism, natural imagery and pictures of the moon, was to be drawn with fine craftsmanship into the long poem we now know as *Endymion*.*

. . .

But before turning to that chapter, let us glance at the last of the 1816 poems to be considered. It stands in a peculiar relationship to, and at the same time in marked contrast with, Mathew's *To a Poetical Friend* of at least a year earlier. Mathew, in alluding to the 'strange tales of the elf and the fay,' had listed, it will be recalled, some twenty incidents in Canto III of *Oberon,* among them this:

> Of giants tyrannic whose *talismans strong*
> Have power to charm the fair ladies astray.

That bouncing allusion, we saw, was to the potent ring which the giant Angulaffer had stolen from Oberon.

Now, evidently in December 1816, Keats, already immersed in the stuff of *Endymion* and its abandoned earlier namesake, wrote another sonnet, which was first discovered in the Woodhouse Book by Miss Lowell.[7] And this is what Keats wrote:

THE POET

1	At morn, at noon, at Eve, and Middle Night	II, 22 †
	He passes forth into *the charmed air,*	
3	With *talisman to call* up *spirits* rare	x, 3; VII, 35
	From plant, cave, rock, and fountain.—*To his sight*	x, 13
5	The hush of natural objects *opens* quite	
	To the core: and *every secret* essence there	
7	Reveals *the elements* of good and fair;	
	Making him see, where Learning hath no light.	x, 13
9	Sometimes *above* the gross and palpable things	

* For some further echoes in *I Stood Tip-toe* see p. 305, note 6.
† These references are to Cantos and stanzas in Sotheby's translation of *Oberon.*

$$\text{Of } this \text{ diurnal} \begin{cases} \text{sphere} \\ \text{ball,} \quad \text{his } spirit \text{ flies} \\ earth \end{cases}$$

11 On awful wing; and with its destined skies x, 19

   Holds premature and mystic communings: x, 20

13 Till such unearthly intercourses shed

$$\text{A visible halo round his} \begin{cases} \text{living} \\ \text{mortal} \end{cases} \text{head.}$$

In this unfinished sonnet one cannot fail to see the theory of the natural source of poetic inspiration. Keats' phrase 'elements of good and fair' suggests the ethical bias of Wordsworth. In the sestet with its flight, however, Finney perceives the influence of Drayton's *Man in the Moone*, which he believes one of the chief sources of the plot of *Endymion*. Now while Keats may very well have owed something to Drayton's flight and such conventional phraseology as 'diurnal' and 'sphere' and 'ball,' it is significant that Drayton's Phoebe transported Endymion into the sky in her chariot after she 'calls down the Dragons that her chariot draw' [8]—in the manner of those of Ovid's Medea. Keats' Poet, on the other hand, explicitly *flies alone* 'on *awful wing*.' He has 'unearthly' insight into 'every secret essence' in nature, 'making him see' as if intuitively where the most learned mortal is blind. Moreover, this Poet 'passes forth into the charmed air, With *talisman to call* up *spirits* rare.' And that is pure daemonology of a very familiar sort. Far more significant here than Drayton's influence, it seems to me, was that of Wieland's Oberon, who possesses virtually every single power Keats bestows on his Poet.*

---

*Besides Titania's gift of pinions in Mathew's 'Lines,' it is noteworthy that in the 'Epistle' *To My Brother George* in which he alluded to the lily and the rose and 'fly from all sorrowing far, far away' and the elements of 'water, earth, or air' in accordance with Oberon's oath, and the 'rich brimm'd goblets that incessant run,' Keats had visioned the soaring power of the Poet's imagination: 'Swiftly I mount, upon wide-spreading pinions.' Again, in *Sleep and Poetry*, where he had identified the hermit's vision of God and spirit-haunted nature with the Poet's experience of high poetic inspiration, he had seen the charioteer and 'shapes of delight' and later had asked: 'The high Imagination cannot freely fly . . .' (*S. & P.*,

In *The Poet* the phrases 'mystic communings' and 'A visible halo round his living/mortal head' remind one of the earlier identification of the poet with the saintly hermit. But the rest is daemonology derived from adjoining cantos of *Oberon,* which Keats knew hardly less well. For Wieland's Oberon wears the *'talisman* . . . by elf and *sprite* ador'd,' (x, 3), by whose power 'Be it or man, or beast, or ghost [spirit], or shade, Lo! at his *beck* it bows, the slave of magic might.' (vii, 35. With this compare K 3.) By day or night in the romance, he

> . . . *wings* along *the air* his viewless course.
> He who possesses [the ring], and knows its force,
> Can, as he wills, alike *o'er earth* and hell prevail!   K 9-11
> (vii, 34)

And the daemon king does so visibly, as Keats knew. He also posts over land and sea at all hours.* And he has other powers. Shortly after the hermit's death, he appears

> . . . *before whose* rays [of *sight*]   K 8
> *All darkness fades,* the guardian god . . .
> While on a heav'n-topt mountain's cloudless brow.
> (x, 13)

And from this mountain-top he not only sees Huon suffering, his image reflected at will in a passing cloud in the sky, but 'from that distance heard, his lowest sigh.' As Oberon observes the sufferer and hears him from afar, moreover, he gazes at the skies and *muses on* the *'secret* influence' of Fate. For he can foretell the

163). In these previous instances where he wrote of *the Poet,* he wrote, we saw, in terms of Wieland's Oberon and Titania, and their aerial spirits, 'shapes of the viewless world.' In *The Poet* what he had previously written naturally recurred to his mind, and his vision, more sharply focused, saw the symbolic images in the same terms but more boldly.

* Cf. K 1 with *Oberon* ii, 22: 'True, known to all, when cocks at *day-spring* crow, Then all the goblery at *noon* of *night* . . . go . . . But the strange sprite' of the enchanted forest 'walks [and flies] at open *day*.' Five stanzas earlier occur the lines: 'In sweet forgetfulness all stilly slept . . .' which we saw in *I Stood Tip-toe.*

future and holds *premature* and *mystic* communings precisely as Keats says (K 11-12). His mind, like his senses, is subject neither to time nor space: *he can see into the soul* of man, as he can commune with and animate nature. Huon in the same passage implies that every grain of sand and every leaf and 'little flint' would aid if Oberon willed. (With this compare K 4: 'plant, cave, rock.') He possesses the awful powers of the monarch of *all the elements* and their animating spirits. As the talisman and his other imagery show, Keats knew all this.

Nothing, however, more clearly reveals the swift flight of his own powers than the contrast between Mathew's allusion to that potent talisman and Keats' full grasp of the inner springs of the romance. Its daemonology, which differs from that of Coleridge, Keats wrought into symbols and imagery with which to convey his own daemonic-angelic version of the theory of natural inspiration. For Wieland's daemon king and 'guardian god' had become a symbol for him of the soaring poetical imagination which, with powers higher than reason, sees into the soul of man and communes with and animates nature—as a great poet does. The imagery of *The Poet* also confirms our suggestions as to the identity of the charioteer who 'talks to the trees and mountains' in *Sleep and Poetry*.

Very probably it was the example of Spenser and Hunt that first led Keats to find an inspiration for poetry in nature. Probably, too, his experiences of nature had been made more meaningful through his reading of Wordsworth. But he had also known *Oberon* since an early date. And the various experiences, while reinforcing one another, had blended in his thought. Certainly, it was with reason that Oberon's unearthly powers were here for the second time transferred to and identified with *The Poet.** In the same manner Keats had identified the hermit's dream-vision with that of *Sleep and Poetry*. The mysterious forces of nature, as sensed

---

* It is suggestive that in the 1819 *Ode on Indolence* Keats still thought of 'my demon Poesy' (line 30).

by the saint and swayed by the daemon king, provided Keats with a new mythology and symbolism, as well as with a world of inspiration. It was probably this, and the crystallizing effect that *Oberon* had upon the formulation of his imaginative perceptions, that led Keats to say: 'What is more full of visions than a high romance.'

But we have only begun to see the intense nature of his absorption in that romance. Again and yet again it provided the stuff of visions, in the genesis of poems not always minor. When Keats as early as 1815 said, 'Nor e'er will the music of Oberon die,' the poet, like the daemon king, had in truth spoken prophetically.

⫸ III ⫷

The Visions, Wanderings, Mission, and Love of 'Endymion'

BY THE END of 1816, when he was living with his brothers in Cheapside, Keats had written chiefly short occasional pieces, a few of which revealed considerable promise. In the Chapman sonnet he had written great poetry. But despite the many lapses in *Sleep and Poetry,* its thrilling notes—of almost religious devotion to art, and of fevered ambition and self-criticism—give a more accurate view of his increasingly tense imaginative life at a time when his intention of forsaking medicine for poetry had barely been realized. The fall of 1816 had been to him a time of troubled thoughts as well as exciting discoveries. Deeply aware that as a medical man he might be both 'Happier, and dearer to society,'[1] he had also had to decide for poetry in the face of his guardian Mr. Abbey, who was incapable of sympathy with a poet's career. Moreover, Keats himself was as yet far from firmly convinced of his fitness for great poetry.

There was reason, on the other hand, for his generally high spirits. Freedom, in the winter of 1816-17, opened ever wider horizons. Besides his brothers, he saw a good deal of Clarke, Leigh Hunt, the young poet Reynolds, and especially of Haydon. From all these and other friends he received affection and encouragement. With Severn or Haydon as guide, he visited the art galleries and the Elgin Marbles and developed an eye for color and line. In Haydon's studio his ambitions were spurred by hours of talk on art and poetry, in the shadow of the grandiose unfinished work from which the painter expected immortality. More than one such evening stimulated Keats. Ironically, it was Haydon who urged him to form regular habits of work and to strive greatly and with faith, to beware of the influence of the facile Hunt, and to guard his health. By Haydon he was encouraged to 'improve' himself and to undertake that long work on Endymion about which he had been thinking for many months. 'Why endeavour after a long Poem?' he had heard Hunt wonder. In the letter where he mentions this, Keats gives the answer. In his opinion, 'Lovers of Poetry' like a 'Region to wander in.' And besides, 'Did our great Poets ever write short Pieces? I mean in the shape of Tales . . .'[2] It was that ambition, to be a great poet, which excited him and which led him to plan Endymion.

All the while he was reading and thinking much. The freer style and diction in the late 1816 poems show that from Hunt he had gone back to the older poets such as Spenser and Chapman, Sandys and Marston, Fletcher and William Browne. He read and reread those 'beautiful tales from the ancient time of that beautiful Greece.' And with his brothers and Haydon he began the serious study of Shakespeare. 'His own intensity of thought and expression,' Clarke noticed, 'visibly strengthened with the study of his idol.' * The Letters reveal how thoroughly Keats saturated himself in the poems and plays of Shakespeare throughout 1817. And the sensitivity of his nature, capable of an extraordinary range of perception, was fostered by those plays, in which he found endless stimulation and delight. It was Shakespeare, too, who led him to ponder more deeply the nature of poetic genius, which readily loses itself in what it contemplates, with that selflessness and 'negative capability' repeatedly discussed in the Letters. It was that same influence, counteracting Wordsworth's, which intensified the conflict in Keats' mind between the claims of beauty and human suffering, between subjective and objective art, between intuition and reasoned knowledge. That conflict, which arose in 1816 and which is apparent in and beyond Endymion, became more and more acute toward the

* Cf. p. 55, above.

end of 1817 and in 1818. By then Keats had greatly matured, and, while still the political disciple of the radical Hunt, he had become more tolerant. Thus thanks also to Bailey, his appreciation of Wordsworth, the mistrusted conservative and poet of the 'egotistical sublime,' came to extend beyond particular passages * and grew increasingly subtle and disturbed.

But now, in the spring of 1817, only a few weeks before he began *Endymion,* Keats' first volume ventured into print. Published at the urging of the sanguine Hunt and his circle, the *Poems,* save for Keats' friends, miscarried. We can only surmise how he himself felt. But the failure did not deter him. The most revealing piece in the volume shows that he had previously been aware of his shortcomings. For in *Sleep and Poetry* he had written

> What though I am not wealthy in the dower
> Of spanning wisdom; though I do not know
> The shiftings of the mighty winds that blow
> Hither and thither all the changing thoughts
> Of man: though no great minist'ring reason sorts
> Out the dark mysteries of human souls
> To clear conceiving: yet there ever rolls
> A vast idea before me, and I glean
> Therefrom my liberty; thence too I've seen
> The end and aim of Poesy.
>
> (lines 284-93)

Keats *had* seen the end and aim of Poesy: through living and thinking and following instinct; perhaps in reading Hunt's remarks on the aims of poetry,[3] and in reading some of Wordsworth; certainly in identifying himself earlier in this poem with the hermit, and the dreamlike and intuitive poetic experience with that sage's self-destroying vision of God. That we saw in the previous chapter. And Keats knew that intuitive perception was his strength. He knew that despite his lack of learning he had that higher power, of immediate insight, to make 'him see where learning hath

* Cf. Bailey in the Houghton Ms. (Colvin, op. cit. p. 145).

no light,' like the daemon king who became *The Poet*. But Keats was humble as well as courageous. In the continuation of *Sleep and Poetry* he had peered into the future and said:

> An ocean dim, sprinkled with many an isle,
> Spreads awfully before me. How much toil!
> How many days! what desperate turmoil!
> Ere I can have explored its widenesses.
> Ah, what a task! upon my bended knees,
> I could unsay those—no, impossible!
>
> (lines 306-11)

And there for 'sweet relief' he had had to turn to less exhausting thoughts of his friends. But his goading ambition clashing with self-mistrust, the desperate turmoil and sense of vastness: these must be borne in mind as we turn to his first long work—in which, I think, Keats tried to unfold something of his 'vast idea.'

In accordance with his brothers' and Haydon's promptings, he left London on 14 April 1817, for the Isle of Wight. Hardly had he reached his quarters at Carisbrooke than he unpacked his Shakespeare and read *Lear*. Shakespeare's greatness, however, depressed as well as stimulated him. In a ferment of hope and fear, inchoate ideas and imaginative conceptions, he could write only the sonnet to the sea. A day or two later he seems to have begun *Endymion*. But solitude and intensity of thought on poetry, 'so long together that I could not get to sleep at night,' upset his digestion and made him flee within ten days to Margate, where Tom soon joined him. His state of mind as he began *Endymion* is revealed in a lost letter to George, written some time early 'in the Spring' and partly quoted in a later letter.

As to what you say about my being a Poet, [he wrote,] I can return no answer but by saying that the high Idea I have of poetical fame makes me think I see it towering to[o] high above me. At any rate I have no right to talk until Endymion is finished—*it will be a test, a trial of my Powers of Imagination and chiefly of my invention* which is a rare thing indeed—*by which I must make 4000 Lines of one bare circumstance and fill them with Poetry;* and when I consider that this is a great task, and that when done it will take me but a dozen paces towards the Temple of Fame—it makes me say—God forbid that I should be without such a task! *

In that spirit he undertook *Endymion,* a long poem which was to him a 'test, a trial,' an important and rewarding experiment. And for all his feverish turmoil, he went about its composition with all his heart and soul, in a self-appraising and thoroughly workman-like manner.

Keats had early been fascinated by the moon. To it, Clarke tells us, he had written an early sonnet, and in the Mathew poems and *I Stood Tip-toe* he had repeatedly alluded to the moon goddess, as if to his guardian spirit, and attributed beneficent powers to her. Since childhood he had loved the nature myths of Greece. But the Endymion legend, of the shepherd of Latmos who fell in love with the moon, had gradually assumed a deep personal meaning for Keats. In country walks and from the windows of the hospitals he must often have noted the silent magic of moonlight which mysteriously transfigures the world of reality and suffering. For Keats that experience was of such profound significance that the story of Endymion became for him a parable. When he came to write his long allegoric romance, he sought to expound that parable as best he might, in the figurative language of poetry. He drew upon his own experience of life and death, joy and suffering, and beauty in nature and everywhere, as well as upon his intense imaginative life in books. His letters are always frank. 'I must work—I must *read*—I must *write*,' he said characteristically,[4] indicating how closely interrelated the processes of absorption and creation were for him. Substantially he followed the salutary advice of Haydon, to 'collect incident, study characters, read Shakespeare'[5]— even though he read far more than that. Young and impressionable,

* *Letters,* 52. Italics mine.

Keats read with the keen and purposeful eye of a poet, 'a reading in which the mind moves like the passing of a magnet'[6] and in which it fastened not only upon pictures of the wandering moon but also upon a myriad of sublunary things to help him fill '4000 lines' with poetry. Indeed, partly because 'All lovely tales that we have heard or read' were to him 'An endless fountain of immortal drink,' as he said with twofold meaning near the outset of *Endymion*, modern critics pretty much agree that in the unusual romance the images, so frequently literary in derivation, are so numerous as to obscure both the theme and the narrative. For Keats lavishly embroidered the legend.

Much has been written in regard to his sources. It has been noted that the familiar and luxurious Huntian style of the earlier poems was modified in *Endymion* by that of the Elizabethan poets. Shakespearean intensity left its marks. And there is little doubt that various archaeological data, from such scholarly works as Potter and Baldwin, were interwoven with the stuff of myth and legend gleaned from Ovid and Bion and other sources. Drayton's 'Festival of Pan' in the *Man in the Moone* provided hints, as did Shelley's *Alastor*. The Wordsworthian experience of the poet's relationship to nature and the 'still, sad music of humanity' affected Keats profoundly and contributed not merely to the theme of his third book, in which Endymion discovers human suffering and the effects of sympathy. Before Miss Lowell,[7] students of Keats had suggested that some of the essential features of his plot may have been drawn from Drayton's *Endimion and Phoebe*, a neo-Platonic allegory, in the highly artificial style of the Renaissance, of the imagination in pursuit of ideal beauty. But that Keats could have known that extremely scarce work has been doubted, and that he must have known it has been questioned among others by Professor Bush.[8]

As for the meaning of *Endymion*, that too has been much discussed. To this day there is a wide divergence of opinion about what Keats intended to convey. The critics have run the gamut, from a charge of complete planlessness to an impression of a transcendent vision of the mystery of life itself. They have seen *Endymion* as without allegoric purpose; as a conventional neo-Platonic quest of ideal beauty; as a philosophical poem about love and beauty; as at least a partial answer to the apparent passivity of Shelley's *Alastor;* as a poet's quest of the ultimate mystery, the meaning of human life, and the stages of experience by which he apprehends the mystery.[9] Because so much has been thought and written, two things are clear: *Endymion* is difficult; and impressionistic criticism, however ingenious, has its pitfalls. Here, at any rate, we must try to steer clear of them. In seeing some fresh evidence of Keats' reading, however, perhaps we may see some new light.

·   ·   ·

Endymion is the work of a young poet whose wings were growing as he flew and whose imaginative control (the very possession of which he doubted) was still imperfectly disciplined. It is a luxuriant poem, often obscure, whose theme is frequently veiled by a too exuberant imagination; a poem whose structure, while consciously planned, is somewhat sprawling, and whose execution is often uncertain. But with all its faults it is a work full of passages of great beauty into which Keats precociously poured some of his most vital intuitions. For that very reason, it is repellent to a 'consequitive man' or logical mind, and those intuitions have not yet been fully understood, for Keats, poet that he was, often wrote elliptically and clothed his perceptions in a symbolism the key to which has not been fully grasped. Yet there was an actual key to Keats' maturing conceptions of life, nature, and art, love and beauty and truth. In *Endymion,* moreover, he merely uttered those conceptions in what proved to be a sort of prolegomenon to his riper masterpieces. This fact and the fascinating process involved in the creation of *Endymion* make it a poem which warrants and repays the minute study devoted to it in the following pages.

Although it has not been realized heretofore, one of the 'lovely tales' that contributed most vitally to *Endymion* was Wieland's *Oberon*. Keats, we saw in the previous chapter, wrote *Sleep and Poetry* in November-December 1816 and in it identified himself with Wieland's hermit. On 18 December 1816, he finished the verses originally called 'Endymion' but now known as *I Stood Tip-toe*. Therein, while momentarily envisaging the 'wond'rous region' into which the poet-maker of the Endymion myth had gone, Keats identified that region with the hermit's and Titania's sanctuary in Canto VIII of *Oberon*. In so doing, in identifying the mountainous sacred groves of Titania and the hermit (and the wanderer Huon and his eastern bride) with the brief vision of the Endymion poet, Keats, wittingly or not, plotted the road for his wanderer. For only four months later he began *Endymion*. And when after further preparation he began writing that romance about 17 April 1817, he clearly saw rising in his mind some of the same scenes and visions that had kindled his imagination in *Sleep and Poetry* and in *I Stood Tip-toe,* and that were now to be transmuted or otherwise incorporated in his long allegory.

Aside from the connection through the earlier 'Endymion,' there were a host of inescapable associations by which the settings, the incidents, and the characters, the very structure and theme of *Oberon* could be drawn into Keats' formative conception of *Endymion*. The name Titania, it is important to remember, was first derived by Shakespeare from Ovid, in whose tale of the metamorphosis of Actæon Titania is a patronym and synonym for Diana or Phoebe, the moon goddess.[10] *Endymion* itself shows that Keats knew this well. Thus Wieland's romance seems to have been recalled to Keats' memory by constantly recurring and basic associations. Moreover, Keats knew early that *Oberon* is the tale of the spiritualizing *visions, wanderings through the elements, mission, and love* of a 'youth, by heavenly power lov'd and led.' * If we examine the four books of *Endymion*, we shall find that essentially

* *End.* III, 708.

they are concerned with these same four themes, or basic structural features. What is more, an examination of the details of settings, and of the characters, imagery, machinery, and allusions in those four structural divisions, indicates that Keats was aware of the parallels; that he alluded to them repeatedly; and that he derived much of his material from *Oberon*. Indeed, that romance seems to have directed or guided the imaginative processes of his mind. It seems to have served as a sort of pattern into whose outline many other elements and ingredients, related by various affinities to the *Oberon* material, were drawn. *Endymion* is long, and the demonstration is difficult. But the attempt to trace its relation to *Oberon* is worth while because the key to Keats' meaning seems to lie in *Oberon*. His own experience, illumined and corroborated by that of Wordsworth and the hermit, found expression in terms of a concrete and poetically conveyed case-history of suffering and beauty that lies at the very heart of *Endymion*. To see this, let us look first at *Endymion* and *Oberon* in their broad structural contours. Thereafter, the detailed evidence will be more clear.

· · ·

In Book I of *Endymion,* after the revealing introductory lines, Keats depicts his setting, nominally the Latmos of the legend, in the *sequestered groves, sacred to* Diana (*Titania*), *atop a mountain overlooking the sea.* At dawn Endymion and others, descending from the mountain, encounter the priest. The festival of Pan begins, during which *the aged priest* and the shepherds see *various spiritualizing visions at sunrise.* After pertinent talk, Endymion, who seemed 'like one who dream'd Of idleness in groves Elysian,' goes off with his reproachful sister, to whom he relates an earlier heavenly vision of his own, the reason for *his renunciation of earthly aims.* Before they return, he tells her his hopes and fears, his idea of *the gradations of happiness* and love, and of a planned *pilgrimage.*

In Book II, after an exordium on love, Endymion *wanders through the mountain forest, along a single path* until he discovers *a cave.* A voice tells him he has too long *'starv'd on the ruth, the bitterness of love'* and that he must wander far in other regions before he can discover his ideal of love. Dejected, he appeals to the moon goddess, and soon an airy voice bids him descend 'through the silent mysteries of earth.' These he explores until he is exhausted. *At his plea vegetation springs up.* He proceeds until he hears faint music, and following it he discovers *a mysterious bower* in which the beautiful (vegetation spirit) Adonis lies in slumber. To him comes shortly the goddess of love, to revive Adonis and bear him up to the light. And since Venus has encouraged Endymion in his love, soon he wanders on, sees further wonders, and is borne off by an eagle. In a bower Endymion falls asleep and *dreams a nympholeptic dream of union with his ideal of love and beauty,* who tells him that she cannot yet 'to starry eminence' uplift him. But *they know 'love's madness' before she vanishes,* and Endymion feels that 'all other depths are shallow' by comparison with physical love. But then he hears the waters Alpheus and Arethusa complaining of their love's frustration; and, pitying them, he appeals to his beloved Diana to 'assuage these lovers' pains' and make them happy. At that moment he feels himself transported to *the bottom of the sea.*

In Book III an exordium attacks worldly power, proclaims higher majesties that *govern the elements,* and finally apostrophizes love as 'potent . . . to teach Strange journeyings' (or exertions) wherever Beauty dwells. As the scene opens, Endymion is resting and thinking of his beloved, the moon. Soon he wanders on and discovers *an aged man who had 'watched for years in forlorn hermitage'* and whom Endymion pities. This sage greets him and tells him that, *if he had never loved, he could not have come to perform his mission.* The aged man, Glaucus, tells Endymion in detail of *his love for an ideal, from constancy to which the enchantress* Circe, the *queen of sensual joys, had tempted him.* Upon his revulsion, she had changed his shape and killed his beloved. The sage produces the instruments with which Endymion, who *has been constant to his ideal love,* is to perform *his mission of reanimating* dead *lovers* at the bottom of the sea. Glaucus tells him that he is a *'youth, by heavenly power lov'd and led.'* Because of this, and of his constancy, Endymion performs the miracle and *soon is welcomed with rapturous acclaim at the palace* of Neptune, where *'dance and song and garlanding'* grew wild and where *pleasure reigned.* Swooning at last, Endymion *is borne away mysteriously,* as the voice of Diana tells him: *'Immortal bliss for me too hast thou won.'*

In Book IV the wanderer awakes back on earth, to the words of a song sung by an eastern maid who is sad and lost. Full of pity, Endymion draws near through the underwood and watches until he feels 'as one by beauty slain.' He feels he is *unfaithful to his vow* of constancy to the heavenly Diana, and that this mortal will be *his executioner.* Envisaging *a fearful storm,* he is calmed only when the lovely lady sings her Song of Sorrow and, against a background of revelry, tells of *her shadowy wooer from the clouds. Carried away by sympathy and thus love for a mortal,* Endymion leans to her, trembling, until a god appears. Upon two steeds *Endymion and his eastern maid are borne through the air* to the very portals of heaven, where he seems to hear the *'marriage melodies'* and to see the immortal gods, the seasons and hours. Awaking, he finds that his dream is true and that he is actually in heaven.

When the vision of the divine beauty vanishes, he urges the steeds back to earth. But as the moon puts forth her first light, the dark-haired maiden by his side vanishes; and, crushed in all his hopes of heavenly and earthly bliss, Endymion sinks into the Cave of Quietude. In his desperate trance he does not hear the 'pinion'd multitude' of *aerial voices warbling sweet as if to greet the wanderer.* At length *he awakes with the eastern maid beside him and pledges constant love to her:* he will live with her 'in love and peace' among the forest wildernesses. For he has been *'presumptu-*

ous against love, against the sky, against all elements.' He renounces solitude and airy visions. In his love for the human eastern
'queen' he feels he will still love his immortal mistress. And *they
will dwell in a mossy cave where the eastern maid 'will joy to live.'*
He will find food for her in the wilderness, and they will be happy.
But the maid says *she is forbidden,* and that *'We might commit
ourselves at once to vengeance; we might die; We might embrace
and die.'* And so they are *'in last extreme.'* But then Endymion's
sister comes to greet the wanderer's eastern bride, only to learn that
*he must and will renounce her. 'A hermit young, I'll live in mossy
cave,'* he says, and in that same void *'white chastity* shall sit.' Renouncing his fondest dream, he takes his leave, expressing the wish
to see them but once more. He broods long and does not hear
Diana's music. Coming to himself at length with a start, he finds
his sister and the eastern maid before him. And before his eyes the
latter changes into the goddess 'Phoebe his passion,' and in a moment after a significant explanation they vanish together.

. . .

Stripped of the heavy veil of beautiful imagery, which obscures
them, the contours of the structure of *Endymion* and through them
glimmerings of what Keats meant by the poem are apparent in this
deliberately bare prose summary. The italicized features, from first
to last, tell a most revealing story. For let us turn to the equivalent
structural features in *Oberon.*

In Canto VIII, in a forest setting upon a wild and sequestered
mountain-top high above the sea, are the groves sacred to Titania.
It is there that the hermit, who had renounced earthly things, had
found peace after a life of suffering. And as the culmination of
his spiritualizing experience, the aged hermit sees at dawn the
radiant visions of God and heavenly spirits in the sunrise. By this
experience of the divine God of Love, the last of a series of gradations of happiness, he has achieved the pinnacle of bliss. It is this

aged sage whom after a long pilgrimage the wanderer Huon encounters upon his descent from the mountains. (Cf. *End*. Bk. 1,
above.)

Huon had discovered the Elysian sanctuary after long and agonized wandering up the mountain crags, through the forests
beyond, along a single path, and through a cavern. He had been
forced to this because he and his eastern bride had felt the vengeance of their heavenly protector, who had left them upon the
desolate shore to starve and taste life's bitterness for having been
unchaste in their love. As if in answer to his prayers, Huon discovers a new world of forest and flowers and fruit-trees: the paradise that had sprung up by Titania's enchantment and in whose
midst is her mysterious bower where Rezia later sleeps in the new
spring. Huon encounters the aged hermit, to whom the wanderer
tells the tale of his pilgrimage and his love: of how he had first
seen his ideal of love and beauty in a dream, and how after their
impassioned caresses she had vanished into a marvelous stream.
(Cf. *End*. II, above.)

Huon having told the rest of his story, the hermit reminds the
wanderer of his mission (to reconcile the estranged fairy lovers
whom Huon had long pitied. Only through the constancy of his
love for his eastern bride can he perform this mission.) Despite the
punishment he has suffered for consummating his love, which
Oberon had forbidden, that guardian spirit who has loved and led
him thus far still hovers over Huon. The hermit assures him that
if he will merit Oberon's favor by chastity and toil, he will achieve
his goal. Thus Huon's love gradually becomes spiritualized. And
eventually (in Canto XII), after a trial of his constancy to his ideal
by the enchantress and queen of sensual joys, Huon and Rezia
perform the mission and are welcomed to the palace of Oberon,
where 'joys eternal dwell' and where they taste the bliss of the
immortals. And since they have restored Oberon's and Titania's
happiness, they are welcomed rapturously amid the song and dance
and garlanding of all the aerial spirits. (Cf. *End*. III, above.)

Now as he told the hermit, Huon had first seen the beautiful eastern princess Rezia, a 'woman like a goddess,' in a prophetic dream. And she had seen him in a dream in which she was saved from death by a dwarf and a beautiful knight who descended from the clouds in a flying car. Later, on the eve of her dreaded wedding she had dreamed of her lover again. Sad and distraught, she had sought her shadowy lover from the skies in the wooded gardens of her father's palace beside the sacred river. At the end of Canto v, Rezia and Huon flee through the air in Oberon's car, lost in heavenly bliss because their dreams have come true. Later on shipboard, though it was forbidden by the heavenly power, they consummate their love because of Rezia's sympathy for Huon's suffering. A fearful storm brings Oberon's vengeance and leads to their being compelled to leap into the sea. By virtue of the talisman (cf. *The Poet*), they are borne through the sea unharmed to the desolate isle, but soon find themselves suffering and in last extremes for lack of food and water. And they, who had been presumptuous against love, against the ruler of the sky and all elements, feel they must die. But Huon bears the 'eastern queen' to a mossy cave in which she delights more than in her father's palace. The wanderer searches out food for her. And such is her devotion and courage that Huon pledges that his love for her will be constant unto death. Soon thereafter he discovers the hermitage, where through the hermit's influence he lives in chastity and gradually is further spiritualized. Thus Oberon is mollified, and the lovers can perform the mission, be welcomed with the marriage melodies at the floating palace of the daemon king, and then awake in the wanderer's own country side by side on a grassy bank. (Cf. *End*. iv, above.)

. . .

Now, though we must remember that much other reading and experience was drawn into *Endymion,* which is a long poem marked by an almost strained idealism, still its structural features offer clear evidence that the parallel plot pattern of Wieland's romance, as well as the theme of the latter, played an unsuspected part in Keats' formative conception. The vital nature of that part is further hinted by Keats' many allusions to *Oberon,* as well as by a great mass of detailed evidence in *Endymion.*

The hermit of the sacred groves reveals many resemblances to Keats' aged priest. The spiritualizing visions at sunrise, which are the culmination of the hermit's gradations of happiness, demonstrably left profound marks upon the visions of Keats' priest and upon Endymion's gradations of happiness, which constitute the crucial thematic passage or preface of *Endymion.* The twofold island setting of *Oberon* colored Keats' Latmos and Pan's 'enmossed realms' each of the three times they appear. And the 'high contemplating,' the mountaineering, and mossy cave phases of the career of Keats' 'wanderer' are identical with the same phases in the pilgrimage of Wieland's 'wanderer.' It will have been realized, moreover, that both Huon and Endymion are fated wanderers 'by heavenly power loved and led.' It is significant that both are youths who are constant to an ideal of love and beauty, and therefore are able to perform a mission or service which is suggestively similar. Both feel that they have been, in Keats' phrase, 'Presumptuous against love, against the sky, against all elements.' Endymion has been presumptuous in that his love for his seeming mortal eastern 'queen'—with whom he would dwell in the mossy cave, but who is forbidden and fears vengeance and death—made him disloyal to his heavenly mistress Phoebe (or, in Ovid, Titania). Huon has been presumptuous in that his love for his mortal 'eastern queen'— with whom he dwells in the same mossy cave—was unchaste and forbidden and almost avenged by death. That love had made Huon disloyal to his master Oberon, ruler of all elements and particularly the sky.

Furthermore, it is clear that the visions and wanderings through the elements of earth, air, and water, are, like the mission and love of Endymion, stages in a spiritual discipline that leads to highest happiness. The mission, a humanitarian service, is the third rung of the ladder to divine fellowship, immortality, and bliss, to which the 'youth by heavenly power loved and led' had steadily aspired. Without unduly laboring the point, Huon too is a youth thus divinely loved and led, who pursued his ideal of constancy unswervingly. And we know that Huon's love for his eastern bride, a 'woman *like* a goddess,' is, like his wanderings through the elements, a graduated spiritual discipline. Only when he happily survives all the trials and suffering born of that love, only when he has been spiritualized, can he accomplish his fated mission of reconciling the fairy lovers and achieve bliss for them and for himself. Despite their divergences, the mission, like the visions and wanderings and love, is essentially identical for Huon and Endymion, identical in both kind and effect.

Moreover, Keats' Glaucus saw his ideal perish because (unlike Huon) he succumbed to the temptations of the 'arbour queen' and 'enchantress,' symbol of sensual pleasure. But Glaucus was redeemed (like Huon in the hermitage, after the sinful consummation of love) by penance and atonement, until with the help of a friend his ideal was restored. It is this aged Glaucus of Grecian myth who becomes Endymion's friend, who reminds him that he is a fated youth, and who reveals the mission. And this Glaucus Keats explicitly likens to the hermit, who had transcended the loss of all he loved through renunciation, through the love of divine beauty in objects, thoughts, and deeds, and through mystical communion with the 'form divine' itself—as reflected in the introduction and thematic passage of *Endymion*.

Equating the patterns farther, we find that it is the hermit who becomes Huon's friend, who reminds him that he is a youth divinely guided, and who urges him to atone for his offense against the heavenly power by chastity. This Huon does; and his love for his humanly embodied ideal of love and beauty, the 'eastern queen' (who is identical from first to last with Endymion's), his love, which had first been commingled of sense and soul, then becomes purified and gradually *spiritualized*. This is brought about by suffering, the contemplation of nature's beauty, the friendship of the sage, renunciation, and the spiritual adoration of his beloved, the 'woman like a goddess,' who more than ever seems to him of heavenly essence.

The effect of this *Oberon* theme upon *Endymion* is revealed not only in the thematic passage or preface but also at the very end of Keats' romance. At the very end of Book IV of *Endymion,* the woman, the eastern 'queen' of the Song of Sorrow, undergoes actual metamorphosis to become the goddess. She explains all to the wanderer:

> '. . . 'twas fit that *from this mortal state,*
> Thou shouldst, my *love,* by some unlook'd for *change*
> Be *spiritualiz'd.*'

Thus the themes, like the visions, wanderings, mission, and love of *Oberon* and *Endymion* are essentially the same. That pervasive sameness does more than shed light upon the creative process; it indicates that *Oberon* served Keats as a sort of pattern into whose outlines autobiographic and other elements and related matter could be drawn. For this assertion, that *Oberon* played the key part in the genesis of *Endymion,* there is further reason: in the fact that many allusions and extensive clusters of details of incident and imagery, in identical sequence, appear within the closely similar structural features. Those details (a few of the most significant of which may be examined in the text below, while the rest will be consigned to the Appendix) will enable us at the end of the chapter to throw some new light upon the meaning of *Endymion.*

II

Immediately after his introduction, to which we shall return shortly, Keats in Book I of *Endymion* naturally sets out to describe the setting on the legendary Latmos. This mountain setting is totally different from the brief, generalized, and highly artificial description in Drayton. Keats reverts to and elaborates his setting in Books II and IV,* until gradually a detailed scene emerges. After thirty lines of description of the 'mighty forest,' with its fertile soil and 'precious fruits' and 'gloomy shades, sequestered deep, Where no man went' (I, 63-8), Keats speaks of the altar 'Full in the middle of this pleasantness.' The dew, he says,

> Had taken fairy phantasies to strew
> Daisies upon the sacred sward last eve.
>
> (END. I, 92-3)

Those floral phantasies are characteristic of Titania's fairies in Shakespeare's play; but Keats immediately goes on to say that it now was dawn. And in the brightness of Apollo's fire

> A melancholy spirit well might win
> Oblivion, and melt out his essence fine.
>
> (END. I, 98-9)

Evidently Shakespeare's and Wieland's Titania (and Ovid's, who is Diana) were closely linked in Keats' mind. For in Canto VIII of *Oberon,* Titania is the melancholy spirit who, separated from her love, had sought oblivion in the sequestered forest upon the mountain-top in the wilderness of crags which is her isle. In its midst, in her sacred groves, no man went but the hermit, who had found a shadowy, enchanted paradise, well watered and fertile, where flowers, fig, and orange trees bloom. These and other features reappear in Keats' Latmos. His allusion to the 'melancholy spirit' was not idle. †

Keats had seen the 'blue heavens o'er enchanted isles' in *Calidore.* And in *I Stood Tip-toe* and earlier he had overheard the tremulous *aerial* music: 'the *groves* among, *Angelic harmonies at distance sung*' and heard *at dawn* by the aged hermit, who then sees the

---

* And in III he alludes to the 'desert shore,' craggy isle, and 'forlorn hermitage.'
† For verbal parallels see App. III, p. 323.

'shapes of the viewless world.' * But now, only fifteen lines after the melancholy spirit sought oblivion in *Endymion,* there occurs the entrance of the troops of children into these 'groves Elysian.' At dawn 'their ears were sated With a faint breath of music . . . airy swellings' lost in the sound of the sea (1, 115 ff.). And after the procession, or, rather, interfused with it, and throughout the greater part of Book 1, we both see and hear Keats' aged priest in this Latmos—and in him, now more, now less, transparently, the form of Wieland's aged hermit—in the familiar mountain and forest topography of the hermitage that had fascinated Keats since the Mathew period. Throughout Book 1, interwoven with data gleaned from pictures and scholarly works on Grecian customs, from Drayton's 'Festival of Pan,' and evidently from seascapes seen in the Isle of Wight, images and incidents from the scenes in Titania's Elysian groves have been clustered or disseminated. Still others reappear, clustered or scattered in the later books of *Endymion.*

Following the children come other figures. And then we see, 'Now coming from *beneath the forest trees,*' a *'venerable priest* full soberly' whose eyes rest upon the turf swept by his vestments. From his right hand swings a milk-white vase, and in his left he bears *'a basket* full *Of all* sweet herbs' (1, 148-56). His 'aged head . . . Seem'd like a poll of ivy in the teeth Of winter hoar' (1, 159-61). After him comes 'another crowd of shepherds' followed by the car of their chieftain-king, Endymion. The youth appears strangely troubled; and when the assemblage has quieted, we see him standing in the circle *'wan,* and *pale,* and with an *awed face'* as he confronts the priest (1, 191). The latter forthwith addresses the shepherds: 'Whether *descended from beneath the rocks That overtop your mountains'* (1, 198-9), and breaks into the paean to Pan. Into this picture (as into a later one in Book II) were absorbed, I think, some vivid recollections of Huon's descent through the mountains

* *Oberon* VIII, 26. And cf. the fairy music and 'shapes of the invisible world' juxtaposed in *I Stood Tip-toe,* the earlier 'Endymion.'

from the top of the crags 'beneath whose dreary height' lie the sacred groves of Titania. For there, beneath the forest trees, Huon, 'worn out, exhausted, pale with ceaseless woe,' in awe and astonishment suddenly confronts the aged hermit.*

. . .

Now Keats appears to have derived suggestions not only from Huon's descent, and the sacred mountain-forest setting, and the meeting with the aged holy man, but also from much that follows. For, omitting momentarily the paean to Pan and the dancing and games in the sacred groves upon the mountain-side, we join those of the shepherds who *at dawn* 'after *brighter visions* stare,' such as a *ship* on the distant *sea.* † At it they stare

> K 349   Until, from the *horizon*'s vaulted side,
>   There shot a *golden* splendour far and wide,†
> 351   *Spangling* those million poutings of *the brine*
>   With quivering ore: 'twas even an *awful shine*
> 353   From the exaltation *of Apollo*'s bow;
>   *A heavenly beacon in their* dreary *woe.*
>
> 355   Who *thus* were *ripe* for *high contemplating,*

cheered and uplifted spiritually by the divinely beautiful vision of the rising sun, 'Might turn their steps.' And they might enter the sober ring where Endymion and the aged priest sat,

> 358   'Mong shepherds *gone* in eld, whose looks increas'd
>   The silvery setting of their *mortal* star.
> 360   There they discours'd upon *the fragile bar*
>   *That keeps us from our homes ethereal* . . .
>   (END. I, 349-61)

---

* For the verbal echoes see App. III, p. 324.

† Just before he meets the hermit, Huon 'bending from the mountain's topmost peak . . . O'er *ocean far and wide* . . . no *vessel*' could espy on the distant sea (*Oberon* VII, 91).

Mystically they converse of 'our duties there,' until, wandering 'by *divine* converse, Into Elysium' (Huon has just wandered into Titania's), each speaks of his *'anticipated bliss'* (1, 373).

Let us now enter into Titania's 'Elysium' and again see the mystical 'high contemplating' of the hermit. His beloved wife and sons and friends had gone to their homes in heaven long years ago.* And he had sought and found solace and peace in the transcendent beauty of this sacred mountainous retreat. And

W 1   Then his half-slumbering ears in trance perceive,
      With shuddering rapture heard, *the groves among,*
3   Angelic harmonies at distance sung,
      For him the inexpressive chorus weave: K 115 †
5   And as he lists he feels *earth's slender wall,*
      That parts him from his friends, *about to fall:*   K 360
7   His spirit swells, *a flame celestial bright*   K 354
      Burns in *his* breast, while rob'd in *heavenly light*
9   Shapes of the viewless world his *soul responsive*   K 355
      call.

These sensations still remain when *at dawn* he sees far more than Keats' sun-god:

11   . . . over all, he sees *the form divine,*
      The Uncreated in his creatures *shine,*   K 352
13   *Bright* as in *drops* of dew *the sun's reflected*   K 351-3
      beam.

He sees the divine beauty of the ultimate Spirit reflected in all created things. But if this vision is much more to him than the sun to the shepherds in their woe, it also enables him to transcend his woe on earth. For

---

* Cf. K 358. Also 'athirst in soul to see again' (385 ff.).

† Above, we saw the children who, at dawn in the groves, heard 'a faint breath of music . . . airy swellings.'

Thus imperceptibly did *heaven and earth*   K 349 *

15   *United* in his soul *together run:*

   His spirit *brightens like* an inward *sun:*   K 354, 347

17   Far from the dissonance of *mortal* birth,   K 359

   From passion's turmoil, in this holy gloom

19   *Joys* that *await the blest* his soul illumine . . .   K 373

(OBERON VIII, 26-8)

Thus, among earthly beauty, all of which he sees transfigured by the divine, the aged hermit, prepared for the most 'high contemplating' by angelic music and radiant visions at dawn in Titania's sacred groves, achieves ultimate vision and joy in fellowship with the divine essence.

In the first 'Endymion,' or *I Stood Tip-toe,* Keats had derived his airy music and 'shapes from the invisible world' from this same passage. † And now, the hermit's mystic vision had become that of the aged priest and shepherds. The former's 'slender wall, that parts him from his friends' in heaven, is the latter's 'fragile bar that keeps us from our homes ethereal,' as both transcend the confines of mortality in sensing the ultimate divine beauty in nature and the radiance of the sun. And the latter's consequent 'anticipated bliss' is the former's 'joys that await the blest.' That is clear. Wieland's mystical imagery, in terms of radiant light, and brightness, and an inward sun, had suggested and was in part transformed into the simpler and paler mysticism in Keats' pagan vision of the rising sun. (The hermit's 'sun's reflected beam' is seen 'spangling . . . the brine' by Keats.) Both visions occur at dawn to analogous characters, who are similarly *spiritualized* by the beautiful vision. They occur in the kindred sacred groves above the sea, and in imagery simplified but less elusive and much more nearly related than a casual glance would indicate. ‡

. . .

* Cf. Keats' 'Horizon.'

† Cf. p. 92.

‡ It is significant, too, that the image clusters we have thus far seen occur in a similar sequence in the two poems.

This same *Oberon* passage left its marks much more deeply elsewhere: in fact at the very heart of Keats' romance. A few hundred lines later in the first book of *Endymion,* in the 'preface' or long passage in which Keats explained the theme of his romance ('such a preface is necessary to the subject,' Keats wrote of this passage to his publisher [11]), he reverted as if instinctively to the hermit's ecstatic vision. Since this passage about the gradations of happiness contains the theme of *Endymion,* it is significant that the immediate stimulus and the symbols for Keats' search for a 'fellowship with essence' again seem to have derived from the gradual spiritualization, the transcendental sensations, and ultimate bliss of Wieland's sage.

Keats' symbolism and imagery, if carefully studied after this crucial passage has first been read, reveal their origins. For in this, the thematic passage of *Endymion,* he wrote:

777	*'Wherein lies happiness?* In that which *becks*	W 9 *
	Our ready minds to fellowship *divine,*	W 11
779	A fellowship with *essence;* till we *shine,*	W 12
	Full alchemiz'd, and *free of space.* Behold	W 14
781	The clear religion of heaven! Fold	
	A rose leaf round thy finger's taperness,	
783	And soothe thy lips: *hist,* when *the airy stress*	W 3
	Of music's kiss impregnates the free *winds . . .'*	

it unbinds songs and prophesyings from the realms of poetry or Apollo.

795	*'Feel we these things?—that moment* have we stept	W 5
	Into a sort of *oneness,* and our state	W 5, 6, 15
797	Is like *a floating spirit's.* But there are	W 9, 3
	Richer entanglements, enthralments far	
799	More *self-destroying,* leading, *by degrees,*	W 17-18

* The references (W 9, etc.) are to conceptual and verbal parallels in the translation of Wieland's lines above.

To the chief intensity: * the crown of these
801   Is made of love and friendship, and sits high
Upon the forehead of humanity.
803   All its more ponderous and bulky worth †
Is *friendship,* whence there ever *issues* forth   W 6-7 ‡
805   A steady *splendour;* but at the tip-top,
There hangs by unseen film, an orbed *drop*   W 13, 12
807   Of *light,* and that is *love:* its influence,
Thrown in our eyes, *genders a novel sense,* §   W 19
809   At which we start and fret; till in the end,
Melting into its *radiance,* we *blend,*   W 15, 16
811   *Mingle,* and so *become a part of it,* ||—
Nor with aught else can our *souls interknit*   W 15, 9
813   So *wingedly:* when we *combine therewith,*   W 9, 3, 15, 19
Life's self is nourish'd by its proper pith,
815   And we are nurtured like a pelican brood.' ¶

Now, having read the key passage through, compare the imagery with the hermit's transcendental vision, on page 118.

In the crystallization of this utterance—of Endymion's concept of the stages leading to highest happiness—Wieland's mystical passage, study of the imagery will show, has been subtly dissolved and reintegrated. No less subtly, since in it Keats also found his symbols, it lays bare the very heart of Keats' message. The symbols and the twofold imagery, daemonic and mystical, in the two passages, are fundamentally identical, even as is the thought: Highest happiness comes of gradually losing one's self in the divine spirit; and to partake in its mystic radiance, one must sense the beauty of the real world, then (in the realm of the ideal) perceive the inner harmonies of earth—the music in the elements—until,

---

* 'Intensity' is at times Keats' word for 'ecstasy' (cf. Murry, *Keats and Shake-speare,* 221).
† Tangible, worldly worth.
‡ Wieland's 'friends . . . flame' provided a symbol.
§ Transcendental.
|| Love.
¶ i.e. by our own better self: spirit, the divine, which is the 'proper pith' or inner-most essence of 'Life's self.'

'that moment,' the restricted earthly vision expands and the shackling bonds of mortality dissolve in a sense of oneness with the eternal and the winged denizens of heaven. Thereupon man is ready 'by degrees' for the 'self-destroying' experience of friendship and love until he can melt 'into *its* radiance.'

It is significant that these sensations are *the identical stages* whereby the blissful hermit '*by degrees*' achieves his sense of immortality and vision of God.* The hermit, consoled in his grief by the beauty of Titania's mountain sanctuary, hears the music of her elemental spirits, and, that moment, 'as he lists, he feels earth's slender wall . . . fall.' And as he longs for the angelic forms of his earthly love and friends, a 'flame celestial bright Burns in his breast' until with 'soul responsive' (Keats' 'ready mind') he perceives 'the form divine' itself,

> The Uncreated in his creatures shine,
> *Bright* as in *drops of* dew the *sun*'s reflected beam.

Thus by the same stages as Endymion he achieves ultimate vision in complete 'fellowship with essence'—essence, or spirit, or the Uncreated, who is (Christ's) God of Love. And significantly the hermit's Love, the Creator of all earthly beauty, is also Keats' Love: an 'orbed *drop of light* . . . *is love.*' This radiant imagery, this key symbol, which has merely been shifted ever so slightly in the new pagan pattern, shows that for Keats too Love is divine.†

This and the other mystical symbols, when once understood in the light of the hermit's experience, are of inestimable value in following Keats' thought. For him as for the hermit, 'The proper pith' or innermost essence of 'Life's self' (K 814) is spirit, or the divine. And only after the same spiritual discipline, by the same 'degrees,' do both achieve that 'novel *sense*' (K 808), which is higher

---

* The hermit, after fearful grief and the renunciation of earthly aims, had '*by degrees* . . . struggled thro' the flood [of grief] That nigh o'erwhelm'd his soul in hopeless death' (*Oberon* VIII, 22).

† And the symbol 'orbed drop of light' came to mean to him, I think: perfect knowing, supreme illumination, God.

than reason, which is transcendental and intuitive, and which reveals to them the source of highest happiness. In the sacred groves, there comes to them both the realization of ultimate love, beauty, and truth—*which is the divine in all things of earth*. And in the divine Love and Beauty both the hermit and Endymion would lose themselves, to attain ultimate vision, immortality, and bliss. The vital message and the symbols, I repeat, in terms of which Keats' creed is expressed, are to be found in Titania's hermitage.

No wonder then that in that sanctuary Endymion's quest begins and ends. For toward the end of the allegorical romance, in Book IV, when on an ever higher plane his visions, and the exploration of the inner principles or harmonies (music) of earth; when humanitarian service (or friendship), and earthly love in various degrees have disappointed the wanderer's hopes of *bliss*, he says to Peona:

> 'Let it content thee, Sister, seeing me
> More happy that betides mortality.
> *A hermit young, I'll live* in mossy cave,
> . . . and lave
> Thy *spirit* in the wonders I shall tell.'
> (lines 858-62)

Already in *Sleep and Poetry*, we saw, Keats had identified himself with the hermit. He had identified the latter's mystical, daemonic, and transcendental sensations with his own ecstatic experience of poetry.* To him poetry, like the hermit's vision, reveals spiritual beauty and the highest truth, by a life of intuitive visions of the ideal (spirit) within and beyond the real (matter).

The evolution and organic unity of Keats' conception, as well as its meaning, are illumined by *Oberon*. His early self-identification with the hermit was merely carried further and more fully developed in *Endymion*. The hermit's renunciation of earthly things, gradual spiritualization, and consequent achievement in a dream-

* Cf. p. 84.

vision of highest bliss and *divine 'truth alone,'* * through real, then spiritual, and finally divine beauty (three manifestations which he perceives to be one), have been assimilated here into Keats' own philosophy of life. And clearly the hermit provided the message and the symbols: the medium of its poetic expression.

Of this there is no dearth of proof. † When *Endymion* was almost finished, Keats wrote in a most important letter to Bailey:

I am certain of nothing but of *the holiness* of the Heart's affections, and *the truth* of Imagination. *What the Imagination seizes as Beauty must be Truth*—whether it existed before or not,—for I have the same idea of all our passions as of *Love:* they are all, in their *sublime, creative of essential Beauty.* In a Word, you may know my favourite speculation from my first book [that is, of *Endymion*] . . . *The Imagination may be compared to Adam's dream,*—he awoke and found it *truth:*— I am more zealous in this affair, because I have never yet been able to perceive how anything can be known for truth by consecutive reasoning—and yet it must be. Can it be that even the greatest Philosopher ever arrived at his Goal without putting aside numerous objections? However it may be, O for *a life of Sensations* rather than Thoughts! It *is 'a Vision* in the form of Youth,' *a shadow of reality to come* . . .

(Letter of 22 November 1817. Italics mine.)

This difficult letter, written when he was twenty-two, is one of the most important witnesses to Keats' evolving inner life.[12]

It is clear that he is defending here a mode of knowing which is higher than Reason. Keats says he is sure only of the sacredness of the feelings of the heart, and of the authenticity, or truthfulness, of imagination—by which he means intuitive perception. For the imagination, or intuition, he says, may be compared to Adam's dream—of God. ‡ Having seen the God of Love in a dream-vision,

---

* *Oberon* viii, 15.

† Another glance at Keats' lines above will prove rewarding. And the revealing continuation of the thematic passage as well as the opening lines of *Endymion* we shall see in a moment.

‡ In Milton's *Paradise Lost* viii, 286 ff. and 452 ff.

Adam awoke and found his vision true, as God, and then Eve, His beautiful creation, stood before him. Moreover, the phrases I have italicized in the letter, and the explicit reference to 'my first book,' all take us back not merely to Adam but to the hermit and his vision of God and divine 'truth alone.

The thought of the letter, which is far more profound—and more intelligible—than its elliptical phrasing would lead one to believe, must be discussed in the notes.[18] Here, only two things need be emphasized. First, that, as in the passage about the gradations of happiness, Keats' Love, as his phraseology and allusions show, is still symbol of the divine. Secondly, and this is of utmost importance, that his yearning *'O for a life of Sensations rather than Thoughts'* has nothing whatever to do with the sensory delight of popular misconception. Rather, that it is the same life of transcendental visions, or super-rational intuitions, of divine love, beauty, and truth as the hermit's.*

. . .

In following the clues in the letter and confirming the symbols and the sublime nature of the key to highest truth, beauty, love, and happiness, that originate and end and are one in the divine, we have not wandered from *Endymion.* In that poem, concerned with all these truths, Keats' thought was expressed poetically: in terms of symbols clearly derived from the hermit's life. Those same symbols first appear in the opening lines of Keats' allegoric romance, the discussion of which has been postponed till now for the sake of clarity. Those lines are steeped in Keats' own experi-

* In the final phrase, 'a life of Sensations . . . is "a Vision . . ." a shadow of reality to come,' Keats means: a foretaste of the heavenly state after death, wherein we shall possess angelic powers of immediate apprehension, like the hermit. Cf. also *Letters,* p. 246 ([16] Dec. 1818): '. . . a direct communication of Spirit . . . will be one of the grandeurs of immortality . . .' And cf. also *End.* I, 797, above: 'like a floating spirit's.' For further discussion, see the notes. The famous phrase, 'life of Sensations,' like many another, has been taken out of context and, handed on from critic to critic, to this day continues to be misconstrued.

ence, confirmed by Wordsworth's (in *Tintern Abbey*) and particularly, as the imagery reveals, by the hermit's. Bearing in mind the latter's experience of utmost despondence, and also his gradual attainment of bliss in the perception of the divine power and source of beauty: with that earlier phase of the hermit's experience in mind, let us now turn to Keats' opening lines.

In the very first lines of *Endymion* Keats wrote of the power of beauty:

> 1   A thing of beauty is a *joy for ever:*
>   Its loveliness increases; it will never
> 3   Pass into nothingness; but still will keep
>   *A bower quiet* for us, and a *sleep*
> 5   Full of sweet *dreams,* and *health,* and quiet *breathing.*
>   Therefore, on every *morrow,* are we wreathing
> 7   A flowery band to bind us to the earth,

that is, each morning as we see it anew, beauty reconciles us and thereby binds us to a life of suffering on earth:

>   Spite of *despondence,* of the inhuman dearth
> 9   Of *noble* natures, of the *gloomy* days,
>   Of all the *unhealthy and o'er-darkened* ways
> 11 Made for our searching: yes, in spite of all,
>   Some shape of beauty moves away *the pall*
> 13 From our dark spirits. Such *the sun* . . .

and the moon, and other beauties of *nature.* But also there is beauty and 'a joy forever' in thoughts of the *immortality* of the 'mighty *dead'* and in

> 22 All lovely tales that we have heard or read:
>   An endless fountain of immortal drink,
> 24 *Pouring* unto us *from* the *heaven's* brink.

All these things of beauty reconcile us to a life of suffering. They are like an immortalizing drink from heaven. For beauty in all things earthly, the hermit had discovered through suffering, is divine and leads in thought to the dead and immortality. All these 'shapes of beauty,' these *glories infinite,* Haunt us till they become a *cheering light* Unto our souls . . .' (29-31).* Precisely thus the hermit was cheered, and the priest and shepherds, by the beauty of the sun in the thematic passage later in the same book of *Endymion.* By that divine beauty they were all prepared for 'high contemplating' beyond the heaven's brink in the divine itself, in whom is highest happiness.

This induction is not a thing merely of beautiful words. It is a part of the same quest for immortality, spiritual happiness, love, and beauty as that expounded in Endymion's gradations of happiness. And it too is clarified by the hermit's experience, which is a succinct case-history of suffering and of the consoling and gradual spiritualizing power of *all* beauty, in which the divine is reflected. That experience resembles yet extends beyond Wordsworth's. And the key significance of the hermit's experience, in the plan of *Endymion* as well as in Keats' own philosophy of life, is clear when we know one of the 'lovely tales' Keats had read: that one from which he drew his symbols, poetic confirmation of his own experience, and truly 'an endless fountain of immortal drink,' in the realization that all beauty ultimately is divine. Since it lies at the very heart of Keats' thought, we must turn for a moment to the story of the hermit's life, told in the stanzas just preceding his dream-vision of God, in Canto VIII.

The *nobly* born Alfonso of Leon, after long devoted service, first had met with ingratitude and ignoble treatment from his royal master. Thereupon he had renounced worldly ambitions and had turned for happiness to his loved wife and friends. But this earthly *'fountain* of his *joy for ever* fails.' † (Cf. K 1 and 23.) For after ten years his three sons had perished of the plague, and his wife had died of grief soon thereafter. (Did Keats, who identified him-

---

* There is also a Wordsworthian echo here: 'The passion poesy, glories infinite, Haunt us till . . .' Cf. *T. A.* 'Haunted me like a passion.'

† *Oberon* VIII, 20. Note the verbal echoes.

self so deeply with the hermit, and who repeatedly derived his symbols from the sage's life, recall his own family? Was there a warm personal bond between the hermit and himself, who had both known the renunciation of worldly aims, and 'the plague,' and three sons, and death, and profound grief and gloom—from which, through beauty, they both arose to the same sublime and heroic vision? Here surely was a vital link!) *

And so Alfonso, having lost all in which happiness lay for him (earthly ambition, friends, and love), had found himself alone in a desolate world, 'his sole sad wish a *grave*' (K 12: 'the pall'). At last he had fled to this island bewildered by 'grief' and in time had found the unexpected. Despite his *'gloom'* and *despondence* and desertion by all his *ignoble* associates (cf. K 9), he had become reconciled to life. And he had found 'peace and content' gradually in Titania's Elysian groves. Thus 'by degrees' (like Endymion in the theme passage †) he arose from thoughts of death to a higher life. For in the divinely beautiful sanctuary of Titania, from whose *silent bower* come the angelic harmonies that he hears in his *dream,*

by degrees he struggled thro' the flood	
That nigh o'erwhelm'd his soul in hopeless death—	
Peace, *still*ness, temperance, zephyr's balmy *breath,*	K 5
His mind unclouded, *purified his blood,*	K 5, 12
And bad[e] *new* hope a gleam of *joy restore.*	K 1, 12
And now he felt *from heaven's exhaustless* store	
That e'en for wounds like his a balsam *flow'd:*	K 23-4
Felt, when the magic of a *sun*-beam glow'd,	K 13, 30
That nature's charms had pow'r to sooth his soul once	K 12 ff.
more.	

(OBERON VIII, 22)

* 'Nothing ever becomes real till it is experienced—,' Keats wrote in April 1818, 'even a Proverb is no proverb to you till your Life has illustrated it.'

† 1, 797: 'But there are Richer entanglements, enthralments far More self-destroying, leading, *by degrees,* To the chief intensity'—a love that is divine.

'New . . . joy restore,' 'from heaven's exhaustless store,' and the last line (so close to Wordsworthian gospel) sum up the hermit's experience of divine beauty in all things—and also the message of Keats' induction. For, as his imagery reveals, they are one and the same: the consoling and healing and spiritualizing power of all beauty, whose eternal fount is heaven.

Moreover, like Endymion (who reaches perception in the thematic passage and achievement at the end of the romance) the hermit by degrees reaches this ultimate truth, and thus highest happiness. For exactly three stanzas later 'he felt a breathing spirit near' and heard the inner harmonies of nature, or the 'angelic harmonies' of Titania's elemental spirits, *in sleep.** Then in the *dream* at sunrise, through perceiving that divine beauty is in all things of earth, he reaches Keats' chief intensity: a fellowship with the divine Love, a sense of immortality, and 'Joys that await the blest' which 'his soul illume.' He reaches this ultimate insight and bliss by stages, like Endymion, after being spiritualized by the power of beauty. (With this cf. K 24 ff.)

It is that divine beauty which reconciles him to a life of suffering, ignobility, disease, death, grief; and which lifts the pall—precisely as in Keats' induction. In the light of the hermit's experience of spiritual regeneration, and of his painfully acquired wisdom, the opening lines of *Endymion* gain a new significance. Keats' 'thing of beauty,' like moonlight, is a thing divine, pours down upon man 'from the heaven's brink,' and acts upon his suffering like the balsam that flowed for the hermit's wounds. That conception of beauty never changed for Keats.

Although *Endymion* reveals that he also owed some of his perceptions to Wordsworth, for whom nature was the 'soul Of all my moral being,' Keats' approach is aesthetic rather than moral as was Wordsworth's. And Keats is concerned not with nature alone but

---

* The hermit's 'felt'—his transcendental power of immediate perception—further clarifies Keats' words to Bailey: 'O for a life of Sensations . . . a vision . . . a shadow of reality to come' after death.

with all beauty and love, which, for him as for the hermit, are closely related. He wrote consistently in symbols derived from the hermit's life. The same clues we have been following shed new light upon the continuation, and therefore upon the whole, of the thematic passage in Book 1. In that continuation (*End.* 1, 816 ff.) the hermit's renunciation of worldly power and ambition, and his and (the wanderer) Huon's experience of an earthly 'love's Elysium' and of love in its various stages, are still part of Endymion's argument. Even as the hermit had seen the divine spirit of love and beauty in all earthly things, so Endymion sees Love as the Creator of beauty in all things. That cosmic perception, reduced to pagan terms, underlies the entire action and meaning of *Endymion.* Its hero, like the hermit, achieves complete spirituality and immortality through experience of the stages of love and beauty even up to the highest. But he does so in terms also of Huon, the sage's disciple. It is for that reason that Endymion near the end of his quest says: 'A hermit young, I'll live'; and that the meaning of the quest is explained: 'from this mortal state Thou shouldst, my love . . . Be spiritualiz'd.'

What the hermit's explicit gradations of happiness meant to him, his thought, and his work, Keats acknowledged to his friend and publisher John Taylor in a letter of 30 January 1818, in which he wrote of the thematic passage:

The whole thing must I think have appeared to you, who are a consequitive Man, as a thing almost of mere words—but I assure you that when I wrote it it was a regular stepping of the Imagination towards a Truth. *My having written that Argument will perhaps be of the greatest Service to me of any thing I ever did.* It set before me at once the gradations of Happiness even like a kind of *Pleasure Thermometer*— and is my first Step towards the chief attempt in the Drama—the playing of different Natures with Joy and Sorrow.[14] (Italics mine.)

And those gradations, which reveal the meaning of *Endymion,* and which differ considerably in kind and number from the two stages (pre-moral and moral) in *Tintern Abbey,* are in the passage of Keats' allegory which is steeped in *Oberon* imagery and the hermit's experience of sorrow and joy. In his life lies the key to Keats' symbolism in (and beyond) *Endymion* and thus to his best thought at this time.*

As the symbolism and imagery in the thematic passage and induction show, the hermit is the vital principle of *Endymion.* His influence extended into all of its body: into the organic function or symbolic meaning of the incidents and into the incidents themselves. These we can now examine rapidly.

In Book 1, after the spiritualizing vision of the divine sun, we left the shepherds in the sacred groves, thinking each one of his *'anticipated bliss'* (1, 373). Those blisses in the next score of lines echo three adjacent passages in the hermitage: Huon and Rezia's spiritualizing winter talks by the fireside with the hermit as he reminisces of his 'earthly walk'; Rezia's joyful anticipation of her child; and Huon's search for his love beneath the blossoming boughs. †
And Huon's somewhat earlier confession, to the hermit, of his sin against the heavenly power, is echoed in Peona's question: 'Hast thou sinn'd in aught Offensive to the heavenly powers?' She suggests that 'Haply, thou hast seen [Dian's] naked limbs among the alders green; And that, alas! is death' (1, 508-14). That suggestion, based on the sin for which Actæon met death in Ovid's tale, the one in which Diana is called Titania, is doubly interesting: for its kind, and for its implications concerning the creative process, in which Wieland's Titania and the moon goddess were closely linked.

Even though some of its details were recalled from Shelley's *Alastor,* in 1, 632 ff., Endymion's erotic dream-vision of his beloved is noteworthy. An initial hint for this vision had appeared in

---

* Since more of that thought appears in the continuation of the theme passage, which is so important for understanding *Endymion,* the reader who would explore it further will find the revealing lines and the hermit's minute transmutations in the Appendix, p. 325.

† For verbal echoes and detailed evidence see App. III, p. 330.

Huon's voluptuous dream of the 'woman like a goddess' in Canto III, a vision mentioned in his confession to the hermit.

Keats' own ambitions and dreams of poetical fame and immortality richly colored the next hundred lines, following which comes the long thematic passage, 'Wherein lies happiness' and its revealing sequel (I, 777-857), conceived in terms of the hermit's experience. Shortly thereafter, 'When last the wintry gusts gave over strife,' Endymion wanders into a mysterious 'grot' (I, 943), the description of whose 'lush screne . . . Thick, as to curtain up some wood-nymph's home,' and location, and encompassing phrases such as 'Faints into sleep' and 'cave is secreter' remind one of Titania's secret grot into which, when winter is over, Rezia wanders at the end of Canto VIII, where her child is born. Her prior sensations beneath the 'naked . . . pillars . . . Of arch'd embow'ring *roofs* . . . Where *nature's temple* tow'rs sublime' in the forest of the hermitage, left their marks on a portion of the Hymn to Pan: his 'palace roof' and some of his less traditional doings (I, 232-54).*
For he has become the spirit of nature: and (I, 288-9)

> Dread opener of the mysterious doors
> Leading to *universal* knowledge.

That, in the light of the hermit's 'truth' and intuitive visions of divine Love in all things earthly, and the gradations of happiness, is not solely a Wordsworthian conception.

· · ·

There is little question that the physical features of Wieland's hermitage, with its Elysian beauty in sacred forest grove, fertile vale, and encompassing mountains above the sea, left their traces chiefly in Book I of *Endymion*—which is concerned with the parallel visions of earthly beauty transfigured by the divine and therefore possessing spiritualizing power. In Book II, although there

---

* For verbal parallels and detailed evidence see App. III, p. 332.

are far fewer incidents derived from *Oberon,* Endymion's wanderings through the mountains reverse Huon's path; and Endymion's
experience of the inner harmonies (elemental music) and mysterious spiritual principle in nature embodies and illustrates poetically
the second stage of the hermit's spiritualization and the gradations
of happiness. In Book II there are also numerous allusions to
Huon's experience of suffering and desolate (or loveless) nature
in Canto VII.

The very first line of Book II: '*O* sovereign power of *love!* O
grief! O *balm!'* echoes Wieland's apostrophe to love: 'O love! thou
only balm of every woe,' * which is prefixed to the incidents of the
lovers' bitter suffering from hunger and thirst on the desert shore in
punishment for their unchaste physical love. And Rezia's love-
wrought reversal of fortune, ('Fav'rites of fortune! now, from empire thrown' *) from the royal throne of historic Bagdad-Babylon
to stark starvation, a state in which love makes her divinely happy,
may well have set Keats off on 'pageant history' and famous lovers
(II, 1-43). Then, Endymion's many days' 'wandering in uncertain
ways,' and significant 'new-born spirit' guide, and 'one track un-
seams A wooded cleft' high above the sea, and his discovery of a
'cavern's mouth' and a fountain that seemed to 'disappear So fairy-
quick' (II, 47-96) reveal the creative process minutely in their
echoes of Huon's motive and wandering toward Titania's sanctuary. Keats' lines, still in the parallel sequence (II, 103-5):

'Youth!
Too long, alas, *hast thou starv'd on the ruth,*
The bitterness of love';

and 'fainting creatures in a desert wild' (II, 119); and the fountain
nymph's origin; and the lines 'After long toil and travelling, to
miss The kernel of his hopes, how more than vile' with their
sequel (II, 144-55) all allude to incidents in the lovers' suffering on the desert shore; their starvation, the vile fruit, Rezia's

* *Oberon* VII, 40.

fainting, and the fountain that arises by Oberon's enchantment.*

Endymion's descent 'into the sparry hollows of the world' and exploration of 'the silent mysteries of earth' are peculiarly interesting in the light of what we just saw: physical love and suffering because Oberon, king of the elements and like the 'god of love,' had withdrawn his protection. For Book ii of *Endymion* is concerned both with the elemental principle of love and with physical love. Endymion, who sees Venus and Adonis, witnesses 'elemental passion' (ii, 375); and incidentally he experiences physical love. In the former he experiences elemental harmony (or spirit music), which is the second stage of his spiritualization and quest of 'immortality' (ii, 212), and also a stage in the hermit's gradations of happiness. Keats' poetical embodiment of this, and the superb architectural imagery and various incidents, owe something to *Alastor* and other sources.

It is noteworthy, however, that the lovelorn Titania is queen of the elements, and that her tale of elemental love and grief is told episodically in Canto viii just after the lovers' spiritualizing talks with the hermit and the cycle-of-nature passage. For Titania's grief-stricken descent into the earth; the vegetation that springs up by her enchantment; Rezia's approach and wandering, through 'Nature's temple' in the spring, into the mysterious bower whence the spirit harmonies emanate; and elements from the childbirth scene (all this in parallel sequence, stanzas 60 ff., toward the end of Canto viii) left their marks on and resemble, if subtly, the sequence of Endymion's descent, his experience of vegetation springing up in desolation (ii, 330-45), and his entrance into the mysterious bower of Adonis, setting for a tale of elemental love, and for winged spirits 'muffling to death the pathos' with flowers (ii, 351-60; 377-427). The bower of Adonis, though a rich composite to which Ovid, Spenser, Shakespeare, Bion, and others contributed, was colored by Titania's bower. Keats, who was still being guided by the pattern of the hermit's and Huon's spiritualization, intro-

---

* For the creative process and detailed evidence, see App. iii, pp. 334 ff.

duced an equivalent, appropriately Grecian myth and gave his bower scene symbolic value: the regeneration of earthly beauty and vegetation (Adonis) through the fructifying power of divine love (Venus).* And that knowledge of elemental love Endymion derives further from the love of the waters Alpheus and Arethusa, subject to the moon.

Endymion's experience of physical love (ii, 714 ff.) again owes something to *Alastor*. But Huon's less voluptuous dream and actual experience of physical 'love's madness' must not be forgotten as a possible hint for the appearance of the episode in the pattern, since that physical love is the cause of the lovers' suffering on the desert shore (cf. above) and is a vital part of his spiritualization. His violation of the divine injunction of chastity † makes the wanderer Huon presumptuous against (elemental) love, the sky, and the heavenly power whom he had pitied, and the reconciliation of whom with Titania constitutes his mission. In *Endymion* the wanderer's exploration of the inner principle of earth (elemental love), experience of physical love, and pity for the elemental lovers Alpheus and Arethusa lead to the third stage of his spiritualization.

Book iii of *Endymion,* whose setting is the bottom of the sea, ‡ abounds in allusions to and incidents from *Oberon*. The rather ranting exordium attacks earthly rulers as devoid of 'sanctuary splendour' (iii, 9), a phrase which recalls the radiance of the spiritualized hermit. And the mystical and daemonic overtones in the lines that follow (iii, 23-35) are revealing:

> No, there are throned seats unscalable
> But by a patient wing, a *constant* spell,

* For verbal and conceptual parallels see App. iii, p. 338 f. In the light of the parallel sequence in *Oberon,* I suspect that this myth was drawn into *Endymion* by the cycle-of-nature passage and the elemental love story of Titania, which appear amid the lover's spiritualization in Canto viii.

† Cf. Dian's complaint (*End*. ii, 800 ff.): 'O I do think that I have been alone In chastity.'

‡ Huon and Rezia, after their experience of physical love's madness, are cast into the sea (vii, 19-32).

Or by ethereal things that, unconfin'd,
Can make *a ladder of the eternal* wind,
And poise about in cloudy thunder-tents
To watch the abysm-birth of *elements*.
Aye, 'bove the withering of old-lipp'd Fate
A thousand Powers keep *religious* state,
In water, fiery realm, and airy bourne;
And, silent as a consecrated urn,
Hold sphery sessions for a season due.
Yet few of these far majesties, ah, few!
Have *bared their operations* to this globe . . .

The last is part of Keats' ambitious purpose and 'vast idea.' But the hermit's gradual spiritualization by a modified *ladder of love* that leads him to the eternal love; his and the constant Huon's experience of the daemon king's spirits and power over the elements: these underlie this passage.*

That circumstance is interesting in the light of the episode of Glaucus. Endymion soon encounters that greatly modified figure of legend, in a mood somewhat like that of Huon's first encounter with the hermit. † And Keats' description of Glaucus (III, 226-7) as

like one whose tedious toil
Had watch'd for years in forlorn hermitage,

and, again, his allusions to 'desert shores' and 'craggy isles' and 'shapes unseen' (III, 339-43) are not idle. It will bear iteration that Huon is spiritualized by suffering on the desert shore, by beauty and love, and by the influence of the hermit who urges him to live in chastity and reminds him of his mission to reconcile the fairy lovers. (Cf. *End.* III, 298-302.) After the hermit's death, Huon's constancy is tried by the heavenly power, who separates the lovers and who (Canto XI-XII) brings about Huon's trial by the 'queen' and 'enchantress.' She lures him into her palace and tempts him

---

* For further echoes see *End.* III, 54-5; 91-4; 164-5.
† Cf. *End.* III, 217-20; 255-7 and *Oberon* VIII, 5-6.

with all manner of sensual pleasures and promises, and when her wiles prove impotent lures him into her twilit bower at dawn. These incidents Keats interwove with the Grecian myth of Glaucus, who tells Endymion of his 'fierce temptations': 'When I awoke, 'twas in a twilight bower . . . a sighing voice expire . . . With tears, and smiles, and honey-words she wove A net' (iii, 418 ff.).*

In the sequel, which reveals the creative process in almost startling fashion, Glaucus' experience of Circe's enchanted forest during the night is a minute re-creation of Huon's experience in Oberon's enchanted forest. After his trial by the sensual queen-enchantress, Huon is borne through the air over land and sea to Oberon's palace, where, his mission accomplished, the lovers are welcomed. That palace, in the enchanted forest, Huon had visited at the outset of his pilgrimage. Huon explicitly recalls his fearful experience: the herd of transformed beasts and the enchanted green fire, the roaring, his encounter with the enchanter, and Oberon's tempest. Imagery and incidents from that early phase of his wanderings were clustered and disseminated through *Endymion* iii, 468-578, in such a manner that we can watch Keats at work, interweaving the *Oberon* material and suggestions therein with stuff gleaned from Spenser and Shakespeare and other sources. †

When Glaucus' composite tale of sensual love has been told, he produces (Prospero's) magic instruments; ‡ and from the scroll (iii, 668-711) he reads to Endymion of the mission he must perform in virtue of his constancy to his ideal of love and beauty and of his being 'a youth, by heavenly power lov'd and led.' § This scroll is important because it throws further light upon the meaning of Endymion's wanderings in Book ii, his exploration of 'all forms and substances . . . to their symbol-essences,' in the course of which

---

* For the verbal echoes, detailed evidence, and interpretation see App. iii, p. 342.
† For that fascinating process see App. iii, pp. 343 ff.
‡ Cf. Oberon's in the enchanted forest after *the tempest*.
§ Much as Oberon tells Huon in the enchanted forest.

he had, like the hermit, discovered the cosmic principle of (divine) love. The mission accomplished, whose resemblances in kind and effect to Huon's we have seen, Endymion in familiar manner is welcomed at Neptune's palace, in which reappear features of Oberon's floating palace and Huon's welcoming there by 'eternal beauty' after the achievement of his mission. (*End.* III, 790-802; 850-7; 933-4; etc.) And like Huon, Endymion is borne back to earth after being assured by his heavenly mistress: 'Immortal bliss for me too hast thou won.' *

. . .

In accordance with the gradations of happiness, love is the last stage of spiritualization. But love, though ultimately divine, exists in many stages. Book IV of *Endymion* accordingly is concerned with the stages of human love (as II is concerned with elemental or cosmic and III with altruistic humanitarian love). From beginning to end, despite many accretions from myth and legend and other sources, Book IV follows the outline of the love story of Huon and Rezia as told the hermit, the story from their first dreamed meeting to their ultimate bliss at Oberon's palace.

The eastern maid's first words (*End.* IV, 30-33) and Endymion's actions clearly allude to Rezia's dreams and departure from her native sacred river Euphrates. In what follows appear unmistakable allusions to her and Huon's dreams of love: the water into which Rezia is cast, and her transformation into a deer (*End.* IV, 40-70). Endymion's 'Thou art my executioner' and vision of the black firmament (IV, 109-25) allude to the black skies and vengeful storm of which Huon had dreamed and which punish him for his unchastity. Into the famous Song of Sorrow, which is another rich composite, further elements from Huon's wanderings and Rezia's dream of her shadowy wooer from the skies have been absorbed (*End.* IV, 182-98; 209-15). And the reason for the appearance of

---

* For verbal echoes and details see App. III, p. 352.

Bacchus in the romance seems to lie in the parallel pattern of *Oberon*.*

Huon and Rezia's blissful flight through the air left some echoes (*End*. IV, 367-70), as did their horror and despair upon realizing their 'heart treachery' (*End*. IV, 468-9). I suspect that Titania's grief, upon being separated from her heavenly lover, sorrow which caused her to sink into her desolate cave, may have suggested Endymion's Cave of Quietude under similar circumstances (IV, 512 ff.). In any case, Endymion's awaking upon earth with the eastern maid beside him, and his long monologue are full of *Oberon* allusions. He would 'live in love and peace' in the forest wildernesses; has been 'presumptuous against love,' the sky, and all elements. The detailed episode of the mossy cave, search for food, fear of death; and the eastern maid's reply: 'I may not be thy love: I am forbidden . . . We might commit Ourselves at once to vengeance' (IV, 635-771): all this minutely follows the sequence of incidents in Huon and Rezia's love and suffering on the desert shore and in the mossy cave of Canto VII, in consequence of Oberon's vengeance. And their suffering, we know, is a stage in the spiritualization of their love and leads to the hermitage. †

Accordingly, Endymion soon renounces earthly love in the line (IV, 860) '*A hermit young, I'll live* in mossy cave . . .' In that 'same void white Chastity shall sit' (to remind us how Huon's love was fully spiritualized and he came to look upon the 'woman like a goddess' as of heavenly essence for spiritual as well as physical reasons). Shortly, the woman changes into a goddess; and Endymion's constancy of purpose having been demonstrated, he reaches the chief intensity in fellowship with the divine after his seeming mortal love explains her transformation:

> ' 'twas fit that *from this mortal state*
> Thou shouldst, my *love*, by some unlook'd for *change*
> Be *spiritualiz'd*.'

* For detailed evidence see App. III, p. 353 f.
† For the detailed evidence see App. III, p. 359 f.

Beauty and love are ultimately one and the same in mortal and divine, the hermit had discovered. But for highest bliss in the divine, he and Huon and Endymion had learned, man must reach higher stages gradually through a long process of spiritualization.

.   .   .

It is clear that *Endymion* is a re-creation and poetical embodiment, in legendary and symbolical incidents, of that message. It is a re-creation at times crude, at times extremely subtle and profound. But the pervasively similar interrelation of theme and characters and incidents, of settings, imagery, and atmosphere—not to mention long verbal and sequence parallels and many explicit allusions —show that from first to last *Oberon*, Keats' pattern, played the determining part in the genesis of *Endymion*. The voluminous evidence, architectural, circumstantial, and thematic, which the allusions corroborate, makes that clear. In the hermit's experience of the divineness of beauty and love in all earthly things lies the key to Keats' meaning in *Endymion* and to some of his profoundest intuitions concerning life and art. Those intuitions were confirmed by his own and by Wordsworth's experience; but they were consistently, and explicitly, formulated in a symbolism derived from the hermit's life. The hermit's influence extended far: to the very verge of the 'reality to come' in Keats' brief life.

There is little need to add that *Endymion,* into which much besides *Oberon* was drawn, is a new creation with a meaning, spirit, truth, and beauty quite its own. Even a partial rereading makes that clear. But the key to its creation, form, and meaning lies in *Oberon,* which enables us to watch Keats at work from the start, now subtly, now crassly absorbing and re-creating, selecting and rejecting, modifying and reintegrating, transmuting or otherwise incorporating the stuff of intense, and evidently synchronous, literary experience. With it he interwove mythical and legendary and other poetic ingredients and accretions, which, the detailed evidence indicates, were drawn into the pattern by associations of one kind or another, many of them suggested by *Oberon*.

In view of all this, there are in literary history few finer instances of irony than a sentence in the notorious review of *Endymion*. Imperfect though that romance was, for Keats it was an artistically profitable experiment, the shortcomings of which he himself saw clearly and publicly admitted. But young Lockhart, tool of the Tories and fresh from Weimar, saw fit to malign the poet as Leigh Hunt's friend and to parade his own new knowledge in *Blackwood's*, in these words:

The old story of the moon falling in love with a shepherd, so prettily told by a Roman classic, and so exquisitely enlarged and adorned by one of the most elegant of German poets, has been seized upon by Mr. John Keats, to be done with as might seem good unto the sickly fancy of one who never read a single line of either Ovid or Wieland.[15]

Though to be sure he had read only Sotheby's translation, Keats must have laughed when he read that, even though Lockhart had in mind not *Oberon* but Wieland's own 'Endymion,' a minor piece of 1771.[16]

Yet in this extraordinary coincidence, too, there may have been the hand of some guiding power, perhaps the same that had led Keats to the enchanted forest and the hermitage, the shadowy gardens by a river side, and other haunts of the daemon king. Without them, *The Eve of St. Agnes,* and *Lamia,* and some of the great Odes would also have been quite different.

III

But, first, what of the meaning of *Endymion?*
In *Sleep and Poetry* Keats had written:

> . . . though no great minist'ring reason sorts
> Out the dark mysteries of human souls
> To clear conceiving: yet there ever rolls

A vast idea before me, and I glean
Therefrom my liberty; thence too I've seen
The end and aim of Poesy . . .

The 'no . . . reason,' 'mysteries of human souls,' 'yet,' and 'thence'
are noteworthy. That Keats intended to convey some of his 'vast
idea' in *Endymion* seems quite clear. That he succeeded in doing
so—notwithstanding the fact that his youthfully exuberant imagination let the lush imagery run riot in the romance and thus conceal
both his theme and the contours of his structural design—is hardly
less clear. For the plan of *Oberon,* by which he was guided from
first to last; and the hermit's visions in a similarly fourfold modified ladder of love, to which he explicitly alludes,* shed light
upon the meaning of *Endymion,* which runs something like this:
Love is the ultimate principle of the universe (1, 814 f., 832). It
is that vital force which leads man to exert himself on 'far journeys'
wherever Beauty dwells (III, 92 ff.). Love is inherent in nature and
beneath nature: it *creates* new forms of vegetation, animal life, and
beauty.† And it is the secret of art and human relations (1, 840-2;
III, 97 ff., and 300). For love is the inner force which animates both.
Without love's devotion the artist does not strive or see. ‡ And those
who 'lord it o'er their fellow men' without possessing such 'sanctuary splendour' or spiritualized love as the hermit has, merely 'singe
Our gold and ripe-ear'd hopes.' § Without love the human being
is selfish, solitary, and sterile, in both a literal and a figurative
sense. || For human love is part of the divine Love which creates
all things. Though human love is on a lower plane, it is essentially
the same vital force as the divine principle of Love (1, 832, 840).
    But to perceive that highest spirit-essence (the Creator); to ap-
prehend that 'form divine' and thereby reach the highest bliss,

---

* Cf. *End.* III, 9, 22-31.
† 1, 835-42; II, 480-500. Venus, goddess of love, is enamored of and revives the
vegetation hero, the beautiful Adonis.
‡ 1, 774; III, 92 ff., 696-703; IV, 957-8.
§ *End.* III, 1-10. (That is, frustrate mankind's spiritual aspirations.)
|| 1, 816 f.; II, 281, 480, 529; IV, 957 ff. (and cf. *Alastor*).

whether in religion like the hermit, in life like Endymion, or in art like the poet, man must be gradually spiritualized.* He must lose himself in devoted love of beauty, wherever it appears. And he must love and pity and serve his fellows. † Only by such 'self-destroying' experience and the renunciation of worldly aims will he be spiritually cleansed and ennobled and thus be prepared for highest happiness: 'in that which becks our *ready* minds to fellowship divine,' a 'fellowship with essence' or spirit, which is the God of Love (I, 777-9, 820; III, 1-31).

A thing of beauty, which can be known only through love, is the bond that binds us to this mortal life of suffering (I, 7). It soothes and spiritualizes man even as the heavenly light of the moon. Beauty, created by love and perceived through love, is divine, a gift from heaven: 'an endless fountain of immortal drink' (I, 20-24). Those who pursue Beauty (progressively more subtle in form and thought and word and deed) with steadfast love, will reach heaven and immortality by a ladder of love, or a process of gradual spiritual perfection, like the hermit and Endymion.

Beauty, however, like its ultimate self the Divine, cannot be fully apprehended save through a 'life of Sensations,' of super-rational intuitions. It cannot be perceived by reasoning alone, but must be sensed in a dreamlike state of intuition which resembles the mystic's ultimate and the poet's imaginative insight. ‡ Hence the visions of Endymion, in which love and beauty and truth and the divine are similarly apprehended. Because of that similarity, intuition and instinctive emotion are sacred and can guide, like the hermit and the daemon king, 'where learning hath no light.' Of that Keats is deeply convinced: like Wordsworth, § he is convinced of the 'holi-

---

* I, 799; III, 675-711; IV, 991-4.

† II, 1015-6; III, 282-90, 701-4; IV, 85 ff. Beauty appears in Nature's Forms, in Eternal Harmonies or Laws, in Humanitarian Deeds, and in Human Love—as the four books of *Endymion* illustrate. Cf. also I, 12 ff.

‡ Cf. *Sleep and Poetry*, p. 88 above; also *Letters*, p. 68; *End.* I, 572 ff., 860, etc.

§ 'That serene and blessed mood In which the affections gently lead us on' (*Tintern Abbey*).

ness of the Heart's affections.' And evidently from Shakespeare's heroes, sublime in their grief and anger, ambition and fear, love and jealousy, Keats has seen that 'all our Passions,' like the hermit's love, are, 'in their sublime, creative of essential Beauty,' which is spiritual.[17] All human passions, that is, if intense and sublimely depicted, create spirituality and thus spiritual beauty in the mind of the beholder. Hence the Song of Sorrow, Alpheus and Arethusa, Glaucus, and, indirectly, the mission.*

These are some of the 'dark mysteries of human souls' that Keats mentioned in *Sleep and Poetry*. All this is his 'vast idea,' first hinted in that poem and illustrated poetically in *Endymion,* in symbols and incidents in large measure derived from *Oberon*. That key makes clear Keats' intention, and the sublime nature of his 'vast idea.' It is clear that for Keats all love (and beauty), however manifest on earth, is part of and therefore ultimately identical with the highest Love (and Beauty), the spirit of God in the realm of timelessness (*End*. 1, 805 ff.; iv, 639 ff.). That is Keats' 'clear religion of heaven' (1, 781).

And it is for that reason that Endymion's visions of beauty—physical, intellectual, and spiritual; in the sunrise, in the laws of the elements, or in woman—his manifold dreams of love and unswerving pursuit of its essence; and his love for the mortal eastern queen—all lead up to the identification of the mortal with the divine Love, which in the legend is symbolized by Diana or the moon. For ultimately vision and achievement, the ideal and the real, are one: for those who pursue their vision without swerving.

---

* The symbolical meaning of Endymion's mission, it seems to me, is this: the poet, after self-discipline through loving exploration of the 'secret mysteries of earth'—whose cosmic principle he perceived to be Love, reanimates through his writings the spirituality of those lovers (of beauty, aesthetic or moral) who have been shipwrecked in the sea of life. (Cf. *End*. 1, 776 and iii, 722. Also Huon and Rezia, and their redemption by the hermit.)

And it is because the fated poet revives their love that he achieves immortality for himself and bliss for the Spirit of Beauty, whose symbol in *Endymion* is the moon goddess. It is she who says, after he has fulfilled his mission: 'Immortal bliss for me too hast thou won' (iii, 1024).

And Love is the ultimate principle which men must obey, if they would know or create either beauty or truth—even as the God of Love creates.

Keats had learned that vital truth from life, deduced it from Wordsworth, and seen it illustrated in the life story of Wieland's hermit. And 'axioms in philosophy,' Keats wrote in a characteristic letter, 'are not axioms until they are proved upon our pulses: we read fine things but never feel them to the full until we have gone the same steps as the author.'[18] His own experience had made him feel the truth of what Wordsworth repeatedly tried to convey and what the hermit's case-history succinctly illustrated. For good reason, therefore, Keats wrote: 'A hermit young, I'll live.'* The three experiences illuminated, corroborated, and supplemented each other. Without knowing all three, as criticism has too well shown, *Endymion* cannot be fully understood.

As the allusions, imagery, settings, characters, incidents, theme, and parallel structure show, *Oberon* contains the key to Keats' imaginative conception. His derivative symbolism and closely parallel structure in *Endymion* make that certain. But he used the plot pattern and incidents of *Oberon* for his own visionary purpose. And in his romance Keats drew heavily upon his own experience of soul-states and greatly elaborated upon Wordsworth's sense of the divine in nature, which is shared by the hermit. I suspect strongly that it was primarily Wordsworth (and Haydon and Bailey) who helped Keats envisage the relation between a poet's life and spiritual discipline. I think it was in part at least for that reason that in November 1816 he wrote the sonnet 'Great Spirits Now on Earth Are Sojourning.'

Moreover, because they are so nearly identical, the Wordsworthian attitude and the life story of Wieland's hermit blended in Keats' mind. For Keats propounded his newly discovered truths,

* *End.* IV, 860. As early as 1816, in *Sleep and Poetry* he had identified himself with the hermit.

of the unity and universal vitality of love and its creative relationship to beauty, in poetical symbols and symbolical incidents which
constitute a language different from Wordsworth's. The latter ex-
pounds his (primarily moral) experience more directly, didactically,
and rationally, in a language closer to prose. Because that was not
Keats' way, because he was no 'consequitive man,' it has been
doubted that he meant anything in *Endymion.* Indeed, for all his
'clear religion of heaven,' it has been doubted, as Arnold's question
implies,* that he had any religious feeling at all, or that his work
contains anything more than 'sensations' of a lower kind. For this
unfortunate and gross misconception his youth was doubtless in
large measure to blame: *Endymion* does not communicate his intuitions clearly, as Keats himself knew before he had completed it.
But in the light of his immediate source, the background of the
unexpressed enables us to see the setting that the legend assumed
in his mind, and his meaning becomes clear.[19] And it helps us
understand what Keats meant in saying: *'The mighty abstract Idea
I have of Beauty in all things.'* [20]

Endymion is a poetic allegory, in a symbolism originally Christian and ultimately Platonic, of a poet's quest for spiritual perfection, (1, 607, 848), immortality, (11, 212), and highest happiness—in
the unswerving pursuit of Beauty, Love, and Truth (1, 769 ff.). It
is the allegorical history of the poet's preparation for his visioned
goal: through suffering, renunciation, and later progressively subtler
stages of perception and spiritualizing experience. These attained,
the hero achieves his goal in a selfless union with the spirit of
beauty, embodied in the 'form divine,' in which is highest happiness
and immortality, and in which purest love and beauty and ultimate
truth co-exist: for the saint (the hermit), the poet (Keats), and
the man Endymion.

* 'Keats . . . is abundantly and enchantingly sensuous; the question with some
people will be, whether he is anything else.'

⋛ IV ⋚

'Visions of Delight,' the Elfin King, and 'The Eve of St. Agnes'

'IF ENDYMION serves me as a Pioneer,' Keats wrote in February 1818, 'perhaps I ought to be content . . . I am anxious to get [it] printed so that I may forget it and proceed.'[1] He had begun revising the long romance early in January but did not finish until March. In the meanwhile he saw a good deal of Haydon and Reynolds, Dilke and Rice. He met Wordsworth several times and also Hazlitt, whose lectures on the English poets he attended regularly. In general, he was perhaps as happy as he was ever again to be. Besides undertaking a short journey to Devon in the spring, he 'feasted upon' Milton by way of preparation for writing *Hyperion,* about which he had been thinking since the first of the year. And all the while he was writing occasional pieces, various songs, and the *Pot of Basil* after Boccaccio. 'I have been hovering for some time,' he wrote in April, 'between an exquisite sense of the luxurious and a love for Philosophy.'[2] Evidently owing to Hazlitt's influence, he now planned a system of study that he might better prepare himself for his life's work.

Soon, however, a crisis arose. His brother Tom had long been ailing; and now George, who for months had been unemployed, decided to marry and emigrate to America. As the time of parting drew near, Keats became increasingly despondent.

I have two Brothers [he wrote Bailey in June], one is driven by the 'burden of Society' to America [;] the other, with an exquisite love of Life, is in a lingering State. My Love for my Brothers from the early loss of our parents and even for earlier Misfortunes has grown into a[n] affection 'passing the Love of Women.' [3]

George departed, nevertheless, late in June. After attending him and his bride to Liverpool, Keats continued with Brown on the long and fateful tour afoot through the North. In the course of walking some six hundred miles, he saw mountains, lakes, and waterfalls to his heart's content. But he also caught a violent cold and further weakened his constitution by fatigue and irregular meals. Forced to return in August, he went to Hampstead and soon was immersed in *Hyperion* and the fever of composition. In September or October he met Fanny Brawne, to whom after a brief courtship he became engaged on Christmas Day. About three weeks earlier, in spite of Keats' devoted care, his brother Tom had died of consumption. Keats, himself no longer in the best of health, never completely recovered from this blow. Numb with grief, at last he went to Bedhampton and Chichester, and in the endeavor to escape from his anguish he set about, toward the end of January 1819, writing *The Eve of St. Agnes.*

Begun only seven weeks after the death of Tom, and not long after the poet had fallen in love, *The Eve of St. Agnes,* the most nearly perfect of his longer pieces, is a tale of love in a setting and atmosphere hostile to happiness. Masterful contrasts mark the poem from first to last. Elemental cold and storm, human hatred and thirst for blood, violent death and slow disintegration in age serve as backdrop to a passion youthfully warm and vibrant. Like shadows of eternity, the backdrop reminds us that love, for all its ecstasy, is perilous: that it surmounts earthly pain imperfectly and leads to a joy that is not unalloyed.

Poignant experience underlay this conception. Sorrow had come to try the resources of Keats' spirit and had turned his mind in upon itself. Clearly his thoughts had reverted to the gradations of happiness in *Endymion.** How recently this had happened is shown

---

* Cf. the echoes and allusions in *Letters,* pp. 246-7 (16 Dec. 1818).

by the three first stanzas of *St. Agnes,* in which light from the ladder of the eternal gleams through clearly. For it is not by chance that the frosted breath of the old Beadsman (*'the eremite'* as significantly he is called *) 'Seem'd *taking flight for heaven, without a death';* and that he is a 'patient, holy man . . . aged . . . and poor,' whose life is solely in God. He makes his way through the icy chapel *'by* slow *degrees.'* And though he hears *'Music's* golden tongue,' unlike Endymion's and Porphyro's, the *'joys* of all his life were said and sung.' These echoes from the thought and phrasing and background of the gradations of happiness (*End.* 1, 777 ff.) are part of the elaborate structure of contrast in *The Eve of St. Agnes.* They remind us at the outset of higher things than human love, which is commingled of joy and sorrow, as the action will bear out.

It is also significant that the hermit, vital principle of *Endymion,* is close to the heart of *St. Agnes.* Porphyro's words to Madeline, 'Thou art *my* heaven, and I thine eremite,' † are meaningful. They too point to the profoundest contrast in the romance: the contrast between spiritual love divine, in which is highest happiness, and sensual love for woman, which is joy of a lower degree. The early appearance in *The Eve of St. Agnes* of the spirit of Wieland's hermit, who had transcended grief, who by degrees achieved highest happiness in God, and who had heard Huon's tale of a dream of love come true, is but one of many clues to the background, genesis, and structure of Keats' masterpiece.

. . .

It is noteworthy, nevertheless, that in his recent study of the romance M. R. Ridley thus summarized our present knowledge of the materials of which it was woven:

I am going to suggest for examination as the four main sources of *The Eve of St. Agnes,* apart from the folklore element, Shakespeare,

* Cf. Keats' canceled stanza iv.
† St. xxxi. Italics mine.

especially *Romeo and Juliet,* Mrs. Radcliffe, the *Arabian Nights,* and a French translation of Boccaccio's *Il Filocolo.*[4]

Mr. Ridley reminds us that, 'on the authority of Woodhouse, "the subject was suggested by Mrs. Jones"'; and that the quite general remarks of Jonson, Brand, and Burton about the rites of St. Agnes' Eve are such as must also have been current in oral folklore.[5] But whether from oral tradition or a chapbook, the folklore basis of the romance consists in the belief that by heeding certain simple but specific observances a maiden might see. her adoring lover *in a dream* on St. Agnes' Eve.

As for Shakespeare, from *Cymbeline, Hamlet,* and *Macbeth* Keats seems to have recalled some minor elements and phraseology. In *Romeo and Juliet,* on the other hand, he knew a tale of electric passion against a somber backdrop. And in that play he found a picture, Mr. Ridley believes, of 'a great house getting ready for an entertainment'; [6] various minor elements; and perhaps the most important of all: 'The general picture of the entry of the lover into the festivities of his foemen [which, thinks Mr. Ridley] is clearly that of *Romeo and Juliet.'* [7]

Mrs. Radcliffe and the *Arabian Nights* would appear to have provided settings and stage properties—Gothic furniture and exotic delicacies. Finally, *Il Filocolo* presents some very serious difficulties. There was no English translation; Keats read Italian only slowly and with painful effort; and the evidence of his having read a French translation, by Mr. Ridley's own admission, is at best unconvincing.[8] Moreover, that romance resembles *St. Agnes* in little more than that a lover in a basket is smuggled into a tower, is concealed in a lady's room by her attendant (who then tells her of a feigned dream of the lover's appearance), and awakens the lady in the night with his impassioned wooing. But the lover's entrance is quite different, the later actions are conventional, and the lovers do not flee.

Even though a composite picture integrated from these several 'sources' be imagined, we discover that crucial elements in *The Eve of St. Agnes* are totally lacking. Allowing fully for Keats' powers of invention, and the profound effect of Shakespearean intensity upon his style, we find that many features of the structure and background as well as various supernatural overtones and allusions in his romance have never been accounted for. No pattern has ever been discovered through whose agency the unrelated threads could have been drawn together and woven into their final form. Again, if the 'general picture' came from *Romeo and Juliet,* whence could the particular pictures of the lover's entry into the festivities of his foemen have derived? Why did the entrance come just when and as it did? Was there no other model for Keats' far larger picture of high revelry and *'thousand guests,'* for the sinister *'hundred swords'* and *'barbarian hordes'* threatening the lover, and for Madeline's actions at that revelry? All these and many other features are totally different from anything in *Romeo.* The hero of that play, who is recognized through his mask by Juliet's father, enters boldly to a 'trifling foolish banquet,' a 'fair assembly.' He does not yet know Juliet, who only flirts and is not given to dreaming. He does not yet know the nurse. The only threat to his life is the single sword of Tybalt. And that 'king of cats' is restrained by Juliet's father himself, who knows Romeo yet shows him courtesy rather than deadly hostility at the revelry. Finally, the lovers in the play do not flee. All this is quite different from *The Eve of St. Agnes.*[9]

As for the other 'sources,' was there nothing more definite than the conjectural 'Mother Bunch' or Mrs. Jones' folklore to color Madeline's actions, her enchanted 'visions of delight,' and panting 'akin to spirits of the air and visions wide'; nothing to suggest the lovers' complex emotions and lute-playing; nothing more than poetic faith to justify 'Love's alarum' and the 'elfin-storm from faery land' into which at last the lovers flee past the benightmared wassailers in the silent castle? I think there was. And I think the hermit of Porphyro's words to Madeline, like the 'eremite' of the opening stanzas, provides but one clue. For Keats had seen all these features in or connected with Canto v of *Oberon*. In much the same sequence they constitute there the tale confessed to the hermit: of how Huon, with the help of Oberon, won his peerless bride and fled with her out of the ghostly castle.*

. . .

That episode, we know from the previous chapter, was the only portion of the love story and spiritualization of Huon and Rezia which Keats had not used in *Endymion*. He had patterned parts of Books II and III and all of Book IV of *Endymion* after the love story in *Oberon*. Into his Book IV he had not only drawn elements from Huon and Rezia's dream-visions of each other and aerial flights in Cantos IV and V; but also he had alluded to or otherwise used all the following incidents occurring in Canto VII: the *consummation of their love* in forgetfulness of Oberon's prohibition, the latter's *alarm*, fearful anger and punitive *tempest*, the suffering on the desert shore and joy in the mossy cave. Probably because it did not fit the design of *Endymion*, he had omitted only the main episode of Canto v, the actual winning of Rezia from under the eyes of the bloodthirsty warrior guests in her father's castle.

But now, when he had come upon the legend of St. Agnes' Eve, a legend of a dream of love, it was inevitable that Keats should have recalled Rezia's dream of love and how it came true. That he did recall it is hinted by the fact that Canto v of *Oberon* bears a striking resemblance to Keats' expanded version of the legend, in his tale of the winning of Madeline and of how her dream of love came true. The similarity is arresting in the light both of clear allusions to *Oberon* in *The Eve of St. Agnes* and of a great deal

---

* For the summary of Canto v see p. 30. As for Huon's confession to the hermit, it occurs only a few stanzas after the sage's vision of highest happiness, in Canto VIII: 'How *love* did *in a dream* at first descend, And with a look enchain him to *his bride*: From Bagdad *how he 'scap'd* . . . And, ah! *the warning* of his fairy friend' (VIII, 35).

of evidence in it of Keats' awareness that Wieland's romance again was serving as a pattern. The resemblance between it and *St. Agnes* consists in general plot contour, from beginning to end. It extends to a considerable number of incidents—highly exceptional as well as more conventional—but always in analogous sequence and configuration. It includes machinery, pictures of settings, not a little atmosphere and furniture, and minutely the interaction and relation of the characters. What is more, Keats even recalled a good deal of exact phraseology. All this points to the nature of the genesis and development of Keats' masterpiece, a process we may observe in examining *Oberon.*

With the action of *St. Agnes* fresh in mind, let us glance first at the pertinent portions of *Oberon* in their outline and sequence:

Shortly before her wedding to a *hated* suitor whom she *scorns* and *disdains,* the lovely Princess Rezia dreams *a dream, sent by her guardian spirit, of a shadowy lover* from the skies. Haunted by his image, *she broods over her dream* for days, until on the eve of the revelry her sleepless anxiety is relieved by the king of the daemons and fairies, who grants her new *'visions of delight':* a second dream of her lover. The vision dispelled, she *dreams awake in her bed* until the nurse comes to wake her, but instead is told the dream and looks about the chamber to see *where the lover is hiding.* While the dreamer is being *robed* by her whispering virgins, *an aged crone is hurried in* who tells and retells of Huon's presence in Bagdad. Meanwhile, *preparations for the regal revelry* have been completed and the great throng of magnificent guests gathers. Amid the music of trumpets, *the splendid procession* begins, until the sultan, the bridegroom, and the bride all have entered. But even *after the revelry has begun* the bride is still *preoccupied with her dream-vision and does not heed* the looks of love cast upon her. Suddenly she is roused from her reverie. For the lover of her dream, the youthful Christian, Sir Huon of Bordeaux, had boldly *entered the closely guarded hall of his* fanatical *foemen,* in a rich disguise provided by *the fairy king.* And as his liege-lord

Charlemagne had commanded, Huon swiftly beheads the bride-groom, the blasphemous *paynim* at the sultan's side. While the thunderstruck revelers gasp, Rezia sees and is seen and is thrice kissed by her lover. In a flash the hot-blooded sultan raves *imprecations,* and the *murder*ous rage of *the barbarian warrior-guests* breaks loose. But a twofold *miracle saves* Huon. In the fearful *elfin storm* the daemon king himself appears in the hall. And while Rezia recalls her *'visions of delight'* and *pants* in his lily fragrance, *the hostile horde lie here and there, deathlike in an enchanted sleep.* Thus *the lovers flee out of the ghostly castle* as Canto v ends.

A careful reading of *The Eve of St. Agnes* shows that Keats not only followed this outline rather closely but that, despite much intervening action in *Oberon,* he also derived hints from another quite different episode in the love story of Huon and Rezia. Various things led him to recall a scene in Canto xi which he had used for Glaucus' temptation by the 'arbour queen' in *Endymion.* For when, shortly after the hermit's death, the lovers have been separated, Huon like Porphyro *attempts to see his immured bride in* this second *festive and hostile castle. By a stratagem of the nurse he is led furtively at midnight through low-arched vaults,* and then by a misunderstanding *to the chambers of the beautiful enamored* queen. There *a feast of delicacies awaits him* and *a lute is played.* And the queen, who had had her own *'vision of delight,'* had hoped to consummate her passion. With some help from Shake-speare, Keats derived various elements from this scene and inter-wove them with the stuff of Canto v. And for sufficient reason.

'Visions of delight.' This was the third appearance of Sotheby's haunting phrase. The three instances are like luminous points in the pattern Keats deftly rearranged. The phrase appears in three provocative scenes of *Oberon,* all of which left their traces in *The Eve of St. Agnes.* Rezia's initial dream of love, with the revelry at the outset of Canto v, was as suggestive for Keats as her vision when the fairy king appears with his fragrance near the end of the canto. And these 'visions of delight' demonstrably blended with the

queen's anticipated visions—of embracing the lover in her chamber, after the midnight revelry in the second castle and the nurse's stratagem had made his furtive entrance possible. This last vision was interfused between Rezia's initial and terminal ones. And the three 'visions of delight' came to limn the main outline of *The Eve of St. Agnes.*

Whence its structure and incidents were derived is attested by the unimpeachable authority of Keats himself. Five times within the compass of his poem he explicitly alluded to elements specific and unique in Wieland's romance: namely, *'visions of delight'* in a dream of love come true; venturing amid revelry into a hostile castle like the *'liege-lord of all the Elves and Fays';* a lovely dreamer's *panting 'akin to spirits of the air and visions wide';* a *'tempest fell'* that was *'Love's alarum';* and the *lovers' flight into the 'elfin-storm from faery land.'* These allusions not only point to Keats' primary source, the folklore element aside, but they define the contours of his poem. They constitute clear evidence that as he wrote Keats was conscious, from first to last, that he was being guided by *Oberon.*

II

Immediately after his picture of the icy chapel and the aged beadsman-eremite, Keats in his fourth and fifth stanzas continued thus:

> K 28   That ancient Beadsman heard the prelude soft;
> And so it chanc'd, for *many a door* was wide,
> 30   From hurry to and fro. *Soon,* up aloft,
> The silver, snarling *trumpets 'gan* to chide:
> 32   The level *chambers, ready* with their *pride,*
> *Were glowing* to receive *a thousand guests* . . .

Omitting the carved angels that support the cornice, we see that

> 37   At length burst in the *argent* revelry,
> With *plume,* tiara, and all *rich array,*

39   *Numerous* as *shadows haunting fairily*
     The brain, new stuff'd, in youth, with *triumphs gay*
41   Of old romance. These let us wish away,
     And turn, sole-thoughted, to *one Lady there* . . .

Now the hermit had heard Huon's tale of what happened in the castle at Bagdad. And if we turn to the beginning of Canto v of *Oberon* and momentarily omit Rezia's dream, the nurse's entrance, and the robing scene, we find that

     Emirs, and viziers, all the courtly *crowd*
     Meantime attendant at the sultan's call,
     With *festal splendor* grace the nuptial *hall*.
     The banquet *waits* . . .
                  (v, 19)

until *soon* 'cymbals, and *cornets,* in imperial *pride' begin* the revelry.* A moment before, cymbals had announced the entrance through a golden *door* of the sultan and his numerous retinue, followed by the princely bridegroom 'with jewels blazing o'er.' Opposite, through an ivory *door,* our one lady there, the Princess Rezia *enters* 'More fair than Mahom's paradise . . . in visionary dreams.' From beneath her silver veil her dazzling beauty seems to fill the hall 'with heavenly *lustre.*'

It is worth emphasizing that Keats' 'triumphs gay' gleaned from 'romance,' a procession into 'chambers ready' and 'glowing,' has a suggestive parallel in Wieland's canto. Besides the similarly luminous quality and the verbal echoes, it is noteworthy that Keats is emphatic about the numerous guests, explicitly 'a thousand.' For Oberon had prophesied that the lover of the one lady there would find a 'thousand' warrior-guests to threaten him.† As for their rich array, Rezia wears pearls in her hair suggestively like a *tiara;* the bridegroom appears in 'proud *array'* and 'high-plum'd in bridal

* v, 22; cf. K 31.
† Cf. Oberon's promise in the enchanted forest (ii, 49).

grace' (IV, 53 and V, 36); while Huon wears the garb the *fairy* king had provided, 'such as highest emirs wear.' It is described in detail: from his caftan's 'golden tissue, *rich* and rare' to the diamond atop the 'turban *shadow'd* o'er with ostrich *plumes,'* while the *silver* garb of his pages is also mentioned. Evidently this and Rezia's lustrous silver veil helped suggest Keats' lines,

> At length burst in the argent revelry,
> With plume, tiara, and all rich array,
> Numerous as shadows haunting fairily . . .

In the last line there was also, I think, another reminiscence.

. . .

This revelry has many other features that we shall see. The important figure is the 'one lady there,'

K 43   *Whose heart* had *brooded, all* that wintry *day,*
       On love, and wing'd St. Agnes' saintly *care,*
45   As she had *heard old dames* full many times declare.

(st. v)

Keats tells us this in the second of the two stanzas above. But now let us glance back at Rezia's two dream-visions. For it is in the hut where Huon meanwhile is concealed that *the old grandam tells* of Rezia's first vision: of how 'She dreamt' of seeing her *shadowy* lover in the dwarf's (*fairy* king's) aerial car, and how 'At once his glance of love her charmed spirit drew'; how

W 3   'The *shadow* flies, but from *her heart* again   K 43
      He *never fades:* the youth with golden hair—
5   Eternally his image hovers there,
      Exhaustless source of *sweetly-pensive* pain,
7   *In nightly visions,* and *in day-dreams* shown.
      Sithence our Drusi prince is loathsome grown,
9   *She hears,* she *sees* him *not* without *disdain*—

Vainly to search the cause all rack the brain:
11　　*She broods* in silent gloom . . .'　　　　　　K 43

(OBERON IV, 46-7, 49)

Of this, Keats' 'shadows haunting fairily' is evidently a subtle reminiscence. Rezia's brooding on her love, and the intervention of her winged guardian spirit by whom her dreams of love were sent, exactly fitted Keats' purpose.

On the eve of her wedding, moreover, Rezia is granted another dream by the fairy king. *In her bed* she is 'sunk in warm fancies of enchanting love.' Breathless, *in her dream she sees her lover,* whose shadowy image approaches her *in the night* with open arms. Her shyness causes the dream to vanish. But when the sun has already ascended high in the heavens,

W 16　　Yet still with Rezia it was ever night:
　　　　While her charm'd soul 'mid *visions of delight,*
18　　Wove in her waking hours anew the dream.

(OBERON V, 6)

This, the first appearance of Sotheby's happy phrase, was the first focal point of associations which led Keats to identify Rezia's story with Madeline's and the legend.

Keats now says the old dames had told the girl:

K 46　　They told her how, upon St. Agnes' *Eve,*
　　　　Young virgins might have *visions of delight,*　　　　W 17
48　　And soft adorings from their loves receive
　　　　Upon the honey'd middle of the *night,* ·　　　　W 15
50　　If ceremonies due they did aright;
　　　　As, supperless to *bed* they must retire,　　　　W 13
52　　And couch supine their beauties, lily white;
　　　　Nor look behind, nor sideways, but require
54　　*Of Heaven* with upward eyes for *all that they desire.*

(EVE OF ST. AGNES, VI)

In these lines Keats artfully embodied the basic folklore of the legend, which, let us remember, concerns only the sight of the lover in a dream. Rezia, we saw, performs all these ceremonies save that of the supperless retiring. And not only her 'visions of delight' but her actions at the revelry and its outcome were circumstantially used by Keats to illustrate the legend.

First of all, he seems to have noted some suggestive elements that occur just after Rezia's visions of delight. The nurse enters, is told the dream of Rezia's lover, and glances about the chamber to see if *he is hiding there.* (Was this a first hint for Porphyro's concealment in the other dreamer's chamber?) Rezia's love having made her desperate, she vows to kill herself before marrying her hated suitor; and when she draws a poniard the nurse cries out and Rezia seals her lips. Then the nurse piously hopes that *'Heaven that has sent the knight will* sure *provide* the rest' of Rezia's *desires,* as the aged 'crone is hurry'd in' (v, 14). (With this compare the pious thought in K 54.) This 'grandam,' who had told of Rezia's dream of love, not only tells of Huon's concealment in her hut, but *'Repeats the wondrous story'* as Rezia bids.* Meanwhile Rezia is being robed 'by her virgins,' † for the revelry is about to begin and like Madeline she is to be 'one lady there Whose heart' still brooded on her visions of delight. Thus far, in short, situation and setting, characters, motivation, and atmosphere, as well as striking phraseology, are closely akin in the two poems.

. . .

Now, alluding to the legend, Keats returns to the revelry:

K 55 *Full of this whim was thoughtful* Madeline: W 5-6
     The *music,* yearning like a God in pain,
57   She scarcely heard: *her maiden eyes* divine,
     Fix'd on the floor, saw many a sweeping train
59   Pass by—*she heeded not at all: in vain*
     Came many a tiptoe, *amorous cavalier,*

* Cf. K 45.
† Cf. K 47.

61   And back retir'd; *not* cool'd by high *disdain*,
      But *she saw not:* her *heart was otherwhere:*   W 8-9
63   *She sigh'd for* Agnes' *dreams,* the sweetest of the year.

      She danc'd along with vague, regardless eyes,
65   Anxious her lips, her breathing quick and short:
      The hallow'd *hour was near* at hand: *she sighs*
67   *Amid* the *timbrels, and* the throng'd resort
      Of *whisperers* in *anger,* or in sport;
69   'Mid *looks of love, defiance, hate, and scorn,*
      Hoodwink'd with faery fancy . . .

                                        (st. vii-viii)

The commentators have been at a loss to explain particularly the
second of these stanzas, with their clear detail and tense and tangled
emotional atmosphere. For Juliet merely dances; and the disdained
amorous cavalier, the whisperers, and looks mingled of love and
defiance, hate and scorn—these certainly are beyond the imaginative
reach of 'Mother Bunch.' Keats' mind, however, was weaving other
threads: still spun by the old grandam. In her recital of Rezia's
first dream, she mentions that lady's 'sweetly-*pensive* pain'; how
her amorous cavalier, 'our Drusi prince,' had become hateful so that
Rezia *'hears,* she *sees* him *not* without *disdain':* because like
Madeline's her brooding heart was elsewhere. A glance at Keats'
lines 60-62 suggests that Rezia's amorous prince had merely multi-
plied in becoming Madeline's luckless suitors! For it is clear that
fragments of Rezia's first vision have been scattered and recombined
in three consecutive stanzas of *St. Agnes.**

      Now the grandam also tells Huon that Rezia's suitor would
'force out favor from the *scorn*ful bride.' † And upon awaking from
her 'visions of delight' Rezia realizes that *'the hour draws near,'*
for her wedding revelry. (Cf. K 66.) And she is so *angry, anxious,*
and desperate that she says, 'Nought like the loathsome . . .

* St. v-vii, cf. p. 157 above.
† iv, 51; cf. K 69.

prince I *hate'* (v, 9, 11). Then she draws the poniard, causes the nurse to scream, and 'seals *her lip'* for fear of discovery. (Did this have something to do with Madeline's 'anxious her lips' in K 65?) At that tense moment a knock is heard and the nurse opens with rapturous emotions that *'her breath* impede' as the old crone is hurried in with her wondrous story of Huon's coming. (Keats wrote 'her breathing quick and short.') That tale told, Rezia's eyes shine, she flushes, and her 'willing *sighs'* so astonish the attendant virgins that:

> 'Is this,' the *whisper* ran, 'the maid forlorn?
> Her whom we late beheld, th' obdurate bride,
> Who in her anguish heaven and earth *defy'd?'*
> (v, 18)

The whisperers pointedly recall all Rezia's emotions—which are precisely those of Keats' picture: 'she sighs Amid . . . the throng'd resort of whisperers in anger or in sport . . . looks of love, defiance, hate, and scorn.'[10]

Keats also knew that two stanzas later the pensive Rezia is 'one lady there' at the revelry, and that she is possessed by the self-same whim as the thoughtful Madeline. Not only are both girls anxious because a 'hallowed hour was near'; not only do both dream of their lovers in the same taut emotional atmosphere. But also, as the (yearning?) *music* of strings and drums or *timbrels* is heard around her, and 'mirth in freer current' inflames the amorous bridegroom, Rezia turns away: *'Casts on the ground* her *looks that never stray'* (v, 34) with precisely the same gesture as Madeline. (Cf. K 58: 'Fix'd on the floor' and 'looks of . . .') In the very next stanza, Huon enters to the revelry and with 'scornful eyes' recognizes the hated prince. (In his two next stanzas Keats also has the lover of the dreamer's 'visions of delight' approach the castle and venture in to the revelry.) But Rezia is still oblivious, even when the guests marvel at the stranger's rich array: 'tranced with fascinated eye,' Rezia *'still views her dream,* and *ever downward bends'* (v, 35) still as if in accordance with the ceremonies due. That facilitated the identification of the legend with Rezia's story.

Both girls are in the same circumstances. Both are oblivious to the whisperers and the music and festivities around them and pre-occupied with their 'visions of delight' or dreams of their lovers. As the legend requires, both 'nor look behind nor sideways' but have their 'maiden eyes fixed on the floor' and heed not at all. As for the amorous cavalier, also present in each scene, he is ignored by both dreamers. If Madeline's high disdain does not *cool* the 'amorous cavalier' because 'her heart was otherwise,' the disdain and scorn Rezia feels for the amorous prince does not cool him. His ardent eye 'discerns Pale Rezia's *look*, more *cold* than Alpine snows' but detects '*love* . . . beneath that icy veil' without realizing that her heart is elsewhere.* All these suggestive features are part of an identical situation, in a parallel action, during the revelry and triumphs gay, in a tale of a dream of love that Keats had used before. In conjunction with the identical 'visions of delight,' the most revealing feature in common is the gesture of 'maiden eyes . . . Fix'd on the floor,' heedless both, of everything but their dreams, oblivious even of the entrance of their lovers.

The legend merely concerns a dream. And as we come to the second part of the pattern, it is significant that the flesh and blood entrance of the lover in both *Oberon* and *St. Agnes* interrupts the description of the revelry attended by the one dreaming lady. Her lover enters at the same point in both romances. The amorous cavalier has no sooner met Rezia's icy look than Wieland tells the whereabouts of her lover. The fairy disguise having been described, Huon's entrance past the great '*portals*' and 'columns' into the closely guarded hall from which he has heard sounds of revelry, occurs immediately. His entrance, it is noteworthy, is screened by the '*mirth*' and revelry, the music and '*song*' within the hall (v, 34).

---

* v, 21-2. Thus a look of love is added to the picture: 'looks of love, defiance, hate, and scorn.' Keats must have known the passage minutely.

In *The Eve of St. Agnes* Keats has no sooner spoken of the scornful looks than he tells the whereabouts of Porphyro. And the parallel interpolation is immediately followed by his entrance, similarly screened by 'the sound of merriment and chorus bland' within the hall. He enters in the ninth stanza, beginning thus:

> So, purposing each moment to retire,
> She linger'd still. Meantime, across the moors,
> Had come young Porphyro, with heart on fire
> For Madeline. Beside the *portal* doors . . .

he stands in the moonlight hoping to catch sight of his love. Then

> K 82   *He ventures in:* let no buzz'd whisper tell:
>   All eyes be muffled, or *a hundred swords*
> 84   *Will storm his heart,* Love's fev'rous citadel:
>   For him, those chambers held *barbarian hordes,*
> 86   *Hyena foemen,* and *hot-blooded lords,*
>   Whose very *dogs* would *execrations* howl
> 88   Against his lineage: not one *breast* affords
>   Him any mercy, in that mansion foul,
> 90   Save one old beldame, weak in body and in soul.
>   (st. x)

All this, we saw, is a very far cry from the Capulets. Keats was well aware, however, that only Rezia's nurse knew of the shadowy lover of her dream.* And it is into Rezia's chamber with its whisperers, just before the revelry, that 'the *happy crone* is hurry'd in' with the tale of Huon's coming. For he had *'chanced* . . . to meet' her, leaning on her 'crutch.' In his next stanza Keats wrote:

> 91   Ah, happy chance! the aged creature came,
>   Shuffling along with ivory-headed wand,
> 93   To where he stood, hid from the torch's flame,
>   Behind a broad *hall-pillar,* far beyond

---

* Whereas Juliet has neither lover nor dream, and her nurse does not know Romeo when he enters—what was surely no 'mansion foul' among 'barbarian hordes.'

95   The sound of merriment and chorus bland:
He startled her . . .

(st. xi)

Huon's entrance is similarly screened. And for this interception there were the two suggestions in *Oberon*.[11]

But now, in the same stanza the aged Angela urges Porphyro:

98   'hie thee from this place;
They are all here to-night, *the whole blood-thirsty race!'*

That too hardly fits the Capulets. But this is what befalls Huon on his entrance. His 'imperial mien' drives back 'the swords' that bar the way; and having entered the hall past the columns and portals and screened by the mirth and song of the revelers (cf. K 94-5), he crosses to the royal table, admired by all the guests save the dreaming Rezia of the downcast eyes. Catching sight of his cowardly foeman of the day before (cf. K 86: 'hyena foemen'?), with one stroke of his scimitar the lone Christian in the sacred Moslem palace beheads the bridegroom in his place beside the sultan. Forthwith the nature of the 'hot-blooded lords' and 'barbarian hordes' is shown:

The jocund *blood* that warm'd each merry guest
Suspends its frozen course in *every breast:*   K 88
Like ghosts, in heaps, all shiv'ring from their seat
They start, and *grasp their swords,* and mark their prey . . .

(OBERON V, 38)

(Keats' 'a hundred swords' and Angela's 'flit like a ghost away' are not idle warnings.) For while *'murder*ous frenzy . . . Glares in each eye,' the bridegroom's blood-spurting trunk paralyzes the Moslem *lords* and 'Each dagger stiffens as it hangs in air, And every *murderer* stands transform'd to living stone' (v, 37). But only momentarily, for in full view of the bloodthirsty throng the stranger thrice kisses the one lady there and puts his only ring, the talisman, upon her finger.* At this the *hot-tempered* sultan is a man possessed: he raves and rages, stamps his feet, pours *execrations* upon the 'Christian *dog*' (cf. K 87), and bids that his blood be drawn drop by drop (v, 42). And at once 'a *thousand*' *swords* storm toward the lover. Then the knight blows the elf-horn as the daemon king had bidden.

In describing his lover's parallel entrance to the revelry Keats wrote that 'a *hundred* swords will storm his heart' and said 'For him those chambers held barbarian hordes . . . hot-blooded lords, Whose very dogs would execrations howl Against his lineage' in that 'mansion foul.' All this becomes clear in the light of the sultan's execrations against Huon's Christian faith and the presence in the hall of the pagan hordes who attack the lover. Angela's warning, 'They are all here to-night, the whole blood-thirsty race' was not provoked by Keats' recollection of the wrangling Capulets, but by the presence, in the pattern he was still following, of the murderous Moslem lords.

In his very next lines, Angela continues:

> K 100 'Get hence! get hence! there's dwarfish Hildebrand;
> He had a fever late, and *in the fit*
> 102 *He cursed thee and thine,* both house and land:
> Then there's that old Lord Maurice, not a whit
> 104 More tame for his gray hairs—Alas me! flit!
> Flit like a ghost away.'
>
> (st. xii)

While embroidering the pattern, Keats was evidently still deriving suggestions from the lords who shivered 'like ghosts' and the old sultan who in a fit of fury cursed the bold lover. In the next lines Angela bids him follow her. Omitting a stanza, we hear her continue:

---

* This (the talisman of *The Poet*), we are explicitly reminded, Huon won from the giant, who had stolen it from 'a *dwarf*.' In the very next line of his next stanza (xii) Keats has this: 'There's dwarfish Hildebrand.'

118   'St. Agnes! Ah! it is St. Agnes' Eve—
Yet *men will murder* upon holy days:'

She is obviously speaking in terms of Huon's would-be murderers. For suddenly the process of creation becomes transparent. In the very next lines Keats has her say:

120   '*Thou must* hold water in a witch's sieve,
And *be liege-lord of all the Elves and Fays,*
122   *To venture so* . . .'

(st. xiv)

Explicitly she likens Porphyro's venture to Huon's. In parallel sequence, amid the revelry the lover of Rezia, the heedless dreamer, ventured into the castle thronging with a thousand hot-blooded barbarian lords who would murder him. And he did so by command of his liege-lord Charlemagne, with the help of Oberon, *who alone is 'liege-lord of all the Elves and Fays.'* Since Huon did this in hopes of finding the lovely seer of 'visions of delight' and planned to 'carry off the bride' (*Oberon* v, 24), he, the lover of her dream, became identified in Keats' mind with Porphyro and *his* venture—even as Rezia had become identified with Madeline, and the aged crone with Angela.*

Keats' explicit allusion, 'liege-lord of all the Elves and Fays,' to the fairy and chivalric features in the *Oberon* episode constitutes clear evidence that he was conscious of the basic analogies we have been tracing in the parallel sequence: the 'visions of delight'; the thronged revelry with its one heedless lady; and the entrance, at the same point, of the dreamer's lover into the festivities of his cowardly and murderous foemen. It is obvious that Keats selected from and re-created the episode, part of which he had previously used in *Endymion*. His new setting here is part English,

---

* Cf. the old crone's words, 'There's *witchery* in the scene'—of the finding in her hut, where Huon is concealed, of the rich array provided by the fairy king. This juxtaposition of witches and king of fairies is that of Angela's words in K 120-1, where only the 'sieve' was added, from *Macbeth*. For further discussion of the circumstantial relation of Angela to the old crone, see App. IV, p. 365.

part Italian, but the oriental coloring of his pattern shines through repeatedly.[12] He followed that pattern from beginning to end. By his own admission Keats knew of Huon's and Oberon's venturing into the castle. And there Huon won the hand of the princess, his actually 'peerless bride,' with whom at the end of the canto he fled into the elfin storm. But first Keats recalled other incidents which fitted his purpose and which illumine the creative process.

. . .

Now although Porphyro's venturing into the castle of his barbarian foemen is explicitly likened by Keats to Huon's entrance into the castle of Rezia's father, the two entrances still differ in part in regard to time, manner, mood, and motivation. Huon entered boldly by day while Porphyro enters furtively in the moonlight. However, as early at least as Books ii and iii of *Endymion,* Keats had seen Huon at great peril venture into another royal castle—this time furtively in the moonlight, but again on an occasion of revelry. 'Facts which sank at intervals out of conscious recollection,' John Livingston Lowes found in the case of Coleridge, 'drew together beneath the surface [of memory] through almost chemical affinities of common elements.'[13] Here, I think, is another case in point. Not only does this second closely related entrance appear to have blended with and modified the former, but with it a protracted parallel sequence of elements consequent upon that second entrance streamed into Keats' tale of the consummation of certain 'visions of delight.' They streamed into his stanzas xvi-xxi and again into four later ones.

Evidently Keats found the motive, manner, and method of Huon's second entrance more appropriate for his purpose. Not only does Porphyro's entrance, in stanza ix, minutely resemble that second entrance in motivation and setting; but hardly has old Angela mentioned his venturing in like the 'liege-lord of all the Elves and Fays' than Porphyro conceives the stratagem that she lead him secretly to the chamber of Madeline and there hide him, after setting out a feast and a lute. This stratagem and its execution with the attendant imagery and atmosphere were clearly patterned after the nurse's stratagem in *Oberon,* whereby Huon, attempting to see his immured bride in Canto xi, is mysteriously guided at midnight through dark passages to the chamber of the enamored queen. It is significant that like Rezia and Madeline, the queen 'calls the night' expectantly. And having prepared a feast and her lute, she too finds the revelry in the castle a screen for the fulfilment of her desires: finds that

> Kind fortune aids her *vision of delight,*
> All obstacles removes . . .
>
> (xi, 53)

This was the third appearance of Sotheby's phrase, each time in a passage magnetic for Keats. Evidently the close affinity of Huon's two entrances, by way of elements common to both—'visions of delight,' lover's entrance, revelry, royal castle, sultan, foemen— caused the two scenes repeatedly and almost visibly to coalesce in Keats' mind. The detailed evidence of this in stanzas ix and xvi-xxi will be found in the Appendix.* Here let us look only at the most revealing stanza.

In stanza xix, Keats explains Porphyro's *stratagem:*

K 163   Which was, to lead him, in close secrecy,
   Even to Madeline's *chamber,* and there *hide*
 165   Him in a closet, of such privacy
   That he might see her *beauty* un*espied,*
 167   And *win* perhaps *that night a peerless bride,*
   While legion'd *fairies* pac'd the coverlet,
 169   And *pale enchantment held her sleepy-eyed.*
   Never on such a night have *lovers met,*
 171   Since *Merlin* paid his *Demon* all the monstrous debt.

* See App. iv, p. 366.

The two first lines as far as 'chamber' are identical with the nurse's stratagem in Huon's second entrance. That is clear. But Huon *won* his 'peerless' bride * after her 'visions of delight' and as a result of his first entrance, shortly after Rezia's *enchanted sleep* in which 'oft mute she stops, oft starts with *pale* delight' (v, 3). Keats wrote: 'pale enchantment held her sleepy-eyed': cf. K 169. It was then that the 'liege-lord of *all* the Elves and *Fays*' visited Rezia's bed with her 'visions of delight' and evidently the 'legion'd fairies' Keats was now recalling. Upon Rezia's awaking, the nurse had looked about 'as if to *spy* the *beauteous* knight' † if he were *hiding in the dreamer's chamber*. Evidently Keats took the hint and, while echoing a phrase from it, recalled the nurse's later stratagem as well. For in the stanza above, two *Oberon* scenes had obviously coalesced in his mind.

And I think Wieland's fairy-daemon lore left yet another trace in that stanza. Just before he chances to meet the old crone who tells of Rezia's first dream of love, Huon rides along beneath the palms beside the Euphrates. (The palms appeared in *Endymion* and the river in *St. Agnes*.) [14] As he rides along he daydreams of Rezia, whom he had just seen in a vision. To find her he would wrest her from the powers of hell—as he does shortly in her father's castle—or even descend into *'Merlin's tomb.'* ‡ That is noteworthy, because Wieland anticipated his *daemon*-sponsored *lovers' meeting* and subsequent flight into the elfin storm by this allusion to Merlin. And in the same manner Keats wrote:

> Never on such a night have lovers met,
> Since Merlin paid his Demon all the monstrous debt.

It is significant that in comparing his lovers with Merlin, Keats acknowledges the daemonic machinery of his romance. For the patterns of daemon-sponsored lovers' meeting are the same in

* The word occurs in x, 49 just before his second entrance.
† v, 7. Rezia's 'visions of delight' appear in v, 6.
‡ IV, 20. In the previous stanza Huon had had 'visions of delight'!

Oberon and *St. Agnes*. Wieland anticipated his meeting with an allusion to Merlin and Keats followed suit. With *Oberon* overlooked, it is no wonder that the presence of Merlin in Keats' romance has vainly haunted the critics since Leigh Hunt's day.[15]

. . .

Keats' two next stanzas, xx and xxi, discussed fully in the Appendix, were modeled after the stratagem of Huon's second entrance into the queen's chamber. But the coalescence of that scene and its central figure, the queen of the 'vision of delight,' with incidents in the main sequence in Canto v and Rezia's 'visions of delight'—that process continued for some time in *The Eve of St. Agnes*. What must have occurred readily enough in the poet's mind can be disentangled only a strand at a time. First, Porphyro is no sooner hidden in the chamber than Madeline ascends the stair. Keats says she 'Rose, *like a mission'd spirit,* unaware' (st. xxii). That supernatural overtone is noteworthy. Mr. Ridley pointed out that Huon appears in Canto v 'like a commission'd angel of the skies' (v, 63). Moreover, just before his second entrance Huon is flown over land and sea, 'borne by a spirit' of the air commissioned by the daemon king himself, who in the chamber of Canto v had granted Rezia's visions of her lover. And Oberon was still hovering in the background.

In Keats' next stanza Madeline enters the chamber, leaving further clues behind her:

> 199   Out went the taper as she *hurried in;* *
>   Its little smoke, in pallid moonshine, died:
> 201   She clos'd the door, *she panted,* all *akin*
>   To *spirits of the air,* and visions wide:
> 203   No uttered syllable, or, woe betide!
>   But to her heart, her heart was voluble . . .
>   (st. xxiii)

* Immediately after Rezia's visions in bed, we saw, 'the happy crone is hurry'd in' to the chamber.

This is the stanza concerning which Sir Sidney Colvin pointed out the echo from *Oberon* which he discovered: 'one instance,' he said he found, 'where a definite phrase from it seems to have lingered subconsciously in Keats' memory and been turned to gold, thus:

> Oft in this *speechless language* glance on glance,
> When mute the tongue, how *voluble* the *heart*.
>
> (OBERON VI, 17)' [16]

The degree of subconsciousness must remain a moot point. But, 'one instance'? It happens that these lines occur a few stanzas after the daemon king appears in the air to warn the lovers to remain chaste, and shortly after they had fled into the elfin storm, during which the ruler of 'spirits of the air' had appeared in the hall of Rezia's father. And on that occasion the 'lovely bride' Rezia *'pants with warm lip'* to inhale Oberon's lily fragrance. We shall see all this again shortly. Here it evoked Keats' 'she panted all *akin to* spirits of the air and visions wide.' And we are reminded thereby that Keats was still following the pattern: that he was being guided particularly by Canto v.

Now both Rezia's chamber and that of the queen (which contained a stained-glass window) are haunted by Oberon and his spirits of the air. Probably it was this which recalled the daemon-haunted chamber of the saintly Christabel in Coleridge's tale.[17] For in his four next stanzas, xxiv–xxvii, Keats, evidently deriving hints from all three chambers (that of Rezia, the queen, and Christabel), describes first the composite window which 'blush'd with blood of *queens* and kings,' and then the virginal Madeline at her prayers.* Then he reverts to the main action, as Madeline *dis*robes, *'dreams awake'* a moment, and finally *gets into her bed,* for the promised

---

* Christabel's prayers are emphasized by Coleridge; and a suggestion for the window appeared in the queen's chamber. See App. IV, p. 369.

visions of delight of her lover. She 'dares not look behind, or all *the charm* is fled.'

All this last resembles the actions of Rezia. In her chamber Rezia appears thus: In her bed, her

> charm'd soul 'mid visions of delight,
> Wove in her waking hours anew the dream.
>
> (OBERON V, 6)

And it is then, when the nurse had sought to espy the lover in the dreamer's chamber, that Rezia is *robed*. Finding that scene and her other actions suggestive, Keats evidently reversed the robing process and the sequence, and described Madeline's actions through the eyes of her concealed lover. The initial suggestion appeared in the *Oberon* pattern of a visionary dream of love come true. Keats' disrobing scene, though it probably came to owe something to Coleridge * and William Browne of Tavistocke, is a thread in that larger design. This circumstance, as well as some verbal echoes and what follows, indicates that Keats derived the original hint from Rezia's robing and with meticulous craftsmanship, much labor, and great delicacy modified the scene with the help of his other models. The evidence of this, and the verbal echoes, will be found in the Appendix. †

The lines immediately after the disrobing are hardly less revealing. For Madeline is soon trembling:

> K 235   Soon, trembling in her soft and chilly nest,
> In sort of *wakeful swoon, perplex'd she lay,*
>   237   Until the poppied warmth of *sleep* oppress'd
> Her *soothed* limbs, and soul fatigued away;
>   239   Flown, like a thought, until the morrow-day;
> Blissfully haven'd both from joy and pain;

* Cf. *Christabel.*
† Cf. App. IV, p. 370.

241   Clasp'd like a missal *where swart Paynims pray;*
        Blinded alike from sunshine and from rain,
243   As though a rose should shut, and be a bud again.

(st. xxvii)

In the light of the fact that the hermit is soon to reappear, the overtones of joy and pain in line 240 are noteworthy. Moreover, just *before* her robing, Rezia, in bed in her chamber, *lies perplexed in her waking dream of her lover* and strives

> To rock herself once more in *soothing sleep,**
> Once more in magic dreams her senses steep . . .

Her 'visions of delight' have already vanished, and soon her lover with the help of the liege-lord of all the elves and fays will enter the *sacred* Moslem castle thronging with a thousand guests, the 'barbarian hordes' of murderous *paynim* lords. It is not strange therefore that Madeline, who is still anticipating her visions of delight, but who lies in the same wakeful swoon, should appear 'like a missal where swart Paynims pray.' Once again Keats is merely letting the oriental background of her prototype shine through. As we shall see, he knew that soon after Rezia's flight into the elfin storm she is converted to Huon's Catholic faith.

Evidently because of some vital elements in common with Rezia's situation, Keats in his next stanza recalled a scene from *Cymbeline,* imagery and phraseology from which contributed for a few lines to the scene in Madeline's composite chamber.[18] Porphyro, 'Stol'n to *this* paradise,'† comes out of his hiding place,‡ listens to Madeline's breathing, crosses the 'hush'd carpet' (not inappropriate, in view of the ultimately oriental background), and then *''tween the curtains peep'd,* where lo!—how fast she slept.' In Rezia's chamber it is the nurse (she suggests the lover's concealment) who 'undraws the curtains of the golden bed' and, looking

---

* *Oberon* v, 5; cf. K 237.
† Another fragment in the structure of contrast?
‡ Like Iachimo in *Cymbeline.*[18]

in, finds the dreamer in the situation we saw above. The hint bore fruit with the help, I think, of Shakespeare. Then, Rezia, having risen, appears 'More fair than Mahom's *paradise* beholds the houri Seen in visionary dreams' and in a moment is robed by the whisperers.

III

Now the imminent consummation of the 'visions of delight,' and Wieland's evocative 'houri' and 'Mahom's paradise,' constituted another evidently irresistible link of association with the enamored queen involved in Huon's second entrance. In connection with stanzas ix and xix of St. *Agnes,* which most clearly reveal how the two entrances fused in Keats' mind,* we saw how the nurse's stratagem led Huon furtively through dark passages to the queen's chambers. Elements from that incident, we saw, coalesced with the legioned fairies and the winning, rather than merely the seeing, of the peerless bride. There is, however, evidence that not only the chambers but their occupants and certain attendant actions blended before entering the pattern of St. *Agnes.* We saw that the queen had had an exotic feast and her lute set out to help her win Huon's love. The oriental setting of this no less than Rezia's presence in Bagdad facilitated Keats' recollection of other voluptuous elements from the *Arabian Nights,* which in due course contributed to Porphyro's feast.

As for the other lover, immediately upon entering the queen's chambers at *midnight,* Huon perceives unchaste luxury. The beautiful jeweled queen appears from behind an *'embroider'd gold'* curtain and is surrounded by alluring dancing girls while music is heard.† She hands Huon a *'cup of gold'* and bids him partake of the *feast.* Keats' art, extraordinarily sensitive here, could in St. *Agnes* have gleaned little from the baroque scene in *Oberon.* But he seems to have selected some features. A 'cloth of *woven* crimson,

* See p. 169 above.
† xi, 48 and 53. And cf. Keats' 'midnight' music.

gold, and jet' is spread by Porphyro upon the table soon to bear *golden dishes* and exotic dainties, significantly from the Levant. These appear in the limpid stanzas, again partly based on the chamber scene in *Cymbeline,* 'And still she slept an azure-lidded sleep' and 'These delicates he heap'd with glowing hand.' [18] For a moment their brightness and fragrance are diffused through the dreaming Madeline's chamber as Porphyro says, 'Thou art my heaven, and I thine eremite.' For Keats had not relinquished the larger design. Nor had he forgotten Rezia's panting in Canto v as 'the fragrance floats around.' The furniture and feast for the lover in the queen's chambers is significant because, since it was in the parallel sequence of the stratagem, it evidently suggested the feast and was the channel through which the *Arabian Nights* contributed their exotic foods. One of them, we saw, first crossed the Euphrates and another 'cedar'd Lebanon' as if with Huon.

. . .

It must be borne in mind that we are still but a few stanzas from that door to which, by dark and devious way, the nurse's stratagem had led Huon. Behind that door, as Keats well knew, many things befall both the lover and the queen, who like Madeline had awaited this night and the consummation of *her* 'vision of delight' impatiently. Thus the queen's actions readily colored Keats' three next stanzas.* In *The Eve of St. Agnes,* following the description of the feast he had prepared, Porphyro tries to awaken his love, and then:

> 280 Thus whispering, his warm, unnerved *arm*
> *Sank in her pillow.* Shaded was her dream
> 282 By the dusk *curtains:*—'twas *a midnight charm*
> *Impossible to melt* as iced stream:

* The process was facilitated by Huon's explicit comparison of the queen with Rezia's 'modest' grace and chaste beauty. And the fusion had begun earlier. For further evidence, see App. IV, p. 371.

284   The lustrous salvers in the moonlight gleam;
             Broad golden fringe upon the carpet lies . . .
                                        (st. xxxii)

Like Madeline's, the dream of Rezia was shaded by the curtains of
her golden bed. But the latter dreamer had fused with the queen.
For now it is *midnight,* and it is the queen (she had just appeared
from behind the 'embroider'd *gold' curtain*) who is in process of
realizing her visions of delight.

W 1   And, tho' she scarce upon herself prevail
        Not to embrace him with *resistless charms,*   K 282
3   And force the *stone* to feel within her *arms,*
        She tries another proof that cannot fail—
5   *Her* winning *lute* she suffers to be brought,
        Then *on a pillowy* throne . . .   K 281
7   Softly *reclines* . . .
                                        (OBERON XI, 60)

Keats probably compounded the queen's 'resistless charms' with
Huon's not melting, to see the 'midnight charm impossible to melt.'
He took the hint of sinking into the pillow and the significant
embrace and transferred all to Porphyro. For in the very next
stanza, having, like the queen, vainly tried to arouse his beloved,

K 289   Awakening up, he took her hollow *lute,*—   W 4-5
          Tumultuous,—and, in chords that *tender*est be,
291   *He play'd* an ancient ditty, long since mute . . .

(with the suggestive title, 'La belle dame sans mercy' *)

293   Close to her ear touching *the melody;*—
          Wherewith disturb'd, she utter'd a soft moan:
295   He *ceas'd*—she *panted quick*—and suddenly
          Her blue affrayed eyes wide open shone:
297   *Upon his knees he sank,* pale as smooth-sculptured
          stone.
                                        (st. xxxiii)

* Suggestive, because as we shall see, the queen's nature was eminently capable
of recalling that title to Keats' mind.

The full import of this stanza will be realized in the next chapter, in connection with *Lamia*. Suffice it to point out here that the picture of the innocent daemon-tranced Rezia evidently has faded imperceptibly while that of the other enamored seer of visions of delight has been superimposed. For after her sinking into the pillow, it is the lovely queen who plays a ditty, like Porphyro. It is she whose fingers 'In sweet confusion [cf. K 290] sweep each . . . string,' and who emits sighs 'from her *pant*ing breast' as does Madeline. 'Sweet was *the melody,* its language plain' since it told of the unhappy love of a female slave (xi, 62). This lute-playing occurs immediately after Huon calls upon Heaven to shield him while the dancing girls gyrate:

W 9   He swears the *vow* anew in holy thought,
        Swears *on his knees* . . .   K 297

his vow to Rezia. (Keats wrote 'Upon his knees he sank' and two stanzas later 'Made tuneable with every sweetest vow.' The sequence is still the same.) It is then that an angel seemed to bring 'a shield from heaven.' * For

W 11   The queen his *speaking features* understands,
        Reads his *chang'd soul;* and as she *clasps* her *hands,*
   13   Swift *ceases* . . .   K 295

not the lute-playing but the voluptuous dance. Keats selected carefully from the cruder but highly suggestive pictures in the queen's chamber, a chamber the lover enters by the same stratagem, for the same purpose, at the same hour as Porphyro. And Keats sublimated and transmuted the selected elements no less carefully. For there is more evidence.

Exactly like Rezia in her waking dream in Canto v, Madeline now appears thus:

_____
* Cf. Porphyro's 'my seraph fair . . . my heaven' (K 275).

K 298   Her eyes were open, but she still beheld,
           Now wide awake, the vision of her sleep:

That picture, however, has blended with one of the queen, for:

300   *There was a painful change,* that nigh expell'd   W 12
         The blisses of her dream so pure and deep
302   At which fair Madeline *began to weep,*
         And moan forth witless words with many a
         sigh;

And features peculiar to the kneeling and praying Huon have been
interwoven—actions which cause the queen to clasp her hands:

304   While still her gaze on Porphyro would keep;   W 11
         Who knelt, with *joined hands* and piteous eye,   W 12, 10
306   Fearing to move or *speak,* she look'd so dream-
         ingly.
                                          (st. xxxiv)

The daemon-motivated temptation scene contained a wealth of
plastic material whose power Keats more than once realized.* The
queen had noted the painful change in Huon, from his 'speaking
features.' In *St. Agnes* the lover 'fears to speak,' yet Madeline, also
reading his features, says *'How chang'd thou art.'* She bids him sing
again and speaks of his 'sweetest vow' and *'looks immortal'* in
the same stanza xxxv.

The queen, thinking the lover quite overcome, drops her lute
and opens her arms to him. But like Madeline's, her dream is ex-
pelled, for Huon will not melt. Instead he seizes the lute and intones a reply to her ditty: 'Firm was his tone, his high heroic *look*
Glow'd *like a god.'* (Cf. Madeline above.) Awakening to reality
at last,

           Th' enchantress, 'gainst her will,
           Feels his superior force—*tears wildly fill*   K 302
           Her eyes indignant . . .
                           (OBERON XI, 65)

---

* This is apparent first in *Endymion* III, then in *St. Agnes,* then *Lamia.*

In other words, like Madeline the queen not only read a painful change from the lover's features, not only panted and sighed in connection with the lute-playing, but also 'began to weep.' But the most significant hint that Keats derived from her actions is the embrace. The queen's 'vision of delight' had promised the consummation of her wild passion and had blended in his mind with Rezia's chaste 'visions of delight.'

All these and some later fragments appeared in the *un*chaste chamber to which the stratagem and the furtive entrance, through dark passages at midnight, had brought the lover. The clues Keats left in his closely analogous sequence reveal the process by which elements in a scene apparently quite different were sublimated and woven into a picture of sweet and innocent beauty. The assimilation of this same 'purple-lined palace of sweet sin' was to take place again some months later: it left its much more transparent marks on *Lamia*.

* * *

But we have not yet done with *The Eve of St. Agnes*. Was that exquisite romance actually a thing of sweet and innocent beauty? Or was there in it too a motif of 'sweet sin'? Another draft of Keats' next stanzas is highly revealing. For lines eight and nine of the present stanza xxxv, containing Madeline's words 'those looks immortal,' were there recast like this:

GK* 314   See, while she speaks, *his arms* encroaching slow
            Have zon'd her, heart to heart—*loud, loud* the *dark winds blow.*

The queen, let us remember, suggestively opened her arms to Huon. And Keats' 'blow' and the repetition of 'loud, loud' were not dictated by rhythm and rhyme. At that point Keats added the stanza (xxxvi) later omitted. Without pause he wrote this:

GK 316   *For on the midnight came a tempest fell.*
           More sooth for that his close rejoinder flows

---

* From a ms. belonging to George Keats. See Garrod, p. 252.

318   Into her burning ear;—and still the spell
         Unbroken guards her in serene repose.
320   With *her wild dream* he mingled as a rose
         Marryeth its odour to a violet.
322   Still, still she dreams—*louder the* frost *wind blows* . . .

                                   (G. Keats)

The word 'For' is noteworthy. And in writing 'marryeth,' as Mr. Ridley showed,[19] Keats indicated that his lovers, the lady who saw 'visions of delight' and the man who entered the castle of the 'barbarian hordes,' had consummated their love.

Now Keats' 'tempest fell,' which occurred at that precise moment, ultimately became part of the retained 'elfin storm' in which the lovers flee. That storm became part of the superb structure of contrast. But originally the two storms were not at all identical. The 'tempest fell' had another meaning, and was derived from quite another scene. And that scene underlies the creative process here. After the lovers' flight in *Oberon* (we shall see the picture very shortly) they are borne through the air ecstatic, as we know from *Endymion*. And Huon having promised his guardian spirit, the 'liege-lord of all the Elves and Fays' and daemons of the elements, to observe his injunction of chastity, the lovers soon board ship in propitious weather. But so great is their love that Huon is compelled to shun Rezia's presence lest, as was Endymion, he be 'presumptuous against love, against the sky, against all elements'— in other words, lest he disobey the daemon king's prohibition. Huon suppresses his passion; but the torture is heightened by Rezia's weeping, which so 'burns . . . his . . . breast' that he sighed out loud as if *'he* soon *must die.'* And in her turn the innocent Rezia is in anguish.*

Then 'like an angel rob'd in light' Rezia one night enters Huon's

* vii, 12. And cf. Madeline's words in the final version. 'For *if thou diest*, my Love . . .' (K 315).

cabin, 'soft pity' heightening her beauty.* And so, overcome at last
by their long suppressed passion, Huon

> Defies the god—*his arms* the maid *enchain.*   GK 314

Thus their love is also consummated. But their elemental guardian
spirit is aroused:

> W 14   *At once* the heav'ns are *dark*en'd, quench'd each
>   star!
>   Ah! happy pair! they knew it not—the wave
>   16   Howls as unfetter'd *winds* o'er ocean *rave:*   GK 315
>   Their *tempest*-laden pinions *roar* from far!   GK 316
>   18   They hear it not—*with rage* encircled round,
>   *Stern Oberon* flying thro' the gloom profound
>   20   Rushes before their face—they hear him not!   GK 319
>   (OBERON VII, 17)

And Keats wrote 'came a tempest fell' and 'loud, loud the dark
winds blow' and yet again 'louder the frost wind blows.' This as
the identical accompaniment of Madeline and Porphyro's consummation of their love! This is that third daemonic storm, 'a
tempest fell' or cruel, which causes Huon and Rezia to be cast
away upon the 'craggy isle' where ultimately, after suffering and
starvation, they find their way to the hermitage and like Endymion
are spiritualized.

But here Keats was concerned with the consummation of 'visions
of delight.' † And by characteristic associations, the queen's voluptuous visions and embrace evidently having recalled the scene on
shipboard, the punitive tempest was drawn into the pattern, where
it blended with the elfin storm of the lovers' flight. The tempest
left its marks even on the final version of *St. Agnes.* For there
Keats omitted the second-draft stanza (xxxvi) and continued thus:

* VII, 15. And cf. Keats' 'She seem'd a splendid angel, newly drest . . .'
† The queen's 'vision of delight' repeatedly fused with Rezia's in Canto V—
which provided the main sequence for *St. Agnes* and terminates in the elfin storm.
Keats' second draft of *St. Agnes* dates from about Sept. 1819, shortly after the
more decadent *Lamia* had been completed. And the heroine of that romance is
no Madeline.

K 316   Beyond a mortal man impassion'd far
         At these voluptuous accents, he arose,   W 18
   318   Ethereal, flush'd, and like a throbbing star
         Seen mid the sapphire heaven's deep repose   W 14
   320   Into her dream he melted, as the rose
         Blendeth its odour with the violet,—
   322   Solution sweet: meantime the frost-wind blows   W 16
         Like Love's alarum pattering the sharp sleet
   324   Against the window-panes; St. Agnes' moon hath
         set.

What underlies this imagery is plain. Almost visibly Keats had identified the impassioned daemon king with Porphyro. Yet Oberon, the 'god of love' defied, who, when carnal love triumphed over spiritual, sent the punitive storm, has become 'Love's alarum.' And Keats continued in his final version:

   325   'Tis dark: quick pattereth the flaw-blown sleet: W 14
         'This is no dream, my bride, my Madeline!'
   327   'Tis dark: the iced gusts still rave and beat: W 16

This is still Oberon's tempest. And 'no dream' indeed. Then suddenly, and I think significantly, we are back, in mid-stanza, in the queen's chamber.   .   .   .

Her wily design Huon resists, though once at least he felt 'nature melt in this voluptuous glow.' (Cf. K 317 and 320: 'Into her dream he melted' and 'at these voluptuous accents.') Dismissed at last, he seems to have provided Keats with some further hints for his parallel sequence. For

              Already in the morning's purple light
      W 22   The mountains gleam, when sunk in deep despair
              Sad Huon hastens back . . .

from the miscarried stratagem for finding Rezia. He accuses the 'pale' nurse of treachery, until he sees 'thou wert thyself deceiv'd—

my evil *stars* prevail' (xi, 66). It is noteworthy that Madeline remarks upon the lover's 'sad eyes' and 'How changed thou art! how pallid, chill, and drear!' And a few lines later, 318-19, appear the 'throbbing star' and 'sapphire heaven's' along with 'voluptuous accents' and 'melted' in the same stanza.

But now let us turn again to the latter half of stanza xxxvii, where still

K 327   'Tis dark: the iced gusts still rave and beat:
         'No dream, alas! and woe is mine!   W 22
329   Porphyro *will leave me here* to fade and pine.'

Did Madeline think so because Huon leaves the queen of the 'vision of delight' in her chamber? In the parallel sequence it is the *lovelorn* and now *cruel* queen who would 'in the *traitor*'s blood allay' her rage, and who *'curses* loud the luckless hour' and the lover and herself. And a few breathless stanzas earlier she says: 'Oh thou belov'd! *my* life on *thine* depends' (xii, 38 and 33). But let us finish Keats' composite stanza. Madeline, still speaking, now says:

330   'Cruel! what traitor could thee hither bring?
         I curse not, for my heart is lost in thine,
332   Though thou forsakest a deceived thing:—
         A dove forlorn and lost with sick unpruned wing.'
                                                    (st. xxxvii)

Here, in the termination of the stratagem of the deceived lover's entrance, is plain evidence not only of the fusing of three scenes of *Oberon* in one stanza of *St. Agnes,* but of the transmutation which elements, selected and sublimated from the episode of the queen, underwent. It was the actions of that impassioned seer of visions of delight which suggested to Keats *cursing* the lover. It was that which led him to make the gentle Madeline utter that apparently inappropriate word. But subtly came the sea-change. Madeline will 'curse *not,*' and the very fact that she will not curse him who she thinks may now leave her (as Huon, in innocence, leaves the queen) brings out the conscious contrast embodied in Madeline's idealized nature. And the creative process is the clearer.

IV

Keats' next stanza is another interesting composite. For Porphyro says:

> K 334   'My Madeline! sweet *dreamer! lovely bride!*
>   Say, may I be for aye thy vassal blest?
> 336   Thy *beauty*'s *shield*, heart-shap'd and vermeil dyed?
>   Ah, silver shrine, here will I take my rest
> 338   *After so many hours* of *toil* and *quest,*
>   *A famish'd pilgrim,—saved by miracle.*
> 340   Though I have found, I will not rob thy nest
>   Saving of thy sweet self; *if thou think'st well*
> 342   *To trust,* fair Madeline, *to no rude infidel.'*
>
>   (st. xxxviii)

This stanza forms the transition from love's consummation and the attendant tempest to Porphyro's proposal, in the next stanza, of flight into the elfin storm. The imagery, seemingly so tortured and excessive, indicates that Keats' mind was not working in a vacuum. Instead he was tying his threads together. First of all, Huon had met his dreamer and 'lovely bride'* while on a pilgrimage to Bagdad; and in the hall of the barbarian hordes he was saved by the miracles * of the liege-lord of all the elves and fays. Again, Oberon's 'tempest fell' had led to the lovers' starvation, which evidently suggested the phrase, now figurative, 'a famished pilgrim.' The stratagem of his second entrance in search of Rezia was effected after 'unsuccessful *toil,* seven tedious days,' and just after he had vowed to seek Rezia 'wherever *beauty* bears the highest rate—There will I *shield* her' (x, 33). The two words 'pilgrim' and

---

* We shall see the phrase in a moment.

'shrine' from *Romeo and Juliet* evidently were drawn in by verbal association.[20] And since Keats was about to have his lovers flee into the elfin storm, in his last lines with their curious 'infidel' his mind obviously had reverted to the main sequence of 'visions of delight' in Canto v. For just before the lovers flee, Oberon appears in the hall and cautions Rezia to consider the step. She, a paynim, nevertheless trusted herself to Huon, who, *'no* rude infidel,' was a Catholic; and so the lovers were ready to flee into the storm. Keats' transition stanza clearly is a fourfold tissue of reminiscences of scenes connected with the outcome of 'visions of delight.'

It will have been observed that the assimilating process we have been tracing differed in both kind and intensity, and that consequently it left now more, now less transparent clues. Unquestionably this is the result of the dissolving and subsequent reintegration of now more, now less resistant elements. Evidently there was little resistance in the main ones which defined the shape of the pattern: the 'visions of delight,' the revelry with its one dreaming lady there, the lover's furtive entrance into the castle of his bitter foemen, love's consummation and a tempest, and now the strikingly similar dénouements. It was said above that originally the two daemonic storms were distinct, because the flight of the lovers in *Oberon* occurred before the consummation of their love amid the 'tempest fell.' Let us now turn to the four last stanzas of *The Eve of St. Agnes* and the parallel action at the end of Canto v of Wieland's poem.

The decapitation of the hated bridegroom and Huon's kissing of his visioned bride having led to the sultan's execrations, Huon sees the swords about to storm his heart. Then as the liege-lord of all the elves and fays had bidden, he blows the elf-horn and provokes the irresistible dance that paralyzes his would-be murderers. When the 'barbarian hordes' have recovered and again seek to attack him, the horn is blown by the squire as if to wake the dead. Straightway the most wondrous things befall:

W 1   Loud rings the castle with rebellowing shocks;
       Night, ten-fold *midnight,* swallows up the day;
3   *Ghosts,* to and fro, like gleams of lightning play,

. . .

       Terrors unknown *the heathen race* confound!
5   *Sight, hearing lost,* they *stagger, drunk* with fear;
       Drops from each nerveless hand the sword and spear,
7   And stiff upon the spot *all lie* in groups *around.*

(OBERON V, 67)

And while with '*miracle* on miracle opprest, The caliph struggles with the pangs of death,' at once *the elfin* '*storm* is hush'd' and the fairy king emerges from the air, 'sweetly breathing o'er the prostrate crowd.' Huon, much more evidently than Porphyro, is in Keats' phrase (K 329) '*saved by miracle.*' And the degree to which the poet was absorbed in this canto could hardly appear more clearly than in that line and in the lines following upon 'trust . . . to no rude infidel' (K 342: cf. W 4 'heathen race').

For now Keats wrote thus:

K 343   'Hark! '*tis an elfin-storm from faery land,*
       Of haggard seeming, but a boon indeed:
345   Arise—arise! *the morning* is at hand;—
       The *bloated wassaillers* will never heed:—   W 5
347   *Let us away, my love, with* happy *speed;*
       There are *no* ears to *hear,* or eyes to *see,*—   W 5
349   Drown'd all in Rhenish and the sleepy mead:
       Awake! arise! my love, and fearless be,
351   For o'er the southern moors I have a home for thee.'

(st. xxxix)

Oberon's elfin storm and the 'heathen race' who 'stagger, drunk with fear' evidently were assimilated differently. The daemonic storm was not naturalized as was the enchanted paralysis of the Moslem lords. 'Stagger, drunk' was a crying hint, and Keats promptly took it—naturalized the condition of the hostile horde, in phraseology, 'bloated wassaillers,' 'Rhenish,' 'sleepy mead,' evidently borrowed from *Hamlet* and the grooms in *Macbeth*. But Wieland's *'sight, hearing* lost,' Keats retained in the phrase 'no ears . . . or eyes.' In the phrase 'the morning' he was merely being consistent with the furtive midnight entrance—and Huon's flight from the queen's chambers and attempted embrace. It is not surprising either that Rezia proposes flight to her lover even before the daemon king appears: 'Oh, *hasten! let* our footsteps *fly* the ground' she says. (v, 51. Cf. Porphyro's 'Let us away, my love, with happy speed.') And when Oberon has appeared, he warns Rezia to ponder well before trusting herself to her lover in a perilous world (cf. 'if thou think'st well to trust, fair Madeline, to no rude infidel'). And the liege-lord of all the elves and fays also explains that

> W 11   'These *sleepers,* seeming dead, without delay
>   Rise at the waving of my potent arm . . .'

and he blesses the lovers with his lily wand and melts into the air (v, 72). But again he left traces in *The Eve of St. Agnes*.

For now, even more clearly, Rezia *is* Madeline, who so recently was awakened ('sweet dreamer, lovely bride': K 334) from her 'visions of delight' in the fragrant chamber. At this crucial point Keats had seen this picture: Rezia

> As if new wak'd from visions of delight,
> The lovely bride, while fragrance floats around,
> Pants with warm lip . . .
>
>   (OBERON v, 76)

This circumstantial hint, of awaking amid fragrance from her dream of love, a hint coinciding with the second appearance of Sotheby's magnetic phrase, Keats had seen early. Not only the echoed phraseology attests that he put it to use: as early as her entering the fragrant chamber in stanza xxiii we saw how Madeline 'panted, all akin To spirits of the air, and visions wide.' 'All akin,' we may be sure, means: 'exactly as on the occasion when' Rezia visioned Oberon, king of aerial spirits, and panted in the fragrance his lily wand diffused. Keats' allusions, here as elsewhere, throw a clear light upon the creative process.

. . .

But let us return to the lovers' flight and the elfin storm. In the same stanza of *Oberon* wherein the 'lovely bride' and the lines above appear, Rezia sees her royal father lying as 'in slumb'rous death' and sighs as 'woes . . . her heart assail.' (Madeline too is depressed on awaking.) But Huon, seeing his 'wan bride with inward anguish grieves' (a further hint?) *urges her to hurry* before their enchanted foes awaken. Folding his arm around her, he *'steals* her from the *hall.'* (Cf. Porphyro's 'rob thy nest' and 'into the wide hall' below.) And *'down the* marble *steps'* (v, 78) Huon bears her to the fairy chariot. All this occurs, let us remember, after their foemen

> W 16   . . . stagger drunk *with fear;*
>   Drops from each nerveless hand the sword and *spear,*
> 18   And stiff upon the spot *all lie around* . . .
>   (OBERON v, 68)

and while around the enchanted sleepers

>   A fearful silence thro' the castle reigns:
> 20   Still as the grave, and peaceful as the dead,
>   The *guards lie* here and there around them spread . . .
>   (v, 79)

It is not surprising that in his next stanza Keats wrote:

> K 352   She hurried at his words, beset with fears,
>   For there were sleeping dragons all around,
> 354   At glaring watch, perhaps, with ready spears—

Note the very rhyme scheme of this and W 16-18.

355   Down the wide stairs a darkling way they found.—
       In all the house was heard no human sound . . .   W 19
                    (EVE OF ST. AGNES, xl)

The scenes, complex as they are, are minutely alike.*
Keats' lovers still follow Huon and Rezia:

361   They glide, like *phantoms,* into the wide hall;   W 3
       Like phantoms, to the iron porch, they glide;
363   Where *lay the Porter,* in uneasy sprawl,   W 21
       With a huge empty flaggon by his side . . .   W 16
                   (st. xli)

Keats had seen the ghosts flitting about the wide hall among the enchanted sleepers *'drunk* with fear,' and also the guards lying about. In accordance with these hints he again partly naturalized the enchantment, and the enchanted guards were modified by Macbeth's drunken porter. But Keats did not omit the supernatural elements in the *Oberon* scene entirely. His last stanza reads thus:

And they are gone: ay, ages long ago
These lovers fled away into the storm.

So far as structure is concerned, Wieland might have written his ending of Canto v just so.

That night the Baron dreamt of many a woe,
And *all his warrior-guests, with shade and form*
Of witch, and *demon,* and large coffin-worm,
Were long be-nightmar'd . . .
              (EVE OF ST. AGNES, xlii)

And with a final glance at the old crone and the dead eremite, the action is ended. But the supernatural elements here were again suggested by *Oberon.*

Probably the witch wandered in with Macbeth's porter. The rest of the phantasmagoria, save for a few details again remembered

---

* For the accretions in the last lines of this stanza see note 21.

from *Christabel*, derives from Wieland's daemonic romance. For this nightmare is the enchanted sleep of Rezia's more exalted father, the sultan and all his warrior guests or 'barbarian hordes,' into whose revelry Huon had ventured with Oberon's aid. The elfin storm that the daemon king provoked, and the enchanted sleep caused by his power, contained hints not lost upon Keats. The imagery of Wieland's scene—sleepers, death, 'as if to wake the dead,' grave, ghosts flitting, daemon king—not only evoked Keats' 'shade,' 'phantoms,' 'demon,' and 'coffin'; he felt the 'terror' of the sultan's guests, and saw nightmares in *their* sleep.*

More significant is the circumstance that the lovers fled from out of the macabre scene in the castle while screened by the elfin storm. That is merely the last of the identical structural elements which reveal how Keats was guided, from beginning to end, by the tale in *Oberon* of a dream of love come true. †

.   .   .

In the light of all the evidence we have seen, there can be little question as to the vital nature of the rôle Wieland's tale played in the genesis and development of *The Eve of St. Agnes. Oberon,* I think it is clear, by virtue of Rezia's 'visions of delight' or expectant dreams of her lover, must have provided a form within whose highly charged contours the creative impulse from the legend was given direction and momentum and the sustenance that enabled it to evolve. Keats and his Angela, in their explicit allusions, made no attempts at concealment.

The Eve of St. Agnes is essentially a new creation with a tone and spirit, a delicacy and verbal felicity utterly different from Sotheby's *Oberon*. The poet who breathed upon that mold and clay first selected and transmuted before he gave it life, and new-

---

* The subsequent details in Keats' stanza xli—the iron porch, watchful hound, chains of the door, and lamp in stanza xl—were recalled from *Christabel* by way, we may be sure, of Oberon's spirits of the air and presence in the daemon-haunted castle. For earlier *Christabel* echoes see note 17.

† Was the Song 'Hush, hush' of Dec. 1818, a preliminary study for *St. Agnes?*

ness, and the intense beauty born of his own genius. The assimilated materials have assumed a new identity, in a new integrated pattern which is the perfection of loveliness. And like the subtle structure of contrast with its shadows of eternity, it has been articulated with a sensitiveness utterly Keatsian.

There is no better way to appreciate this than to watch the mutations by which his masterpiece came to be. One value of the evidence we have been watching, it seems to me, is that the process of re-creating the stuff of recent literary experience appears in a compass probably unique in its compactness. And that, with its transparency, lends it a peculiar fascination.

❧ v ❧

The Nature, Metamorphoses, and Torment of 'Lamia'

THE YEAR 1819 was Keats' harvest time. He reaped swiftly and in great abundance, but all the while storms gathered and broke about him, buffeting him without mercy; for this period of high achievement was more deeply troubled than any other. He was harassed alike by weeks of sorrow and hours of joy, by fretful indolence and feverish creation. Still torn between a hunger for knowledge and the yearning for beauty, he found, too, that as his love for Fanny Brawne grew it clashed with his lofty ambitions and passion for poetry. While his wants increased, illness imposed new restraints, and his hopes of fame met with little promise of fulfilment. He had to struggle against grief and frustration, financial strain and incertitude; and as his health became increasingly delicate, he found his faith shaken and creative moods more difficult to attain. Throughout the year of climax he suffered inner conflicts the intensity of which the letters but seldom reveal.

Having finished *The Eve of St. Agnes,* he returned to Wentworth Place in February with a throat persistently sore. Soon, nevertheless, he was at work on the fragment, *The Eve of St. Mark.* By March he found both his health and his affairs interfering with poetry. Since a chancery suit threatened to leave him penniless, repeatedly from then on he thought of resuming his medical studies and becoming a ship's surgeon. He was, however, reading Beaumont and Fletcher, Chaucer, Dante, and Milton, Dryden, Voltaire, and Burton. In April he wrote to his brother George: 'I am still at a stand in versifying.' [1] Yet within a few days he composed *La*

Belle Dame sans Merci, while experiments with a new sonnet form led to the writing in April and May of some of his greatest odes. Nevertheless, he said early in June: 'I have been very idle lately, very averse to writing; both from the overpowering idea of our dead poets and from *abatement of my love of fame.'* The same day he told his sister, 'I am in so unsettled a state of mind about what I am to do. I have given up the idea of [being a surgeon on] the Indiaman: I cannot resolve to give up my studies.' Instead, he had decided to live cheaply in the Isle of Wight and 'set my Mind at work once more.' Although his financial resources had dwindled alarmingly and both George and Mr. Abbey were in trouble, Charles Brown had persuaded him to postpone inquiries 'for a situation with an Apothecary' and to 'try the press once more.' If luck failed him this time, he wrote Haydon on 17 June, ' "ye hear no more of me." ' [2]

Full of determination, he departed ten days later for Shanklin, where he stayed a few weeks with his ailing friend Rice. Within a few days of his arrival he was at work on *Lamia,* and writing the first of the letters to Fanny Brawne that reveal the strained and divided state of his mind. After long unhappiness over Tom, he now felt trammeled by his love—which had cost him his freedom. He yearned to be with her constantly but was compelled to live upon 'hope and chance.' Unless his luck changed, he told her, he would not return to London. Thus he steeled himself, and within two weeks he had finished Part I of *Lamia.* A few days later Charles Brown had arrived and the two friends began their joint venture, the tragedy *Otho the Great.* They hoped that with Kean in the starring rôle, a few performances would replenish their empty purses. Working steadily, they had brought the play nearly to completion by 12 August; then, Keats needing a library, they removed to Winchester. Both the tragedy and Part II of *Lamia* had been finished by 5 September.

* *Letters,* p. 347. Italics mine.

All this time, Keats avoided Fanny Brawne. 'You absorb me in spite of myself,' he had written one day. And in August he wrote:

The thousand images I have had pass through my brain—my uneasy spirits—my unguess'd fate—all spread as a veil between me and you— Remember I have had no idle leisure to brood over you—'tis well perhaps I have not. I could not have endured the throng of Jealousies that used to haunt me before I had plunged so deeply into imaginary interests.[3]

While he had fallen deeply in love, he knew that young and conventional as she was, she did not, could not love with his intensity. He knew that not only his future but that even his passion was precarious. He could not understand her coquetry and love of pleasure: feared that she, his 'bright reality,' was too worldly. Since she distracted him and led him to torment himself, now that he was 'in complete cue—in the fever' of poetry, he must continue alone for a time. Months later, just after his illness had entered upon its fatal stage, he wrote in retrospect:

When I look back upon *the pains and torments* I have suffer'd for you from the day I left you to go to the Isle of Wight; the extasies in which I have passed some days and the miseries in their turn, I wonder the more at *the Beauty which has kept up the spell* so fervently. (Italics mine.) [4]

In this flood of anguish and conflict *Lamia* was written. That poem came to reflect the torment and one of the fundamental ironies of life.

. . .

Like a good many other features of the romance, however, this does not appear to have been generally discerned. It has long been known that *Lamia,* in which for the first time Keats sought to please the public, was avowedly a stylistic experiment in emulation of Dryden's verse as shown in his *Fables.* The commentators have pointed out, too, that the romance abounds in reminiscences of

Milton, and that it is notable for the close articulation of its structure, its swift narration, and economy of effects. Some critics have sought to explain the curious difference in the tone of Parts I and II in terms of the change in Keats' mood in the interval between their composition. But the question of the nature of his heroine, like that of the meaning of his poem, has led to wide difference of opinion.

Thus Sir Sidney Colvin spoke of the poet's Lamia as 'the serpent, at once witch and victim of witchcraft.' He found that the

one fundamental flaw in *Lamia* concerns its moral. The word is crude: what I mean is *the bewilderment in which it leaves us* as to the effect intended to be made on our imaginative sympathies. *Lamia is a serpent-woman, baleful and a witch,* whose love for Lycius fills him with momentary happiness but must, we are made aware, be fatal to him . . .

Why are we asked to take sides with the enchantress, ignoring everything about her except her charm, and against the sage? If she were indeed *a thing of bale under a mask of beauty,* was not the friend and tutor bound to unmask her, even though the pupil lacked the strength of soul to survive the loss of his illusion? *

The crux of the question is this: Was Keats' Lamia 'baleful and a witch'? Was she in Keats' mind 'a thing of bale under a mask of beauty'? It seems to me that Colvin, and many a later writer, have misunderstood Keats' intention. They have confused the figures of sinister legend with those in the romance. Bewilderment consequently was inevitable, for Keats' figures are no longer those of the legend: they have been crucially modified.

In his acknowledged source, Burton's brief outline of the legend in the *Anatomy of Melancholy,* Lamia as from time immemorial had been thought merely a phantasm, an evil bloodthirsty serpent who assumed the form of a beautiful woman in order to lure hand-

* Colvin, op. cit. 407-9. Italics mine.

some young men to their destruction. In Burton's version of this ancient tale, moreover, Lamia appeared only in her woman's guise and not till her meeting with the youth. A comparison of this with Keats' poem enables us at once to perceive some of his purpose, which was quite different.* Keats first shows us his Lamia as serpent and then as woman. We see her well before her meeting with the youth. And in a line here and there Keats tells us a good deal about the past, the identity, and the nature of his heroine, who among other things is thought 'high inspired' and 'of heavenly progeny.' His Lamia, in short, acquired traits both human and supernatural for which Burton offered hardly the slightest hint. But what Keats tells us throws flashes of light upon the background and the realm of the unexpressed, in which the shadowy figure of a new Lamia took shape in his mind, to become the conception embodied in his poem. It so happens that the clues and allusions in the poem enable us in large measure to reconstruct this background and thus to grasp more fully the design and significance of what he did express. As Colvin's honest bewilderment shows, it is worth while attempting to understand how Keats' conception came to change—in a direction that owes little to Burton. The latter was merely the groundwork of Keats' structure. Its relation to various other works must be established before we can arrive at a clearer understanding of the moral or inner meaning of *Lamia*.

For this purpose, there is again plentiful evidence to show, one of the most important works is *Oberon*. To realize its importance in the genesis of *Lamia* and its contribution to the ideas of which Keats made the poem a vehicle, we must first glance back a moment at *Endymion* and then at the opening lines of Part II of *Lamia*.

It will be recalled from our study of *Endymion* that in its Book III Keats remodeled the myth of Glaucus in accordance with his larger purpose. He had conceived of Glaucus as a poet, brought up

---

* For Philostratus' tale as summarized by Robert Burton, see App. v, p. 373.

in *spiritual purity* 'in forlorn *hermitage,*' who had vainly pursued his ideal of love and beauty, and then turned in despair to the *'arbour queen' and enchantress* upon feeling 'distemper'd longings.' Keats had derived hints for her actions and nature from the enchantress-queen in *Oberon* who tempts and is thwarted by Huon. Glaucus, however, had *succumbed to her sensual joys* and as a result Endymion had seen *his punishment,* been told of *the death of his ideal love,* and overheard him say in his torment:

> 'What shall I do? where go,
> When I have cast *this serpent-skin of woe?*'
> (END. III, 240)

The italicized concepts are peculiarly pertinent in connection with the theme and metamorphosis of *Lamia.* For substantially those concepts reappear in much the same relationship in that romance.

Let us turn to the opening lines of Part II of *Lamia.* Like much else in the romance those lines have been interpreted without reference to their background, and hence have been misunderstood. Colvin found in them 'a new note of idle cynicism.' And despite Keats' apologetic apostrophe to Love,* a later student believed that 'Keats began the second part of *Lamia* with a cynical and Byronic comment on love.' [5] But let us see what Keats said:

K 1   Love in a hut, with water and a crust,
      Is—Love, forgive us!—cinders, ashes, dust;
3   Love in a palace is perhaps at last
      More grievous torment than a hermit's fast:—
5   That is a doubtful tale from faery land,
      Hard for the non-elect to understand.
7   Had Lycius liv'd to hand his story down,
      He might have given the moral a fresh frown,
9   Or clench'd it quite: but too short was their bliss
      To breed distrust and hate, that make the soft voice hiss.

---

*A cosmic principle and divinity, let us remember, in *Endymion.*

11   Besides, there, nightly, with terrific glare,
       Love, jealous grown of so complete a pair,
13   Hover'd and buzz'd his wings, with fearful roar,
       Above the lintel of their chamber door,
15   And down the passage cast a glow upon the floor.

       For all this came a ruin: . . .

namely, the 'bliss' in the palace of the enchantress which we shall
see in due time. First, however, in the light of subsequent *mis-*
understanding, Keats wrote 'Hard for the non-elect to understand'
in the best of faith. And his epithet 'doubtful tale' does not mean
that he disbelieved in the moral, but rather that he felt his readers
would disbelieve what was really his cryptically worded partial plot
summary of the fairy tale. That 'tale from faery land' is not hard
for the elect to understand.

   'Love in a hut' is a clear allusion to the spiritualizing hermitage in *Oberon,** where Huon felled wood to build his royal
bride a hut—for Rezia's 'hut to form a roof' (viii, 40). We know,
too, that earlier he and his eastern bride had been punished for
their sinful consummation of love, first by the daemon king's
'tempest fell' † and then by the agonized torment of hunger and
thirst. Shortly thereafter, their penance and spiritualization had
proceeded under the influence of the hermit, whose simple fare
they shared for some years. To this Keats was now alluding in the
phrases 'water and a crust' and 'grievous torment . . . hermit's
fast.' Moreover, after the hermit's death the paradise wrought by
Titania's enchantment had reverted to its original desolation, of
bleak volcanic rock and cinders. Thus *physically* and quite literally
the spiritualizing 'Love in a hut' idyll became Keats' 'cinders, ashes,
dust'!

   What is more, this termination of the hermitage is adjacent in
Oberon to the trial by sensual pleasure, or the queen's *'Love in a*

---

* Background of the 'ladder of love' or 'pleasure thermometer' in *Endymion.*
† Cf. *St. Agnes.*

palace—even as in Keats' revealing lines. For almost immediately after the hermit's death Rezia is kidnaped; while her lover, abandoned in the forest of the sacred isle, appeals to his guardian god, and is borne aloft through the air to the queen's gardens, where that enchantress confronts him one evening. It is she who lures him lamia-like into her magnificent chambers.

All this left its traces in *Lamia*. Keats' allusion, in the opening lines of Part II of his romance, to 'Love in a palace' is *not* idle. It is clearly an allusion to that scene in Canto XI of *Oberon* which had left its marks upon Glaucus in *Endymion*, and some sublimated aspects of which had already been interfused in the chaster *Eve of St. Agnes*. Colvin's 'new note of idle cynicism' is quite beside the point, for the lines are neither new, idle, nor cynical. They do, however, afford a clue to a most important element, hitherto óverlooked, in Keats' conception of his Lamia. In contrasting 'Love in a hut' with 'Love in a palace,' much as in the episode of Glaucus with its allusions to 'forlorn hermitage' and 'arbour queen,' Keats was using the phrases cryptically: as symbols of spirituality and sensual pleasure, even as Wieland did. Evidently with Lycius and his own life in mind, Keats meant to say that the ascetic's love of a spiritual ideal is less of a torment than the love of sensuous pleasure. The significance of his symbols and their juxtaposition as in *Oberon* are vital for understanding *Lamia*.

Another glance at Keats' lines, particularly 7 to 10, shows that he explicitly alluded to 'the moral' of the 'tale from faery land.' The moral is that 'Love in a palace is perhaps at last More grievous torment than a hermit's fast.' In part Keats drew this conclusion from the torment of the frustrated queen in Wieland's fairy tale. And as the phrases *'his* story,' 'the moral,' *'fresh* frown,' and 'clench'd *it* quite' show, Keats, even as he was weaving the pattern of his tale of 'Love in a palace,' was conscious of some basic analogy with Wieland's episode of love in a palace and its moral. In the light of the machinery of *Oberon,* and of the queen's nature and part in the action, the reason Keats alluded to the fairy tale is clear enough. For in that tale, among other things, 'Love in a palace' instills jealous 'distrust and hate' in the queen, who vainly seeks bliss in sensuousness. And in Keats' phrase 'make the soft voice *hiss*' lurks another clue: to his realization of the dual nature of Wieland's African queen, and to the manner in which *Oberon* with its curse and threefold theme of penance came to help modify the traditional character of Lamia.

This is further hinted in the six last lines of the passage:

> Besides, there, *nightly*, with *terrific glare*,
> *Love,* jealous grown of so complete a pair,
> *Hover'd* and buzz'd his *wings,* with fearful *roar,*
> Above the lintel of their chamber door,
> And down the passage *cast a glow* upon the floor.
> *For all this came a ruin: . . .*

This angry, terrifying, and luminous Love clearly is no conventional Cupid or winged cherub. He is, rather, a malevolent figure who guards the chamber of Lamia and Lycius in their 'palace of *sweet sin*' (*Lamia* ii, 31). Keats' allusion to 'the moral' of the 'tale from faery land' makes his identification simple. This Love is a composite of recollections of daemonology: he is Oberon as he appears in Wieland's allegoric fairy tale. Keats had first seen the winged daemon in the forest of the sinful men transformed into the shapes of beasts. (And that concept had not been lost upon the creator of Glaucus and Lamia.) In that forest Oberon appeared in the guise of 'a boy more beauteous than *the god of love*' (*Oberon* ii, 28). Again, Keats had seen this Love form in the air in Canto v after the elfin 'storm is hush'd that *roared* so loud'—enabling the lovers to flee, as in *St. Agnes.* Then he had seen Oberon *wrathfully hover over the sinful lovers* in Canto vii until, their passion consummated despite his warning, the daemons of the elements were unleashed whose 'tempest-laden *pinions roar* from far.' Keats, whose similar imagery in *Lamia* is significant, knew too that, just before 'Love in a palace' begins, Oberon, *'before whose rays All darkness fades,* the *guardian god'* of chaste love, observes Huon in the forest from a distant mountain peak (*Oberon* x, 13). Then by Oberon's power Huon is borne through the air to the meeting with the queen. Since upon the outcome of that trial the reconciliation of Oberon and Titania depends, the daemon king and his invisible spirits hover near the enchantress-queen's chamber as if to shield Huon during his temptation by 'joys that seduce' from constancy to an ideal. All this is part of the background of *Lamia.*

For Keats' 'Love' is the same god on guard above the chamber door. Above the lovers, the scholar and the enchantress, in the dark night he emits a 'terrific glare' and 'cast a glow.' * And he hovers and buzzes his wings 'with fearful roar.' In the light of Keats' imagery, his allusion to 'the moral' of the 'tale from faery land,' the telling details of the scene in the chamber of the enchantress and the phrase 'For all this came a ruin,' there is little question that Keats had adopted some of Wieland's machinery. Keats' 'Love' is Oberon, the 'guardian god' and 'god of love.' And the daemon king † insists upon spiritual purity, constancy, and chastity; while Keats implies in the phrase *'For* all this came a *ruin'* that there was a causal connection between the presence of the guardian Love in that palace and the frustration of Lamia's sensuous love. The transitional 'For' and the colon after 'ruin' are expressive. But the human note in 'too short was *their* bliss' and explicitly Keats' 'Besides,' in line 11, indicate that this causal connection was only partial: that the daemonic guardian was conceived as only part of the cause of the ruin. Part, however, it was; and it was derived from *Oberon,* the fairy tale to whose moral Keats so plainly alluded. The lines at the opening of Part 11 of *Lamia* constitute a focal point of imagery whose radiations spread farther and farther over and beneath the surface of the romance. They provide a clue to the nature

---

* Whereas in *The Poet* Keats conceived of Oberon's insight figuratively, in these lines he took Sotheby's 'rays' and 'darkness' literally.

† He of both *The Poet* and the *Ode on Indolence* with its three daemons: Love, Ambition, Poesy.

of Keats' Lamia, who differs greatly from Burton's, and whose final defeat is duly brought about by the strange 'demon eyes' of Apollonius.

II

The continuation in the second part of *Lamia* reveals how many hints and how much imagery Keats derived from the furniture, action, and motivation of 'Love in a palace' in *Oberon*. More important than these details, however, is the guidance which particularly Cantos x to xii of the fairy tale provided for both Parts i and ii of Keats' romance.* Let us therefore turn next to the structural similarities between the two poems: architectural features whose essentially parallel sequence reveals how profoundly *Oberon* affected the genesis of *Lamia*. After first glancing at these features in their broad contours we shall examine in detail a few of the most significant.

We know from both *Endymion* and *The Eve of St. Agnes* that long before coming upon Burton's summary of the legend of the lamia, Keats had been sensitive to various phases of the temptation of Huon by the voluptuous queen in *Oberon*. In Burton Keats read of a 'phantasm' who meets a handsome youth, lures him into her palace, and tempts him with all manner of sensual pleasure, only to be frustrated and exposed, as a serpent in the guise of a woman, when she marries him. As he read this ancient tale, a light must have dawned in Keats' mind, since the basic likeness to the *Oberon* episode of the queen did not escape him. For that 'enchantress' meets the handsome Huon one evening, becomes enamored of him, lures him into her palace, and tempts him with all sorts of sensual pleasure. Finally she proposes marriage, but in this too finds herself thwarted. In her fury, honey becomes gall, as her true nature, that of *'a wily snake,'* is dramatically revealed. Her tortured soul, that of a schizophrenic, is dramatically bared in two violent scenes strangely suggestive of transformation.

* Cantos x-xii of *Oberon* are summarized on p. 44 f. above.

From earlier episodes in *Oberon* Keats knew, too, that the queen or 'wily snake' is the embodiment of the daemon king's curse of 'woe and pain' *—upon 'faithless' and 'deceitful' woman, whose voluptuous passions are those of the *'bosom snake'; upon 'joys that seduce';* and upon *'syren pleasure on a proffer'd throne.'* Keats knew that that curse was evoked by Titania's sympathy with the deceitful May, because of which the elfin queen had been banished in penance and sorrow to her sacred isle. Keats' allusion to the 'tale from faery land' and its moral of 'grievous torment' makes clear that Burton's vague phantasm and Wieland's sensual, demonically tormented enchantress speedily became identified in his mind. When Keats came to create his heroine, the enchantress-queen helped him to animate and individualize Burton's lifeless abstraction. Not only the mortal queen in her palace, but her connection with the elfin queen Titania and the daemonic world of Oberon's curse and punitive power over sinners, profoundly influenced his conception. This is hinted at the very outset of *Lamia.* For whereas Burton began his tale with the meeting of the sinister 'gentlewoman' and the youth, Keats begins his romance at an earlier point, with some significant lines and incidents full of eerie overtones.

Thus in the opening lines of Part I of *Lamia* there is an allusion scarcely less significant than the later one to 'Love in a hut.' This is what Keats first wrote:

K I   Upon a time, before *the faery broods*
       Drove Nymph and Satyr from *the prosperous woods,*
3   Before *King Oberon's* bright diadem,
       Sceptre, and mantle, clasp'd with dewy gem,
5   Frighted away the Dryads and the Fauns
       From rushes green, and brakes, and cowslip'd lawns,
7   The ever-smitten Hermes empty left
       His golden throne, bent warm on amorous theft:

* Cf. *Oberon* VI, 100 ff. on p. 36 above.

9   From *high Olympus* had he stolen light,
       On this side of Jove's *clouds,* to escape the sight
11   Of his great summoner, and made retreat
       Into *a forest on the shores of* Crete.
13   For somewhere in *that sacred island* dwelt
       A nymph, to whom all hoofed Satyrs knelt . . .

But some other personages dwelt there too.

'The opening of the poem,' Douglas Bush pointed out, 'seems to be much elaborated from the story of Mercury, Herse, and Aglauros at the end of the second book of the "Metamorphoses." ' [6] The title of that source is significant. But perhaps it would be more nearly correct to say that that much elaborated incident has been transferred to a new setting in a Gothic forest, and that it has been interwoven with an incident from the 'tale from faery land.' For while the nymph for whom Hermes 'burnt' is evidently Herse, we might just as well be back in the mighty forest on the sides of Latmos with Endymion, since this *sacred island* of Crete is really the sacred island of the penanced Titania. As the sequel makes quite clear, the time is shortly after 'Love in a hut' had become 'cinders, ashes, dust.' Keats' imagery shows that memories of another forest had arisen too: the 'prosperous woods' of the 'faery broods' and King Oberon's wand or sceptre, with its powers of punitive transformation.* But let us continue somewhat farther.

Hermes having been introduced, we see him as

K 27   From vale to vale, from wood to wood, *he flew,*
       Breathing upon the flowers his passion new,
29   And wound *with* many *a river to its head,*
       To find where this sweet nymph prepar'd her secret bed:
31   In vain; the sweet nymph might nowhere be found,
       And so *he rested, on the lonely ground,*
33   *Pensive,* and *full of pain*ful jealousies
       Of the *Wood-Gods,* and even the very trees.

* Seen by Glaucus, of the 'serpent-skin of woe,' in *Endymion.*

35   *There as he stood, he heard a mournful voice,*
Such as once heard, *in gentle heart,* destroys
37   *All pain* but *pity:* thus *the lone voice spake:*
'When from this wreathed tomb shall I awake!
39   'When move in a sweet body fit for life,
'And love, and pleasure, and the ruddy strife
41   'Of hearts and lips! Ah, *miserable* me!'

(LAMIA I, 27-41)

Already in 'this wreathed tomb' there is a hint of a weird penance. And what the voice desires is significant.*

But now let us turn to Canto x of the 'tale from faery land': to a point alluded to by Keats, between 'Love in a hut' and 'Love in a palace'—or, to the time when the former had become 'cinders, ashes, dust' with the reversion of Titania's paradise to its volcanic state. The hermit has died; Rezia has been kidnaped; and Huon, badly wounded and awaiting death, has been abandoned *in the lonely sacred isle:* 'bound to an oak on that deserted spot.' Suddenly, in the very next line we see Oberon again, still separated from the penanced Titania, as

. . . he, before whose rays
All darkness fades, the guardian god, delays . . .

We already saw this luminous god in Keats' jealous guardian Love and his 'terrific glare' in the palace of Part II. But now:

. . . the guardian *god, delays:*   K 32
While *on a heav'n-topt mountain's cloud*less brow,   K 9-10
That shades *the sources of old Nile* below,   K 29
He drinks the balmy gale that round its summit plays.

(OBERON X, 13)

And Oberon's actions closely resemble those of Hermes.

* Cf. the voice of the transformed elephant heard by Glaucus, in Circe's (Oberon's) wood—where the power of the sceptre or lily-wand is revealed. (*End.* III, 500; and App. III, p. 346.)

For the winged Hermes, who had flown from the heavenly mountain Olympus this side the clouds, 'wound with many a river to its head' until he rested and heard the 'mournful voice.' And much like him the winged Oberon, the 'guardian *god,*' rests on the lonely cloudless summit of a heaven-topt mountain at the *head of the river* Nile. And what does he do there? He

> Fixes, where Huon droops, his *mournful* eye,   K 35
> While from that distance heard, his lowest sigh . . .

strikes the daemon king's ear. Oberon groans on seeing 'poor Huon's *miserable* form' (cf. Lamia: 'Ah, miserable me!'); and he is so sad that, daemon as he is, he 'from sight withdrew'—as did Hermes' nymph, we soon learn, by Lamia's power.

At last a 'gentle fay,' seeing his sovereign's *pain,* near *'pensive* Oberon drew' (cf. K 33: Hermes, 'pensive, and full of painful . . . the Wood-Gods,' of whom incidentally Oberon is one and king *). Oberon lets the devoted spirit glimpse the wretched Huon, who appears amid the deep forest of the sacred isle, reflected in a cloud. Then, like Hermes, Oberon *hears the mournful voice:*

> W 1   'How at my woes all peaceful as before!
>   How tranquil *all!* un*pity*ing of my *pain:*   K 37
> 3   No being feels with me—no viewless grain,
>   No, not a grain of sand upon *the shore*   K 12 †
> 5   Stirs from its place! From off the woodland glade
>   No, not a leaflet falls a wretch to aid!'

And then the 'lone voice' of Huon appeals to the invisible Oberon:

> W 7   'Yet, if thou didst but will it, thou! whose aid
>   Unhop'd, has sav'd me oft when most distrest,
> 9   *Didst thou but will,* my soul would sink to rest,
>   Each twig that trembles in the woodland shade

* Cf. 'the wood-god's ire," *Oberon* VII, 81.
† 'Deep in the *wood,* at distance from the *shore*' (*Oberon* IX, 63). With this compare K 12: 'Into a forest on the shores of Crete,' where Lamia is miserable and Hermes' invisible nymph strays even as does Titania in the lonely sacred isle.

11   Would at a wink, *transform'd beneath thy sight,*
Stretch forth a guardian hand!' *Celestial light*
13   Swift *vibrates,* as he spoke, *thro' every bone:*
His bands at once are loos'd—he tumbles prone,
15   Safe in the viewless arms of some protecting sprite.

              (OBERON X, 17-18)

These stanzas teemed with hints that were vital for Keats.

The daemon king, still angry with Huon, had caused his penance to begin anew. But the *'gentle* fay' had *pitied* the miserable sufferer and interceded with the 'guardian god.' Keats' echoed 'all pain but pity' shows the origin of his 'gentle heart.' But now Oberon charged this gentle aerial spirit:

      'Haste! thy fleet course *to yonder island wing:*   K 9, 12
W 17   Bear *the poor wretch from that abandon'd spot,*
      To Tunis bear, before the lowly cot
19   Of aged Ibrahim, gard'ner of the king.
      Speed thro' the paths of air his viewless way:
21   Then on a bank of stones the wanderer lay
      Close by the cottage door. Quick! leave the place,
23   But *fly unseen* along th' ethereal space . . .'

            (OBERON X, 21)

Thus Huon, his penance ended, is borne aloft through the air to the palace gardens and his meeting with the lovely temptress, the African queen and 'wily snake,' Lamia's human and regal counterpart.

Let us look more closely at the process of assimilation and recreation so strangely revealed here. The lone and mournful voice that the resting and pensive god Hermes hears from the forest not far from the shore of the sacred island, echoes some of the very words which the resting and pensive god Oberon hears from the forest not far from the shore of the penanced Titania's sacred island. Obviously Huon's 'abandon'd spot' *is* Hermes' 'lonely ground'; even as the *'celestial light'* that 'swift *vibrates'* through the former's *'every bone'* (W 12) is like the 'celestial heat' that 'burnt' from Hermes' 'winged heels to either ear' (*Lamia* 1, 22). Yet Hermes' rôle is based upon that of Oberon, while he flies to the sacred isle like Oberon's gentle aerial spirit.

A rereading of Keats' lines reveals the creative process. As the italicized elements show, settings and incidents, characters and imagery, no less than phraseology and overtones indicate how many ideas and hints Keats derived from the *Oberon* passage—as well as what came of them when interwoven with Ovid. But while Huon's words and Oberon's actions helped Keats to create the sufferer's voice and elaborate the actions of Hermes, the hints in the machinery and moral of *Oberon* were more important. The most provocative lines that Keats saw evidently were these words of the mournful voice undergoing penance: *'If thou didst but will'* it, that something be *'transform'd beneath thy sight.'* This not only recalled Oberon's powers of punitive transformation, but with a subtle difference is precisely what Hermes is about to will for the mournful voice he heard. Instead of Huon's twigs, we are to see Lamia herself transformed beneath our sight. We are to see the miserable serpent transformed and borne aloft through the air (like Huon) to the meeting with Lycius.

For Keats took the momentous hint. And having adopted the daemon king's powers of transforming men and beasts twice before in *Endymion,* he now transferred them once again to Hermes.[7] Keats modified the hint in accordance with what Huon (and Glaucus) had seen in Oberon's 'prosperous wood' on his first visit there. The poet who alluded to that wood and the sceptre, to 'Love in a hut' and 'Love in a palace' and 'the moral' of the 'tale from faery land,' found in the designated portions of *Oberon* the crucial hint for penance and transformation and invisible conveyance through the air. The hint was crucial, because it was peculiarly instrumental in evoking that portion of *Lamia* which is quite outside the scope of Burton: the complex nature of Lamia, the idea of her penance and 'grievous torment,' and particularly her amazing metamorphosis. Oberon is at once the Hermes of Part I and the guardian Love in Part II. As both his parallel sequence and the ideas in his sequel show, Keats was being guided by the moral and machinery as well as by the characters and incidents in the daemonic world of *Oberon*.

. . .

Keats' next lines are full of significant overtones. Hermes approaches the mournful voice and finds not Huon but the gorgeous snake. Her dazzling coloration, we shall see, was not new. The dissolving patterns include some significant symbols, but her identity is most clearly hinted if we know to whom the 'sacred island' really belonged. For Keats tells us that

> She seem'd, *at once,* some penanced lady elf,
> Some demon's mistress, or the demon's self.
> (LAMIA I, 55-6)

She has a woman's mouth, but 'Her throat was serpent.' Yet she has such strange powers of enchantment and supernatural insight that Hermes believes her to be 'high inspired.' She has other powers which we shall examine somewhat later. But the second most important revelation as to her nature is this. She tells Hermes:

> 'I was a woman, let me have *once more*
> A woman's shape, and charming as before.'
> (I, 117-18)

In other words, in form *she is essentially a woman who had been changed into a serpent*—not, as in Burton, a serpent in the guise of a woman. This distinction is deliberate and significant. In answer to her plea, the god touches her with his charm and she begins shortly to transform, visibly 'beneath' our sight—even as Huon had suggested. Then, like him, she is borne aloft through the air to the meeting, for she had become 'a lady bright.' When we have seen a little more of the background and her human prototype, we shall examine the metamorphosis of the serpent and 'brilliance feminine' in detail, for then its subtlety will become apparent.

With the help of Burton and details evidently gleaned from Potter's *Antiquities* or elsewhere,[8] Keats next describes the place near Corinth where in her restored woman's form she awaits the youth. Then Keats tells us of her intuitive love-learning and, in happier lines, of powers more rare and revealing, among them

> how she could muse
> And dream, *when in the serpent prison-house.*
>
> (1, 202-3)

The overtone of penance and punitive transformation is again un-mistakable. He tells of how her senses transcend elemental space, and of how she had become enamored of the mortal Lycius. Then, taking up her human phase, Keats turns in lines 235 ff. to the meeting.

With Keats' allusion to 'Love in a palace' in mind and also the parallel sequence in the 'tale from faery land,' it is clear that the protean Lamia is for the time being the lovely queen at her first meeting with Huon in those palace gardens to which, like Lamia, he had just been borne through the air. While Keats greatly ex-panded the meeting and dialogue of the 'lady bright' and the youth and had them shed further light upon the supernatural side of Lamia's nature, he was guided in broad outline by the meeting of Huon and the queen. For that enchantress and 'wily snake' appears full-bodied for the first time in Part 1 of *Lamia,* only some three-score lines after the elusive transformation of 'smooth-lipp'd serpent' into woman. Thus at last Lamia beholds Lycius *that evening:*

> K 235   His phantasy was lost, where reason fades,
>   In the calm'd *twilight* of Platonic shades.
>
>   237   Lamia beheld him coming, *near,* more near—
>   *Close to her passing,* in indifference drear,

239 *His silent sandals swept the* mossy *green;*
  So neighbour'd to him, and yet so unseen
241 *She stood:* he pass'd, shut up in mysteries,
  His mind *wrapp'd* like his mantle, while *her eyes*
243 *Follow'd his steps,* and *her neck regal* white
  Turn'd—syllabling thus, 'Ah, Lycius *bright,*
245 And will you leave me on the hills alone?
  Lycius, look *back* . . .'

And he does, astonished, then adoring, until *'Her* soft *look* growing *coy,* she saw his chain so sure.'

At her first meeting with Huon, Almansaris doesn't quite bid the indifferent youth to look back. But it is also evening, just at twilight. And Huon who, like Lamia, had been borne through the air from the sacred isle, is disguised as a gardener as he seeks *silently* within the forbidden gardens for sight of his bride—his ideal of love and beauty.* Bearing on his arm a *basket full of* fruit and *flowers freshly picked,* he rounds a hedge and quite *near him stands* the languorous and lovely queen. (Cf. K 237, 241.) 'What dost thou here?' she inquires not too sternly of this fairest youth her eyes had ever seen. Dropping to his knee, he offers her the basket submissively and begs pardon for his bold intrusion. His handsome and noble mien not lost upon her, she nods half regretfully that he go. As he obeys,

In pensive silence *wrapt* she paces slow,   K 242
Bends *her fair neck* stretch'd *back* in fond presage, K 243-5
And feels her bosom throb with sudden rage,
That he at once obey'd the wink to go—
Was he too *coy* to read *her look* aright?
       (OBERON XI, 16)

And already jealous, she would know whether he had come to seek some form 'less *bright.'*

Not only the echoed phrases but the time and setting, the charac-

---

* Significantly, Lycius is dreaming on 'Platonic shades' at the parallel moment.

ters and their actions and thoughts indicate how many hints Keats derived for this first meeting. Huon's coolness was as suggestive of Lycius' 'indifference drear' as the lovely queen's gesture, of turning back her regal neck, was of Lamia's identical action. And if Huon with his basket 'near *the goddess'* drew, Lycius says 'Ah, Goddess, see'; and Keats duly wrote that he

> . . . leant thoughtfully
> At Venus' temple porch, 'mid *baskets heap'd*
> *Of* amorous herbs and *flowers, newly reap'd*
> *Late on that eve* . . .*

If from one have come many, this, we may be sure, is still Huon's basket and the flowers he had gathered for the harem.

The shifting pattern, with oriental harem gardens refashioned into Grecian temples, and Gothic forests with their transformed denizens changed into island fanes, sufficiently illumines the ways of the creative imagination at its work. The dialogue between the *regal* Lamia and Lycius suggests even more vividly the imaginative control Keats was exercising in the creative synthesis, by which the natural and the preternatural were constantly intermingled in the richly composite being which is his Lamia. For if she is now the queen, Lycius also believes her a goddess; and his other suggestions as to her identity contain yet another modification of her supernatural lineage. But of that, more later.

Notwithstanding her significant replies, as 'lady bright' her chief prototype is the enchantress-queen. Lycius falls 'into delight' to hear her whisper 'woman's lore so well.' There Keats interpolates the unfortunate lines 'Let the mad poets say whate'er they please' of 'Fairies, Peris, Goddesses.' I suspect that he caught the tone for these 'Byronic lines' from Wieland's somewhat jocular description (just before the meeting) of the charms of the queen, whose every feature and limb is likened to that of a Venus, Helen, Erigone.

---

* *Lamia* I, 316-9. Cf. also the queen's *'Venus* frame,' *Oberon* XI, 8.

For in the adjoining lines we are for the first time momentarily within the queen's palace, as Keats says:

> Thus gentle *Lamia judg'd,* and judg'd aright,
> *That Lycius could not love in half a fright,*
> *So threw the goddess off,* and won his heart
> More pleasantly by playing woman's part,
> With *no* more awe *than what her beauty gave* . . .
>
> (LAMIA I, 334-8)

When Huon first entered the chamber of 'Love in a palace,' he was startled by the pomp and jeweled splendor of the queen's garb. And that lady, seeing the youth's confusion as he 'views the *goddess* face to face,' changes her tactics, descends from her throne and 'ready seems to *lay aside* that pomp' whose dazzling splendor might *'the youth affright.'* Precisely like Lamia 'she wishes *no* advantage *but her charms'* (*Oberon* XI, 50-51). And Lamia is on the point of luring the youth into the same palace, of sensuous joy and torment.

For we are almost at the end of Part I. The distance to Corinth by a 'spell' of that enchantress, who is and yet is not a mortal, shrinks to a few paces. Then Keats interpolates the superb description of the 'populous streets and temples lewd.' Burton reappears momentarily with Apollonius, 'the ghost of folly haunting my sweet dreams,' and then we are before the palace. But like Lamia herself, the palace is no simple conception. 'A few Persian mutes' remind us that the queen, Lamia's human other-self, has mortal slaves in her palace. But Lamia is also 'some demon's mistress, or the *demon's self.'* And probably for that reason in part, 'Sounds Aeolian breath'd from the hinges' of her palace, which is here that of Mulciber, the builder of the hall in 'Pandaemonium,' the abode of Satan and all demons in *Paradise Lost.* For Milton helped furnish the threefold amalgam which is the 'faery roof' of Keats' daemonic romance.

III

The key to the genesis of *Lamia,* however, is in that revealing allusion to *Oberon,* its moral and machinery, in the lines 'Love in a hut' and 'Love in a palace' and their continuation, with which Part II opens.* Of that sensual palace and its occupants Keats said:

K 8   He might have given the moral a fresh frown,
          Or clench'd it quite: but too short was their bliss
10   To breed distrust and hate, that make the soft voice hiss.
          Besides, there, *night*ly, with terrific glare,
12   Love, jealous grown of so complete a pair,
          Hover'd and buzz'd his wings, with fearful roar,
14   Above the lintel of their *chamber door,*
          And *down the passage cast a glow* upon the floor.
16   For all this came a ruin . . .

In the phrase 'too short was *their* bliss' Keats, I think, was writing partly in terms of the 'pleasure thermometer' and experience, which played an increasingly important rôle in the psychology of Part II. The verb 'hiss,' on the other hand, recalls the 'smooth-lipp'd serpent' and her regal exemplar, the 'wily snake.' And the next lines remind us of the identity of the angry guardian Love, the Oberon who is also Hermes, and his causal connection with the ruin. But it is the imagery and the sequence of incidents in what follows that reveal how many ideas for the furniture of the costly and dazzling chamber and for the actions and emotional reactions of the occupants Keats derived from the episode of the queen in *Oberon.* Though he interpolated many other reminiscences and symbolical and other matter, he never lost sight of the fairy tale and continued for some time to follow its pattern. This is shown by his broadly parallel sequence. As we resume our examination of the structural similarities, we shall glance at those elements which are most illumi-

* Cf. p. 197 above.

nating. But, lest we lose sight of larger issues, verbal parallels and other detailed evidence, fascinating though it is, must for the most part be consigned to the Appendix.

First, however, let us follow Keats' lines somewhat farther. In the very next lines he wrote thus:

16   For all this came a ruin: *side by side*
       They were *enthroned,* in the even tide,
18   Upon *a couch, near to a curtaining*
       Whose *airy texture,* from a *golden* string,
20   *Floated* into the room . . .

22   . . . *there they reposed,*
       Where use had made it sweet . . .

until the interruption comes. Certainly this and what follows is the temptation scene in the queen's magnificent chambers. In tracing the poet's tracks in *The Eve of St. Agnes,* we saw Huon at *midnight* carry out the nurse's stratagem, which led him *silently* through the *dark passages* to the door where his guide left him, despite *his whisper of inquiry.* (Keats' 'whispering in midnight silence, said the youth' occurs in a moment within the door. *Lamia* II, 84.) At Huon's soft tap, *'the door* expands—*a tender gleam* . . . Soft *on* a suit of endless *chambers* plays.' (*Oberon* XI, 46. This imagery throws more light upon K 14-15: 'chamber door . . . down the passage cast a glow.') As Huon steps out of the dark passage, suddenly lighted by the opened door, he finds himself within the queen's chambers. And there

A curtain flies away that play'd his eye before.

    .   .   .

On either side back *flies* th' embroider'd *gold*—
A scene celestial fascinates his gaze!
On *throne* of gold a dame in beauty's blaze,
Glows like the form that thoughts entranc'd behold,

> When by the warmth of youthful fancy won
> A Venus smiles in *airy texture* spun.   K 19
>
> (OBERON XI, 47-48) [9]

After the youth has marveled at her dazzling beauty, the slaves
grouped around her, and the splendor of the regal furnishings
(which substantially reappear, disseminated in Lamia's palace); and
after she has laid aside pomp and reached him a cup of gold, and
the slaves have begun and ceased to dance at her bidding,*

> Her winning lute she suffers to be brought,
> Then *on a* pillowy *throne for pleasure wrought,*   K 17, 22
> Softly *reclines* . . .
>
> (XI, 60)

and causes Huon to sit beside her. Only ten stanzas later her
'pillowy throne' is exchanged for her silken 'damask *couch*' of torment, that is like Lamia's (K 18).

This kindred appearance, in the same setting, of the 'dazzling'
enchantress of 'Venus frame,' who like the Lamia of the 'dazzling
frame' had lured the youth into her palace; the identical situation
of the queen who reclines on a throne near an airy golden curtain
just within her chamber door of the 'Love in a palace' scene to
which Keats had just alluded—this does not require much comment. Keats, selecting carefully from a scene much of which was
crude, derived his setting and some of his mood from it.[10] But in
the light of the moral of the 'tale from faery land' and the identity
of the guardian Love above the chamber door, a deeper resemblance
is significant. It is revealing to compare the queen reclining on
'pillowy throne for *pleasure* wrought' with Keats' more sensitive
but even more suggestive 'enthroned . . . upon a couch . . . *where
use had made it sweet.'* For his scene is in the 'purple-lined palace
of *sweet sin*' (*Lamia* II, 31). That conception, together with 'use
had made it sweet,' bears out the causal connection between the
guardian Love (the daemon king who insists upon chastity and

* Cf. *Lamia* II, 206-8, 265, etc.

constancy to an ideal), his jealousy of 'so complete a pair,' and the
ruin of sensual pleasure palace and its inmates. That moral, of
the punishment of sensuousness by 'grievous torment,' was still part
of Keats' intention. His Lycius is a scholar no longer constant,
because betrayed by his senses. And that, while also symbolic, is a
thematic overtone from the fairy tale, an overtone not quite lost
in Keats' larger purpose.

. . .

Now Huon's temptation by the daemonically accursed 'joys that
seduce' runs the gamut. He witnesses a voluptuous dance, is offered
a feast of delicacies and wine in a golden goblet from which the
lovely queen first drinks.* Like Burton's Lamia, she plays and sings
for him and offers herself to his embrace.† But because Huon, unlike Glaucus and Lycius, is constant to his ideal, her joys do not
seduce him. Since he resists her every wile and 'vows anew in holy
thought' his constancy to his bride, the enchantress reads in his
features the painful change that her sensuality had evoked. In tears,
she soon dismisses him; and left alone on her couch, 'wild passion
raging in her fiery breast,' she ponders her frustration and con-
vulsively bares all her soul, voluptuous and now cruel.

> These thoughts to maddening rage her soul inflame:
> Death, tenfold death, shall expiate the offence!
> How loath'd the monster that bewitch'd her sense!
> A dragon seems far lovelier to the dame.
> Now pride and jealousy the wretch detest,
> The furious fit now dies, by love supprest—
> Desire and vengeance swift as thought succeed:
> Before her, drop by drop, the wretch shall bleed!—
> Now, in her arms enchain'd, she dies upon his breast.
>
> (OBERON XII, 2)

* Cf. *Lamia* II, 206 ff.

† Another of many close resemblances which helped the integration of queen and
Lamia.

There was much in her tormented fury to stimulate Keats, who had realized all the implications of fiery torment, expiation, 'bewitch'd . . . sense,' serpent lore, beauty, jealousy, vengeance, blood, and death—long before he wrote 'grievous torment' and 'make the soft voice hiss.'

This enchantress, at last subdued by her love for the youth, somewhat later tempts Huon again, in the arbor-grot.* And finally she visits Huon mysteriously in the night, in that prison into which her deceit had caused him to be cast. Her crown glittering upon her head, the 'wily snake' *proposes marriage,* offers him the throne and *'fame'* and *'glory';* and she *falls at his feet* in a passion of tears, *takes his hand,* and *begs him to change his purpose*—of being burned at the stake rather than proving inconstant to his vow.† Soon thereafter, the raging queen having left the stage, as the constant lovers find themselves reunited at the stake and the flames have already risen, the daemon king intercedes and the sensual queen is completely frustrated.‡ And while their exhausted *foes gasp and choke* about them, Oberon's aerial *car* descends into *the thronged streets* to bear the lovers to *the bridal pageant* before the tenuous fairy palace in the enchanted forest. Keats, still following this pattern, demonstrably drew inspiration, ideas, and imagery from all these scenes. In uncanny fashion, what he had gleaned he interwove within the framework of the legend, in a sequence slightly modified but essentially the same.

Thus Huon's 'painful change' and the queen's reactions in her two fits of frenzy colored the actions of both Lycius and Lamia. In parallel sequence Lycius, 'his passion cruel grown,' proposes marriage. But let us glance a moment at Keats' scene. Hardly have Lamia and Lycius appeared on the couch 'where use had made it sweet,' than an interruption comes:

* Which Glaucus had entered in *Endymion* III.
† Cf. *Oberon* XII, 32 ff.
‡ Cf. the 'demon eyes' of Apollonius.

came a thrill
Of trumpets—Lycius started—the sounds fled,
But left a thought a-buzzing in his head.
For the first time, *since first he harbour'd in*
That purple-lined palace of sweet sin,
His spirit pass'd beyond its golden bourn
Into the noisy world almost forsworn.

(II, 27-33)

This trumpet call is clearly symbolic of the call to fame in the
world of achievement.* And while, as we shall see, it is a clue to
Keats' larger meaning, as an interruption of the enchantress' bliss
it is a mere modification of the parallel interruption of 'Love in a
palace' in *Oberon*—and of the queen's offer: *'wake* to fame . . .
glory' (XII, 34). This is revealed by Keats' next lines:

> K 34   *The lady, ever watchful, penetrant,*
>   *Saw this with pain,* so arguing a *want*
> 36   *Of something more,* more *than her empery*
>   *Of joys;* and *she began to moan and sigh*
> 38   *Because he mused beyond her,* knowing well
>   That but a moment's thought is passion's passing bell.

Save for the last line with its deeper overtones, this is precisely
the reaction of the queen during the first phase of Huon's temptation by 'joys that seduce.' Huon thinks beyond her, of his constancy
to his ideal, his bride; and the queen, like Lamia 'ever watchful,
penetrant,' reads the change in his mood from his features. And
Keats' phrase 'empery of joys' is significant. †

What follows is also most revealing. For the youth Lycius, who
like Huon had been lured into the palace, adds:

> K 40   'Why do you sigh, fair creature?' whisper'd he:
>   'Why do you think?' return'd she tenderly:

* Cf. *End.* I, 737.
† For verbal parallels and the detailed evidence in *Oberon,* see App. V, p. 373.

42   'You have deserted me;—where am I now?
      'Not in your heart while care weighs on your brow:
44   'No, no, you have dismiss'd me; and I go
      'From your breast houseless: ay, it must be so.'

The human note in 'care weighs,' and the last phrase, came of the
conflict and sorrow of Keats' personal experience. But 'you have
dismiss'd me' reminds us that Huon's dismissal by the thwarted
queen appears in the parallel sequence. It is also clear from Lamia's
phraseology that Keats, led by the scene in *Oberon,* which he had
previously used, here recalled the identical pattern in Madeline's
chamber in *The Eve of St. Agnes,* where there was also 'a painful
change.' At this point, for some dozen lines, Keats proceeded to
retrace his own earlier steps and to write in terms of imagery in
the dialogue of Porphyro and Madeline. Lamia's reactions are thus
in part those of the queen of the 'visions of delight' and in part
those of Madeline. In the process of coalescence, Keats was unwittingly illumining the 'ways of the imagination' in the subtle
affinity and contrast between the moods and imagery of the two
poems, where that imagination was differently focused.*

But Lycius, who had won the chariot race, reveals his hunger
for fame in expressing his desire for a public bridal pageant. (Huon
despite the queen's joys and offer of fame and glory had been
thinking of his ideal, while the 'chariot' or 'car' and the bridal
pageant were soon to appear in *Oberon.*) And Lycius' next words
show that Keats had returned to the pattern in the fairy tale. For
the lover now says:

K 62   'Let my foes choke, and my friends shout afar,
       'While through the thronged streets your bridal car
64   'Wheels round its dazzling spokes.'—The lady's cheek
       Trembled; she nothing said, but, *pale and meek,*
66   *Arose and knelt before him, wept a rain*
       Of sorrows at his words; at last *with pain*

* The passages will repay careful study. See App. v, p. 374.

68   *Beseeching him,* the while *his hand she wrung,*
      To change his purpose. He thereat was stung,
70   Perverse, with stronger fancy to reclaim
      Her wild and timid nature to his aim:
72   Besides, *for all his love, in self despite,*
      Against his better self, he *took delight*
74   Luxurious *in her sorrows,* soft and new.
      His *passion, cruel grown, took on a hue*
76   *Fierce and sanguineous* as 'twas possible
      In one whose brow had no dark veins to swell.
78   Fine was the mitigated *fury,* like
      Apollo's presence when in act to strike
80   *The serpent*—Ha, the serpent! certes, *she*
      Was none. She *burnt,* she *lov'd the tyranny,*
82   And, *all subdued,* consented to the hour
      When to the bridal he should lead his paramour.
84   Whispering in midnight silence, said the youth: *
      'Sure some sweet name thou hast, though, by my truth,
86   'I have not ask'd it, ever thinking thee
      '*Not mortal, but of heavenly progeny,*
88   'As still I do. Hast any mortal name,
      'Fit appellation for this *dazzling frame?*'

As in most of *Lamia* the overtones in this passage are rich, steeped as they were in a personal passion. The allusion to Lamia's being of 'heavenly progeny' is nonetheless another clue to her composite nature—of which the 'dazzling frame' of the queen was but a part. But it was the queen's actions, in her two attacks of schizophrenia 'self-subdued,' which provided the hints for the fury of Lycius and for the actions of the subdued Lamia. Keats' psychology became more subtle, and Lycius' 'stronger fancy' that of the domineering male. But the queen tried '*to bend the spirit*' of Huon to her aim. †️ And Keats' imagery reveals how carefully he had studied the

---

* Cf. Huon, p. 215.
† *Oberon* xii, 37. Cf. K 71.

'grievous torment' of the queen, who provided the impulse for this scene.*

Keats' words, 'fine was the mitigated fury,' exactly describe what had happened: they express as if subconsciously the volition underlying the creative vision. He had mitigated the queen's 'furious fit.' It is noteworthy, too, that the convulsive torment of the queen *and* 'wily snake' led him to think of the 'act to strike the serpent'; and that Lamia's subdued nature, humanized further in the light of Keats' experience of love, evoked the emphatic assertion, 'The serpent! certes, she was none.' This was again deliberate. For Lamia, with a form essentially that of a regal woman, probably had always been more gentle than the mortal queen. And her 'sorrows new' and 'wild and timid nature' are further clues hinting that she had undergone more than one metamorphosis.

. . .

First, however, let us finish with the structural features of Keats' romance. Oberon's bridal car in the streets thronging with the choking foes evidently suggested the marriage customs, which Keats seems to have verified in Potter's *Antiquities* and elaborated with the help of the bridal pageant before Oberon's palace. † But Keats' sequel was further embroidered with threads from the 'airy texture' of the queen. The latter's preparations for the feast in her palace where 'slaves at will start up to *serve her subtle* mind' helped Lamia, 'regal drest,' to prepare her banquet with the help of 'her subtle servitors.' She was also helped by the pageant attended by heavenly music at Oberon's shimmering palace, woven of crimson twilight. Some of its sylvan features seem to have been transferred within doors to Lamia's haunted palace, which was interwoven of elements Keats had found in the palaces of Mulciber, Oberon, and the enchantress-queen. From the last he borrowed a good deal of furniture.

---

* For the detailed evidence, see App. v, p. 375 f.
† For *Lamia* ii, 105 ff., see App. v, p. 378.

The contribution from Oberon's daemon-haunted palace, however, is more important. It was there that Titania, her penance ended, reappeared in her vestigial moonlight, with winged spirits no longer 'viewless.' And the natural and the preternatural were constantly mingled both in Lamia's palace and in herself, who 'faded at self-will' and 'mission'd her viewless servants' and 'subtle servitors' for a reason. She was in part at least, as we shall see, of 'heavenly progeny.' * . . .

It is noteworthy that in his selection of stuff from the *Oberon* pattern, Keats was governed by considerations of its fitness for his legend frame. Though his conception of the legend had greatly evolved and deepened, it was still defined by the traditional fate of Lamia. Thus as he drew toward the end of the tale, he followed Burton more closely; but he introduced further symbolism and modified the traditional conclusion in accordance with his larger purpose and, evidently, used hints remembered from *Oberon* and elsewhere. For in his *Lamia,* amid the terror of the suddenly silent guests, Lycius dies—the bridegroom at his own wedding feast. This was exactly what happened at the wedding feast interrupted by the daemon king in Canto v, † where the blasphemous bridegroom is slain by Huon with the help of Oberon. That Keats' mind reverted to that scene is revealed by his imagery, some of which in parallel sequence was recalled from *Oberon* and *The Eve of St. Agnes.* ‡

Keats must have remembered, too, the death of his own Ludolph on his wedding night in the synchronous *Otho the Great;* and the death of Sir Huldbrand in Fouqué's *Undine* (that tale of an elemental spirit and her mortal lover by which Keats' conception of his Lamia seems to have been further modified); and also the death of Glaucus' ideal of love and beauty in *Endymion.* In *Lamia,* at any rate, Lycius dies, while his beloved suffers final defeat through

* For the evidence in *Lamia* II, 110-31 ff., see App. v, p. 379 f.
† The canto so vital in the genesis of *St. Agnes.*
‡ For the verbal parallels and detailed evidence, see App. v, p. 383 f.

the malevolent 'demon eyes' of Apollonius—as if in conformity with the presence of the guardian Love, who is Oberon, and the promised 'for all this came a ruin.' For Keats' allusion to 'the moral' of *Oberon* is corroborated by much evidence, all of which suggests that the accurst 'joys that seduce' brought ruin to 'Love in a palace': to the sensuous love of Lamia, and to Lycius the scholar betrayed by his senses and inconstant to 'Platonic shades.' Within the framework of Burton's tale, Keats was clearly guided by the pattern of *Oberon,* to whose moral and machinery he repeatedly alluded.

The creative process, however, which governed the evolution of Keats' conception and the genesis of *Lamia,* was the most subtle, it would seem, of that of any of his longer narratives. That conclusion is supported by the detailed evidence in the Appendix, which, too voluminous for ready reading, makes fascinating material for study. The creative process often becomes visible and much of the genesis of *Lamia* is laid bare if one compares Keats' imagery with that of the 'tale from faery land,' by which once again he was profoundly influenced. Not only the structural features of *Lamia* attest this.

IV

Now that we have seen both the background, which repeatedly shines through the surface of Keats' romance, and the relationship between the human-regal phase of his heroine and the nature and function of the queen in *Oberon,* we can turn to the question of Lamia's nature and her powers and metamorphosis. That new and protean being unmistakably possesses traits both natural and supernatural for which there was small warrant in Burton. Those traits, once understood, can dispel a good deal of the bewilderment of which Colvin complained. Let us therefore try to reconstruct quickly the process by which Keats' conception appears to have evolved and review the traits we have seen. We shall then try to understand his meaning.

By Keats' own admission the initial impulse for his poem came from Burton. In the latter's brief outline of the legend, however, Lamia was a vague 'phantasm' or illusion who, after luring a youth into her palace, was exposed as *a serpent in the guise of a woman.* Led by inevitable associations and the close affinities in the episode of Wieland's more tangible enchantress-queen, Keats soon identified Lamia with her, who was much more than an illusion. Huon's temptress was first of all a beautiful African queen, even as was that Lamia, the legendary queen of Libya or Africa, who, loved by Zeus, was punished with madness and cannibal traits by the jealous Hera.* This African queen Lamia was the archetype of the later traditionally bloodthirsty seducer of handsome youths, known generically as a lamia. Eager student of Greek mythology that the author of *Endymion* and *Hyperion* was, when he had become interested in Lamia Keats may well have inquired into her antecedents. If he knew them (and since he knew the 'Historical Library' of Diodorus, he must have [11]), here was yet another striking reason for his identification of Wieland's African queen first with Burton's traditional one and then with his own Lamia.

But while Burton's 'phantasm' was essentially a serpent, Wieland's lamia-like temptress, besides being an African queen, was essentially a mortal woman possessing a striking resemblance to the fays of medieval romance, with their characteristic vein of allegory.[12] And Almansaris was also the embodiment of Oberon's curse: a voluptuous, deceitful schizophrenic: a tormented woman, only figuratively 'a wily snake.' Conceived literally, however, that trait was electric. For it recalled another tradition:

in religious and poetic tradition from the myth of Adam and Eve to Coleridge's *Christabel,* the serpent has been represented as a form of natural life *in which evil demons, especially female demons, are condemned to pass a part of their existence.* †

* Cf. the affinity in the queen's thirst for Huon's blood in her furious fit.
† Finney, op. cit. p. 701. Italics mine.

Keats, of course, knew this. His own Glaucus in a situation anticipating Lamia's spoke of this 'serpent-skin of woe.' In his favorite *Paradise Lost* he had seen Satan, 'the Enemie of Mankind, enclos'd In Serpent, Inmate bad,' who tempts Eve (*P. L.* ix, 521-2). And well before his Scottish tour of 1818 Keats had read *Christabel,* in which Geraldine, who hisses and has serpent's eyes and is familiar with all those who 'live in the upper sky,' laments her 'bosom and half her side' which had been transformed as a penance.

Thus in the light of both the ancient tradition of the serpent and his knowledge of Oberon's curse on the 'bosom snake,' powers of punitive transformation, and the penance of Titania, Keats came to conceive of the serpent-woman (Burton's 'phantasm,' embodied for Keats in Wieland's accursed queen, who had become Lamia) as *a penanced demon with serpent's traits.* This conception was inevitable since he knew that the 'wily snake,' queen

> Almansaris, in whose empassion'd blood
> A sly seducer creeps, her soul resigns,
> Follows where'er th' infernal fiend inclines,
> And sinks in willing slavery, self-subdu'd.
>
> (OBERON XII, 7)

She was visibly inflamed by the 'fiend Asmodeus,' evil demon of lust, and explicitly connected with Satan, the archetype of penanced snake and 'demon's self.' That connection probably was another reason why Lamia came to reside in a palace partly the queen's, partly Mulciber's, and partly Oberon's.

His conception of Lamia having come to embrace phantasm, queen, woman, snake, penanced demon, Keats proceeded to envision her daemonic lineage in terms of Oberon and Titania, those regal elemental spirits of the air whose forms are essentially human. It was primarily their supernatural powers which the new Lamia came to acquire. And since the penanced Titania is angelic rather than diabolic, Lamia tended to become a gentle d*ae*mon who had erred rather than the traditional evil demon. Partly through Titania,

Lamia's originally evil traits were profoundly modified; and Keats, filled with pity, evidently fell victim to her charm for some further reasons.

But the *tradition* of the lamia demanded a compromise. And the connection of Huon's queen with Oberon's curse upon the 'bosom snake,' or type of voluptuous and deceitful woman whose arts are the 'joys that seduce,' seems to have led Keats to conceive of his Lamia as a daemonic transgressor punished by the daemon king in terms of his awful curse. This is revealed not only by the forest setting and Oberon's sceptre in the scene of Lamia's visible trans-formation,* but also by the forest scene in *Otho the Great,* Keats' tragedy whose period of composition overlapped that of *Lamia.* In Act v of that play Ludolph curses the faithless and deceitful Auranthe who had been the *mistress* of another, and he does so in the very words of Oberon's curse! What is more, Ludolph explicitly terms the sensual Auranthe a *'sylph'* and *'cockatrice,'* or serpent, who should be transformed in punishment. That synchronous con-ception identifies Auranthe with Lamia, that 'penanced lady elf' and 'demon's mistress' who had been transformed into the 'gor-geous snake,' and whom we later see in her real woman's form in her 'palace of *sweet sin.'* The reason Keats conceived of Lamia as having been transformed lies in Oberon's powers, in his curse upon 'the joys that seduce,' and in the lamia-like queen's embodi-ment of that curse. This is revealed by Act v of *Otho the Great.* More plainly than *Lamia* that play shows what conceptions of sensuality and punitive transformation were in Keats' mind at this period, when personal torment led to his fascination by the tor-mented 'wily snake' who lamia-like lured Huon into her palace to try his constancy to an ideal. †

. . .

---

* Oberon's powers are revealed to Huon in the forest of Canto II, used by Keats in *Endymion* III.

† For the startling evidence in *Otho,* see App. v, p. 387 f.

That the moral, machinery, and characters of *Oberon* were all drawn into *Lamia* is clear through Keats' allusions. And that Titania, the penanced 'elfin queen,' blended in his mind with the mortal enchantress-queen is no less clear. For the impassioned blood of that tormented serpent-queen was almost visibly diluted with fairy ichor in Lamia's first appearance in the sacred isle. We saw the setting in its place in the structure and know that the time was shortly after 'Love in a hut' became volcanic ruins. And we saw how, like Oberon, Hermes heeded the mournful voice which in its 'wreathed tomb' yearned for its 'woman's shape' and 'love and pleasure.' * But after proceeding, somewhat like the queen and 'wily snake' in her gardens one evening,[13] Hermes found this:

K 45   he found a palpitating *snake,*
            Bright, and cirque-*couch*ant in a dusky brake.

47   She was a gordian *shape of dazzling* hue,
            Vermilion-spotted, *golden,* green, and blue;
49   Striped like a zebra, freckled like a pard,
            Eyed like a peacock, and all crimson barr'd;
51   And full of *silver moons,* that, as she breathed,
            Dissolv'd, or *brighter shone,* or interwreathed
53   Their *lustres* with the gloomier tapestries—
            So rainbow-sided, touch'd with miseries,
55   She seem'd, *at once, some penanced lady elf,*
            Some *demon's mistress,* or *the demon's self.*
57   Upon her crest she wore a wannish fire
            Sprinkled with stars, like Ariadne's tiar:
59   Her head was serpent, but ah, bitter-sweet!
            She had a woman's mouth with all its pearls complete:
61   And for her eyes . . .

they wept they were 'so fair'; while 'her *throat was serpent'* and yet she spoke with human voice (*Lamia* 1, 45-62). This is one of the most crucial passages in the romance.[14]

* Cf. p. 205 above.

The most striking features of the gorgeous vision are the dazzling luster half lost in the coloration of fluid patterns. Perhaps Douglas Bush is right in thinking the picture 'overdone in coloring,' but it seems doubtful that it owes much to 'hints taken from more restrained descriptions' of serpents in the *Aeneid*.[15] Keats was sensitive to the beauty of goldfish, and a good many of this serpent's colors were remembered from his own description of the nymph's fish in *Endymion*.* Be that as it may, here Keats stressed the strange brilliance: *dazzling, golden, silver, 'brighter shone,' moon, fire*. And this woman-serpent, the 'brilliance feminine' has a crest, a 'starry crown' as well as a 'woman's mouth with all its pearls complete,' and other jewels revealed later, while 'her throat was serpent.' Although the crown is conventional in serpent lore, I still suspect that this crown and the extraordinary dazzling quality and the jewels may owe something to the serpent's regal other-self, that 'wily snake,' the crowned and dazzling and jeweled queen, embodiment of the daemon king's curse upon the voluptuous *'bosom snake,'* whose *'throat* was *serpent'* only figuratively. Lamia the serpent is after all not merely a serpent, and the convulsed queen on her couch is not merely a woman; and the strange metamorphosis of the one into the other is almost at hand. The overtones in Keats' picture are not nearly so simple as has generally been thought.

One wonders too whether it is not misleading to say that 'Keats is quite deliberately discarding the method of *Christabel* and considers that the gain will more than counterbalance the loss. The contrast between the two poems, both dealing with a serpent-woman, is most illuminating.'[16] The contrast is illuminating and on Keats' part probably deliberate. Coleridge had used the 'suggestive method' as to the identity of his 'lady of a far countree' with brilliant irresolution. But while Keats shows us that the lady of his poem is a snake-woman by first showing her as snake, we

* Cf. 'All my clear-eyed fish, *Golden* or *rainbow-sided,* or purplish [*green and blue*], *Vermilion*-tail'd or finn'd with *silvery* gauze . . .' (*End.* ii, 109-11.) Cf. also *Letters*, p. 287 (March 1819).

hardly 'know from the outset exactly where we are and what the revelation is to be.'[17] Keats uses the suggestive method too, if less obtrusively than Coleridge. Keats characterizes his 'palpitating snake' with apparent vagueness: 'She seem'd,' he says knowing full well what she is, 'She seem'd, *at once,* some *penanced lady elf,* Some *demon's mistress,* or *the demon's self.*' The delicately composite nature of Lamia is hinted in the significant phrase 'at once.' This too is the suggestive method, and Keats' conception is only gradually becoming clearer in the light of the daemonology of *Oberon.*

The setting in the sacred isle where the penanced Titania strays, lovelorn and invisible, identifies the 'penanced lady elf.' And evidently it is her 'silver moons' that 'brighter shone.' In seeing 'the demon's self' Keats evidently saw Satan as serpent. But Oberon (Hermes) was still hovering in the background with his sceptre, that of the daemon king who lent some of his powers to Lamia. By 'demon's mistress' Keats may have meant Titania. But the overtones also recall the 'wily snake' and 'dazzling' enchantress subject to Asmodeus and Satan himself. 'Mistress' also suggests both Auranthe, 'sylph' and 'cockatrice,' and Lamia's desire for 'Love and pleasure' soon to be realized in her regal 'palace of sweet sin.' Not least significant, however, is the crucial phrase 'at once' which reveals her composite origin.

That is yet more brilliantly disclosed in her extraordinary metamorphosis, a hint for which Keats had heard in Huon's pleading voice.* For Oberon's wand having been exchanged as in *Endymion* † for Hermes' more appropriate 'lythe Caducean charm,' the pitying god puts it to proof, and shortly we see this:

> K 146   Left to herself, the serpent now began
> To change; her elfin blood in madness ran,
> 148   Her mouth foam'd, and the grass, therewith besprent,
> Wither'd at dew so sweet and virulent;

* Cf. p. 207 above.
† See note 7 to this chapter.

150   Her eyes in torture fix'd, and anguish drear,
       Hot, glaz'd, and wide, with lid-lashes all sear,
152   Flash'd phosphor and sharp sparks, without one cooling tear.
       The colours all inflam'd throughout her train,
154   She writh'd about, convuls'd with scarlet pain . . .

However regretfully, we must pause there. The process is the product of no simple vision, and the serpent's metamorphosis was as
complex as it was violent. 'Her elfin blood' needs no comment; the
scene is still Titania's isle. But Keats, we know, had seen deeply
into two violent scenes in the 'Love in a palace' episode of *Oberon*.
And Lamia's human prototype, the dazzling queen Almansaris into
whom the 'smooth-lipp'd serpent' is visibly changing, was herself 'a
wily snake' whose furious fit, provoked by Huon, helped conceive
the 'mitigated fury' of Lycius.* But that furious fit had also recalled serpent metamorphosis to Keats' mind. For he wrote: 'Fine
was the mitigated fury, *like* Apollo's presence When in *act to strike
the serpent.*' Why did he write 'like'? Was he thinking of Hermes'
striking the serpent Lamia? Let us glance quickly at the scene in
Almansaris' chamber where the answer may lie.

That queen, we know, is *left to herself* (cf. K 146) after the frustrated embrace ended the first phase of the youth's temptation. And
she tries to rest on her *couch,* but her soul is 'on fire, Wild passion
raging in *her fiery breast*' for 'wild groans the demon of *desire.*'
(Cf. Lamia! †) To *'madden*ing rage' (cf. K 147) her thoughts *'inflame*' her soul (cf. K 153), and we see the *'wily snake*' change indeed. Now she 'loath'd the *monster* that *bewitch'd* her sense' and
a 'dragon' (reptile?) seems more attractive. She would have him
suffer, 'drop by drop the wretch shall bleed' (suffer *scarlet pain,*
like Lamia? ‡) And she lies there mortified and sleepless, almost
visibly writhing in her impassioned frenzy, *convulsed* by opposite
passions.

* Cf. p. 221.
† The 'demon's self,' who desires 'love and pleasure.'
‡ Did it occur to Keats too that Huon is bleeding in the forest while his mourn-
ful voice hints Lamia's transformation and 'scarlet pain'?

I suspect strongly that many of the scattered fragments of Keats' picture lay here in this highly charged scene in which the 'wily snake,' Lamia's regal and human likeness, at first so *sweet* became so *virulent*. Keats, I think, realized the suggestions in the elements italicized, and challenged by them let their rich overtones become dominant and their values, both literal and symbolic, become visible actuality, even as Huon's words, 'transform'd beneath thy sight' hinted. For, let us remember, Lamia, the 'palpitating snake' couched in the forest, is in process of becoming the queen; and, full-bodied, within sixty lines she is to begin luring Lycius-Huon into 'Love in a palace' and 'more grievous torment.' Lamia the demon-snake is becoming Wieland's queen, herself a snake possessed by a demon. For all their complexity the characters are one and the same. And surely there was a reason for Keats' 'mitigated fury like . . . act to strike the serpent.'

Let us remember too that Wieland's queen in the prison scene beseeches Huon to change his purpose as Lamia does later. *Her crown* on her head, arrayed in her gorgeous robes, the dazzling queen, whose glittering jewels make her another 'brilliance feminine,' appears mysteriously in the night. Her wiles proving useless, lost in pain and desire she implores his pity.* Then, cursing his 'hell-assisted power,' 'wild *foams her lip,* her *eyes like lightning glare.*' Did that violent picture escape Keats, who wrote of his maddened snake: 'her mouth foamed' and 'eyes in torture fix'd and anguish drear . . . Flash'd phosphor and sharp sparks'? There were these and yet other hints in that 'Love in a palace' pattern to whose moral of 'grievous torment' he alluded.

But if the serpent is in process of becoming the tormented queen, she also has intermingled in her veins that *'elfin blood'* of which Keats reminds us at the very outset of Lamia's subtle metamorphosis. And in the very process of tortured change, whose setting is Titania's *volcanic* isle, that 'penanced lady elf' seems to have left her shimmering moonlight. For now Keats wrote:

* Much as does Lamia of the god before her change.

K 154   She writh'd about, convuls'd with scarlet pain:
        A deep *volcanian* yellow took the *place*
156   Of all *her milder-mooned body's grace;*
        And, as *the lava ravishes the mead* . . .

What could possibly have suggested so remote a figure here, but the ravished paradise of Titania, who when her penance has ended appears beside her fairy palace 'in moonlight's modest ray.'

157   And, as the lava ravishes the mead,
        Spoilt all her silver mail, and golden *brede,*
159   Made gloom of all her frecklings, streaks and bars,
        Eclips'd her *crescents,* and lick'd up her stars: *
161   So that, in moments few, she was undrest
        Of all *her sapphires,* greens, and *amethyst,*
163   And rubious-argent: of all these bereft,
        Nothing but *pain and ugliness* were left.
165   Still *shone her crown;* that vanish'd, also she
        Melted and disappeared . . .

in the air, like the 'demon's self' Oberon that she is too.[18]

But she is soon to reappear—as 'lady bright' with 'regal neck,' and mistress of 'royal porch.' She is to appear within a few lines as the queen herself, at the meeting with the youth. And since she is to be 'regal drest' like the queen, perhaps the crown and elusive jewels of her vanishing serpent phase came of her 'dreaming on things to come.' For the queen first appears in her *golden* bower from behind the airy curtains thus:

The queen in *brilliancy* of art array'd,
Jewels and *pearls* in *many a* curious *braid,*   K 158
Shews that th' unnotic'd *diamond*'s *sun*-like rays
Fail to *eclipse* the self-resplendent blaze . . .   K 160
             (OBERON XI, 49)

Both the 'wily snake' and the serpent, both the queen and Lamia are a vision of 'brilliance feminine.' The scattered fragments of the

* Another allusion to the moon, as the 'stars' show.

picture of the queen are too many and too suggestive, it seems to me, to be fortuitous. Stimulated by that picture, Keats evidently transmuted much of the imagery: at times its literal, at times its symbolic values were absorbed.* But, like the moral, that imagery provided quickening hints which miraculously left their traces, now more, now less visible, as, most appropriately in the light of Part II, the serpent 'beneath our sight' became the queen.

. . .

In Part I, however, Lamia is still part elfin queen and elemental daemon as well as part enchantress-queen. She is an enchantress in virtue of her kinship both with Titania and the mortal queen, of 'Love in a palace.' It is her 'elfin blood' that the critics have quite overlooked. Keats tells us explicitly that she is 'at once . . . penanced lady elf . . . demon's mistress . . . demon's self' as well as 'regal drest.' And Lycius thinks her 'of heavenly progeny' for sufficient reason: like Titania Lamia is evidently of that 'angelic band' of 'virgins' with 'ever-blooming cheeks' who appear before Oberon's tenuous fairy palace at the bridal pageant. Before her transformation into a serpent, Lamia says she had 'a woman's shape'—like Titania.† She acquired her supernatural powers directly from that queen and mistress of daemons and from the daemon king himself.

Thus she shortens the distance to Corinth by 'a spell,' even as Huon is instantaneously conveyed through the air to Tunis by Oberon's power. She melts into the air like the daemon king. And truly a 'smooth-lipp'd serpent,' she is 'surely high inspired': her long dialogue with Hermes dispels all doubt on that score. All mortals' ignorance, 'all darkness fades' before her eyes even as before Oberon's—those of *The Poet*. She knows Hermes' thoughts and motives with precisely such insight as Oberon has; and like

---

* Thus 'Nothing but pain and ugliness were left' is true both of Lamia, the serpent changing into the queen, and that queen in her furious fit which reveals the 'wily snake' possessed by a demon.

† Cf. Titania, 'a woman veil'd' in the elfin grot, p. 255.

his so do her senses transcend elemental space.* She saw Hermes depart from Olympus, even as Oberon, atop the mountain by the Nile, from afar sees and hears the mournful Huon in the sacred isle. She saw Hermes break through the clouds to that same sacred isle—like Oberon's 'viewless' gentle sprite. She tells Hermes of his nymph who, like Titania, 'free as the air invisibly . . . strays . . . by my power'; and at her will the nymph once more becomes visible. Oberon has this power over all beings in virtue of the talisman. †

Lamia's daemonic nature again becomes explicit at her meeting with Lycius when, among other things, she says:

> 'Thou art a scholar, Lycius, and must know
> 'That finer spirits cannot breathe below
> 'In human climes, and live: Alas! poor youth,
> 'What taste of purer air hast thou to soothe
> 'My essence? What serener palaces,
> 'Where I may all my many senses please . . .'
>
> (LAMIA I, 279-84)

Then she rises 'Tiptoe with white arms spread,' like one of her aerial kindred. At the same time, however, she 'Put her new lips to his' the more surely to lure the youth into her palace. Later, in her composite enchanted palace with its 'noise of wings' she 'faded at self-will' and has just such 'viewless servants' as Oberon.

In that palace, of course, she is primarily the mortal queen. But in Part II there are also hints that her protean nature underwent further modification. For while Keats derived his daemonology consistently from *Oberon,* during the composition period of *Lamia* he also read Fouqué's *Undine,* that charming romance of a lesser daemonic princess, the elemental water spirit, who upon falling in

---

* Cf. *Lamia* I, 200 ff.: 'how she could muse and dream . . . of all she list . . . how ever, where she will'd, her spirit went' through the four elements of air, water, earth, and fire. The passage is pure daemonology.

† Not only is he invisible at will, but he can compel all beings into his presence: 'shall *any* being stand before his sight? Let him but press the ring . . . Be it or man, or beast, or ghost [spirit], or shade, Lo! at his beck it bows . . .', VII, 35.

love with a mortal acquires a soul and its sorrows. Ultimately Undine returns to her watery element, and her lover having proved unfaithful dies on his wedding night. We have seen the death of Lycius. But earlier he suspects that Lamia is 'a Naiad' whose 'far wishes . . . streams obey' (1, 261 ff.). And there are many other echoes and phrases in *Lamia* which strongly suggest that in Keats' poem, which had become a daemonic romance through *Oberon,* the untraditional nature of Lamia (who *is* 'of heavenly progeny') was further modified by that of Undine.*

Finally, however, Lamia, the penanced lady elf, was profoundly humanized: she became a 'real woman' because her creator had come to feel the spell of a woman's beauty and had known torment at first hand.

V

Thus we come to the meaning of *Lamia.* While he also drew upon other materials, his allusions and the restored background make clear that Keats in conceiving his romance was profoundly influenced by the structure, incidents, machinery, and imagery, as well as by the characters and moral of *Oberon.* It would seem that, when in a period of personal torment he had come upon the sinister legend in Burton, Keats was led by characteristic associations to identify the traditional Lamia with the tormented and snakelike African queen in *Oberon.* Her function, as an agent of the daemon king, was to tempt the youth she lured into her palace, and with *sensual 'joys that seduce' test his constancy to an ideal of love and beauty.* Keats, torn between love for a woman and desire for immortality, significantly contrasted 'Love in a hut'—where the hermit found immortality in spiritual love of the divine—with sensual 'Love in a palace.' Evidently the queen's function and fate in *Oberon* helped Keats identify the lamia legend with his own tormented existence: in which the single-hearted ascetic's life, in the transcendent visions of Poetry, had been terminated by fate and

* For evidence of this, see App. v, p. 393.

love of woman.* No longer could he say as in *Endymion,* 'a hermit⧓ young I'll live.' He had lost his freedom for that, lost it to love and its torments.

Oberon enabled Keats to reject Lamia's traditionally evil traits, to pity her, and to conceive of her as a gentle penanced lady elf. It helped him to expand and transpose the legend, as he had that of Glaucus, and to create the machinery and incidents of his poem, which became a daemonic romance. But it was his own experience of a multiple conflict which lent that romance its poignant life and passion. There is little question that, with help from the moral of *Oberon,* in the course of its genesis *Lamia* acquired symbolical values born of the poet's own anguish: *in the inner clash of the sensuous man*—and his need for beauty, pleasure, woman—*with his spiritual nature*—his hunger for knowledge and achievement, fame and immortality.† In his own life at this time Keats craved yet sought to reject the 'joys that seduce' from constancy to his quest of fame. Young and harassed as he was, he knew not how to reconcile his desires.

Thus his Lamia—'the serpent! certes, she was none'—is no more 'a thing of bale' or 'a witch,' but a lovely elemental creature of passion. An elfin being, she is also a 'real woman' whose beauty, like that of the Fanny Brawne of the letter,‡ trammels the lover's senses in her potent spells without satisfying his restless ambition and intellectual needs. In view of her daemonic powers, she may well have been intended also as a larger symbol.[19] For her lover Lycius, while like Glaucus both the youth of the legend and Sir Huon in the 'purple-lined palace of sweet sin,' in part is Keats himself—and eternal young manhood torn between two fundamental needs, of body and soul. In part he is the poet-scholar in love with sensuous beauty—a beautiful woman, who is incapable

---

* In other words, spiritual 'love in a hut' had for him become 'cinders, ashes, dust.'

† Hence Lycius hears the trumpet call from the world of achievement. Cf. p. 219.

‡ Cf. p. 194.

of satisfying the needs of his reason but for whom nonetheless he is inconstant to his spiritual ideals or 'Platonic shades.'

Apollonius and the guests have also become symbols of forces Keats had felt: the forces that, released by a trumpet call from the world of fame and care, destroyed the 'sense of oneness' and his soul's inner peace, the sufficiency of beauty, and eventually the dream realm and the living vision of beauty. If the guests are the world which the poet-lover cannot ignore, Apollonius is his teacher, 'philosophy' and insistent reason. With 'eye severe' and 'patient thought' he is reason and knowledge in the realm of intuition: the coldly critical mind inimical to imaginative insight as to dreams of beauty and illusions of joy. He is the wisdom which Keats as intuitive poet felt to be folly: as Lycius says, the spirit or 'ghost of folly haunting my sweet dreams.' [20]

Thus *Lamia,* while at first without a 'palpable design upon us,' came to reflect the sympathy of self-projection. It came to touch upon Keats' wavering constancy of purpose, or 'abatement of my love of fame'; and upon his life-long struggle to reconcile intuition and reason, imagination and thought, sensation and knowledge, spirituality and sensuousness, beauty and man's suffering. And it came to touch upon one of the essential ironies of his and all human life: the simultaneous ripening of body and mind—powers so often antagonistic, intellect and sex.[21] Their conflict in Lycius, who with 'bewitch'd . . . sense' hungers after fame, and for whom 'a moment's thought is passion's passing bell,' makes universal and inevitable the human tragedy of Lamia's love, a tragedy which the intervention of Apollonius merely hastens. Before his arrival Lamia, the lovely woman, feels deserted for fame and says, 'Ay, it must be so.'

Ultimately the taut romance, so complex in its genesis and so closely related to the 'pleasure thermometer' in *Endymion,* was enriched by sorrowful overtones. *Lamia* became a confession piece which, while not always unified, or consistent in its intention, or perfectly integrated with the legend, is close to tragic reality.[22]

❧ VI ❦

Symbols and Overtones: 1818-1819

BOTH *Lamia* and *The Eve of St. Agnes* are romances based upon legends of earthly love. Both were more or less closely connected with portions of *Endymion,* and therefore indirectly with 'Love in a hut' in *Oberon.* The central figure in that spiritualizing episode Keats had had in mind when writing the induction and the thematic passage of *Endymion,* concerning which he had written to John Taylor early in 1818:

My having written that Argument will perhaps be of the greatest Service to me of anything I ever did. It set before me . . . the gradations of Happiness even like a . . . Pleasure Thermometer . . .[1]

In saying this Keats was not exaggerating. The philosophy of life and art in that argument—of the gradations of happiness, as culminating in communion with the divine, and of a life of transcendental sensations and highest contemplation, which reveal the divine Love and Beauty as ultimate Truth: that philosophy was uttered in more works than *Endymion.* And since Keats had formulated his creed in symbols derived from the hermit, those symbols also reappear again and again. In more than a dozen poems of 1818-19, including *Lamia* and some of the great 'Odes, the symbols based upon the hermit's experience of gradual spiritualization and the divine fountain of purest joy reappear. With the key in mind, various thoughts in those poems become more clear, and the essential unity of Keats' message is emphasized. In this chapter, accordingly, we shall examine the shorter pieces and try to interpret those symbols which he had derived from Titania's *Elysium.*

While still engaged in copying *Endymion* (in the fourth Book of which he had said: 'A hermit young, I'll live in *mossy cave* . . . and lave Thy spirit in the wonders I shall tell'), Keats wrote, in February 1818, the *Lines on the Mermaid Tavern*. They begin thus:

> Souls of Poets dead and gone,
> What Elysium have ye known,
> Happy field or *mossy cavern*,
> Choicer than the Mermaid Tavern?

In this twofold Elysium the joyous field is Grecian, but the mossy cavern is that of Titania's isle where dwelt the ascetic hermit-sage.

In September-December 1818 Keats wrote *Hyperion, a Fragment*. Its opening lines contain echoes from two stanzas of *Oberon*, which adjoin elements drawn into both *Endymion* and Madeline's 'visions of delight' in *The Eve of St. Agnes*. And Titania's grief in her cavern seems to have left traces in the famous description of the den of the Titans in *Hyperion* ii, 6 ff.[2]

Shortly after the death of Tom Keats, in December 1818, in *Bards of Passion and of Mirth* the overtones from the hermitage seem particularly rich. Keats wrote that the immortal bards have left their souls on earth, yet have souls in heaven too. There they commune with sun and moon, and are

> Seated on *Elysian* lawns
> Brows'd by none but *Dian*'s fawns
> Underneath large blue-bells tented,

an allusion to the fairies of Shakespeare's Titania-Diana? But

> Where the daisies are *rose*-scented,
> And *the rose* herself has got *
> Perfume which on earth is not;
> *Where the nightingale doth sing*
> Not a senseless, tranced thing,
> But *divine* melodious *truth*;

* Emblem of Wieland's Titania-Diana.

Philosophic numbers smooth;
Tales and golden histories
Of heaven and its mysteries.

The stream of associations is characteristic: moon, Diana, a two-fold Titania. 'Elysian,' and 'Dian,' and 'the rose' all point to Titania in the hermitage. The divine truth, which the hermit had discovered there through suffering, now is sung by the mystical nightingale. It is noteworthy that the 'nightingale upperched high' had sung of 'her love' a few lines beyond 'love's elysium' in the thematic passage of *Endymion*.[3] There God is Love and highest beauty and truth. And in that 'love's elysium' the hermit and the lovers strayed and the former found highest bliss and immortality.

Evidently Keats had recalled this. For now that poet and 'hermit young' wrote of his *blissful bards:*

> Thus ye live on high, and then
> On the earth ye live again;
> And the souls ye left behind you *
> *Teach us,* here, *the way to find you,*†
> *Where your other souls are joying,*
> Never slumber'd, never cloying.
> Here, your earth-born souls still speak
> To mortals, of their little week;
> Of their sorrows and delights . . .‡

But Keats meant that the bard in Elysium is a sage who, like the hermit in Titania's Elysium, had achieved immortal bliss in God. Like the nightingale, who sings 'divine melodious truth . . . of heaven,' the bard, through his art and poet's (cf. mystic's) vision, teaches mortals how to achieve bliss in heaven. Like the hermit, of the gradations of happiness and 'fellowship with essence,'

* In your poems on earth.
† In heaven.
‡ Note the overtones from the 'pleasure thermometer' in this line.

> Thus ye teach us, every day,
> *Wisdom,* though fled far away.

Keats, the 'hermit young,' had identified himself and his master
with the bards.[4]

    .   .   .

It was, however, during the feverish year 1819 that Keats' absorption in Wieland's romance bore its richest fruit. Besides its
vital connection with the genesis first of *The Eve of St. Agnes*
(January) and then of *Lamia* (summer), *Oberon* left its traces next
in three poems written within a few days of one another, toward
the end of April 1819. I refer to the *Song of Four Fairies, La Belle
Dame sans Merci,* and the first of the great Odes, *To Psyche,* all
of which Keats copied into the long journal-letter to George Keats,
in which he wrote of the 'vale of Soul-making' and less significant
topics.[5]

The 'tripping little fragment' or composite *Song of Four Fairies*
is not merely an interesting experiment in rhythmical variation.[6]
It reveals Keats' continuous preoccupation with the daemonology
of Wieland's romance and of Paracelsian fable, as well as a characteristic fusing process. The fairies, as their names show, are elemental spirits of fire, air, earth, and water. Yet the water spirit
Breama derived a thought from the *Midsummer Night's Dream*
in saying:

> 'Like our Queen, when she would please
> To sleep, and Oberon will teaze.'

These are obviously Shakespeare's Oberon and Titania. But it is
the aerial spirit *Zephyr,* most appropriately, who replies:

> 'Come with me, *o'er tops of trees,*
> To my *fragrant palaces,*
> Where they ever *floating* are
> Beneath the cherish of a star

Call'd Vesper, who with silver *veil*
Ever hides his brilliance pale,
Ever gently-drows'd doth keep
Twilight for the Fayes to *sleep.*'

This is a reminiscence of the diaphanous palace of the aerial spirits
in Wieland's romance. It is the palace of *Oberon,* girt with fragrant
rose trees amid the enchanted forest, as beheld from the aerial car
'While *zephyrs* fan the clouds that round the chariot flew.' It is
the daemons' palace that appears where 'twilight sweeps Her veil
of shapeless mist' and the moon admires her image that 'calm beneath her sleeps' in many a lake, while 'as if woven from the rosy
eve, Radiant before their sight *a floating palace* springs.' (*Oberon*
xii, 67-8.) It had already left its mark on Neptune's home (*End.* iii)
and was yet to color the faery roof of *Lamia.* But its appearance
here, together with elements gleaned from Shakespeare and Paracelsian lore, is peculiarly illuminating, for it is a transparent example in miniature of a typical coalescence of related conceptions.

Now it is important to remember that it was into the same journal-letter on the same 28 April that Keats, preoccupied with Wieland's daemonology, copied his dreamlike ballad *La Belle Dame
sans Merci.* The connection of that ballad with *Oberon* is suggested
not only by its exact concurrence in date with the 'Fairy Song,' but
also because there was another link with the romance: namely, the
circumstance that Keats had first mentioned the title of the ballad
a few months earlier, as that of the 'ancient ditty long since mute'
sung by Porphyro in *The Eve of St. Agnes.** He had mentioned
it there in the lute-playing scene which owed so much to the queen
of the voluptuous 'visions of delight.' But in connection with 'Love
in a palace' in *Lamia,* we saw the cruelty of that same queen, who
with 'bewitch'd . . . sense' feels that 'Death, tenfold death, shall
expiate the offence'—the offence of the youth who spurned her love

* Cf. stanza xxxiii and ch. iv, p. 176 above.

and whom later she lures into her shadowy grot. In conjunction
with the somewhat similar theme of Keats' ballad, all this is not
without significance.* And in connection with the wild demonic
nature of Wieland's enchantress-queen, the title of Porphyro's
'ancient ditty' was peculiarly apt.

The queen, we know, was soon to become the human and regal
counterpart of Lamia and was to lend herself readily to the genesis
of that romance for many reasons. Not the least of them was her
close affinity with those traditional fays of romance familiar to
every reader of medieval story as regal enchantresses, often mortal
and residing in glamorous remoteness, who seek the love of a
mortal knight. † This circumstance is significant here because La
Belle Dame, who lures a youth into her grot, obviously is some
such enchantress, destructive and sensual like the traditional Lamia
and the queen. And there is evidence in the magical ballad that
Keats conceived of her nature as a composite one, somewhat as he
was to envision Lamia's infinitely more complex nature, in the light
of 'the moral' of the 'tale from faery land,' some few months later.

The cause of the conflict Keats was experiencing in these months
has already been discussed. And La Belle Dame's victim is a
'wretched wight, So haggard and so woe-begone.' ‡ He has 'a lilly'
on his brow ('death's lilly,' Keats first wrote) and 'a fading rose'
withers in his cheek. Like Sir Launfal and many another knight
he had met 'a lady in the meads' (originally Keats wrote 'wilds'),
a lady who was a strange and subtle being. For she was

K 14   Full beautiful, *a faery's child* . . . §

He set her on his pacing steed; and

* Cf. also Glaucus' 'arbour queen' of sense.
† Cf. Introduction, p. 11.
‡ The text of the ballad given here is that of *The Indicator,* as printed in the Oxford Standard Authors edition, edited by H. Buxton Forman, 1929, p. 354 f. This
version differs in a few details from extant copies, notably in the opening lines and
in the transposition of stanzas v and vi; but it contains several other features significant here. For all variants, see Garrod, op. cit. p. 441 f.
§ Cf. Titania.

K 19   . . . sideways would she lean and *sing*
         A faery's *song.**

21   I made a garland for her head,
         And bracelets too, and fragrant zone; †
23   *She look'd at me as she did love,*
         *And made sweet moan.**

25   She found me roots of relish sweet,
         And honey wild, and manna dew;

As Endymion did in the mossy cave episode—like Huon for Rezia
in the mossy cave, when they had been punished for sinfully consummating their love.

K 27   And sure in language strange she said,
         I love thee true.

As the princess Rezia did in the mossy cave. ‡

K 29   She took me to *her elfin grot,*
         And there she gaz'd and sighed deep,
31   And there I shut her wild sad eyes—
         So *kiss'd to sleep.*

Can the lovers' grot have coalesced with Titania's and the queen's?

33   And there *we slumber'd on the moss,*
         And there I dream'd, ah woe betide,
35   The latest dream I ever dream'd
         On the cold hill side.

37   *I saw pale kings,* and *princes* too,
         Pale *warriors, death-pale were they all,*
39   Who cry'd—'La belle Dame sans merci
         Hath thee in thrall!'

* Cf. the queen.
    † Cf. Huon, who weaves garlands for Rezia just before his trial by the queen
(*Ob.* xi, 2).
    ‡ Huon reproaches himself for his sin and its punishment: 'To see thee thus
from every bliss remov'd, All that *in Bagdad* serv'd' and loved (vii, 70). But Rezia
('' Tis my heart speaks') replies with ardent faith: 'I did it for myself, because I
lov'd' (vii, 77). Keats' 'language strange' was an oriental tongue, I suspect.

And that bondage and their appearance are as significant as this:

> 41   I saw *their starv'd lips* in the gloam
> With horrid warning gaped wide,
> 43   And I awoke, and found me here
> On the cold hill side.

The ballad is sheer witchery, the diction no less than the spirit. As has long been thought, Keats may possibly have drawn upon Spenser's Phaedria and even some lines in Shakespeare's *Pericles*.[7] But with the moral and incidents of the fairy tale in mind, Keats' magical sequence of pictures becomes highly significant and, I think, more meaningful. For the fated lovers in *Oberon* had been involved in a similar series of pictures, in almost identical reversed sequence.

First they had witnessed a macabre scene, on fleeing from the deathlike enchanted palace of Rezia's *kingly* father and his emirs or *princes* and all his warrior guests (cf. K 37-8) with the help of the daemon king's elfin storm. As they fled, Rezia

> . . . with side-glance upon her father cast,   K 19
> Who seems in *slumb'rous death* to *stare aghast*,   K 33, 38, 42
> . . . sighs, while stealing woes . . . her heart assail.
> (v, 76)

But more than her father lay thus. For when the lovers are gone,

> A fearful silence thro' the castle reigns:
> Still as the grave, and peaceful as *the dead*,
> The guards *lies here and there around them* spread.   K 38
> (v, 79)

All the inmates, princely and others, of the enchanted castle lay as in death through Oberon's power.

Keats had used this scene, so like the wretched wight's dream, only a few months before he wrote *La Belle Dame;* that is, in the

last stanza of *The Eve of St. Agnes,* only nine stanzas beyond
Porphyro's singing of the ancient ditty, after which the ballad was
named. And he had transmuted it thus:

> And they are gone: ay, ages long ago
> These lovers fled away into the storm.
> That night the Baron *dreamt* of many a *woe,**
> And all his *warrior*-guests, with shade and form
> Of witch, and demon, and large *coffin*-worm,
> Were long be-nightmar'd . . .

How came the wretched knight, victim of La Belle Dame, to
dream much the same dream: 'I dream'd, ah woe betide' a vision of
'pale kings' and princess and 'warriors' lying as in death? Much
the same dream it is, and for good reason. The Baron, we know,
was originally a king, a sultan to be precise. And the wretched
knight seems to dream of him with Sir Huon's reminiscent eyes.
Keats, I think, was in part retracing the earlier pattern. He evidently saw the scene of the lovers' flight as if in a fearful dream
dreamed by Huon in the mossy cave of penance—penance for the
sinful consummation of love. And in the process a phrase from his
own *St. Agnes* was drawn in.

What had happened, after the flight and vengeful tempest, to
Huon and Rezia? Their sin against spiritual love had caused them
to be cast up on the desert isle (VII, 38). Huon had borne 'the
eastern queen' to the mossy cave.[8] First they had been rapturous:
'O love! thou only balm of every woe'; and Rezia in *'this* savage
grot' had been more happy than in 'golden halls by pomp imperial
trod'; † while Huon 'to her bosom prest becomes a god'—a manifold hint Keats had taken for *Endymion.* Then another phase of
Oberon's punitive power is brought into play and the pictures
change. For soon Huon, still in the mossy cave episode, exclaims
over his love:

* Cf. *La Belle Dame,* lines 34 and 38.
† VII, 39-41. Note the link with the king in his hall.

'Keen *famine* o'er thee hangs, and eyes *thy swift decline!'*
(VII, 45)

(Why did La Belle Dame's victims have 'starv'd lips'?) And both
sinful lovers seem about to perish, and full of 'heart-tormenting
anguish,'

. . . *pale* as the cheek with *death-dew* icy cold,
They on each other gaze; heart-broken pair.   K 30
(VII, 53)

(Keats wrote: 'I see a lilly on thy brow, With anguish moist and
fever dew' (K 9-10). Was the lily an emblem of more than the
knight's 'swift decline'?) And after Huon *sought food for his love*
(K 25) and the golden fruit proved bitter and rotten, Rezia in
her punishment,

Yet still, and meek and mild, with rayless eyes,
Parch'd lip, and pallid cheek . . . sighs,   K 41, 30
'Oh! let me on thy breast . . . expire!

'And ah! how sweet to die upon thy breast!
And thanks to *the avenger,* kind in *death . . .'*
(VII, 54-5)

Explicitly, sensual love is linked with this, the daemon-avenger's
punishment: a mossy cave, two lovers, lily, rose,[8] starvation, anguish, death-dew, pallor, parched lips, death. And these concepts
were linked, through Huon's bitter self-accusation, with Bagdad
and its macabre scene of the deathlike king and princes and
warrior-guests, other victims of Oberon's power.

Is the similar configuration—of setting, images, spirit—in Keats'
ballad multiple coincidence? In the light of *St. Agnes,* the 'Fairy
Song' written the same day as the ballad, and *Endymion,* it hardly
seems possible. Moreover Huon's agonized prayer for water for
Rezia is heard by Oberon.* And *in their grot,* refreshed and with
new hope:

* As by the 'fountain nymph' in *Endymion* (II, 119), for Keats had used this
scene before.

Their meeting arms *embrace,* all woe forgot:
. . . when *their lips* once more had drain'd the   K 32
bowl,
Sleep, balm of grief, mild soother of the soul,
Deigns with light touch their weary limbs unbind;
And *on the moss* that fring'd the rill, reclin'd   K 33

they slumber (vii, 60). Keats' lovers kissed and 'slumber'd on the
moss' in the elfin grot. The pictures are substantially the same. And
Keats' wretched knight forthwith dreams a more sinister counterpart of Huon's vision of the royal hall in Bagdad.

Evidently all these pictures that he knew so well had blended in
Keats' mind. For his Belle Dame is a strange composite. She is a
'faery's child' and 'wept, and sigh'd full sore' in her 'elfin grot' like
the penanced Titania. And she lures a youth into her grot, looks
at him 'as she did love,' and sings and 'made sweet moan' like the
accurst queen of 'bewitch'd . . . sense'—who had promised 'death,
tenfold death' for the youth's offense. Yet La Belle Dame declares
her love, slumbers on the moss, receives 'kisses four,' and is involved
in the search for food and the dream of death—much like Rezia in
the mossy cave of penance. All this seems another typical coalescence of related conceptions: a coalescence of three grots linked
with sensual love, and of three lovely ladies who undergo a penance. It would seem that through the 'almost chemical affinities'
of elements in common, the grots and the ladies had coalesced in
Keats' mind and had become a new composite in which features
of all are blended.*

The composite seems to have derived its meaning from the enchantress-queen, who had hovered in the background when

---

* It is suggestive that as early as in the 'Epistle' *To My Brother George* there
is this: 'For there *the lily* and the musk-*rose* sighing, *are emblems* true *of hapless
lovers dying.'* In connection with that same poem we saw that 'From [Titania's]
pale *cheek* the *withering roses fell.'* And in *La Belle Dame* Keats wrote: 'death's
lilly . . . And on thy cheek a fading rose Fast withereth too.'

The ballad is clearly a tissue of recollections blended deep in 'the well' of subconscious memory.

Porphyro played the ancient ditty 'La Belle Dame.' It was the queen who *lured* the knight into her grot and promised death, for she was the embodiment of sensual love. What else was La Belle Dame?

The latter seems to have fulfilled the queen's threat and to have actually destroyed the pale kings and princes, as if by Oberon's power over the deathlike sleepers. And to the wretched knight who seems on the point of death (like Huon in his punishment by Oberon), the warning that 'La belle Dame . . . Hath thee in thrall' reveals both the moral and the identity of the lady, who, patently like the queen, is the symbol of sensual love.

The subliminal coalescence, and the telescoping of concepts, and the intensification by focusing the pictures more sharply, make the ballad particularly fascinating. It is the quintessence of the theme of sensuality and torment. The wretched knight undergoes Huon's experience of some phases of the punishment meted out by the daemon king—namely, feverish anguish, and sensations of imminent death. Huon's starvation, on the other hand, has become part of that other phase of punishment which he witnessed in the royal hall (namely, deathlike sleep of those enchanted), and which has changed into the wretched knight's dream in the composite grot. The manifold punishment of sensuality is the same, but in the ballad it has been reapportioned.

Notwithstanding their new intensity, the pictures and the pattern and the moral and the creative process of fluid integration anticipate *Lamia*. Like the latter, and the tale of Glaucus, and that of Auranthe, the ballad concerns the punishment of sensual love. But in the ballad almost the same ingredients blended completely. So subtly interwoven of recollections of sweet sin and anguished penance, the ballad, infused with the 'true wild weird spirit' of balladry and romance, is a transmuted product of the imagination at highest tension. The ingredients have been dissolved and their identity distilled in a dreamlike masterpiece.

.   .   .

Particularly in 1819, Keats was intensely absorbed in *Oberon*. It is a visionary as well as daemonic romance, in which the second phase of penance leads from the mossy cave directly to the hermitage. Let us bear this in mind. For the *Ode to Psyche* was composed almost at the same time as the 'Fairy Song' and the ballad and was copied into the same journal-letter only two days later than they, namely, on 30 April. In the letter Keats reverted to the 'vale of Soul-making'—his significant phrase for a world of suffering. And in the Ode, it is clear, Titania's elfin grot in the silent daemon-haunted forest enclosed by steep mountains in several wild ridges that cross the lonely isle, recurs too. It appears, however, in its visionary phase, as the site of the hermit's or aged priest's highest contemplating, as in the thematic passage of *Endymion*. It reappears in the *Ode to Psyche,* or soul, as the haunted grove and fane amid the mountain forest sacred to Titania-Diana. In the Ode, for several good reasons, Keats reverted to his derivative Latmos and its prototype in *Oberon,* the resort of 'shapes of the viewless world' and angelic harmonies that emanate from Titania's elfin grot.

In the composite Ode Keats laments the neglect of the worship of Psyche, who has 'no *shrine,* no *grove,* no oracle.' He says:

K 36   O brightest! though too late for antique vows,
         Too, too late for the fond believing lyre,
  38   When *holy* were the *haunted forest* boughs,
         Holy the *air,* the *water,* and the *fire* . . .

Where the daemonic elements appear in Keats, Oberon their ruler is not far off. He had not been far off in the 'Fairy Song' and the ballad, and Titania hovers invisible here too. For in the next stanza Keats, evidently with his Latmos and *Endymion* in mind as well as their source, says:

K 50   Yes, I will be thy priest, and build a fane
         In some untrodden region of my mind,
  52   Where branched thoughts, *new grown* with *pleasant pain,*
         Instead of pines shall murmur in the wind:

54   Far, far *around* shall those *dark-cluster'd trees*
        Fledge the *wild-ridged mountains steep* by steep;
56   And *there by zephyrs,** streams, and birds, and bees,
        The moss-lain Dryads *shall be lull'd to sleep;*
58   And in the midst of this wide quietness
        A rosy sanctuary will I dress
60   With the *wreath'd* trellis of a working brain,
        With *buds* . . .

In small compass this fascinating stanza reveals the weaving of the poet-priest's 'working brain,' as, led by the mysterious powers of association, it wanders among the dissolving scenes of memory.

Transparently his mind breathed the pure air of Latmos, and felt the spiritualizing power of nature (cf. K 56). And as in the opening lines of *Endymion,* the hermit-priest-poet were one. 'In some untrodden region' Endymion had wandered and seen visions until he found the rose tree. A rose had budded beneath his sight, from which emerged a golden butterfly. The wanderer had followed it 'like a newborn spirit' (cf. K 52), until he descended into the underworld and discovered the bower of Adonis—which had been colored by Titania's elfin grot and the childbirth scene. Did Keats remember? The italicized images read consecutively answer that question.

Keats' mind was retracing a portion of the *Endymion* pattern and its radiant background. The reason, I think, was in the budding rose. For the butterfly that emerged from it was the symbol of Psyche. By way of that recollection the whole tissue of thought and pictures, their coloring and symbolism flashed upon his inner eye and so poured forth as by magic. His mind had flown 'quick as fairy thought' to the local habitation of *Endymion.* And somehow, from the hermitage and Titania's rosy sanctuary in the sacred grove enclosed by steep mountains, his thought fled down a year to the mountains of Wales where he had used the verb 'fledge' in

* Aerial spirits, as in the *Song of Four Fairies.*

a letter to Tom that he had recently reread.[9] Endymion and the hermit's vision, in Titania's paradise, since it resembles Adam's vision in Eden, seems to have recalled Milton, who also left his marks on the Ode.[10] And the thought of fanes and temples and soul seems to have awakened a slumbering line from Spenser.[11] All poured into the Ode and blended, but the hermitage that so profoundly affected Keats' deepest thoughts of 'Soul-making' left the most visible and most numerous traces. Examining them with the raw stuff at hand illumines the creative process. What therefore had Keats seen in the hermitage that was recalled in the Ode?

Among a profusion of pictures, he had seen these. From the mossy cave (of the ballad), the grot near the shore of 'the desert isle *untrodden* far and wide' he had seen Huon ascending despite the '*wild* confusion' of crags and cliffs, until he finds the single path through the wooded pass that leads to the edge of the *holy* and *haunted* hermitage (cf. K 38). There he had seen 'the wanderer' sink as if spellbound into

A little dell with twilight shade o'ercast.
His wearied limbs with nameless shudders thrill,
Slow as he totters down the gloomy hill.
It seems as if terrestrial footsteps rude   K 51
On the dark *shrine* of loneliness intrude,   K 34
And dare invade . . .

the *silent* realm of shades, as the main *ridge* is overpassed (*Oberon* viii, 1). We saw that Endymion followed the same path as Huon's —'Thro' the *steep mountains* to a dell profound' (viii, 3. Cf. K 55) and that both encounter the hermit-priest. Huon meets him where

No trace of man had ever cheer'd his sight,   K 51

· · ·

Where *from the* rocks that every way *surround,*
O'ershadowing fir-*trees* spread a *gloom* profound . . .   K 54
(viii, 5)

and where Titania's sanctuary is. That site, where

> . . . the *mountains round* in guardian rows   K 54-5
> Shelter the bosom that their heights enclose,
> (VIII, 12)

is Keats' 'untrodden region of my mind.' The verbal echoes are as revealing as the topography and the sanctuary itself.

But Titania's elfin grot now underwent a metamorphosis. Precisely as Keats says (K 58), it is 'in the midst of this wide quietness'—that of a silent realm of shades. Toward the end of Canto VIII Rezia is guided invisibly through the murmuring forest and 'the incense' of blossoming boughs, until mysteriously she enters the otherwise inaccessible ivy-screened elfin grot of Titania (cf. K 59). And Rezia's hour having come, she feels sharp pains shoot through her body and *lies* upon *roses* and *moss*. (Cf. K 57: the 'moss-lain Dryads.') Then softly her senses dissolve and she beholds this vision:

> It seems, that o'er her eyes pale moon-beams glide,
> Gradual, in deep and deeper shadow dy'd,
> Till softly *hush'd to sleep*, oblivion stills her heart.   K 57

That picture is doubly significant, for it suggested Keats' *'The moss-lain* Dryads shall be *lull'd to sleep'* (K 57) by way of some 'low lull'd echoes' in the next *Oberon* stanza. From the same picture of Rezia slumbering, lulled to sleep in the elfin grot, also came a line in *La Belle Dame sans Merci*.*

But let us go on with Rezia's vision:

---

*Written about the same time as the Ode, *La Belle Dame* reads thus in the same journal-letter: 'She took me to her elfin grot And there she wept, and sigh'd full sore.' (Titania sighs and weeps and grieves for Oberon in her penance, contiguous stanzas show.) 'And there I shut her wild wild eyes With kisses four. And there *she lulled me* asleep . . .' La Belle Dame is still partly the penanced elfin queen, and the knight for the moment is Rezia, who is lulled just so in the elfin grot. Did the kisses come from Huon's three in Bagdad, before the eyes of the king and princes and warrior-guests?

. . . from within her a confusion gleams
Of lovely shapes; some o'er her sweep, some roll'd,
Each in the other floating, fold on fold;
Mixture of wond'rous mood—and now it seems
Before her knees three lovely angels stand:

the aerial spirits, the zephyrs of the 'Fairy Song' and of K 56.

Clear to her gaze their mystic rites expand:
And, lo! a woman veil'd in roseate ray,*
Holds to her lips, as dies her breath away,
A *wreath* of *roses* fresh that *bud* beneath her hand.   K 59
(VIII, 71-2)

And that, occurring in the 'rosy sanctuary,' clearly became 'the wreath'd trellis of a working brain, With buds.' In *Endymion* the golden butterfly, symbol of Psyche, had flown from out a rose that 'buds beneath his sight.' Visibly the patterns had overlapped.

The working brain also performed other wonders. For Rezia's slumber, in the 'elfin grot' of *La Belle Dame* or the 'rosy sanctuary' of the Ode, continues thus:

For the last time her higher beating heart
Thrills *with* a short and softly-silenc'd *pain*—   K 52
The forms are fled away—she swoons again—
And now, without remembrance of a smart,
Wakes to *soft notes,* and seems *afar* to hear   K 53
Their low-*lull'd* echoes dying from the ear . . .   K 57
(VIII, 73)

Those 'lull'd echoes' are the fading music of the aerial spirits, or zephyrs, by which not only Rezia but 'The moss-lain Dryads shall be lull'd to sleep' (K 56-7). Not only did Keats transmute the mountain hermitage and that aerial fairy music which we have heard repeatedly. Occurring in the elfin grot in the childbirth scene, that music seems to have blended with Keats' '. . . branched

* Titania.

thoughts, *new grown* with *pleasant pain.*' The verbal echoes and contiguity with the rosy sanctuary in the same untrodden mountainous region hint that the 'branched thoughts' were born in Rezia's pleasant pain. In like manner, her mortal child was probably brother to Endymion's 'new-born spirit' that guides him to the slumbering figure in the bower of Adonis.

A rereading of Keats' transmuted stanza in the light of all these pictures that he knew so well is most rewarding. Yet at the same time it confronts us with the mystery which is the creative imagination. In the distilling and transmuting process, Titania's elfin grot was transformed again and again as the shaping imagination, controlled by the poet's will and the determining pattern, would have it transform. We can watch the mutations of the ingredients. We can see how grot and aerial music and charming childbirth scene, aerial spirits, and Rezia visibly dissolve by some magical alchemy. But what came of the mixture is each time something new and different and unpredictable. Here clearly it produced a stanza in an ode to the soul, in a vale of soul-making.

*   *   *

The conflict he was undergoing explains in considerable measure why Keats was so deeply absorbed in *Oberon* during 1819. He was repeatedly preoccupied with the moral of the tale from faery land, the torment caused by sensuality and 'sweet sin,' and the trial by 'joys that seduce' from constancy to an ideal of love and beauty. Simultaneously he was fascinated by the tale of earthly love, as *St. Agnes* and *To Psyche, La Belle Dame, Otho the Great,* and *Lamia* have shown. His feeling for Fanny Brawne doubtless had a good deal to do with this. But I suspect that the lovers' spiritualization through the hermit, and their achievement of a bliss higher than sensual love can yield, also contributed to his fascination. For evidently the anguish born of the death of Tom had lent the hermit's message of soul-making a deeper vitality.

We have seen that toward the end of April 1819 Keats' thought was hovering about Titania's elfin grot and the Elysian hermitage, in terms of whose central figure he had symbolized the gradations of happiness in *Endymion*. And we know their profound significance to him from the letter to John Taylor. It is important to remember this, because the *Ode on a Grecian Urn* was composed at about the same time as that to Psyche. The subject of the famous Ode was linked with *Oberon* by some lines in *Endymion*. Near the beginning of Book III (the tale of the hermit Glaucus) Keats had written that worldly monarchs have

> not one tinge
> Of sanctuary splendour.
> (END. III, 9-10)

By this he meant, as the adjoining lines in the passage indicate, that they have nothing of the radiant spirituality of the hermit, who after intense suffering (or soul-making) had by degrees come to know the spiritualizing power of nature's beauty, and ultimately highest Truth and Beauty in fellowship with essence, which is God. A few lines later Keats had written of higher than earthly thrones:

> A thousand Powers keep religious state,
> In water, fiery realm, and airy bourne;
> And, silent as *a consecrated urn,*
> Hold sphery sessions for a season due.
> (END. III, 30-3)

This urn, so intimately linked in thought with the daemonic elements ruled by Oberon, and with religion, was a symbol of something—something peaceful, spiritual, sacred—as a consecrated soul that communes with heaven, as do the hermit and Oberon in *The Poet?* At any rate it is significant that the hermit's 'sanctuary splendour,' a soul-splendor attained through suffering and purification, and the daemonic elements, and a consecrated urn had been closely intertwined in Keats' thought. In the *Ode to Psyche,* two of those strands reappear. And in the Ode on the Urn, written at about the same time, the third strand emerges.

The *Ode on a Grecian Urn* is not the greatest of the Odes, poetically speaking. But it is, I think, perhaps the most succinct poetic-symbolic utterance of Keats' philosophy of life and art. As such, it was intimately connected with the 'gradations of happiness.' Inevitably, therefore, it was also linked with the wisdom of the blissful hermit-sage from whose life of woe Keats had learned so much, and from whom he had derived his symbols. Those symbols throw some light, I think, upon the famous Grecian Urn, which, whether itself a symbol or a remembered actuality or both, expresses the essence of Keats' thought. In the Ode, moreover, there are some suggestive images.

In the light of *Oberon, La Belle Dame,* and the imagery of *To Psyche,* the opening phrase is curious:

> Thou still unravish'd bride . . .

Did Keats mean to imply that the spirituality or spiritual purity of the Urn is something lovelier than earthly love?

> Thou still unravish'd bride of quietness,
> Thou foster-child of silence and slow time,
> Sylvan historian, who canst thus express
> A flowery tale more sweetly than our rhyme . . .

And he goes on to describe the teasing 'leaf-fring'd legend' of 'What wild ecstasy.' In the phrase 'more sweetly' he is comparing two media of art.

In the second stanza, perhaps recalling a line from Wordsworth,[12] he writes:

> Heard melodies are sweet, but those unheard
> Are sweeter; therefore, ye soft pipes, play on;
> *Not* to the *sensual* ear, but, *more* endear'd,
> Pipe to the spirit ditties of no tone:

Explicitly he is contrasting things of sense and tangible reality with things of the spirit and mind and the ideal. And he goes on:

> Fair youth, beneath the trees, thou canst not leave
> Thy song, nor ever can those trees be bare;

Because the art work, which is of the spirit and ideal, is enduring, where nature in an impermanent world of flux is not.

> Bold Lover, never, never canst thou kiss,
> Though winning near the goal—yet, *do not grieve;*
> She cannot fade, though thou hast not *thy bliss,*
> For ever wilt thou love, and she be fair!

And that is reason for not grieving. 'Thy bliss' of earthly love could not endure. In the ideal representation of an art work, that bliss is higher in degree, for neither it nor her beauty can fade.

In the third stanza the same thought is developed further:

> Ah, *happy, happy* boughs! that cannot shed
> Your leaves, nor ever bid the Spring adieu;
> And, *happy* melodist, *unwearied,*
> For ever piping songs for ever new;

New, because in the mind of the beholder, who hears with his own ideal inner ear. Note, too, the emphatic repetition of 'happy.'

> *More happy* love! more happy, happy love!
> For ever warm and still to be enjoy'd,
> For ever panting, and for ever young;
> *All* breathing *human* passion *far above,*
> That leaves a heart high-sorrowful and cloy'd,
> A burning forehead, and a parching tongue.

'Again the insistence upon a higher degree of happiness.

In the fourth stanza a new figure is introduced, who in the light of the gradations of happiness is peculiarly suggestive. The imagery also becomes vaguely familiar:

> Who are these coming to the sacrifice?
> To what green altar, O mysterious *priest,*
> Lead'st thou that heifer lowing at *the skies,*
> And all her silken flanks with garlands drest?

Did Keats, pondering the gradations of happiness, remember the festival on Latmos, and the high contemplating that came of it?

> What little town by river or *sea shore,*
> Or *mountain*-built with *peaceful* citadel,
> Is emptied of this folk, this *pious morn?*

The high contemplating occurred at dawn, when aerial music—or 'spirit ditties'—was heard in the silent peaceful grove in the untrodden region upon the mountain overlooking the sea.

> And, little town, thy streets for evermore
> Will silent be; and not a soul to tell
> Why thou art desolate, can e'er return.

Keats was visualizing the imagined scene in its literal sense—with how sensitive an inner eye!

In the last stanza the message comes home:

> O Attic shape! Fair attitude! with brede
> Of marble men and maidens overwrought,
> With *forest* branches and the trodden weed;
> Thou, silent form, dost tease us out of thought
> *As doth eternity:* Cold Pastoral!

There let us pause a moment. Thus far Keats has spoken of physical nature and earthly love, than which art is 'more happy.' He has also urged, 'Not to the sensual ear, but, more endear'd . . . the spirit ditties of no tone,' which are more beautiful because they are ideal and hence 'for ever new.' He has insisted upon the gradations of happiness, and upon the greater happiness in art, the realm of ideal or spiritual beauty, which is 'all breathing human passion far above.' Let us bear this, as well as the image of the priest, in mind, and also the lines just quoted:

> Thou, silent form, dost tease us out of thought
> As doth *eternity* . . .

The work of art teases us out of thought of what—of reality? It teases us out of ourselves and our earthly problems 'As doth eternity.' But thoughts of eternity are the province of religion and the priest. Did Keats, 'a hermit young,' mean that art is, like religion, essentially spiritualizing or 'self-destroying'? * That thought and his imagery and the priest, and the insistence upon the ideal and greater happiness: all recall the thematic passage of *Endymion*. †

In it, happiness is in the form divine. Its symbols derive from the hermit and his mystical vision of God, the 'form divine' of Love, to whom *in his woe* he turned, and in whose supernal essence he found selflessness and highest bliss. 'To truth alone' the hermit had 'turn'd his mental ear.' Thence, through his life of highest contemplation, came his vision of Beauty in all things, that essential Beauty which is of the spirit or essence of God. And *in Him truth and beauty are coexistent,* one, indivisible. With that mystical message in mind, which the hermit had perceived after the gradual spiritualization that enabled him to transcend all earthly woe: with that message in mind, and also the 'consecrated urn' of *Endymion,* let us turn back to the last lines of the *Ode on a Grecian Urn:*

> Thou, silent form, dost tease us out of thought
> As doth eternity: Cold Pastoral!
> When old age shall this generation waste,
> Thou shalt remain, *in midst of other woe*
> Than ours, a friend to man, to whom thou say'st,
> *Beauty is truth, truth beauty,*—that is all
> Ye know on earth, and *all ye need to know.*

That is all that we mortals, under the shadow of eternity, need to know: For highest bliss, 'all breathing human passion far above.'

The Beauty of which Keats speaks, or rather the priestlike consecrated Urn, is spiritual beauty, divine beauty; the beauty of eternal essence or spirit which is of God, in whom truth and beauty, beauty

---

* He had said so as early as in *Sleep and Poetry*, 25-6. (Cf. p. 82.)
† Cf. p. 120 above, and the continuation in App. iii, p. 325.

and truth are one. Such beauty is the ultimate truth man can perceive. And nature, earthly love, the spiritual beauty and happiness
in art are gradations to Him in whom is highest and eternal bliss.

In a world of death and anguished suffering, Beauty, a manifestation of the highest truth or spirit of God, is a divine consolation—even as the hermit had revealed to the young poet. To him,
the artist, the mystic's 'form divine' could be an art form, whether
an urn or pure poetry, in which is revealed truth *in* beauty to men
capable of intuitive vision.*

The message that the Urn breathes is the quintessence of the first
lines and of the 'wherein lies happiness' passage of *Endymion.* They
were formulated in symbols derived from the hermit's experience
of deepest woe. Those symbols and overtones reappear in the *Ode
on a Grecian Urn,* which is also concerned with the 'vale of Soul-
making' and the 'untrodden region of my mind.' The message is
the poetical embodiment of the Platonic ladder of love, a Christian
version of which Keats found in his spiritual master, the blissful
disinterested hermit-sage, with whom, 'a hermit young,' he had
deeply identified himself. The Ode is a pendant to the opening lines
of *Endymion,* 'A thing of beauty is a joy forever,' a joy and a step
toward 'fellowship with essence.' It is a reaffirmation of a timeless
creed, profound as Christ and as seemingly simple: a creed that
every generation must learn, 'in midst of other woe.'

.   .   .

It is noteworthy that in *Bards of Passion* and its Elysium

> . . . the nightingale doth sing
> Not a senseless, tranced thing,
> But divine melodious truth . . .

'Of heaven and its mysteries.' That was significant because of the
contiguity of the 'nightingale upperched high' with 'love's elysium,'
where the hermit and the lovers wandered, in the thematic passage

* That is, 'a life of Sensations,' and highest contemplation.

of *Endymion*.* But the nightingale becomes even more interesting now.

Only a week or two after the *Ode to Psyche,* and very soon after that *On the Grecian Urn,* very soon after they had visibly taken him back to the untrodden regions of the hermitage, Keats heard the immortal nightingale in Brown's garden. And on Sunday, 11 April, as Professor Garrod pointed out, Keats had met Coleridge and walked two miles with him while that incomparable talker characteristically held forth on a dozen favorite topics, among them nightingales and poetry. For all his levity in reporting the meeting to George, the youthful Keats must have listened spellbound. Professor Garrod has indicated the evident connection between Coleridge's brilliant monologue, his unmelancholy nightingales, and Keats' own bird of 'happy lot.'

From our wanderings in the hermitage with Endymion and Rezia, we know that Keats long since had heard the nightingales in Titania's sacred groves, just before the childbirth scene (*Oberon* VIII, 51). Evidently he remembered them and much more besides. For in his *Ode to a Nightingale* he would 'fade away into the forest dim,' somewhat as in the 'Epistle' *To My Brother George,* where the world,

> Thy dales, and hills, are fading from my view:
> Swiftly I mount, upon wide spreading pinions . . .

But now he would

> Fade far away, dissolve, and quite forget
> What thou among the leaves hast never known,
> The weariness, the fever, and the fret
> Here, where men sit and hear each other groan;
> Where palsy shakes a few, sad, last gray hairs,
> Where youth grows pale, and spectre-thin, and dies;
> Where but to think is to be full of sorrow
> And leaden-eyed despairs,

* Cf. p. 325.

> Where Beauty cannot keep her lustrous eyes,
> Or new Love pine at them beyond to-morrow.

Was there possibly a connection between the 'Epistle' to his brother George and the image of the dying Tom? The other thoughts are much like those of the Ode on the Urn. And now:

> Away! away! for I will *fly* to thee,
> Not charioted by Bacchus and his pards,
> But on the *viewless wings* of Poesy,
> Though the dull brain perplexes and retards:

The 'viewless wings' are those of *The Poet* and the daemon king. And I suspect that the chariot drawn by leopards is his too by way of Rezia's first dream-vision of Huon in Oberon's leopard-drawn * chariot, the passage that colored the Indian maid's lament for her shadowy wooer from the skies near the beginning of Book iv of *Endymion* with its triumph of Bacchus. For now Keats proceeds:

> Already with thee! tender is the night,
> And haply the *Queen-Moon* is on her throne,
> Cluster'd around by all *her starry Fays* . . .

That beautiful image was wrought of the identification of Titania with Diana as in Ovid and *Endymion*. The fays are those of the former, who has visibly coalesced with the moon goddess. So vital to his thought was *Oberon* that images and symbols were drawn into poem after poem, by one association or another.

The *Ode on Indolence,* apparently written in May, contains a familiar symbol that we first saw in *The Poet,* where Keats identified the daemon king's preternatural powers with those of the visionary poet. In this Ode, significantly,† he writes of the three shadowy visitants Love, Ambition, and Poetry, one of whom: 'I

---

* Cf. *Oberon* ii, 27.
† In the light of *Lamia,* shortly to be written.

knew to be my *demon Poesy.*' In the next line, 'They faded, and, forsooth! I wanted wings.'

Only two months later Keats was at work on *Otho the Great,* of the 'spotted souls,' and on *Lamia,* in which the moral of the 'tale from faery land' and the daemonic phase of the romance engrossed him.

Hardly had the play and *Lamia* been finished and *The Eve of St. Agnes* revised than Keats began work on *The Fall of Hyperion* in an attempt to reconstruct his earlier vision. In the 'Fall' there are a number of familiar overtones and at least one symbol from the visionary phase of *Oberon.* He begins thus:

> Fanatics have their *dreams,* wherewith they weave
> A *paradise* for a sect; the savage too
> From forth *the loftiest fashion of* his *sleep* *
> Guesses at *Heaven* . . .

As in *Sleep and Poetry,* this imagery suggests that the hermit's blissful visions are not far below the threshold of consciousness. And Keats says three lines later:

> For Poesy alone can tell her dreams . . .

Soon the vision begins:

> Methought I stood where trees of every clime,
> Palm, myrtle, oak, and sycamore, and beech,
> With Plantane, and spice-blossoms, made *a screen;*
> In neighbourhood of *fountains,* by the *noise*
> Soft-showering in my ears; and, by the touch
> Of scent, not far from *roses.* Turning round,
> I saw an *arbour* . . .

The configuration hints at Titania's elfin grot or rosy sanctuary, amid her well-watered paradise where dwelt the hermit-sage-poet. The 'fabled horn' and delicious food appear magically, as do these:

* Note the characteristic identification of mystical vision and sleep.

All in a mingled *heap* confus'd there lay
Robes, golden tongs, censer, and chafing dish,
Girdles, and chains, and holy jewelries.

(FALL OF HYPERION, 78-80)

These may well be the fairy gifts the lovers found after emerging
from the daemon king's palace and awaking from enchanted sleep
when their mission had been accomplished:

And there in heaps upon the bushes round,
Stores of bright armour, and rich robes were found:
Armour for princely knight, and robes for royal bride.

(OBERON XII, 75)

The fairy jewel-casket was there too. And Keats had just said:

How long *I slumber'd* 'tis a chance to guess.
When sense of life return'd, I started up
As if with wings; but the fair trees were gone,
The mossy mound and arbour were no more;
I look'd around upon the carved sides
Of an old sanctuary . . .

(FALL, 57-62)

I think he had just seen Oberon's aerial spirits start up with wings,
a few stanzas before the lovers, magically transported through the
air to Paris, awake.

But all these are small things. Far more important is the last appearance of the most vital symbol Keats had gleaned from Wieland's romance. As in *Bards of Passion,* the poet who had long
since said 'A hermit young I'll live,' in his last poetic-symbolic utterance about his art, wrote in *The Fall of Hyperion:*

'. . . sure not all
Those melodies sung into the world's ear
Are useless: sure *a poet is a sage;*
A humanist, *Physician to all men.'*

And a few lines later:

'The poet and the dreamer are distinct,
Diverse, sheer opposite, antipodes.
The one *pours out a balm* upon the world,
The other vexes it.'

(lines 187 ff.)

While this is Keats' ideal of poetry, the 'balm' is the same 'balsam' that 'flowed' from the springs of heavenly Truth and Beauty for the hermit's earthly wounds: * that hermit-sage of 'woe-bewildered mind' who found peace and immortality in the divine Love, and who helped teach a poet an enduring creed of spiritualization and the gradations of happiness and the divine consolation of Beauty. With that mentor Keats still walked, in the very shadow of eternity.

* Cf. App. III, pp. 329 f.

The Weariness, the Fever, and the Fret

THE VISIONARY and the daemonic features of *Oberon* had left their marks on no less than ten of Keats' poems of 1819. But in that year of extraordinary creative activity there was yet another work, the last he wrote, which bears evidence of his intense absorption in the fairy tale. That last work, written between November 1819 and February 1820, or else October-November 1819, was the unfinished mock-heroic *jeu d'esprit, The Cap and Bells,* whose final stanzas 'were the last verses of poetry which he composed.' [1]

As Sir Sidney Colvin was the first to suspect, *The Cap and Bells* contains innumerable traces of *Oberon*—elements which differ from those in the earlier works in being disseminated at random throughout Keats' satire, and in being cooler reminiscences devoid of the intensity that had helped to make masterpieces. These echoes seem to suggest that after Keats' exhausting creative fever and saturation in the 'tale from faery land' through most of 1819, he had become surfeited with romantic escape and in the reaction had satirized his favorite world without quite throwing off its spell.

Keats' comic romance, as Professor Finney reminds us, is a compound satire aimed primarily at the notorious Prince Regent and his enforced marriage to the Princess Caroline of Brunswick. Its tone is somewhat that of the Byronic 'flash poem,' which is visibly parodied in more than one instance. A few elements, moreover, were derived from the *Midsummer Night's Dream;* Spenser contributed the fairy emperor Elfinan's name and that of his capital Panthea; [2] Drayton may have contributed a phrase; and Ben Jonson and Chaucer apparently lent some alchemist's jargon; while Keats' own unfinished *Eve of St. Mark* also was taxed. But primarily the leisurely piece abounds in topical allusions. And *Oberon* seems to have contributed more ingredients than any other single source. This evidently is what Sir Sidney Colvin first implied.

In his discussion of *The Cap and Bells,* Colvin spoke of the choice of the Spenserian stanza as unfortunate, said that 'Keats had probably wished to avoid seeming merely to imitate Byron as he might have seemed to do had he written in the ottava rima.' Colvin thought, however, that 'not even Keats' power over the Spenserian stanza could make it a fit vehicle for his purpose.' And he added:

Though Thomson and Shenstone had used it playfully, to bite in satire or sting in epigram it cannot effectively be bent. To my sense *the precedent most in Keats' mind was* not these but *the . . . translation of Oberon . . .* Sotheby had invented a modified form of the Spenserian stanza riming abbaccddc . . . and keeping the final alexandrine. *Much of the machinery and spirit of the Cap and Bells—the magic journeys through the air—the comic atmosphere and adventure of the courts— are closely akin to the jocular parts of this Oberon.*[3] (Italics mine.)

If later critics have perhaps regarded the poem more sympathetically than Sir Sidney, they have neglected his suggestion concerning the part of *Oberon* in its conception. In the light of later discoveries, Colvin's surmise was unquestionably correct.

There is small need to go into the evidence very deeply. But to round out the story of *Oberon's* influence it is essential that *The Cap and Bells* be examined from our present vantage point. In our brief survey we shall repeatedly traverse familiar ground, for in this, Keats' last romance, comic though it was, pictures he had transmuted in *Endymion, The Eve of St. Agnes,* and *Lamia,* flashed through his mind as in a dream. But for once the poet's imaginative control of the flow was noticeably slack.

In *The Cap and Bells* Keats borrowed from all three *Oberon* palaces: the floating one of the daemon king (which had appeared that year in both the 'Fairy Song' and *Lamia*); the palace of the enchantress-queen of Tunis (the setting of 'Love in a palace' in *Lamia* and, in part, of Porphyro's furtive entrance and actions in *St. Agnes*); and the palace of Rezia's royal father in Bagdad (which became that of Madeline's father in *St. Agnes*). To all three of these settings Keats again and again alluded, for the last time. At the very outset he says that 'there stood, or *hover'd, tremulous in the air, A faery* city.' Though he may have recalled Drayton's line 'This palace standeth in the air,' Keats, as his stanza iv shows, certainly had not forgotten the bridal pageant before Oberon's floating fairy palace, tremulous 'as if woven from the rosy eve.' In the second stanza he speaks of the reaction to Elfinan's *amorousness:* 'For *ruin* and dismay' the priests foresaw. 'They wept, he *sin'd,* and still he would sin on . . .' For all the levity, one is reminded by this of the daemon-guardian Love in *Lamia* and 'for all this came a ruin' in the 'purple-lined palace of sweet sin.'

The fourth stanza contains an early topical allusion to the Prince Regent's dictated courtship of the unhappy Princess Caroline. Then immediately we are back before Oberon's palace, as Keats speaks of the fluttering embassy: to

> . . . bring the weeping *bride* away;
> *Whom, with but one attendant,* safely lain
> *Upon their wings, they bore in bright array,*
> *While little harps were touch'd by many a lyric fay.*

And lest we be confused in our bearings, he adds this:

> As in old pictures *tender cherubim*
> *A child*'s soul thro' the sapphired canvas *bear,*
> So, *thro' a real heaven,* on they swim
> With the sweet princess on her plumag'd lair,
> Speed giving to the winds her lustrous hair;
> And so she journey'd, sleeping or awake . . .
> (CAP AND BELLS, iv-v)

His allusion to 'old pictures' was, I think, an after-thought. For Keats seems first to have recalled an incident in the bridal pageant and the welcoming of the lovers to Oberon's floating palace (counterpart of the lovers' welcoming to the floating palace of Neptune in *Endymion* III). During that procession celebrating the reconciliation of the daemon king and queen, amid the songs of the fairies and the playing of *fairy harps* three winged aerial spirits (cf. cherubim) descend from a cloud bearing Rezia's child to restore it (*Oberon* XII, 73). That child, born in the elfin grot, had been abducted by the fairies from the hermitage after 'Love in a hut' became 'cinders, ashes, dust.' It was probably by way of that incident that the changeling motif from the *Midsummer Night's Dream* was drawn into *The Cap and Bells,* where Bertha Pearl's origins are explained in its terms by Hum (st. xliv). As for the aerial journey of the bride and her one attendant, the Princess Rezia and her nurse Fatme are transported with the squire and Sir Huon through the air in the chariot drawn by swans. Their second aerial journey immediately precedes the return of the child and takes them from the last of their trials in Tunis to Oberon's palace and the bridal pageant in the enchanted forest.

With fine disregard for sequence, the next *Oberon* reminiscence that came to Keats' mind, by way perhaps of the affinities between Rezia's and the Princess Bellanaine's hatred of the prospective bridegroom, was the scene in Rezia's chamber in the palace in Bagdad the morning of her dreaded wedding and the revelry that was to be interrupted by the 'liege-lord of all the Elves and Fays.'* The Princess Rezia is awakened from her 'visions of delight' by her *nurse and confidante* to whom, just before the robing scene, she says in anger and scorn provoked by her imminent wedding, 'Nought like the . . . Drusi prince *I* hate' (v, 11). And she draws *a poniard.* Bellanaine's nurse fears 'a sharp needle,' and her young mistress says, '"my tongue shall not cease Till from this hated match I get a free release"' (st. vii). The nurse seeks to hush that

---

* Here we are back in the scene drawn into *The Eve of St. Agnes.* The contrast is instructive.

princess even as Fatme attempts to quiet the indignant Rezia.* That Keats, while writing of fairies, reverted to the Bagdad palace is further indicated by Hum's phrase *'Commander of the faithful'* (st. xli), the traditional title, of course, of Harun-al-Rashid, the caliph of the *Arabian Nights.* He evidently was drawn in by way of Rezia's father, sultan of Bagdad. Before that allusion appears, however, the next dozen stanzas are full chiefly of the troubles of the Prince Regent and parliament, as H. B. Forman showed. At their close, various scattered fragments of the oriental settings of *Oberon* appear.

It will be remembered that the snakelike consort of the African queen tempts Rezia, to whom he offers both his hand and throne. Her steadfast refusal finally puts that enamored sultan into a towering passion in which he condemns Rezia to death at the stake along with her constant lover. As his many other reminiscences from Canto xii suggest, Keats was probably alluding to this scene when he wrote:

> *Love thwarted in bad temper oft has vent:*
> *He rose, he stampt his foot,* he rang the bell,
> *And order'd some death-warrants* to be sent . . .
>
> (CAP AND BELLS, XX)

Eban, 'this was his page, a fay of colour,' and the allusion to bowstring and the descriptions of elaborate oriental costumes are further elements suggested by the palaces of Bagdad and Tunis. On Huon's entrance to the former, with the aid of Oberon, his princely *golden dress* and diamond-studded *turban* 'shadow'd o'er with ostrich plumes' and *jeweled scimitar* are described in detail as we know. † And here Keats described Eban's multicolored dress and his 'turban wreath'd of gold . . . and his sabre keen' (st. xxxi). Only ten stanzas later appears the phrase 'Commander of the faithful,' evi-

---

* A moment later Rezia relates her dream of Huon and the nurse hunts about the chamber for 'the beauteous knight.' And Bellanaine, dreaming of Hubert, says: 'Ah, beauteous mortal!' 'Hush!' quoth the nurse.
† Cf. ch. iv, p. 157.

dently recalled by Rezia's father, sultan of Bagdad, who raged at Huon.

Ten stanzas beyond that, there is another allusion, to the aerial flights of the daemon king and queen and the conveying of their mortal protégés, Sir Huon and his bride. Keats writes, remembering evidently the sleepy nurse's panic,* 'And as *she would be frighten'd wide awake, To travel such a distance through the sky'* (st. lv); and again *'Uplift her from the ground, and swiftly flit* Back *to your palace'* (st. lviii). In the latter instance he evidently heard again the mournful voice and the guardian god's charge to the pitying spirit: *'Haste! thy fleet course* to yonder island *wing: Bear* the poor wretch from that abandon'd spot *To Tunis'* and the gardens of the palace of the enchantress-queen. That Keats went with him and retraced the steps leading to the meeting with Lamia's regal counterpart and the scene in the chamber of 'Love in a palace' seems likely since Hum says shortly: 'This room is *full of jewels as a mine.'* The queen's golden chamber was so filled with 'gold and lazuli . . . o'erlaid' that all 'Siam and Golconda's rifled mines' seemed to have poured their treasures there.†

In the contrast of these weak echoes with those in the *Lamia* pattern, it is instructive to see Keats at work when he had no longer that 'suspension of disbelief which constitutes poetic faith.' When he had that faith, it enabled him to transmute often common clay into the stuff of visions. *The Cap and Bells,* on the other hand, is merely full of 'the untransmuted shapes of many worlds.'

In the stanza preceding the instructions to bear Bertha through the air, appears another unmistakable fragment, Hum's *'bright casket of pure gold'* wherein *'in wool* or snow' there 'lay an old . . . legend-leaved book, mysterious to behold.' Actually, and the process illumines in little the ways of the imagination, Keats saw the golden casket wherein *in cotton lay* the teeth and beard of the sultan, the

---

* Immediately after the flight into the elfin storm (*Oberon,* end of v).
† With this cf. ch. v, pp. 215 ff.

fantastic tokens demanded by the vengeful Charlemagne to insure Huon's death. Provided painlessly by the daemon king, the casket is delivered to the emperor at the end of the romance immediately after the lovers' return from the fairy palace.* Several other of Oberon's effects appear subsequently in *The Cap and Bells:* 'my wand' (st. lxi) and *'an invisible ring'* (st. lxvii). But how prosaic have the awful talisman and the shape-shifting sceptre become! Mere fragments in an instance of joiner's work here, they had enabled *The Poet* to soar and had transformed the 'palpitating snake' *Lamia.*

The 'invisible ring' gleams upon Oberon's hand only in the bridal scene before the floating palace, and the circumstance shows that though features of all three palaces were interwoven, Keats derived most of his matter and machinery from the last canto of *Oberon.* At this point in *The Cap and Bells* we are at the edge of what amounts to a cluster of images derived from Canto xii, namely, the scene in *the thronged streets* of Tunis on the festive occasion of the intended execution, when Rezia and Huon are to be burned at the stake. *The fire* is lighted, it will be recalled, and the flames rise. Then suddenly there is a clap of thunder, the flames are extinguished, the ropes fall, and the elf-horn hangs again from Huon's neck. When he blows it softly, all the motley throng whirl in the irresistible *mad dance.* It is then that Oberon's aerial chariot appears drawn by swans, and as if prophetic of a later day bears the lovers and the squire and the nurse of the princess up into the air from among the gasping, whirling throngs. Then the visionary scene of the enchanted forest and the floating fairy palace woven of crimson twilight is revealed. As in *Endymion* and *Lamia* and the *Song of Four Fairies,* reminiscences of that provocative episode appear in *The Cap and Bells.*

As Elfinan is about to depart through the air to Canterbury to fetch Bertha, the 'morn is full of holiday . . . Light flags stream out

---

* *Cap and Bells,* lvii; and *Oberon* xii, 92 and x, 32; and the 'cotton' in vi, 7.

like gauzy *tongues of fire;* A metropolitan murmur . . . Comes
from the northern suburbs' and

> . . . now *the fairy escort* was seen clear,
> Like the old pageant of *Aurora's train,*
> Above a pearl-built minster, *hovering near* . . .
> (CAP AND BELLS, lxiv-lxv)

Elemental earth spirits or gnomes precede the rest of the winged
train, in whose midst the bride, 'the fair Princess in full view [is]
Borne upon wings,' somewhat as the Princess Rezia is borne to the
bridal procession before the hovering fairy palace. Crafticant's
whimsical diary tells us too that they flew over the Gobi desert and
a volcano (Huon and Rezia were borne through the air from
African Tunis to the enchanted forest, while Titania's flight above
her volcanic isle may also have provided a hint.[4]) The diary also
tells us that *'The city all her* unhiv'd *swarms* had cast, To watch our
grand approach, and hail us as we pass'd.' * After an echoing of
Shakespeare's 'Middle summer's spring,' he tells us further how
'Onward we floated o'er *the panting streets,* That seem'd throughout with upheld faces paved' (st. lxxxii) and of 'the *strangest sight*
—the *most unlook'd for* chance—All things turn'd topsy-turvy in *a*
devil's dance' (st. lxxxiv). It is clear enough from this peculiar sequence of descriptive details that Keats was in Tunis for the time.
And 'the fluttering ensigns' and 'bright standards,' the 'row of lords
and ladies' who 'make show Submissive of knee-bent obeisance' in
the same stanza are elements which were probably gleaned from
Huon's and Rezia's almost immediate triumphant return to Paris,
their momentary presence at a colorful tourney of which Sir Huon
is declared champion, and their happy progress through the welcoming streets to the court of Charlemagne where Huon does
obeisance and is restored to favor.

* This may have been suggested also by the welcoming throngs of Paris who
greet Sir Huon and his bride at the end of Canto XII.

Possibly the Princess Bellanaine's 'Master Hubert' was suggested by Huon. And the last echo, the

> brilliant crowd
> Cinque-parted danced, some half asleep reposed
> Beneath the green-fan'd cedars, some did shroud
> In silken tents.
>
> (st. lxxvii)

reminds one of Huon's progress down the cedared heights of Lebanon and his vision from afar of the brilliant tents and knightly retinue of the prince of that land, whose bride had been stolen by the giant—from whom Huon recovered the stolen talisman. That is the same ring of the daemon king by which Keats and George Felton Mathew had been beguiled in the days of the former's apprenticeship, five years earlier. It is the same talisman with which *The Poet* had soared and called up spirits rare.

But now, only a few stanzas later in *The Cap and Bells,* the weary poet was interrupted as he came to write the ominous last line: that he would tell

> The sequel of this day, though labour 'tis immense!

Therewith a last effort, heroic rather than mock-heroic, had exhausted itself. After a year of feverish creation, Keats had brought his meteoric course and the development of his genius to the brink of timelessness.

⊱ VIII ⊰

The Forgotten Realm

IN A STUDY of one facet of a great poet's life it is difficult yet essential to approximate wholeness of impression. Keats' work, we have seen, was intimately related to his own life experience and the aspirations, events, and conflicts that shaped his swift career. Besides such personal influences as those of Clarke, Hunt, George and Tom Keats, of Haydon, Hazlitt, and Bailey, there were many strong literary influences other than *Oberon*—namely, Greek mythology, Spenser and his eighteenth-century imitators, Hunt, the Elizabethans and Shakespeare, Wordsworth, and Milton—who awakened or gave direction to his genius. Yet Wieland's poem, read with boundless admiration at an early and impressionable age, obviously set his imagination afire. Though other creeds became to him outworn, and other loyalties shifted, he seems to have read and reread *Oberon* until he must have known it almost by heart. It was to Keats an inexhaustible source of story and creative impulse. So much was it on his mind and so intimately did it come to blend with his own experience, that gradually it became inwoven in his deepest thought, and its images and symbols were drawn by one association or another into poem after poem. Though hitherto overlooked, *Oberon* constitutes one of the most momentous chapters in all Keats' poetical life.

The spell of the romance was never broken. In the 'Shell Stanzas' of 1815 he had said as if prophetically: 'Nor e'er will the music of Oberon die.' And for him it never did.

> . . . its music long,
> Like woven sounds of streams and breezes, held

> His inmost sense suspended in its web
> Of many-coloured woof and shifting hues.

From the time of his discovery of it in 1815, Keats' interest in the romance grew and evolved, even as did his own powers. After his interest in allegory and chivalry had been aroused by Spenser, Keats happened upon *Oberon*. From fanciful allusions gleaned from its surface, he penetrated gradually to its inner springs. From the incidental high coloring of its marvels and chivalry, his attention turned to its essence. And there, beneath its shell of sophistication, he probed until he had grasped its machinery and allegoric meaning and had become saturated in them, as in its rich and sensuous imagery.

In 1816, with freedom, came time for thought and self-orientation. He had, moreover, discovered Wordsworth, whose greatness gradually grew upon him. The priestlike devotion of the poet to his art; the sense of mission and of the need of spirituality in its service; the recognition of nature as an instrument of divine revelation; and the turning from the beauty of sensuous phenomena to the exploration of the inner and eternal harmonies, in the consciousness of the mystery of life and human suffering: these are typically yet not exclusively Wordsworthian doctrines. In all probability the influence of Wordsworth, through the lyrics and *Tintern Abbey* and portions of *The Excursion,* materially helped Keats to find himself in his art. Yet Wordsworth's bent, not purely poetic, was moral and didactic, subjective and doctrinaire. In many ways it was repulsive and antithetic to that of Keats, the intuitive lover of beauty who soon came to worship Shakespeare's dramatic objectivity and 'negative capability.' What is more, according to Bailey Keats did not know Wordsworth deeply until the year 1817 was well advanced. But he had discovered Wordsworth about 1815, almost simultaneously with *Oberon*. And while Wordsworth corroborated and may even have opened his eyes to the meaning of the hermit's story in Wieland's romance, it was Keats' own insight that revealed the truth and poetic vitality of that succinct tale of regeneration.

Thus in 1816, in the central portion of *Sleep and Poetry* in which he identified the poetic experience with a dream-vision, Keats with a new intensity of insight and expression derived his symbols from the hermit's spiritualizing vision of the Godhead. For the first time he sensed the import of the hermit's life. In the lift of that revelation he identified himself explicitly with the sage, who felt 'a glowing splendour round about me hung.' In the light of that vision, in Titania's mountain-girt Elysium, which he identified with the 'sanctuary' of Poesy, Keats with the help of *Oberon* achieved the sheerest poetry, excepting the Chapman sonnet, which he had written till then. In the act he divined that mystical symbolism which he developed more fully a few months later in *Endymion*. In *Sleep and Poetry* for the first time, too, he assimilated and transformed Wieland's daemonology. In its visible animation of nature he saw a new source of poetic material. Only a month or so later he wrote *The Poet,* in which he distilled that daemonology, and in which, most fittingly, the daemon king became a living symbol to him for the poetic imagination. By the end of 1816 he had thus realized both the visionary and the daemonic phases of Wieland's romance. From it with increasing sensitivity he drew inspiration, substance, and symbols.

Fruition came in 1817 while he was composing *Endymion*. For though its allegory owes something to the Elizabethans, to Shelley, and to Wordsworth's doctrines, from beginning to end the romance bears the marks of Keats' absorption in the wanderings through the elements, the gradually spiritualized love, and the fated mission of Wieland's hero. From *Oberon,* which plainly played the dominant part in the genesis of *Endymion,* Keats derived crucial inspiration. In it he found a model for most of his settings, much of his plot, many incidents, and his character interactions. As we saw, he re-created from it with varying intensity. The love story, the temptation, and the mission he re-created variously, and from almost every portion of *Oberon* he derived unnumbered hints.

Most significant of all, with some help evidently from Wordsworth, he wrought a philosophy of life from the hermit's experience of anguished suffering and the loss of all earthly things 'where happiness' had been. For Keats emulated the four stages of his spiritualization and devotion to divine Love and 'truth alone.' From this and the hermit's communion with the fount of highest bliss and the Beauty that is eternal Truth, *Keats formulated his own philosophy of life*. From the hermit's visions, too, he derived the symbols in which he conveyed his message in the opening lines and in the key passage of *Endymion:* 'Wherein lies happiness? In . . . A fellowship with essence'—which is God and the cosmic principle of Love. Thus, far more deeply than in *Sleep and Poetry*, Keats in *Endymion* identified himself with the hermit-sage. It was in terms of his life of transcendental sensations that Keats thought, and that he wrote, among other things, 'O for a life of Sensations . . . a shadow of [heavenly] reality to come.'

The vital and lasting significance to him of the hermit's gradations of happiness and life of 'highest contemplating' in good part explains the intensity and endurance of Keats' absorption in the romance. Such is the variety of *Oberon,* moreover, that at sundry stages and in different crises of his career he could find in it some portion or feature to interest him afresh. When the legend of St. Agnes' Eve attracted him, the basic affinities in Rezia's dream of love, come true with the help of the 'liege-lord of all the Elves and Fays,' caused the *Oberon* episode and several related scenes to become the shaping matrix within whose bounds the tiny seed of the legend was nourished, developed, and molded to its superb form. In the genesis of *The Eve of St. Agnes,* which we have watched, *Oberon* played the crucial part, even as in the genesis of *Lamia.* In the latter case the accursed 'wily snake' and enchantress-queen possessed affinities with the legend of the lamia. Hence the machinery and moral of the 'tale from faery land,' as well as many incidents and other elements, came to help Keats embody and expand and modify the legend, as he hinted in the opening lines of Part II of *Lamia*.

Thus for three of his great romances, all of them works that helped make him immortal, the malleable tale of the daemon king furnished substance and form and suggestions which governed their conception, their growth, and their meaning. And in many shorter poems and more than one letter, as we have seen, the symbols and overtones from the hermit's message reappear repeatedly. That message endured for Keats, just as the romance continued to fascinate him throughout his career. *It seems to have left its traces in more than a score of his poems,* among them most of his very greatest.

In this vast and rich impregnation; in its significance and scope; in the potency and endurance of the influence upon Keats, we are confronted with one of the most extraordinary instances of literary stimulation on record.

II

How did the romance, in a translation fearfully shackled at times by the poetical mannerisms of an earlier day, come to exert so great an influence? What was there in its nature that attracted Keats? Why did the spell remain unbroken? These questions have already been answered in part, but they warrant more narrow scrutiny now that all the evidence is at hand.

In November 1819, in a letter to John Taylor, Keats wrote: '*As the marvellous is the most enticing and the surest guarantee of harmonious numbers* I have been endeavouring to persuade myself to untether Fancy and let her manage for herself.' * Significantly this was written toward the close of his career. And it reveals a temperamental bias: 'the marvellous is the most enticing.' As at the end, so in the beginning in his 'prentice days, it was the same enticing

* *Letters,* p. 439. Italics mine.

marvelous quality in *Oberon* which first attracted him and Mathew to 'strange tales of the elf and the fay.'

Beneath this, however, lay a mine of riches, for to an unusual extent *Oberon,* despite its early date, was a focal point of tendencies —imaginative, intellectual, and poetic—that were increasingly current toward the close of the eighteenth century and the beginning of the nineteenth. Into its tapestry Wieland had interwoven the stuff of marvels and chivalry, of the Orient and the world of faërie; neo-Platonic daemons, and the nostalgia for romantic escape to lands remote; it was a tale of travel, love, and visions of this world and that beyond. All these characteristic interests of the age, scattered in other works, were concentrated in *Oberon*. It was a convenient handbook of romantic materials, embodied in poetry. And as Keats' poems show, its kaleidoscopic variety of settings and episodes, its wealth of incident and highly visualized imagery—in short, the manifold romantic nature of *Oberon*—struck him early. It touches each phase and facet of the romantic's dream. Replete with the wonder of the natural and the supernatural, the strange and the familiar, it reflects the beauty of sun and moon, forest and mountain, sea and sky. That beauty is linked with the eternal by the visionary gleam, the transcendental sense of animating spirit, of the ideal within and beyond the real. Hovering aerial shapes like angels, and the radiance of the Form Divine reflected in His creatures, endow that beauty with ultimate truth. All this is in Wieland's romance beneath its superficial glamor—for him who has eyes to see. Keats, child of the romantic age, had most penetrating vision. Almost all the riches of *Oberon,* poetically blended and embodied as they were, struck an answering chord in him, for not merely the marvelous appealed to his nature.

Unquestionably other temperamental affinities were also involved. The most momentous surely was that between Keats' spiritual nature and the mystical hermit-sage, with whom repeatedly he identified himself and his aspirations. Keats did so with all the fervor and intensity of his deeply idealistic, intuitive mind. His own recurrent experience of profound grief, in the death of father and mother, of grandmother and then of Tom, made him the more intensely receptive to a kindred experience depicted in art. For 'Nothing ever becomes real till it is experienced—,' Keats wrote, 'even a Proverb is no proverb to you till your life has illustrated it.' Thus the hermit's experience became real, passionately real and alive to him. The anguished man's experience of the loss of his loved ones and, gradually, of the spiritualizing power of beauty, was more than a homely truth. It was an epitome of life to Keats. The spiritual exaltation which the sage achieved through suffering or 'Soul-making'; his finding of highest bliss in devotion to divine Truth and Beauty; the saintliness that spiritualized earthly love and rose to assured immortality—this was more than something read. To Keats it was a way of life: the core of a philosophy of soul-making that he understood in his own inmost being, with all the sensitivity of his nature. It was a philosophy he could utter fully: one he could develop to meet his own needs. And it was a timeless message to be sung in poetry.

Keats' sympathetic understanding of the hermit, his eager assimilation of the saint's every word and thought, underlie the vital centralness, the persistence, and the extent of the influence of *Oberon* upon him. That influence varied: it exerted itself upon the matter, the form, the spirit—upon one or all of these, isolated or in combination—in more than a score of individual poems, as well as in his evolving but abiding philosophy of life. It was an influence, the evidence attests, second perhaps only to Shakespeare's in the directing of his genius and its characteristic expression.

For sufficient reason, too, *Oberon* affected Keats diversely. The hermit was its spiritual center, upon which revolved the fate of the 'youth by heavenly power loved and led.' Keats' concentration upon that luminous center led his kindling eye down the radii to other portions of the romance. And the center lent meaning to all: the love story, the temptation, the fated mission—revealed in the daemon king's vow and curse—a mission capable of completion only by one spiritualized and constant to an ideal. (Here, incidentally, is the heart of *Endymion*.) Thus the hermit sustained and fostered the increasing potency of the spell, as well as its endurance, while the importance of his message helps explain the overlapping of patterns that is apparent in Keats' work.

For this, however, the exuberant density of the romance was also visibly responsible. Various portions had affinities with legendary tales. And those tales became alive for Keats in terms of the affinities and the rich pattern of which in *Oberon* they were a part. Hence the mutations and heterodox features of *St. Agnes* and *Lamia*, on themes of earthly love: a love linked in *Oberon* with the curse upon sensual love, the gradations of happiness, and the lovers' spiritualization by the hermit. The protean nature of Wieland's threefold theme of sin and penance, a theme exalted by the hermit's gradations of happiness, readily lent itself to all manner of adaptation and remodeling. This aided the fecundation hardly less than the richness of *Oberon*. The causal relation between the opulence of that poets' poem and its extraordinary provocativeness, which made it the beginning of so many visions, can perhaps be best explained by a conclusion reached by John Livingston Lowes, in his study of Coleridge and the ways of the imagination:

. . . the more multifarious, even the more incongruous and chaotic the welter, the freer play it offers to those darting and prehensile filaments of association which reach out in all directions through the mass. The more caleidoscopic the chaos of shattered fragments of memory, the more innumerable the reflections and refractions between the shifting elements.*

Apply that to *Oberon*, and the reason it enriched so many creations becomes clear.

But there is another significant factor. *Oberon* contained within itself the potent links of association to catch together the innumerable threads composing its own rich fabric. We saw what came of

* *The Road to Xanadu*, p. 60.

this, for instance, in the coalescence of Huon's two entrances into a castle in the case of *St. Agnes*. Also, *Oberon* possessed affinities with five of Keats' favorite poets. Through Titania-Diana and Oberon's powers of metamorphosis, it was linked with Ovid. Through its theme, and its hero Sir Huon, and its title, it was linked with Spenser's *Faerie Queene* and the book of Sir Guyon or Temperance and the bower of bliss. Through Oberon and Titania it was linked with Shakespeare. Through the hermit's paradise and dream-vision of the 'form divine' it was linked with Milton's *Paradise Lost* and Adam's dream. And through the hermit's experience of nature, it was linked with Wordsworth. These links of association visibly affected the genesis of more than one of Keats' poems, as we have repeatedly seen. The linking elements, both internal and external, the manifold affinities, proportionate to the intricacy of its pattern, readily enabled *Oberon* to complicate, to an extraordinary degree, the weavings of the poet's working brain. Keats doubtless perceived this early. So many were the threads that they were capable of an infinite number of new combinations. This, no less than the vital nature of the hermit's influence, explains the persistence of the fascination and the wonders that it wrought.

III

The evidence that we have examined is voluminous. Considered piece by piece, however, in connection with what it enriched, it is seen to differ progressively in kind, in complexity, in extent—even as does its value and the influence which it defines.

At the outset in 1815, aside from establishing Keats' knowledge of the romance, it shows how *Oberon* lightly spurred his fancy and added somewhat to his stock of images. Thus the echoes in the 'Shell Stanzas' and the later 'Rose Sonnet.' But by 1816, in *Sleep and Poetry* and *The Poet* for example, the romance was already enriching his thought both subtly and profoundly at its roots. At the same time that it was stimulating his imagination, it was providing symbols that fostered intensity and conciseness of utterance in the artist.

By 1817, as the opening lines and the thematic passage of *Endymion* show, Keats was reacting to the influence at its profoundest. He was deriving enduring spirit from the hermit. Yet in the same work, doubtless in consequence of the effect upon its spirit, there is evident a pervasive imitation or emulation of the matter and form of Wieland's poem. Thus too in the *Lines on the Mermaid Tavern* and *Bards of Passion* and the Odes, the influence was on spirit and matter in varying degree.

In *The Eve of St. Agnes* the influence was on form, in the architectonic sense, and on matter, and to far less extent on spirit. In *Lamia* it was a combination of matter, form, and spirit. But the proportions were as different as the intention, as various as the subtlety and complexity of the creative process.

• • •

The value of the evidence attesting all this is no less various. For, first of all, Keats' relative susceptibility to the same provocative materials at different stages of his career, and what he made of them, throws new light upon the phenomenal development of his powers as thinker and poet. Thus he grew from the languid sentimentalities of the Mathew period to the lush profundities of *Endymion* within some eighteen months. Yet at both stages he was susceptible to the same passages of *Oberon,* although to phases significantly different.

In brief compass, his use of that poem reveals his receptivity to the increasingly profound elements of life and art, as he felt the stimulating influence of sundry more subtle phases and features of the same romance. What he rejected is as revealing as what he selected, for apathy is as eloquent as sympathy. The different ways in which he reacted to that deepening influence reveal how and in what direction his powers of perception, his sense of form and artistic fitness, his resourcefulness and intensity of poetic expression evolved as his mind and art matured. In the light of Wieland's romance—in terms of which Keats saw so many visions—the record is illumined: from the pedestrian Mathew verses, through *Sleep and Poetry*, to the masterpieces of 1819.

His experience of *Oberon* clarifies some cardinal facts about his life and work. It reflects his eager faith and high seriousness of purpose, as it does his deep idealism and constant quest of perfection. It reveals his devotion to his art and abiding concern with its problems: the ends and means; the aims and purposes; the domains and values, forms and powers of 'pure poetry.' It clarifies the evolution of his concept of poetry, from escape in 'the most heart-easing things' to the searching out and affirmation of timeless truth that 'pours out a balm upon the World.' It illuminates his thought on the poetic imagination: as daemonic and intuitive and unconfined by time or space, or as transcendental power of dream-like vision of a beauty that is divine and that exalts spiritually. It shows that Keats' frequent use of the imagery of sleep and dreams is a manifestation of his intense interest in the phenomena of intuition and the transcendent creative vision which revealed to him ultimate truths of life as in a dream.

His experience of *Oberon* sharply focuses the conflicts, philosophical and poetical, by which his life was marked: the search for faith and a philosophy; for certitude in regard to the validity of knowledge and imaginative insight, and about the nature of Truth and the power of Love and Beauty. It reflects the conflicting claims of spirituality and sensuousness, of sensuous poetry and the poetry of revelation, to both of which he was drawn. No less clearly it illumines the personal conflicts: between humility and high ambition; lofty aspiration and sense of imperfect achievement; worldly success and artistic integrity; love and fame; earthly happiness and immortality. It clarifies these personal conflicts because Keats' interest in the various portions of *Oberon* was largely determined by the crises and problems of his own life.

Thus, too, it sheds light upon the outcome of the conflicts: upon

Keats' 'criticism of life'—his thought on this life of suffering, from 'A thing of beauty,' the gradations of happiness, and the cosmic principle of love in *Endymion,* to the cryptic message of the Grecian Urn. It establishes *the centrality of the gradations of happiness in his thought and art* and emphasizes the essential unity of Keats' thought, which evolved and unfolded without changing basically.

· · ·

There is another value. For *Oberon* reveals the close interdependence of many poems he wrote, in virtue of their visibly overlapping patterns. Repeatedly the poems show how in the same passages he sought material or stimulation; how his mind often reverted to the same scenes—with similar or else totally different results. The same inspiration affected him differently at nearly the same or at widely separated periods. But the diverse as well as the kindred results point out unsuspected relationships among poems which on the surface seem utterly unrelated in topic or time. Of this the *Ode to Psyche* and *La Belle Dame* are as typical as *Lamia* and *Otho the Great,* or again *Lamia* and the tale of Glaucus in *Endymion.* These and other strange overlappings, within the confining bounds of the same inspiration, form a fascinating if shadowy pattern. Even if that pattern must always elude full comprehension, to attempt to chart it is not without value since it may serve a higher purpose than to clarify further the nature and potency of the *Oberon* spell.*

Aside from the illumination afforded by the overlapping patterns and interdependence of so many poems; in addition to throwing new light upon the crises in Keats' life and the evolution of his thought and art, the evidence has a still greater value. For the poet often writes with intense compression. He often suggests rather than states. And since he frequently conveys his elliptical thoughts in meaningful symbols, their value to him is vital—even as it is to us who would understand his thought. In the case of Keats, many of his best-loved poems, from *Sleep and Poetry* and *Endymion* to

* Cf. App. vi, p. 397.

St. Agnes and *Lamia* and the great Odes, are unutterably clearer and richer in meaning for being read in the light of the setting they had in his creating mind. Their background in *Oberon* shows that Keats lived and thought and wrote in the shadow of eternity.

We have seen how many of his works are clarified by that romance from which he derived ingredients—ideas and suggestions for plot or incidents, machinery or moral, characters or imagery. We have seen how the hermit became his central symbol. And the hermit is the key to some of Keats' most vital thought on art and beauty and life. For Keats as for the hermit Beauty in all its guises is a manifestation of the divine. To commune with it is to know spiritual exaltation and highest happiness. That is the ultimate Truth man can know in a world of suffering. In this lies Keats' 'clear religion of heaven'—and the answer to Arnold's question, whether Keats is anything more than 'enchantingly sensuous.'

Oberon clarifies this central question in the interpretation of Keats, as it does the meaning of *Endymion*. It also makes clearer the meaning and intention in *Lamia* and *La Belle Dame* and *The Poet*, as it does the overtones in *To Psyche, On a Grecian Urn,* and *The Eve of St. Agnes.* It explains innumerable lines, passages, and allusions. The introductory lines in Part II of *Lamia*, for instance; the structure of contrast and allusions to Merlin and 'Love's alarum' in *St. Agnes;* the crucial 'Beauty is truth' in the cryptic Ode.

It does this inevitably in lighting up the mine from which the ore came, quick with galvanizing power. By exploring that forgotten realm of gold where Keats traveled, with greater frequency, intensity, and profit than in any other excepting Shakespeare's, his thought and his craftsmanship, his art and his very soul are revealed. What he loses of inventiveness, he gains anew in depth. Keats as man and artist, even as Shakespeare in the light of the sources from which he derived so much, becomes yet more of a miracle.

IV

For whether in Shakespeare or Homer, Simon Lake or Mme. Curie, in Coleridge or in Keats, the shaping mind never works in a vacuum. In Mary Shelley's words:

Invention, it must be humbly admitted, does not consist in creating out of void, but out of chaos; the materials must, in the first place, be afforded; *it can give form* to dark, shapeless substances, *but cannot bring into being the substance itself.**

That is as true of the creation of submarines as of an *Odyssey* or an *Oberon,* of creeds outworn as of marvels and masterpieces yet undreamed. The imagination is a shaping power which, however diversely, operates according to more or less uniform laws. The substance upon which it works is the stuff of experience, in its broadest sense.

Thus, of necessity, if the 'dark' but not always 'shapeless substances' of experience can be recovered, the process of giving form, which is the essence of creation, will be clarified. Hence the evidence of Keats' use of *Oberon* assumes another value, which extends far beyond the domain of Keats.

The literary creator works in a medium of self-expression that is more permanent than most. The 'dark, shapeless substances' to which he gives form and life and beauty, derive, perhaps as often as not, from the same indestructible medium: the printed word. Thus the genetic study that is supported by copious evidence and that can marshal the antecedent materials beside the finished form, can throw light on the nature and quality of the creative process involved.

On many occasions we have watched the substance of *Oberon* in the very act of undergoing the mutations, the dis- and reintegrations, of which came many a poem—poems great, and new, and

---

*From the 1818 Preface to *Frankenstein.* Italics mine.

totally different. In seeing the substance and hints, which with kindled eye Keats drew from the complex tale; in watching the material *and that which came of it,* the manner in which he formed it into patterns and combinations new and strange, time and again we can observe the very act of creation. Again and again we can see the clay, which many another passed by: clay which is shapeless until its potentialities have been realized, taking form in a master modeler's hands. That spectacle is perhaps unique for its transparency, no less than for its extraordinary compactness. The influence of *Oberon* upon Keats throws a penetrating light upon art in the making: upon the various processes and differing intensity of the shaping imagination at its mysterious work.

Nothing perhaps is more fascinating than that spectacle: of the manner in which an intense human mind seeks and sees and appropriates the stuff of experience, whether that experience is sensory or intellectual and literary; the process by which the mind selects and rejects, dissolves and remolds the fragments of experience into new combinations and new integrated patterns. Those patterns, we have seen, are determined not so much by the ingredients as by the focus and purpose, however attained, to which the controlling will would shape them. Of the same picture can come a 'palace of sweet sin' and the chaste and fragrant chamber of a Madeline; of the same image can come a sanctuary of Poesy and a lovers' elfin grot. The completeness of the shaping depends upon the degree of intensity exerted in the process, no less than upon the degree of sensitivity and discipline that the shaper's sense of fitness has achieved—fitness of form and matter, of spirit and expression—a sense which hovers over the work like a guardian spirit.

It is a process inconceivably complex in its fluidity and its elusiveness, its subtlety and multiplicity. Here repeatedly it appears in conjunction with the same ingredients. That static sameness, like a control in experiment, lends the evidence immeasurable value, owing to Keats' repeated use of the same materials, which time and again he rewrought differently. This makes possible several kinds of revealing comparison. It enables us to compare many phases of the creative process as manifested in Keats. For example we see embodied in *The Poet* imagery that was to serve a quite different purpose in *Endymion* and *Lamia*. Or again we see the same theme of the torments of sensual love diversely assimilated, and conformed to various patterns, in *Endymion, and St. Agnes, La Belle Dame, Lamia,* and *Otho the Great*. In the second place, it makes possible a comparison of the phases of the creative process at different dates and stages in the career of an artist visibly maturing, but the creative process focused, nevertheless, upon the same substance. Repeatedly we see the tentacles of thought in identical areas of the romance, selecting and fastening first upon the same and then upon neighboring fragments. Yet what came of them was never the same.

At times we see fragments so electric as to bring whole clusters in their wake: so electric as to galvanize all that they touch. Some are passive and inert; others so dynamic that they determine and dominate their new setting, or bring to the surface particles derived we know not where, that long had slumbered in the poet's memory. But whether isolated or in clusters, whether what came of them was crass or as sensitive as in *The Eve of St. Agnes* where the bounds of the pattern helped stay a hand firm and sure, the fragments and the rejected residuum are most revealing when examined with that which came of them.

Repeatedly we have seen Keats refit and dovetail the fragments without materially changing their essential nature. We have seen them scattered more or less widely, or with their original grouping retained. We have seen him distill poetry—from Wieland's machinery into *The Poet,* from the substance of Oberon's curse into *La Belle Dame* or *Lamia*. Within the limits of *Endymion* we have seen him engaged in the process of repeating simply or by transposition the untransmuted stuff of recent literary experience. And in the same book of the same work we have witnessed that synthesizing, the transmuting and blending of many elements into one, which is 'the prime and loftiest' phase of imagination. The love story of *Endymion* is a case in point, wherein Bacchus and Oberon's aerial car, the legendary Diana and the Princess Rezia's visions and life have blended almost irresolvably, while the mossy cave that remained unchanged is quite another matter. The contrast between the genesis of *Lamia* and *The Cap and Bells,* or that between the *Ode to Psyche* and *La Belle Dame* is even more obvious. For while each group was composed at nearly the same time, in the second and third poems we see more or less conscious joinery, whereas in the others the ingredients have lost all identity and have been blended into a new pattern in which they have been utterly transformed.

The different types of assimilation and re-creation are illumined, too, by the changes that elements in *Oberon* underwent. Huon the wanderer is, yet is not Endymion; he is and yet is not Porphyro in *St. Agnes,* and Lycius in *Lamia.* Rezia is the eastern queen who, 'woman like a goddess,' metamorphosed into Phoebe. She is and yet is not Madeline of the 'visions of delight.' Oberon is *The Poet,* who was Keats. He is both 'Love, jealous grown of so complete a pair,' and Hermes in *Lamia.* And the hermit is Keats, the intuitive poet and seer: the hermit speaks in Keats and Endymion, and he animates an Urn; his features appear in Glaucus, and his shadow emerges a moment in *St. Agnes* and 'Love in a hut' in *Lamia.* Titania is Lamia, the 'penanced lady elf,' and partly *La Belle Dame* of the 'elfin grot'—that grot whose shape and texture themselves shifted *at will.*

At will, it would seem. For the purpose that the artist consciously wills evidently helps vitally to determine the pattern. It directs the focus of his mind, and hence the seeking after models and materials. Energized by the will, it stirs those regions of memory which are somehow related, however remotely, to the congregating elements of conscious thought. In the act it opens the channels of association by which the purposed pattern will be enriched from the reservoir of remembered experience, in the manner and to the extent that the shaper's judgment permits.

The creative imagination that sees form in chaos and that can realize its visions is an organism indescribably complex, composed of an infinite number of integrating parts. The blending power of the subconscious seems to act reciprocally upon conscious thought, which partly directs its activities and is partly directed by it and by the shadows of experience how, when, or wheresoever gleaned. As impression or image or thought strikes down among the slumbering denizens of an area with which it is somehow related, the shadows of experience surge upward into the realm of consciousness. And judgment, intent to record, selects and rejects from the welter. But it does so in accordance with what it has itself experienced—of images and forms, concepts and words. The conscious power of judgment and subconscious powers of memory interpenetrate when energized by the will. But the artist's purpose is the determinant in the complex creative process. It first directs the focus of thought upon this or that area of experience and thus stirs the deeps. It releases a flow, which judgment controls and will shapes as is found fitting. The richer the area of experience and the more sensitive the judgment, other things being equal, the richer and subtler can the work become that the shaper strives to create.

V

Thus Keats' prodigious four years of artistic creation, even when beheld in the light of his indebtedness to Wieland's romance, seem more miraculous than ever. As Mr. Murry says:

In four years to have achieved, with no advantages of education and against the dead-weight of a Cockney tradition, *the opulent perfection of language, the living depth of poetical thought* which is in *Hyperion* and the *Eve of St. Agnes* and the great Odes! It is a miracle.*

* *Keats and Shakespeare*, p. 13. Italics mine.

It is that, incontrovertibly. Keats gave imperishable form to the stuff of experience. He created new beauty and living truth, and in more than one vision he reached the form divine.

His was a penetrating mind, boldly and fruitfully speculative. Young and self-taught though he was, he steered his way surely through aesthetic and metaphysical perils with a rare clear-eyed saneness and soundness. He sought and saw truth, with a fresh immediacy of perception. He saw beauty and man's suffering; joy and sadness; the physical and the spiritual; the temporal and the eternal. These are but a few of those opposites the reconciliation of which was for him an abiding problem. In this, as in his constant preoccupation with the eternal questions, values, and verities of life and art, lies some of his claim to being a philosophical poet. The gradations of happiness were at all times close to the heart of his speculation and of his life, even as *St. Agnes* and *Lamia,* the *Ode on a Grecian Urn* and *The Fall of Hyperion* have revealed. Unmistakably he was of those 'to whom the miseries of the world Are misery, and will not let them rest.' His poetry, rich in 'the ardors' as well as 'the pleasures of song,' is far more than an expanding of the range of sensory delights. If its appeal is ageless because of its vital fullness of beauty and enchanting felicity, beneath the perfection of its loveliness lie profound spiritual truths. They are there, even if, like his deep religious spirit, they have been too often unnoticed.

He was first and foremost a poet, never a doctrinaire. And he was a passionate lover of beauty. Yet he loved not merely the forms but '*the principle* of beauty in all things.' * Heroic and noble in character and mind, he was essentially naive and simple, intuitive and creative rather than erudite. Yet he had a profundity of insight, a piercing depth of vision, only less phenomenal than his powers of growth and the extraordinary intensity and sensitiveness of his mind.

* Cf. *Letters,* p. 468 (Feb. 1820?). Italics mine.

Like Shakespeare, Keats invented none of his plots but re-arranged and articulated with great intensity those of earlier narrative. He used them with conscious emulation, humanized the characters, and re-created the features of whatever was guiding him with a depth and delicacy and range of perception, both sensory and spiritual, that have seldom been surpassed. The completeness and subtlety with which he made the assimilated materials his own; the skill, sensitiveness, and energy with which time and again he exerted his shaping power of imagination, in seeing new forms within the old forms that were his chaos, and then in realizing his vital visions: this shows how triumphantly his writings are his own.

Keats happened to express his reactions largely to imaginative experience; and of the 'lovely tales' that he had read, particularly *Oberon* was to him 'an endless fountain of immortal drink.' But the nature, even as what came of *that* experience, was peculiar to John Keats. It was the stamp of his genius, the 'precious life-blood' of his spirit, that wrought his imperishable masterpieces. The element of mystery, which is of the mind, particularly of genius and its works, can never be dispelled for all the transparency of its weavings.

One thing more is clear. His lofty ambition and flaming will traversed no ordinary world. In an orbit narrowed by fate he sought experience instinctively in the realms of gold. And fate relenting, he came upon an enchanted realm: an English translation of a German poem. There Keats the creator—who felt early that 'invention . . . is a rare thing indeed'—found much of his 'chaos.' In him

> All is concentr'd in a life intense,
> Where not a beam, nor air, nor leaf is lost
> But hath a part of being . . .

He brought this intensity to his reading as completely as to his feeling, and thinking, and writing. He *lived* books. And his utter concentration upon their substance made him see 'where learning hath no light.' This intensity again and again stimulated his preternaturally sensitive brain to the working of poetic and perceptual miracles. It enabled him to see, and assimilate, and create. What did it not enable him to *make* of *Oberon!* In what was only potential, he saw life. Through its crust of sophistication he saw its basic idealism. And he molded his visions in the breath of his own spirit into living shapes of beauty.

In the 'life intense' which came to him readily from his contact with books, he transcended the narrow confines of his own real experience and mounted easily to that realm of 'eternal day' in whose radiance he saw with the eyes of the sage that the real world, whether micro- or macrocosm, is a 'vale of Soul-making.' By transcendental sensations he perceived the eternal principle as in 'a shadow of reality to come.' And he, who had known suffering, became physician to all men: physician to the soul, whose sovereign restorative is the consoling and spiritualizing power of Love and Beauty. Intensity enabled him to surmount the narrowness and obstacles of this world, to see and to sense beyond them. It gave him, who was a mere youth, sight and speech such as only seers and angels know.

❧ NOTES ❧

INTRODUCTION: SECT. i

1. W. H. Bruford's excellent study, *Germany in the 18th Century: the Social Background of the Literary Revival* (Cambridge, 1935), is particularly helpful for understanding some of the subtler aspects of the time.

2. For literary history, see K. Francke, *A History of German Literature*, N. Y., 1916; J. G. Robertson, *History of German Literature*, N. Y., 1902; Paul Wiegler, *Geschichte der deutschen Litteratur*, Berlin, 1930; Heinrich Hettner, *Geschichte der deutschen Litteratur im 18. Jahrhundert*, Leipzig, 1929; Josef Nadler, *Litteraturgeschichte der deutschen Stämme und Landschaften*, 2nd ed., 1924.

3. For biography, the *Allgemeine Deutsche Biographie* (Leipzig, 1897, vol. xiii) is as reliable as any. That by J. G. Gruber (in four volumes, as Bde. 50-53 of *Wielands Werke*, Leipzig, 1828) is hopelessly outmoded, but there are several monographs on periods of his long life. Perhaps the best brief sketch of his life and works is that in *Der Grosse Brockhaus . . .* 15th ed., 1935.

4. C. E. Vaughan, *The Romantic Revolt*, N. Y., 1907, p. 192.

5. Cf. Julius Steinberger, *Bibliographie der Wieland Übersetzungen*, Göttingen, 1930. And the list is not complete.

6. Gotthold Klee in his valuable Introduction to *Wielands Werke*, Leipzig, 1900, I, 29.

7. Cf. Kuno Francke, *History of German Literature*, p. 263.

8. Cf. F. W. Schroeder, *Wielands Agathon und die Anfänge des modernen Bildungsromans*, Königsberg, 1904.

9. G. P. Gooch, *Germany and the French Revolution*, N. Y., 1920, pp. 142, 150.

10. G. Klee, op. cit. I, 11.

11. Ibid. I, 38 ff.

12. C. E. Vaughan, *The Romantic Revolt*, p. 193.

13. K. Francke, *History of German Literature*, p. 262.

14. For most of these data and references I am indebted to G. Klee's excellent Introduction to his selected edition of Wieland's Works (cf. op. cit. I, 6-7).

15. S. T. Coleridge, *B. L.*, p. 300 (Everyman ed.).

16. Cf. *Cabal and Love* II, i: 'Wahr ist's, er kann mit dem Talisman seiner Grösse jeden Gelust meines Herzens, wie ein Feenschloss, aus der Erde rufen . . .'

17. Klee, op. cit. p. 7. Schiller borrowed a scene for *Don Carlos*.

18. Cf. A. B. Faust, ed., *Oberon*, A Poetical Romance in Twelve Books translated from the German of Wieland (1799-1801) by John Quincy Adams, N. Y., 1940, p. v.

19. William Beattie, *Life and Letters of Thos. Campbell* (3 vols.), London, 1849, I, 342.

20. V. Stockley, *German Literature as Known in England: 1750-1830*, London, 1929, pp. 6, 78.

21. See F. W. Schroeder, op. cit. . . . for a good sketch.

22. *The Romantic Revolt*, p. 194. And cf. Newman Ivey White's *Shelley* (2 vols., N. Y., 1940, I, 349, 701) for Wieland's influence on *Alastor*, etc.

23. *The Gentleman's Magazine*, vol. xxxii (Part I), pp. 285 and 598. Also *Monthly Magazine*, xxxv, 366.

INTRODUCTION: SECT. ii

1. Edited by S. L. Lee for the Early English Text Society, Nos. 40, 41, 43, 50. London, 1882.

2. Alice D. Greenwood, 'English Prose in the XVth Century,' in *The Cambridge History of English Literature*, II, 385.

3. Minor Latham, *The Elizabethan Fairies*, pp. 178 ff.

4. Ibid. p. 181.

5. *Oberon* was first published in Wieland's *Teutsche Merkur* in 1780. A discussion of sources, and textual criticism and notes are appended to the definitive, collated edition of Wilhelm Kurrelmeyer, vol. xiii of *Wielands Gesammelte Schriften*, Herausgegeben von der . . . Preussischen Akademie der Wissenschaften, Berlin, 1935.

6. For sources, see Heinrich Düntzer (*Erläuterungen zu Wielands Oberon*, 2nd ed., Leipzig, 1880) and Max Koch (*Das Quellenverhältnis von Wielands Oberon*, Marburg, 1880). Also cf. Heinrich Gundolf and others below.

W. Kurrelmeyer (op. cit. p. A47) points out one or two minor borrowings from Ariosto and follows Düntzer in regarding the *Insel Felsenburg* as a partial source of some incidents in Canto VIII.

It seems to me that Wieland may also have taken hints from Shakespeare's *The Tempest*, particularly from Caliban's lines in III, ii: '. . . the isle is full of noises, Sounds and sweet airs that give delight'; '. . . and then in dreaming, The clouds methought would open, and show riches . . .' Herein may well have been a germ of Alfonso's dream-vision in *Oberon* VIII. And that Elysian episode was further colored, I think, by Milton's paradise; for see Chap. III, note 13, below.

7. Cf. G. Klee, op. cit. p. 8.

8. Alice D. Greenwood, 'English Prose in the XVth Century,' loc. cit.

9. There is some difference of opinion as to whether Wieland used

Chaucer's tale of Januarie and May, or Pope's adaptation, or both (cf. Klee, op. cit. p. 8). Oberon's oath and curse, at any rate, are Wieland's own.

10. See the prefatory essay to *Agathon*, concerning his use of the 'Symposium' therein ('Über das Historische im "Agathon" ' in Klee, op. cit. III, 22). Wieland translated widely from the Greek, for a time was professor of philosophy, and enjoyed an international reputation as a scholar.

11. Besides *The Tempest* (cf. note, p. 15 above) see *MND*, II, i, the opening lines. But that allusion to the four elements is nowhere borne out in the play, and the Shakespearean Oberon remains a modified folk-fairy.

12. Cf. the early theory, no longer accepted, of the origin of the folk-fairies, in M. W. Latham, *The Eliz. Fairies*, pp. 41 ff.: ' ". . . fallen Angels . . . the departed souls of men and women . . . middle between Heaven and Hell . . ." '

13. Friedrich Gundolf (*Shakespeare und der Deutsche Geist*, Berlin, Bondi, 1920, p. 181): '. . . Nicht Feenmotive, sondern Feenluft, Elfenspiel, Mondscheinlandschaft und die sinnige Verknüpfung von Schicksal und Stimmung, von Sinnlichkeit und Schicksal; die sprachliche Lockerheit, die sich den sinnlichen Eindrücken anschmiegt und sie wiedergibt, die Wechselbeziehung zwischen Tonfall und Stimmung, der Gebrauch farbiger Effekte, saftiger Worte, um phantastische Vorstellungen zu erwecken, kurz die Eroberung der deutschen Sprache als Klang und Ton für die Sinnlichkeit und für die Phantasie: das ist hier Shakespeares Einfluss.'

INTRODUCTION: SECT. iii

1. *The Gentleman's Magazine*, vol. liv, Part II, p. 837 (Nov. 1784); continued and expanded in ibid. lv, Part I, p. 202 (Mar. 1785).

2. *Deutsches Museum*, Leipzig, Weygandt, vol. II, pp. 238 ff. (Sept. 1784). This translation sample was rediscovered by W. A. Colwell ('The First Translation of . . . *Oberon*' in *Mod. Lang. Notes*, vol. xxii, for March 1907), and has been discussed very fully by Miss V. Stockley (*German Literature as Known in England*, pp. 90-3).

3. William Hazlitt, *The Spirit of the Age*, p. 293 (Everyman ed.).

4. *The Monthly Review*, vol. xxiii (N.S.), pp. 576-84.

5. Cf. my articles, 'Coleridge, Wieland's *Oberon*, and the *Ancient Mariner*' in the *Review of English Studies*, vol. xv, No. 60, pp. 401-11 (Oct. 1939), and 'Coleridge . . . *Oberon*, and the *Wanderings of Cain*' in ibid. vol. xvi, No. 63, pp. 274-89 (July 1940).

6. Cf. H. N. Coleridge, *Specimens of the Table-Talk of the late S. T. Coleridge*, London, 1835, I, 345.

7. V. Stockley, op. cit. p. 95. The translation is discussed there in some detail.

8. *Oberon, a Poem from the German of Wieland*, by William Sotheby Esq. (2 vols.), London, Cadell and Davies, 1798, II, 10.

9. Most of the reviewers, unfamiliar as they were with the original, judged the translation on its English merits as of high quality. Wieland himself wrote in his *Merkur:* 'Mr. Sotheby's translation gave me a surprising pleasure felt in no similar instance, for it is a real masterpiece' (cf. Stockley, op. cit. p. 98). William Taylor, writing in *The Monthly Review* (vol. xxvi, N.S., p. 567, Aug. 1798), was at first disappointed in Sotheby's choice of stanza and the consequent diffuseness, but closed with the comment: 'he has effected much . . . in having naturalized so well a poem . . . remarkable for a versatility of style which has no model among our native writers.' The *Analytical Review* gave it fifteen pages, likened 'the ever-teeming fancy of Wieland' to the Shakespeare of Dr. Johnson's 1747 'Prologue' ('Each change of many-colored life he drew . . .'), and concluded with thanks for 'this elegant and harmonious translation' (cf. vol. xxviii, pp. 279-93, Sept. 1798). The *Critical Review* (vol. xxiv, Series ii, pp. 58-66, Sept. 1798) alone was a bit carping on moral grounds, felt that *Oberon* 'contains little that can elevate the mind or amend the heart,' but said 'it will be popular because it is lively and licentious.' But the *British Critic* (vol. xii, pp. 513 ff., Nov. 1798), church mouthpiece though it was, was highly impressed by 'this beautiful poem' and felt it 'will delight all those for whom poetry has any charms. As a translator Mr. Sotheby is judicious and able.' For many months thereafter correspondence concerning it appeared in the periodicals. Crabb Robinson's letter, written shortly before his departure for Weimar, is especially noteworthy: 'Unquestionably,' he wrote, 'the most valuable present to our national literature from the German is Wieland's *Oberon;* and our obligations to Mr. Sotheby are very great' (*Monthly Mag.,* ix, 23, Feb. 1800). William Taylor personally called it to Southey's attention and thus brought about its influence on *Thalaba* (cf. Theodor Zeiger, *Beiträge zur Geschichte,* pp. 53-6). When he reviewed the second edition of Sotheby's version, Taylor mentioned another translation in Chaucerian stanza that had circulated in mss. (concerning which see Stockley, op. cit. p. 99); and he concluded: 'It is beautiful; it will prove an enduring accession to our literature: and *may arouse the emulation of living bards to attempt some analogous exertion.' (Annual Review,* London, 1806, v, 503. Italics mine.)

10. A two-volume octavo and a one-volume quarto. The latter has been overlooked by Miss Stockley. But J. Steinberger (*Bibliographie der Wieland Übersetzungen,* p. 39) has seen it.

11. Cf. V. Stockley, op. cit. p. 99.

12. The 'licentious' and a few other passages were expurgated: iii, 24 and 61 (line 3) to 62 (line 2); iv, 2; vi, 32, 35-84, 90-7; vii, 11, 14, 15, 16, 36, 87; viii, 24; xi, 11, 57, 61, 63; xii, 16. (Cf. A. B. Faust, ed., Adams' translation, p. xxix.)

13. This edition has been overlooked. But see the *English Catalogue* of Books and Periodicals, 1801-36, p. 636: '2 vols. Fcp., 8vo., 15 s., Cadell, July '06.'

14. John Genest, *Some Account of the English Stage from 1660 to 1830,* Bath, 1832, VIII, 535. His epithet 'celebrated' is noteworthy.

15. Ibid. IX, 349; also *Dictionary of National Biography,* London, 1922, IV, 1024. This adaptation was overlooked by Miss Stockley. There is a copy in the New York Public Library.

16. H. C. Colles, ed., *Grove's Dictionary of Music and Musicians,* 3rd ed., 1928, V, 656.

17. Thomas Carlyle, *Life of Schiller,* 2nd ed., 1845, p. 187.

CHAPTER I

1. *The Letters of John Keats,* edited by Maurice Buxton Forman, 2nd ed. with revisions and additional letters. N. Y., 1935, p. xv.

2. Ibid. p. xiv.

3. Ibid. p. xv.

4. H. W. Garrod, ed., *Poetical Works of John Keats,* Oxford, 1939, p. lxxii. (Cf. also *Notes and Queries,* vol. 181, pp. 174 and 264.)

5. The Letters of George Felton Mathew, Charles Armitage Brown, Benjamin Bailey, Richard Woodhouse, and Cowden Clarke have never been published. Of Keats' other intimates, the letters of Hunt, Haydon, Severn, and Reynolds have been published, but only in part, as their several editors make plain. For the early years only Mathew and Clarke are vital here.

6. Dorothy Hewlett, *Adonais,* New York, 1938, p. 52.

7. Charles and Mary Cowden Clarke, *Recollections of Writers,* London, 1878, pp. 122 and 123.

8. Colvin, op. cit. p. 12, from Houghton Mss.

9. Ibid. p. 16, note.

10. Clarke, op. cit. p. 125.

11. Ibid. p. 135.

12. C. L. Finney, *Evolution of Keats's Poetry,* Cambridge (U. S. A.), 1936, I, 23.

13. Colvin, op. cit. p. 24.

14. Finney, op. cit. I, 33.

15. 'It was reviewed at length in all the leading periodicals, and attracted much attention' (V. Stockley, *German Literature as Known in England,* p. 10. Cf. also E. G. Jaeck, *Mme. de Staël and the Spread of German Literature,* London, 1915).

16. To Woodhouse he mentioned 'the fairy tale Undine' and Schiller's 'Armenian' [*Geisterseher*] (letter of 21 Sept. 1819: *Letters,* pp. 389-90); and a little later he mentioned Goethe's Werther in the journal letter to his brother George (*Letters,* p. 401).

17. Mme. the Baroness de Staël-Holstein, *Germany.* Trans. from the French. In 3 vols., London, 1813, I, 239 ff.

18. Ibid. I, 317 ff.

19. Cf. *Edinburgh Rev.*, xxii, 214 (Oct. 1813); also *Quarterly Rev.*, x, 361 (Jan. 1814). Latter article begins on p. 276.

20. Finney, op. cit. 1, 44. Cf. also Edmund Blunden, 'Keats's Friend Mathew' (in *English*, the Magazine of the English Association, 1936, 1, 46 ff.) for a vindication and some biographical data, etc.

21. John Middleton Murry, *Studies in Keats, Old and New*, London, 1939, p. 5.

22. It is noteworthy that Tasso, like Wieland, is not directly mentioned in extant letters of Keats.

23. I am using H. W. Garrod's edition of *The Poetical Works of John Keats*, London, 1939.

24. Oberon says to Puck, in the famous passage, only that 'I know a bank where the wild thyme blows . . . Quite over-canopied' with flowers, a bank where Titania sometimes slumbers (II, i). Again, to end the quarrel over the changeling, which has lasted only since 'the middle summer's spring,' Oberon squeezes the flower on Titania's eyelids and bids her 'love and *languish* for his sake'—Bully Bottom's, as it turns out.

Virtually all the action occurs 'in a wood . . . a league without the town' (I, i).

Oberon expresses no sorrow until after their reunion. Then in reply to Puck's warning of the coming of dawn, Oberon says: 'Then, my queen, in silence sad . . .' we must depart—which is the nearest he comes to sorrow (IV, i).

Titania bids her fairies to 'sing me now asleep' (II, ii); Oberon later says, 'Titania, music call . . .' (IV, i); but there are *no* fairy instruments in the play nor does Oberon play one.

The fairy chorus (II, ii) merely bids 'Philomel, with melody Sing *in* our sweet lullaby . . .'

25. And cf. *Oberon* III, 52: 'At once before his sight a stately *tent* arose.' Cf. also the 'rich tents' in III, 1. All my references are to *Oberon*, a Poem from the German of Wieland, by William Sotheby Esq. (2 vols.), London, 1798.

26. Of Keats' long and complex configuration, only 'languish' and 'over-canopied' and the idea of diminutiveness and possibly a reminiscence of the phrase 'And that same *dew* . . . like round and orient pearls, Stood now within the pretty flowerets' eyes, Like *tears*' (IV, i) could derive from the *MND*.

27. Cf. *PMLA*, XI, No. 1 (March 1930). Mathew's poem was discovered there by Miss Roberta Cornelius.

28. *Studies in Keats*, p. 2.

29. The text is that of the original version in the Woodhouse Book; see App. I.

30. Lowell, op. cit. 1, 84.

31. Finney, op. cit. I, 70. Also compare Colvin (op. cit. p. 25) who cites Mathew's 'Recollections' to Lord Houghton thus: Keats *used to spend many evenings reading to me.*

32. The massed fairies appear thrice in *MND*. The first time Oberon's abrupt 'Ill met by moonlight' provokes Titania's 'Fairies, skip hence' (II, i). And Oberon refuses to attend the 'moonlight revels' that *never appear* in the play. The second time (II, ii) only Titania's train is present and again there is no jubilation. The trains of both rulers meet for a moment only in the palace of Theseus on an occasion of rejoicing. But that is not on the green, not beneath the moon, not particularly quaint (cf. v, i).

CHAPTER II

1. It is not impossible that he did attend. For on 25 March 1817, he wrote Clarke: 'When shall we see each other again? In Heaven or in Hell . . . or jumbled together at Drury Lane Door?' (*Letters*, p. 16). By that time he was evidently thoroughly familiar with the famous old house.

2. See p. 51 above: Canto XII, 69-74. And cf. also the *Epistle to . . . Mathew*, the 'fairy jubilee.'

3. It was natural because there are numerous resemblances between the two chivalric romances: between Spenser's Sir Guyon [or Temperance] and Sir Huon and the theme of *Oberon*. Spenser owed a good deal to Wieland's source *Huon of Burdeux* and moreover mentions Oberon in his fanciful genealogy of the fairy sovereigns in the Book of Sir Guyon (*F. Q.*, II, x, 75). I suspect that consciously or not Keats' mind was led to associate the two chivalric romances by these links as well as by their titles. See his grouping of Spenser and the un-Shakespearean fairy queen Titania in the 'Shell Stanzas,' the *Epistle to . . . Clarke*, and the 'Epistle' above. And we shall see more evidence.

4. Cf. Canto II, 27; v, 80; VI, 1; VII, 66; and XII, 66. The second is particularly noteworthy: 'O'er earth's dim speck the self-raised *chariot* float'; while in the third, a few stanzas later, 'The *aerial steeds* descending touch the land.' These flights, as we shall see, are particularly visionary.

5. Finney, op. cit. I, 172.

6. Did Titania's gesture in the night of the hermit's death, his serene 'bursting of our mortal bars,' have something to do with Keats' superb 'Full in the speculation of the stars'? For 'That very night . . . the fairy queen Lifts her sad eye' and sees 'how in aspect dire *the stars* combine' (*Oberon* IX, 32).

It is also noteworthy that very early in *I Stood Tip-toe* Keats seems to have recalled a bit of natural imagery appearing in the enchanted forest of Oberon, which significantly contributed also to *Endymion* (and Mathew's 'Lines'). In *I Stood*, Keats wrote: '. . . *sweetly* they *slept* On the blue fields of heaven, [cf. the heaven over the enchanted isle. Was it a link?] and then there *crept* A little *noiseless* noise among the *leaves* . . .' (9-11). As for *Oberon*, this from a daemonic passage: 'In sweet forgetfulness all stilly slept; Along the *wood* no nightly murmur crept, All noiseless as the dead' (II, 17).

7. Lowell, op. cit. I, 163.

8. Finney, op. cit. I, 177.

CHAPTER III

1. 'Epistle' *To My Brother*, August 1816.

2. *Letters*, pp. 52-3.

3. Finney, op. cit. I, 77.

4. *Letters*, p. 270.

5. Ibid. p. 28.

6. J. L. Lowes, *The Road to Xanadu*, Boston, 1930, p. 34.

7. Cf. Colvin, op. cit. p. 216.

8. Douglas Bush, *Mythology and the Romantic Tradition*, pp. 99-101: 'one may think that *Endimion and Phoebe* was at any rate not necessary.'

9. Cf. C. DeW. Thorpe, *The Mind of John Keats*, New York, 1926, for a persuasive and cogent interpretation.

10. In Book III of the *Metamorphoses*. And this is noteworthy because it has long been known that Keats derived various incidental myths interwoven in *Endymion* from the 5th, 10th, 13th, and 14th books of Ovid. (Cf. Finney, op. cit. I, 256.)

11. *Letters*, p. 91.

12. I have quoted this letter, of extreme importance for understanding Keats, from Murry's study, *Keats and Shakespeare*, 1935, p. 28. The brackets are his.

13. The letter to Bailey is important here because it confirms the divine nature of Keats' symbol *Love*. In *Sleep and Poetry* Keats had likened poetry to religion, and a poet's power of insight to the hermit's mystical dream-vision of God and 'truth alone.' But in the letter to Bailey, Keats used Adam's vision to illustrate his conception of the Imagination. The reason for this interchange is not far to seek. Bailey evidently was not familiar with the hermit; and Keats had seen that the hermit's vision and Adam's experience are closely similar. Possibly this realization was the reason that as early as Mathew's 'Lines' an allusion to Milton had appeared amid a great cluster of allusions to Wieland's hermitage. (Cf. p. 318.)

There is a striking resemblance between the hermit's experience in *Oberon* and Adam's in *Paradise Lost:* a resemblance in setting, action, imagery, and atmosphere. If *P. L.* VIII, 286 ff., be compared with *Oberon* VIII, 10 ff., it will be found that in both poems the scene is an enclosed paradise, on a mountain-top, wooded, with fruit-trees and bowers. And both Adam and the hermit in sleep, in a dream, see the 'shape Divine' (*P. L.*), the 'form divine' (*Oberon*). Again, in *P. L.* it is God who says: 'This *Paradise* I *give* thee, count it thine To Till and keep, and of the Fruit to eate' (VIII, 319-20), and it is Adam who *falls at the feet* of the Creator. In *Oberon* the hermit says to Huon: 'Share all I have, where peace and quiet reigns—For thee my paradise its sweets bestows.' And it is Huon who falls at the feet of the hermit. Keats must have caught these and other echoes—which hint that Wieland, who read Milton early, owed something to *P. L.*

More important here is the circumstance that the close resemblance between Adam's and the hermit's visions made possible the interchange or transference which underlies Keats' words to Bailey: 'The Imagination may be compared to *Adam's* dream.' For that dream of God, and its counterpart, the hermit's, indicates that the transcendental faculty seemed to Keats as valid in poetry as in religion, and that Love is consistently his symbol for the divine creative spirit governing the universe.

There are several other interesting overtones in the letter to Bailey. It seems to me that Wordsworth's experience, as recorded in *Tintern Abbey*, blended in Keats' mind with Adam and the hermit, doubtless because Wordsworth had helped focus Keats' attitude toward poetry. Keats wrote to Bailey: 'I am certain of nothing but of the *holiness* of the Heart's *affections* and the truth of Imagination.' And Keats knew Wordsworth's 'serene and *blessed* mood, In which the *affections* gently lead us on . . . Until . . . we are laid asleep In body and become a living soul' (*T. A.*).

And from the same poem Keats knew Wordsworth's attitude: 'Therefore am I still a *lover* of the meadows and the woods, And mountains . . . both what they half *create* And what perceive.' Keats doubtless had noted that in Wordsworth's experience, too, Love implicitly leads to creation and perception. And that thought, universalized, is part of the theme of *Endymion*, in which Keats was profoundly concerned with the relationship of Love and Beauty, as with the stages and powers of Love.

As for the key phrases in the letter, in saying that *'What the imagination seizes as Beauty must be truth'* Keats seems to have meant this: What the Intuition apprehends as Beauty [which is God-created and the manifestation of the divine; and which, as illustrated in the four Books of *Endymion,* may be natural, intellectual, moral, or physical-spiritual] is the ultimate perception and highest experience of which man is capable. Hence this intuitive perception must be the truth or certainty for which man seeks, most often in vain because with the barren reason alone.

The letter shows that for Keats intuition is as vital and authentic in philosophy and affairs as in religion and art. And Keats, who was still groping to clarify his evolving conceptions, is here [as Thorpe pointed out] overstating the potency of intuition, which, like Wordsworth, he came to realize must be steadied and controlled by reason and by knowledge if it is to illuminate life or to solve man's creative problems.

In saying to Bailey: *'I have the same Idea of all our Passions as of Love: they are all, in their sublime, creative of essential Beauty'* Keats' speculations seem to have taken a dubious turn—dubious, despite 'the holiness of the Heart's affections.' This is not the place to discuss his merely tentative aesthetics. It may be noted, however, that Keats was steeped in the Shakespearean tragedies at this time and that within a month he was to write his reviews of Kean's acting. It is that circumstance which makes me suspect that, whether or not Keats thought all human passions capable of being sublime, his glimmering of truth was glimpsed in the passions of Shakespeare's heroes. It was, I think, Lear's anger and grief, Macbeth's ambition and fear, Othello's love and jealousy which led Keats to believe that, when sublimely depicted in art, all human passions can spiritualize or create spiritual beauty in the mind of the onlooker—even as Love (the Creator) does. And this conception, in turn, seems to underlie the inclusion of the Song of Sorrow, Alpheus, Glaucus, etc. in the spiritual pilgrimage of *Endymion*.

What he is saying in the letter to Bailey is that all our passions when sublime are, like sublime Love, creative of essential Beauty. And sublime love, the creative force, is, in terms of Adam and the hermit, to whom Keats refers, the God of Love, the Creator. For Keats' symbolism, despite his elliptical phraseology, is consistent.

14. *Letters*, p. 91. The hermit's 'by degrees' is noteworthy in connection with this Pleasure Thermometer.

15. *Blackwood's Magazine*, III, 52. (August 1818.)

16. Wieland's early interest in the Endymion legend is repeatedly reflected in *Oberon:* in the frequent images of the moon, and especially in the circumstance that his Titania's derivation from Diana is much more obvious than Shakespeare's. In *Oberon* Titania is always attended by moonbeams— as Keats had discovered when he replied to Mathew's 'queen of those regions of air' in his own 'Epistle.'

17. *Letters*, p. 67.

18. Ibid. p. 142.

19. For want of the key, only De Sélincourt, Murry, and especially Thorpe, to my knowledge, have come close to grasping its full import. Cf. *The Mind of John Keats*, p. 53 ff., for a very persuasive interpretation. One of Mr. Thorpe's most valuable conclusions is that the Indian maid or eastern queen is the symbol for humanity, in love for which Endymion penetrates to the threshold of heaven. Her Song of Sorrow, I believe, is of Wordsworthian timbre: 'the still sad music of humanity.'

20. *Letters*, p. 241.

CHAPTER IV

1. *Letters*, p. 108.
2. Ibid. p. 135.
3. Ibid. p. 152.
4. M. R. Ridley, *Keats' Craftsmanship*, p. 103.

5. Ibid. p. 108.

6. Ibid. p. 114.

7. Ibid. p. 124.

8. *Il Filocolo* as a possible source was first suggested by Prof. H. N. McCracken many years ago (cf. Lowell, op. cit. II, 158). Mr. Ridley has revived the theory and modified it to the extent of assuming that Keats read a French translation of Boccaccio's work. 'There is . . . no intrinsic improbability in the conjecture,' says Mr. Ridley in his valuable study, 'that Keats read Boccaccio's tale *in French,* and if he had read Mirabeau's [French] translation of the *Decameron,* he might well have looked round for other French translations' (op. cit. p. 106). One trouble with this 'conjecture' is that by Mr. Ridley's own earlier admission, 'I do not think that these [earlier] parallels amount at all to evidence that Keats had read Mirabeau's translation' (ibid. p. 56). With that one must agree. In general *Il Filocolo* is tedious and conventional enough, and the diction the stock in trade of a sufficiently commonplace type of romantic literature.

9. It is old Capulet himself who says to Paris, 'This night I hold an old accustom'd feast Whereto I have invited many a guest' (I, ii) and who later says to the masked but recognized Romeo, 'We have a trifling foolish banquet towards' (I, v). At the start of the latter scene we see the musicians waiting and the servingmen moving about. But despite the phrase 'many a guest,' the guest list of the servingman whom Romeo intercepts is not long, and anything but martial ('A fair assembly: whither should they come?'— I, ii).

Juliet's nurse, it has been argued, is the lover's only friend in the house of Capulet. But does either the lady or the nurse know him when he enters? The influence of the play on *St. Agnes* was very slight in tangible features. Intensity and delicacy of style are another matter, not readily measured. Only in that way can the tragedy have affected the genesis of *The Eve of St. Agnes* deeply.

10. Capulet's 'whispering tale told in a lady's ear' (I, v) occurs in no such peculiar conflux of emotions, specific and clashing.

11. Hardly has Huon arrived in Bagdad than 'they *chance* . . . to meet, Propt on her *crutch,* a little *aged crone'* (IV, 36). She hides the lover in her hut and tells of Rezia's haunting dream of her shadowy lover over whose image she broods; and of how in the dream Rezia was retransformed into human shape by Oberon's *wand.* Absorbed into *Endymion* IV and *St. Agnes,* v-vii, did this interception and gossiping tale also provide a hint for Porphyro's concealment and the 'ivory wand' of Angela? There is reason to think so, since the latter is the one who knows the 'liege-lord of all the Elves and Fays.'

12. The name of Porphyro is given as 'Lionel' in earlier drafts, and other English names are Madeline and Maurice; while 'southern moors' separate Porphyro from his home. The word 'signor,' obviously an after-

thought, occurs in one draft. On the other hand, the oriental setting of the prototype reappears in 'swart Paynims,' 'barbarian hordes,' 'no rude infidel,' Samarkand, Lebanon, Euphrates, etc.

13. (*The Road to Xanadu*, p. 58.) Unless Professor Lowes has written his classic study in vain, it has since been realized that the imagination works according to more or less uniform principles which, while differing in degree, apply to Keats as well as to Coleridge and the many other witnesses Professor Lowes summoned.

14. Cf. *Endymion* IV, the Song of Sorrow, p. 357. 'And sugar'd dates that o'er Euphrates fared' appears in a rejected holograph reading of *St. Agnes*, xxx. Incidentally, the old crone's hut (cf. note 11 above) stands quite near the river, and she serves some oriental fruits to Huon (cf. App. IV, p. 365).

15. Cf. Ridley, op. cit. p. 137, where the logomachy is summarized. But the reason for Keats' allusion to Merlin is clear enough.

16. Colvin, *John Keats*, p. 87.

17. In Christabel's chamber, 'carved so curiously, *Carved* with figures strange and sweet,' and containing the *'lamp* with two-fold silver *chain* . . . fastened to an angel's feet,' the saintly girl is told to disrobe by Geraldine. That daemonic lady speaks familiarly of 'all those who live in the upper sky' and of a 'guardian spirit' and also disrobes: 'Her silken robe and inner vest, Dropt to her feet, and full in view, Behold her bosom and half her side.' Suggestions of prayer abound. In the Second Part, Bard Bracy tells of the *dove* Christabel *'swelling* its *neck'* in the coils of the serpent.

It has long since been pointed out that *Christabel* left some traces in the final stanzas of *St. Agnes*. The reason is clear: both Coleridge's tale and *Oberon* are daemonic romances haunted by spirits of the air and boasting chambers in which the heroine dreams. *Oberon* contained the links of association that drew minor images from *Christabel* into the pattern of a dream of love. The latter poem may have left some slight traces in *St. Agnes* as early as stanzas xxii-xxiv. For Madeline, in the stanza before 'spirits of the air' appear, comes 'like ringdove fray'd.' In the next stanza the nightingale 'swells Her throat.' And a few lines later the casement in Madeline's chamber appears 'All garlanded with carven imag'ries' beneath which Madeline prays and then disrobes. Probably Keats studied Coleridge's manner of handling the scene of Geraldine's disrobing. In stanza xxxvi Keats likens Madeline to 'a deceived thing, A dove forlorn and lost.' And three stanzas later appears the 'chain-droop'd lamp.' In stanza xli Keats mentions 'the iron porch,' the 'wakeful bloodhound' and chains of the door as the lovers flee out of the silent castle. These are probably reminiscences of the iron gate, little door, and wakeful mastiff which Christabel and her unholy guest pass on their entering her father's castle. And these reminiscences were probably evoked by the daemon king's appearance in the hall of Rezia's father just before the lovers flee into the elfin storm.

18. I think Keats derived a few more hints from Shakespeare's dramatic romance than has been realized. Thomas B. Stroup pointed out (cf. *E. S.*, xvii, Aug. 1935, p. 145) that Keats' *'azure*-lidded sleep' and *'tinct* with' are phrases evidently recalled from the brief scene in Imogen's chamber (*Cymbeline* II, ii). That sleeper's eyelids are 'white and azure, lac'd with heaven's own tinct.' The reason Keats recalled this lies, I think, in *Oberon*. For like Rezia of the visions of delight, Imogen is a *princess* beset by 'a *wooer* more *hateful.*' A few lines later, as she is about to fall *asleep,* we hear her say: 'From *fairies* and the tempters of the night Guard me.' Rezia's situation, in the pattern of a dream of love which Keats was following, could not have failed to recall Imogen. And it is noteworthy that no sooner is the latter asleep than the villainous Iachimo comes out of the trunk where he has been concealed, observes her beauty carefully, and says: 'fresh lily, *whiter* than thy *sheets'* and ' 'Tis *her breathing* that Perfumes the chamber thus.' The lily and perfume were further links to *Oberon* in the hall of Canto v, and were probably instrumental in the coalescing process.

For Madeline is no sooner asleep than Porphyro, lover rather than villain, comes out of his hiding place, notes how she sleeps 'In *blanched linen,'* and 'listen'd to *her breathing.'* I suspect that the hints for imagery and action came from Iachimo; that his actual concealment in a lady's chamber reinforced and was modified by the lover Huon's suggested concealment in the dreaming Rezia's chamber. For Keats had just been describing the dreaming Madeline in terms of Rezia, 'where swart Paynims pray.' This and other elements that we have seen show that Keats recalled both Rezia's and Imogen's chambers almost simultaneously. And in both chambers he saw a hint for Porphyro's concealment.

19. Cf. Ridley, op. cit. p. 171, where is quoted Woodhouse's revealing letter of 20 Sept. 1819, to Taylor, concerning Keats' revisions.

20. In his first speech to Juliet, Romeo says: 'If I profane with my unworthiest hand This holy *shrine* . . . My lips, two blushing pilgrims . . .' (I, iv).

21. Aside from the echo from *Christabel,* in this stanza Keats, thinking of the elfin storm and the earlier 'tempest fell,' also has: 'the besieging *wind's* uproar; And the long *carpets rose along the gusty floor.*' He may have been recalling a scene in *Oberon* which he had used as early as the 'Shell Stanzas.' For in describing Oberon's fairy canopy, Wieland mentioned its 'silken *carpet* spread upon the ground . . . Whose airy swell at every touch *ascends'* (III, 53).

CHAPTER V

1. *Letters,* p. 320.
2. Ibid. pp. 348 and 352.
3. Ibid. p. 369.

4. Ibid. p. 468 (Feb. 1820).

5. C. L. Finney, op. cit. II, 696.

6. Douglas Bush, 'Notes on Keats' Reading' in *PMLA*, L. 3, p. 789. Ovid's tale also helped Keats conceive of the fading of Lamia at the end of his poem.

7. Cf. *End*. IV, 66 (' "O for Hermes' wand" ') and its background in *Oberon* IV, 48, in ch. III, p. 354 f.

8. Cf. Bush, op. cit. p. 786.

9. This 'blaze' and 'glows' so close to the chamber door probably had something to do with Love's 'terrific glare' and 'glow' above Keats' chamber door.

10. In Coleridge's phrase, he 'dissolved, diffused, dissipated' the baroque scene, selected what he found fitting, and discarded the rest. Its elements appear now in clusters and now scattered throughout Part II of *Lamia*.

11. Concerning Keats' knowledge of Diodorus and the antecedents of Lamia it is noteworthy that 'Perhaps the two best specimens of the handling of the myth [of Lamia, the African queen] are those by . . . Diodorus Siculus, and his . . . predecessor, Duris of Samos' (A. H. Nethercot, *The Road to Tryermaine*, 1939, p. 86). And to Diodorus, John Livingston Lowes long since pointed out, Keats owed some features of the Triumph of Bacchus in *Endymion*. Similarly he 'was especially indebted' to Chapman's Homer, to Hesiod, Ovid, 'and Booth's translation of Diodorus Siculus's Historical Library' for the mythological matter in *Hyperion*, according to C. L. Finney (op. cit. II, 494).

12. The queen and *'enchantress* summons [Huon] to a splendid hall' where 'a second veil flies back *by magic* call' and 'a godlike feast' waits, 'whose taste might life recall' (XI, 52). Such concepts not only facilitated coalescence with the elfin queen, who is another sort of enchantress, but also were capable of recalling the fays of medieval romance. These fays (of whom Keats' own lady in *La Belle Dame sans Merci* is one) were believed to be 'mysterious ladies, "primarily enchantresses" and "often regarded as mortal" with "no limitations of beauty, age, or resources." ' (With this conception compare Wieland's enchantress-queen.) They dwelt in 'some inaccessible country concealed from human eyes by glamour, or in some mysterious islands . . . or in the far-off *island paradise* of Avalon . . .' (Precisely as did Titania in her banishment in the sacred isle.) 'They came into a world of mortals to gain a knight's love' and were often regarded as a 'queenly princess'—like Lamia and Wieland's queen, whom the German poet had humanized and motivated daemonically. The fays of romance were a vital link between Titania and that queen. For the nature of the fays see M. Latham, *The Elizabethan Fairies*, p. 37, whence the above is cited.

13. While 'The God, dove-*footed, glided silently* Round *bush* and tree . . . Until *he found a* palpitating *snake,*' the 'goddess' queen seeks Huon (of the mournful voice). And 'Her noiseless feet advance where the light

branches were in motion seen. 'Twas but a lizard . . . From the green bush . . . glide' (xi, 19). This scene, which occurs just after the meeting with Huon and the turning back of her regal neck, may well have suggested Hermes' action. And is the dove-snake imagery a recollection from *Christabel?*

14. It will be recalled from our study of Book iii of *Endymion* and Keats' assimilation of the scene in Oberon's forest, that Huon, shortly after being warned by his superstitious squire, sees the herd of harts and hinds. 'Their ceaseless groans like warnings strike the ear, And their *large eyes* o'erflow with many a *tear.*' These beasts, the squire says, had been

> '*Men once* as good as we, in *form* the same.
> Heaven knows in *what wild skin* our human frame
> Shall be ere dawn array'd *to make the demon sport.*'
> (ii, 11)

The gorgeous snake Lamia has eyes that wept they were so fair; and she says: 'I was a woman, let me have once more A woman's shape . . . Give me my woman's form.' These echoes need not be illusory in the light of Keats' allusion to 'the prosperous woods' and 'King Oberon's . . . sceptre,' and the evidence, in *Otho the Great* and *Endymion,* of his minute knowledge of Oberon's power over sinful men: punitive transformation.

15. Bush, 'Notes on Keats' Reading,' p. 789.

16. M. R. Ridley, *Keats' Craftsmanship,* p. 251. The *Letters* show that Keats knew *Christabel* as early at least as his visit to Burns' cottage. And *The Eve of St. Agnes,* we saw, contains a few reminiscences. It is quite likely that Keats, with Oberon's curse on the 'bosom snake' in mind, owed the idea of partial transformation, of a woman of daemonic lineage into a serpent, to Geraldine's bosom, 'the mark of . . . shame' and 'seal of . . . sorrow,' which is her penance.

17. Ridley, op. cit. p. 252.

18. Cf. 'Swift *melting into air* the fairy flies'—that is, the daemon king, Oberon (vi, 10).

19. In view of her daemonic powers, 'high inspired' and intuitive, it may well be that Lamia was intended by Keats to symbolize not merely sensuous beauty but also sensuous poetry, which can dream at will in the prison house of the body, and with music build in air its castles of delight for its lover: such poetry as he himself had written particularly at the start of his career. That Keats intended Lamia as some such symbol is hinted by his sympathy with her, by the conflict in Lycius, and by the abiding conflict in himself between love for sensuous poetry and love for the poetry of revelation or 'knowledge.

Moreover, the nature of his symbol is even more strongly hinted by his repeated use of the aerial spirit as a symbol for the poetical imagination and poetry. Thus, besides the imagery of *The Poet* and 'my demon Poesy' in the *Ode on Indolence,* it is also noteworthy that in his review of Kean's acting in *Henry IV* (the review appeared in the *Champion* for 28 December 1817) Keats wrote thus: 'the poetry of Shakespeare is generally free as the wind—*a perfect thing of the elements, winged* and sweetly coloured. *Poetry* must be free! It *is of the air,* not of the earth; and the higher it soars the nearer it gets to its home.' (Cit. by Lowell, I, 539. Italics mine.) Consistently Keats' symbol for poetry was the aerial spirit or daemon who resembles not only Wieland's Oberon and Titania but also Lamia, 'the demon's self' of the 'faery roof' with its 'noise of wings.'

In this connection, too, compare the three 'demons' Love, Ambition, and Poesy in *On Indolence* with 'Love,' the 'demon eyes' of Apollonius, and Lamia 'the demon's self' of 'heavenly progeny.' I suspect that the two sets of symbols are essentially the same.

20. Cf. *Letters,* p. 142: ' "Knowledge is Sorrow" . . . "Sorrow is Wisdom"—and for aught we can know for certainty "Wisdom is Folly." ' Cf. too, the letter to Bailey, p. 124 above.

21. I am indebted to Professor Emery E. Neff of Columbia University for suggesting to me this aspect of the conflict.

22. Through self-projection and probably his heroine's background in the 'tale from faery land,' Keats came to sympathize deeply with his penanced 'gentle Lamia.' But to the average reader, and even to so great a critic and biographer as Sir Sidney Colvin, this sympathetic attitude has been bewildering because of Lamia's traditionally evil nature. In choosing her history as a theme, Keats put himself in the perilous position of the dramatist who, unable to rewrite history, tries nevertheless to make a hero of a well-known figure condemned by history, in terms of which he must act and still be heroic.

But there is another flaw in *Lamia.* Keats' purpose became more and more complex, even as his own problems did, as he proceeded. And his daemonic machinery in the romance was imperfectly integrated with the legend and his own symbolism. Thus we are told that the guardian Love with his 'terrific glare' contributed to Lamia's frustration: 'For all this came a ruin.' To be consistent with this and the legend, Apollonius would have to be the agent of Love. But while Apollonius is thought by Lycius to have 'demon eyes' like that guardian god, who demands purity and constancy and who punishes those betrayed by sensual 'joys that seduce'; and though Apollonius enters the 'palace of sweet sin' and is the teacher and sage, he is thought by Lycius, with whom Keats sympathizes, to be 'the ghost of folly haunting my sweet dreams.' Thus Apollonius is at once the defender of such constancy as Lycius [cf. Glaucus] lacked, constancy to spiritual ideals, and a destroying force with which Keats is bitterly impatient.

This cleavage evidently was born of Keats' own inner strife and of his sympathy with the subtle being, of 'heavenly progeny,' which he had created: a being who had become the symbol of the dream world of sensuous beauty and imagination. Yet that conception also ran afoul, afoul of 'sweet sin' and the ethical bias of the legend. The hand that guided the shuttle deserted the pattern still further for an aside, the subject of favorite speculation: reasoned philosophy versus the intuitive 'life of sensations.' In the pursuit of that thought Keats became polemical and introduced additional symbols and the attack on Apollonius with its romantic anti-intellectualism, even though this attack harmonized with neither legend nor daemonic machinery, and so broke up the unity of the design without itself being sustained or consistent.

Ultimately *Lamia* reveals several strata of symbolism and a bold but divided intention. For further discussion of the attack on Apollonius, see App. v, p. 396.

CHAPTER VI

1. *Letters*, p. 91.
2. In conjunction with a stanza of the Indian Maid's Song of Sorrow in *End.* iv: 'Beneath my palm trees, by the river side' we saw this stanza of *Oberon:*

> Where high Euphrates winds its gentle tide,
> Onward they took their solitary way,
> Beneath o'er*shadow*ing palms that dim the day.
> Enchanting land! creation's fairest pride!
> Slowly they went: *still*, pensive, neither spoke:
> Each inly mus'd—*no voice* the *silence* broke.
> *The* balmy *breath of morn*, her roseate gleam,
> The birds' gay melodies, the murmuring *stream*,
> To visions of delight enchanted fancy woke!

In the next lines 'Merlin's tomb' appears. And the visions above anticipate Rezia's by a few pages, those other 'visions of delight' drawn into *St. Agnes.* But now, a few stanzas later, Huon first sees Bagdad thus:

> *Far in a vale* that stretch'd before their way,
> The gleams of evening to their gaze expose
> Where crown'd with many a tower that stately rose,
> The queen of cities spreads her golden scene—
> A Paradise expands, for ever green,
> And here the Tigris winds, and there Euphrates flows.
>   (OBERON iv, 19 and 31)

With this compare the opening lines of *Hyperion:* 'Deep *in* the *shady* sadness of *a vale Far* sunken from the healthy *breath of morn* . . . *Still* as *the silence* round about his lair . . . A *stream* went *voiceless* by' (lines 1-11).

And there may be some faint echoes of Titania's grief ('beneath the cave' in her craggy isle, 'Pil'd up with monstrous ruins height on height'—viii.

60-1) in the famous description of the den of the Titans in *Hyperion,* ii, 5 ff. For while that description owes a good deal to the scenery of the Scottish tour, Keats in line 30 wrote: 'Far from her moon had Phoebe wandered,' Phoebe who is Titania.

3. Cf. App. iii, p. 325 (*End.* i, 823 and 828).

4. Cf. too Wordsworth's *Personal Talk,* 53-4, which may also have provided a hint.

5. Cf. *Letters,* p. 335 et seq. in which are some interesting phrases, overtones and symbols, from the 'Pleasure Thermometer' and its mystical reservoir.

6. Cf. Lowell, op. cit. ii, p. 229.

7. Cf. *The Faerie Queene,* ii, vi, and *Pericles,* i, i, 34-40, as De Sélincourt suggested. And Colvin found a phrase perhaps echoed from William Browne and another from Wordsworth.

8. '*Moss* the *cavern* strews . . . And far more fragrant than . . . From *lily's* . . . breath, or scent of vernal *rose*' (vii, 41. Cf. K 9 and 11).

9. Cf. Finney, op. cit. ii, pp. 618-9. The verb 'fledge' (K 55) is a direct reminiscence from the Welsh letter to Tom of 29 June 1818. Mountains evidently were the link.

10. In connection with the Ode, Mr. Finney (ii, p. 617) pointed out that 'Keats dissolved Milton's stanza [the 19th of the Hymn on Christ's Nativity] into its primal elements and shaped the elements into a new and original whole.' As a matter of fact, other echoes from later stanzas also appear in the *Ode to Psyche,* which is a composite.

11. Douglas Bush (op. cit. p. 802) pointed out the line in the *Amoretti,* xxii, of Spenser: 'Her temple fayre is built *within my mind,*' reminiscence of which seems to have blended with Titania's 'untrodden regions' (K 51)—by way of *Faerie Queene?*

12. Cf. Wordsworth's 'sweetest melodies are those that are by distance made more sweet,' lines 25-6 of *Personal Talk,* published in the 1807 volume. Murry (*Studies in Keats,* p. 140) goes so far as to believe that the germ of Keats' entire Ode was in Wordsworth's sonnet on the sight of a picture by Sir George Beaumont. But wasn't the Ode the natural outgrowth of the gradations of happiness and a dualistic view of the universe?

CHAPTER VII

1. Finney, op. cit. ii, p. 740.

2. Cf. *The Faerie Queene,* ii, x, 72-4.

3. Colvin, op. cit. p. 445.

4. Titania flies from the volcanic isle just before we hear Huon's mournful voice from the forest: the voice heeded by Oberon at the source of the Nile and by Hermes in *Lamia.*

⚛ APPENDIX I ⚛

(Keats and Mathew's *To a Poetical Friend*)

I am deeply indebted to the Trustees of the Pierpont Morgan Library and to its director, Miss Belle da Costa Greene, for permission to print from my transcription not only the text of the early version of George Felton Mathew's *To a Poetical Friend* but also Woodhouse's notes to the poem.

Both text and notes, in the autograph of Richard Woodhouse, are to be found in the *Woodhouse Book*, folios 52-3, in the Morgan Library.

As footnotes to lines 37, 40, and 43 of his text, Woodhouse added the following under the last line of Mathew's poem:

> ¹, ² Alluding to Keats's then profession of a Surgeon.—
> ³ 'Mongst boughs pavilion'd, where the Deer's swift leap
> 'Startles the wild bee from the foxglove bell.'—
> Keats's 7th [?] Son. p. 85.

N.B. Most of the pieces underwent alteration previously to being published; and it ~~was~~ [?sic] is probable that the allusion to this Sonnet, as originally written, was even more perfect than at present.

Written in a different ink, these notes may have been added by Woodhouse some time after he had copied the text of the poem.

Prefixed to the fair copy of Mathew's 'Lines' appears this:

One of Keats's Epistles (p. 53) is addressed to Geo: Felton Matthew [sic], who is very flatteringly hailed as a brother poet.—The verses (p. 29 of Keats's poems) I am informed were sent to the Misses Mathew, cousins of the above Gentleman, then at Hastings; & that Mr. M. was then with them. —The next copy of verses (p. 32)—'on receiving a shell and verses from the same ladies.'—appear to be addressed to *Mr*. Mathew.—I am not aware that Mr. M. has ever published any of his compositions: I have obtained the follow [sic] copy of verses, which were written by him, and clearly refer to the copy sent to him by Keats, & published p. 32.—How far Mr. M. is entitled to the poetical character assigned to him by Keats, it would be scarcely fair to judge from this one specimen. — ——

. . .

317

Although it seems to have been unknown to Woodhouse, who may have 'obtained the . . . copy of verses' from Keats himself, Mathew revised and polished his 'Lines' *To a Poetical Friend* and then published them in the *European Magazine* for October 1816. His revisions are for the most part minor (cf. lines 4, 8, 9, 10, 11, 12) and do not conceal their origin. A major change is the interpolation of the four new lines following the fifth quatrain.

I give this revised version from Mr. Murry's transcription (*Studies in Keats*, 1939, pp. 1-2):

To a Poetical Friend

O Thou who delightest in fanciful song,
  And tellest strange tales of the elf and the fay;
Of giants tyrannic, whose talismans strong
  Have power to charm gentle damsels astray;

Of courteous knights-errant, and high-mettled steeds;
  Of forests enchanted, and marvellous streams:—
Of bridges, and castles, and desperate deeds;
  And all the bright fictions of fanciful dreams:—

Of captures, and rescues, and wonderful loves;
  Of blisses abounding in dark leafy bowers;—
Of murmuring music in shadowy groves,
  And beauty reclined on her pillow of flowers:—

O where did thine infancy open its eyes?
  And who was the nurse that attended thy spring?
For sure thou'rt exotic to these frigid skies,
  So splendid the song that thou lovest to sing.

Perhaps thou hast traversed the glorious East;
  And like the warm breath of its sun, and its gales,
That wander 'mid gardens of flowers to feast,
  Are tinctured with every rich sweet that prevails?

O no!—for a Shakspeare—a Milton are ours!
  And who e'er sung sweeter, or stronger, than they?
As thine is, I ween was the spring of *their* powers;
  Like theirs, is the cast of thine earlier lay.

It is not the climate, or scenery round,
  It was not the nurse that attended thy youth;
That gave thee those blisses which richly abound
  In magical numbers to charm, and to soothe.

O no!—'tis the Queen of those regions of air—
The gay fields of Fancy—thy spirit has blest;
She cherish'd thy childhood with fostering care,
And nurtur'd her boy with the milk of her breast.

She tended thee ere thou couldst wander alone,
And cheer'd thy wild walks amidst terror and dread;—
She sung thee to sleep with a song of her own,
And laid thy young limbs on her flowery bed.

She gave thee those pinions with which thou delightest
Sublime o'er her boundless dominions to rove;
The tongue too she gave thee with which thou invitest
Each ear to thy stories of wonder and love.

And when evening shall free thee from Nature's decays,*
And release thee from Study's severest control,
Oh warm thee in Fancy's enlivening rays;
And wash the dark spots of disease from thy soul.

And let not the spirit of Poesy sleep;
Of Fairies and Genii continue to tell—
Nor suffer the innocent deer's timid leap
To fright the wild bee from her flowery bell.

                                      G. F. M.
* Alluding to his medical character.

We are not concerned with the poetic merit of these lines or with
their lack of it. Their value is of another sort. In this revised version
the interpolated stanza, beginning 'O no!—for a Shakspeare—a Milton
are ours,' contains one interesting feature. Since Mathew's verses are
full of allusions to Sotheby's translation of Wieland's *Oberon*, the phrase
'are *ours*' may well be a note of patriotism. And the linking of Wieland with Shakespeare and Milton is even more interesting, for Keats
came to associate the three poets more than once in his later years. He
also reverted to several other conceptions that first appear in Mathew's
To a Poetical Friend.

                        .   .   .

(Further echoes of Mathew's 'Lines' in Keats' 'Epistle to Mathew')

Mathew's fanciful tribute to Keats, ' 'tis the Queen of those regions
of air . . . thy spirit has blest' (M 25-6) was based, we saw, upon the

identification of Keats with Rezia's infant, who was attended at birth by Titania. And Mathew's line evidently evoked the Ovidian metamorphoses which Keats had Mathew undergo in his answering 'Epistle.' Keats wrote (lines 76-9):

> For thou wast once a flowret blooming wild,
> Close to the source, bright, pure, and undefil'd,
> Whence gush the *streams* of song: in happy hour
> *Came chaste Diana from her shady bower* . . .

The phrase 'the source . . . of song' is noteworthy in the light of the allusions to *Oberon* VIII in Mathew's *To a Poetical Friend*. And the italicized words also are revealing. For the childbirth scene takes place in Titania's moonlit and rose-filled bower or grot, which is situated in the flowering paradise that abounds in pure streams. And as Keats knew, in Ovid 'Titania' is a synonym for Diana, the moon goddess. Thus by an eminently characteristic fusion, which we shall see again elsewhere, the Gothic [Shakespeare-Wieland] figure of Titania seems to have blended in the lines above with the figure of classical myth. But the italicized imagery above is a direct echo of Canto VIII by way of Mathew's tribute and his picture of Rezia: 'beauty reclined on a pillow of flowers' in Titania's shady bower. The various metamorphoses that Mathew undergoes in the continuation of Keats' 'Epistle' to him, are thoroughly Ovidian.

✍ APPENDIX II ✍

(Keats, Clarke, and *Oberon*)

In the 'Epistle' *To Charles Cowden Clarke* (September 1816), in which he acknowledged his deep indebtedness to his friend and former teacher, Keats again mentioned Titania. First he alluded to Ovid; then, much as in the 'Shell Stanzas,' to Tasso and Spenser. Then, immediately after those two writers of chivalric romance, he wrote of Clarke as one

> Who had of all that's sweet tasted, and seen,
> From silv'ry ripple, up to beauty's queen;
> From *the sequester'd haunts of* gay *Titania,*
> To the blue dwelling of divine Urania . . .
> (lines 38-41)

It is noteworthy that Shakespeare is nowhere mentioned in the list of debts. And we saw that the epithet 'sequester'd' and the very phrase 'sequester'd haunts' occur only in *Oberon* in connection with Titania. The first phrase was used by Sotheby to describe her island retreat when 'far, far away,' and the second to describe the environs of the enchanted forest, alluded to in Mathew's 'Lines' and in Keats' 'Shell Stanzas.' Moreover, Keats' Titania above is mentioned in conjunction with two chivalric romances as if in a logical grouping of poems according to type. In saying that Clarke had 'seen . . . the sequester'd haunts of . . . Titania,' did Keats mean that Clarke had read *Oberon* before him and introduced him to that chivalric romance too? It is impossible to say.

But it is also noteworthy that it was to Clarke that Keats said (*after* the Mathew poems had been written) that the sunbeam coming into the lecture room had brought with it 'a whole troop of *creatures floating in the rays,*' and that that picture had lured him off 'to Oberon and fairy land.' In *Oberon* 'spirits . . . in groups, their king surround' on the mountain-top (x, 14). And a whole troop of creatures floating appear visibly in the enchanted forest at the fairy jubilee beneath the

321

moon, on the occasion of the 'airy march' into the diaphanous palace of Canto XII, as in Keats' 'Epistle to Mathew.' Shakespeare's fairies are terrestrial garden fairies, while Wieland's are aerial spirits and 'sylphs' (one is explicitly called 'the son of light'—*Oberon* x, 19) who visibly fly and float through the daemonic romance. Keats and Mathew knew this early, as the illusions to 'Fairies and Genii' and 'the Queen of those regions of air' plainly indicate. But one wonders whether Clarke understood Keats' allusions fully. It is not impossible that he did, and that in saying 'to Oberon and fairy land' Keats meant 'to *Oberon* and fairy land.'

All that we can know with certainty about Keats' earliest familiarity with Wieland's romance is that he read it with George Felton Mathew in 1815 and that both thought very highly of it. The rest must remain surmise.*

* Cf., however, Mary Cowden Clarke's references to the première (1826) of 'von Weber's enchanting fairy opera . . . a never-to-be-forgotten occasion' (*My Long Life*, London, 1896, pp. 38-9). Her husband was well read, and may have known Sotheby's version more than a decade earlier.

⚞ APPENDIX III ⚟
(Addenda to *Endymion*)

1, 63-8 (p. 115):

Immediately after the opening lines and after speaking of sending his 'herald thought into a *wilderness*,' Keats begins thus:

> Upon the sides of Latmos was outspread
> A mighty forest; for the moist earth fed
> So plenteously all weed-hidden roots
> Into o'er-hanging boughs, and precious fruits.
> And it had gloomy shades, sequestered deep,
> Where no man went . . .

Titania's mountain sanctuary above the sea lies 'far *sequester'd* from the world of tears' (*Oberon* VIII, 9); amid the deep, rock-girt forest whose *'O'ershadowing* fir-trees spread a *gloom profound*' (VIII, 5). It is on the far side of the mountain barrier, separated from the wilderness of desert by towering crags; and it comprises the sacred groves where no man went but the aged hermit, until the wanderer and his eastern bride arrive as if by miracle. And

> In other worlds, in realms of fairy land   K 1, 92 *
> She seems to pass; and sure, had never seen
> The heaven so blue, the lap of *earth so* green,
> Or leaf so fresh on vernal bow'r expand;   K 1, 85 †
> For where the mountains round in guardian rows
> Shelter the bosom that their heights enclose,
> And fence from blasts that on their summits beat,
> *Grapes* richly clustering swell with genial heat,
> Dark hangs the *ripen*ing *fig,* the golden *orange* glows.
>   (OBERON VIII, 12)

It was so fertile because of 'a spring that playful burst' (VIII, 8) and because

---

* 'fairy phantasies.'
† 'freshness of heaven . . . the blue.'

From bubbling rills the purling currents stray
Down the green *moss* . . .

(VIII, 51)

I, 251:

And Keats duly mentions Pan's 'enmossed realms . . . fig trees . . .
ripen'd fruitage . . . golden honeycombs,' all in conjunction with the
sacred groves of the spiritualizing visions.

I, 148-56 (p. 116):

Having wandered 'Thro' the steep *mountains* to a dell profound,'

From the last step as Huon faint *descends,*
Gay smiles, like Paradise, the lovely scene:
A man before him stands of noble mien . . .

(OBERON VIII, 3-4)

the silver-bearded hermit, *beneath the forest trees.* And

. . . weak with hunger, with fatigue o'erdone,
Amid these cliffs, *beneath* whose dreary height
No trace of man had ever cheer'd his sight,   K 68 *
Where *from the rocks* that every way surround,
O'ershadowing fir-trees spread a gloom profound . . .

(VIII, 5)

the astonished and awed Huon, 'worn out, exhausted, pale with ceaseless woe' (VIII, 7) thinks the hermit a ghost. But soon the old man
'Fruits *of all* kinds . . . in *a basket*' brought. The aged priest in
Endymion comes from 'beneath the forest trees' and in his left hand he
held 'a basket full Of all sweet herbs.'

I, 189-91; 198-9:

It is this same aged priest who says to those who 'paled gently for
slight fear' and to Endymion who stood 'wan, and pale, and with an
awed face':

'Whether descended from beneath the rocks
That overtop your mountains . . .' †

* I, 68: 'Where no man went.'
† Just before he encounters the aged hermit, Huon 'bending from the *mountains'*
*top*most peak' strains his eyes 'o'er ocean far and wide' in the manner of Keats'
shepherds somewhat later.

Keats seems to have derived further suggestions from the ghostly meeting for Endymion's meeting with Glaucus (cf. III, 217-20; 255-7).*

. . .

(Pp. 120 and 121):

The thematic passage, or gradations of happiness, of *Endymion* continues thus:

K I, 813	'when we combine therewith,
	Life's self is nourish'd by its proper pith,
815	And we are nurtured like a pelican brood.†
	Aye, so delicious is the unsating food,
817	*That men, who might have tower'd in the van*
	Of all the congregated world, to fan
819	And winnow *from* the *coming* step of *time* ‡
	All chaff of custom, *wipe away* all *slime*
821	*Left by men*-slugs and human serpentry,
	Have been content to let occasion die,
823	*Whilst they did sleep in love's elysium.* §
	And, truly, I would rather be struck dumb,
825	Than speak against this *ardent* listlessness: ‖
	For I have ever thought that it might *bless*
827	The world with benefits unknowingly;
	As does the nightingale, upperched high,
829	And cloister'd among cool and bunched leaves—
	She sings but to *her* love . . .'

There let us pause a moment. We saw from the symbolism in I, 807, that Keats' Love is divine, the universal spirit of God the Creator. And in this cryptic passage, Keats is still writing in terms of that conception and of the hermit, who had come to see visions of God in his sleep in Titania's divinely beautiful Elysium (cf. K 823). There it was that he attained highest happiness in 'fellowship divine, a fellowship with es-

* And in *End.* I, 182, the *Ancient Mariner* seems to have left a trace—by way, probably, of the hermit.

† By our own innermost [divine] spirit.

‡ To prepare themselves for death and heaven, like the hermit.

§ Titania's, where the hermit found the Love sublime of God, in his dream-visions in sleep; but also where the mortal lovers, the wanderer and his eastern bride, found their love spiritualized.

‖ Mystic's passiveness which revealed love to the hermit.

sence.' It is for that reason that Rezia on first seeing him notes how 'His
eye a smile on *all creation* beam'd.' For

W I   *Time* from his features long had *worn away*   K 820
       The *rust* of earth, and passion's gloomy frown:
3   He would not stoop to grasp a falling crown,
       Nor bend the sceptre of a world to sway.   K 817-18
5   Free from the vain desires that earth enthrall,
       Free from vain terrors that mankind appal,
7   Untouch'd by pain, and unassail'd by fear,
       To *truth alone* he turn'd his mental ear:
9   Alone to nature tun'd, and her sweet simple call.
                                        (OBERON VIII, 15)

In all that 'nature' and 'all creation,' we know, the hermit had come
to see divine beauty. And the 'truth alone' that he had sought is also
God, the ultimate spiritual Truth and Beauty which the hermit 'by
degrees' had found: in dream-visions of immortality. These visions came
to him long after he had fled to Titania's sacred groves

10   . . . with woe-bewilder'd mind:
       And found, what grief had never hop'd to find,
12   Peace and *content* as tardy years retreat.   K 822
       Tho' worldlings from the wretch had *basely flown* . . .   K 821
                                        (VIII, 21)

It is to this experience—of the power of love and beauty, which the
hermit found to be divine, after he had 'by degrees . . . struggled thro'
the flood' of grief *—that Keats alluded in the opening lines of *Endymion,* in the gradations of happiness and their continuation above, and
again in the lines that follow.

If we bear in mind the hermit's sense of the presence, in 'all creation,'
of the divine Love (the Creator), then Keats' next lines are significant.
Speaking of the nightingale, he says:

I, 830   'She sings but to *her* love, nor e'er conceives
         How tiptoe Night holds back her dark-grey hood.
832   Just so may *love,* although *'tis understood*
         The mere commingling of passionate breath,
834   *Produce more* than our searching witnesseth:
         What I know not: but who, of men, can tell

* *Oberon* VIII, 22. Cf. p. 128.

836 That flowers would bloom, or that green fruit would swell
   To melting pulp, that fish would have bright mail,
838 The earth its dower of river, wood, and vale,
   The meadows runnels, runnels pebble-stones,
840 The seed its harvest, or the lute its tones,
   Tones ravishment, or ravishment its sweet,
842 If human souls did never kiss and greet?'

Like the hermit, in other words, Endymion says that love 'in *all* his creatures' shines. Endymion's is a cosmic restatement of the same religious truth. And that truth is part of the theme of *Endymion,* whose thematic passage now shows further how closely Keats had identified himself with the hermit's life and experience. For Endymion proceeds thus:

843 'Now, *if* this earthly *love has power to make*
   Men's being *mortal, immortal;* to *shake*   W 6 *
845 *Ambition from their memories,* and *brim*   W 3
   Their measure of content; what merest whim, W 12
847 Seems all this poor endeavour after fame, †
   To one, *who keeps* within his *steadfast* aim
849 *A love immortal,* an *immortal too.*
   Look not so wilder'd; for these things are true . . .'

In the ultimate sense, in which essential Beauty is Truth: in the light of the 'shadow of reality to come' which is immortality in God, these things were true and prophetic for Keats precisely as he says. And they represent some of the profoundest elements of his own philosophy of life: that renunciation of earthly ambitions, for love of the divine principle or cosmic law of Love, can bring man immortality.

As for its derivation, and that of the symbols in which poetically it was uttered, a reading of the italicized image-concepts with the hermit's life in mind will once again show what Keats learned from the blissful sage and mystic. After intense imaginative perception Keats had identified his yearning for highest beauty and immortality with the hermit's. He saw the sage's life as symbolic of a way to the highest life, even as he had in *Sleep and Poetry.* He saw how the hermit had transcended

---

* Also the hermit's sense of immortality and state of bliss: 'Joys that await the blest his soul illume' (VIII, 28).

† That is, earthly fame, as Peona's reproaches have made clear (cf. I, 737).

all earthly illusions, passions, ambitions, woes, through the consoling and spiritualizing power of divine beauty and love in all things earthly; how he had come to perceive spiritual beauty informing the real and tangible; how *'by degrees'* he had perceived the divine itself; and how in losing himself therein he had arrived at the highest bliss, the 'chief intensity' which is Love the Creator of all beauty, and far above the earthly love and friendship he had lost.

And all this had happened to the hermit, Keats knew, after

> The fountain of his [earthly] *joy for ever* fails—
> How insupportable the friendless cot
> *Where happiness* once fix'd her chosen place!
>   (OBERON VIII, 20)

'Wherein lies happiness?' Keats had echoed. And he had also answered in terms of the hermit: 'in that which becks our ready minds to fellowship divine, a fellowship with essence.' Keats had perceived the power of every thing of beauty ('a joy forever') in terms of its divine origin, its consoling and spiritualizing power and mediation between earth and heaven, even as the hermit had. For the induction and the thematic passage of *Endymion* are parts of the same message, which the entire action of the romance illustrates. And the symbols in which Keats conveyed that message reveal the creative process of absorption, distillation, and re-creation, as well as his meaning.

In studying those symbols in their source, where they appear compactly in fourteen stanzas within the space of a few adjoining pages, ours is merely the privilege of seeing the light more fully as we watch the artist at work, the 'hermit young' who like his saintly teacher achieved the kingdom of heaven.

In part, both *Sleep and Poetry* and the letter to Bailey confirm the key significance of the hermit in Keats' intuitions. Both show that the sage had helped him formulate two aspirations: to renounce worldliness and seek highest happiness in a poet's quest of beauty, essential truth, and immortality; and through that 'life of Sensations,' of intuitive visions and highest contemplation of the spiritual—that life which foreshadows the heavenly state or 'reality to come'—to transcend earthly reality and penetrate as in a dream vision of the 'form divine' to that Beauty which is also Truth. For the artist, however, the form divine may be ideal beauty. And for the mystic—'To *truth* alone he turn'd his mental ear'—the form divine, Truth, Love, and Beauty are one in God. Keats' symbolism comprehends both. Ultimate truth is apprehended by super-rational intuitions in art as in religion, by the hermit as by Keats. And the hermit's gradual spiritualization, moreover, was vital to the 'pleasure thermometer,' for it was 'by degrees' that he achieved fellowship with the divine and ultimate immortality. Those degrees closely resemble Endymion's four stages. Like Endymion a leader in the 'congregated world,' the hermit had come to perceive its vanity and illusion, its ignoble deception, and the 'o'erdarkened ways' of a world of impermanence, grief, and death—even as is reflected in Keats' opening lines and in the continuation of the thematic passage above. When the hermit arrived in Titania's paradise, he wanted only a grave to end his earthly woe. But then he found what he had never expected to find:

1. That the beauty of the real or visible world can uplift and heal the spirit: 'Peace, stillness, temperance, zephyr's balmy breath, His mind unclouded, purified his blood, And bade new hope a gleam of *joy* restore. And now he felt from heaven's exhaustless store That e'en for *wounds* like his a *balsam* flow'd: Felt, when the magic of a sunbeam glow'd, That nature's charms had pow'r to sooth his soul . . .' (*Oberon* VIII, 22).

2. The *magic* of a sun-beam is a glimpse of the spiritual beauty irradiating the physical beauty of earth. And when he settles in Titania's groves 'He feels affliction from his soul withdraw: He feels *his spirit* glowing with delight, Rous'd from the tortures of a fev'rous night, Soar to the twilight of eternal day' (VIII, 23). And so, gradually, in labor and spiritual enjoyment he is 'Lost to the world, its miseries . . . A childish dream;' and 'conscience, *health*,* and *peace*, his *spirit* daily blest' (VIII, 24).

3. Then, when all alone, 'his spirit turn'd to that celestial shore, Where all he lov'd [his *friends* and *love* on earth] did with their God reside.' And then at night 'as external senses die . . . Oft on his cheek he felt a breathing spirit near' (VIII, 25). And he overhears the divine spirit of nature and its ideal harmony or music: 'Angelic *harmonies* at distance sung.' And as he listens he feels earth's 'slender wall, That parts him from his *friends,* about to fall' and he sees them, 'rob'd in heavenly light, Shapes of the viewless world his soul *responsive* call' (VIII, 26).

4. Soaring yet higher, and completely spiritualized, at dawn he reaches the twilight realm of the eternal itself in a dream-vision [cf. the creative

* Keats' 1, 5: 'health and quiet breathing.'

imagination] of God, the 'form divine,' and blends into the divine Love in whom is *highest bliss,* immortality, and essential, ideal, eternal Truth and Beauty (VIII, 27-8).

The stages or gradations of happiness are here, including Keats' music. And Keats' similar stages (earthly beauty, music, friendship, love-Love divine) are formulated in symbols consistently derived from the hermit's. The poet had identified religious with poetic vision as early as *Sleep and Poetry* and had merely changed those symbols and their correlation slightly. The hermit's mystical philosophy is Christian mysticism, which was based upon Plotinus' neo-Platonic philosophy, which in its turn was based upon the Platonic ladder of love, revealed in the *Symposium* by Diotima to Socrates, whose interlocutor is Agathon.* Wieland's vision was itself based upon the Platonic ladder of love, as modified in Christian thought. †

Keats seems not to have known Plato directly. But he said in *Endymion: 'a hermit young I'll live . . .* and *lave . . . spirit* in wonders.' And he meant precisely what he said. He lived and laved *his* spirit in that of the hermit, with all the sublime intensity of his intuitive and idealistic nature. It was primarily thence that he learned the 'Neo-Platonic philosophy of beauty.' Thus when he came to write *The Fall of Hyperion, a Dream,* he still wrote in terms of the hermit's teaching: '. . . sure not all those *melodies sung into the* World's *ear* Are useless: sure *a poet is a sage;* a humanist physician to all men.' And a few lines later: 'The poet and the dreamer are distinct . . . The one pours out a balm upon the World, The other vexes it' (I, 189 ff.). It is the same balsam (cf. the hermit's first stage, above), the divine beauty that from 'the heaven's brink' flowed for the earthly wounds of the hermit, the sage who helped teach a poet that all beauty is divine.

I, 372-91 (p. 131):

A few lines after the shepherds and aged priest, like the hermit, 'discours'd upon the fragile bar That keeps us from our homes ethereal,' they speak 'each one' of 'his own *anticipated bliss.'* And

* Wieland used that very passage for his best novel, *Agathon.*

† And Keats, 'voyaging on strange seas of thought, alone,' as if instinctively used the image of the ladder. For in his Book III, 26, before and after alluding to the hermit ('sanctuary splendour' or spirituality, and 'forlorn hermitage'), Keats wrote that one 'Can make *a ladder of the eternal* wind . . .'

K 374   One felt heart-certain that he could not miss
          His quick gone love, among fair blossom'd boughs,
376   Where every zephyr-sigh pouts, and endows
          Her lips with *music* for the welcoming.

(The hermit longed to join his earthly love as he heard the 'angelic harmonies.' And Huon searches for Rezia beneath the blossoming boughs, when she wanders into Titania's grot, where the child is born and from which the angelic music issues.)

378   Another wish'd, *mid that eternal spring,*
          To meet his rosy child, with feathery sails . . .

(In the spring, Rezia 'in prescient rapture . . . Clasps a sweet child . . . to her breast' before its birth. That is her anticipated bliss.) *

385   Some were athirst in soul to see again
          Their fellow huntsmen o'er the wide champaign
387   In times *long past;* to *sit with them,* and *talk*
          Of all the chances in *their earthly walk;*
389   Comparing *joyfully,* their plenteous stores
          Of happiness, to when upon the moors,
391   Be*nigh*ted, close they *huddled from the cold* . . .

The hermit of the visions actually saw his loved ones in heaven, the wife and sons and friends he had lost before he achieved highest happiness in God. And of his earthly career he talks to Huon and Rezia whose love has already become so spiritual that Huon sees in her 'an angel of the heavenly choir.' In the next stanza

  . . . oft *between them* plac'd the father *sits,*   K 387
And to his wistful guests in lively strain,
(While scenes *long past,* in memory rise again)
Thro' half the swift-wing'd *nights,* relates by fits
Some bold transaction *of his* days of yore:
And as they glow th' eventful story o'er,
Warm'd by their fire his spirit warmly glows . . .   K 391
               (OBERON VIII, 47)

Not the imagery and verbal parallels alone, but the circumstance that the hermit's recollections are part of the process of spiritualizing 'the youth, by heavenly power loved and led,' indicates Keats' interest in the

* Keats' 'feathery sails' seem indirectly to allude to Mathew's 'Lines.'

hermit's every thought and feature. That absorption led him to assimilate phrases and minute imagery and to re-create the very setting and atmosphere, time and time again.

I, 232-54 (p. 132):

The cluster above is noteworthy too because only three stanzas later in *Oberon* occurs the description of the changing cycle of nature:

W 1   Thus imperceptibly the winter past—
      And now awakening from her long repose,
3   *Spring o'er* the *lap* of earth gay *verdure* throws:
      No more the forest bows before the *blast,*
5   A *naked* wreck—but where the *pillars* stand
      Of arch'd embow'ring *roofs* that shade the land,
7   Where *nature's temple* tow'rs sublime in air,
      The pomp of foliage thickens full and *fair,*   K 375 *
9   And clustering leaves on leaves, *religious gloom* expand.

      The earth is deck'd anew with flow'ry *bloom,*
11   Fair budding smile the garden, grove, and plain,
      Charm'd echo trills the birds' melodious strain,
13   And rocks are wreath'd with plants that breathe perfume.
      From bubbling rills the purling currents stray
15   Down the green *moss,* and wind their silver way:
      And thro' the night, from time to time renew'd,
17   The lonely bird amid the thickening wood
      Trills to the silent moon her melancholy lay.

19   Rezia, whose time now ever nearer draws,
      Seeks pathless solitudes, and deep alcoves,
21   Where *branches* thickly-arch'd *o'ershade* the groves:
      There *loves to lean* in still *and solemn pause,*
23   *And mark* with *trembling* joy the vernal strife,
      The motion, *murmur, universal life,*
25   That *teem* around—in prescient rapture prest,
      Clasps a sweet child in spirit to her breast . . .   K 378 *
                (OBERON VIII, 50-2)

This passage, to the middle lines of which Keats seems to have alluded as early as the Mathew poems, is still a vital part of the lovers' spiritualization by the hermit and by the divine beauty of Titania's sacred groves.

* See page 331.

That circumstance probably had something to do with the appearance, in the identical setting, of Keats' spiritualizing rites of spring. Near the beginning of his address, the hermit's counterpart, the aged priest, says (1, 216 ff.):

> Have not rains
> *Green'd over* April's *lap? No howling* sad   W 3-4
> Sickens our fearful ewes; and we have had
> Great bounty from Endymion our lord.
> *The earth is* glad . . .   W 10

The verbal echoes and sequel, no less than the setting and parallel theme, are significant. For after he had interpolated about ten lines of Grecian local color, ideas for which Keats seems to have drawn from the first volume of Potter's *Antiquities of Greece,** the chorus launches upon the Invocation to Pan:

> 'O thou, *whose* mighty *palace roof* doth hang   W 5-7
> *From jagged trunks,* and *overshadoweth*   W 21
> Eternal whispers, *glooms,* the *birth, life,* death W 9, 24
> Of unseen flowers in heavy peacefulness;   W 9-10
> Who *lov'st to see* the hamadryads dress   W 22-3
> Their ruffled locks where meeting hazels darken;
> And through whole *solemn* hours dost *sit,* and *hearken* W 22
> The dreary melody . . .'

Happy suggestions for this passage evidently were derived from Rezia's actions before the *birth* of her child. Ten lines later Keats specifies 'en*moss*ed realms,' '*fig* trees,' '*mountain pine*'—all of which also mark the exotic clime of Titania's haunted grove, or 'nature's temple' whose roof is formed by the arching 'naked . . . pillars' or trunks of trees. That religious spirit, born of the hermit's presence, the hermit who had come to see the ultimate Truth of God in these groves, is significant. For as all the spiritualizing visions and the gradations of happiness of Book 1 hint, the hermit no less than Wordsworth had something to do with Pan's transformation into the spirit of nature and (1, 288):

> Dread opener of the mysterious doors
> Leading to *universal* knowledge.   W 24

* Cf. Bush, 'Notes on Keats' Reading.'

The first of the shepherds' spiritualizing visions occurs some fifty lines later.*

II, 47-94 (p. 133):

Almost immediately after the opening apostrophe to love and 'pageant history,' Endymion sets out on his wanderings and reverses Huon's path:

> For many days,
> Has he been wandering in uncertain ways:
> Through wilderness, and woods of mossed oaks;
> Counting his woe-worn minutes, by the strokes
> Of the lone woodcutter.

(As part of his spiritualization in the adjacent hermitage, with its thick oak woods, the woe-worn Huon fells 'the groaning wood till twilight's shadowy gleam,' Oberon VIII, 39.)

Endymion finally sits down and sees 'a wild rose tree' from which he plucks a bud which 'flowers beneath his sight.' From it flies a golden butterfly, symbolic of the soul, whose flight the wanderer follows 'like a new-born spirit.' This is significant because at the end of Book I, he had discovered a wood nymph's home—'the cave is secreter'—even as Rezia discovers Titania's secret grot. And while the child is being born, Rezia sees Titania hold 'to her lips, as dies her breath away, A wreath of roses fresh that bud beneath her hand' (VIII, 72). It was the imminent birth of the child that led Huon to fight his way up the towering crags, to discover the single path at the summit, and so to find the sacred groves and the hermit. All this Keats knew.

For now the golden butterfly leads Endymion

> K 73   Through buried paths, where sleepy twilight dreams
>   The summer time away. One track unseams
> 75   A wooded cleft, and, far away, the blue
>   Of ocean fades upon him; then, anew,
> 77   He sinks adown a solitary glen,
>   Where there was never sound of mortal men,
> 79   Saving, perhaps, some snow-light cadences

---

* The figure 'mysterious doors' seems to be that of the Mansion of Life letter (Letters, p. 143) and hints at the coalescence in Keats' mind of Tintern Abbey and Wieland's hermit because of their close resemblance.

Melting to silence, when upon the breeze
81   Some *holy* bark let forth an anthem sweet,
To cheer itself to Delphi. Still his feet
83   Went swift beneath the merry-winged guide,
Until it reached a splashing fountain's side
85   That, *near a cavern's mouth,* for ever pour'd
Unto the temperate air.

And it is this peculiar fountain which vanishes:

92   . . . to *disappear*
So *fairy-quick,* was strange! *Bewildered,*
94   Endymion *sought around* . . .

After Wieland's apostrophe to love, Keats had seen the lovers' suffering and joy in the mossy cave.* And at length he had seen Huon, who
for many days wandered uncertainly high up among the wild cliffs and,
'bending from the mountains' topmost peak, Strain'd his dim eye o'er
ocean far and wide. (vii, 91. With this cf. K 47-8 and 76 above.) A few
stanzas later Huon stands 'beneath o'ershadowing crags That low'r
before him like a ruin'd world' in 'rude magnificence.' Urged by despair
and a lover's fear for Rezia, he climbs from perilous crag to crag until
he finds *one path that leads through the wooded pass.* (Cf. K 74-5.)
That path widens 'as his step ascends' until he passes the summit. Unwittingly on the edge of the hermitage, he finds himself, 'By fir-trees
vaulted from the light of day,' sinking down into a

. . . little *dell* with *twilight* shade o'ercast.   K 73, 77
His wearied limbs with nameless shudders thrill,
Slow as he totters down the gloomy hill.
It seems as if *terrestrial* footsteps rude   K 78
On the dark *shrine* of *loneliness* intrude,   K 77, 81-2
And dare invade the realm of lifeless shadows . . .   K 78
(OBERON VIII, 1)

Huon follows the path down to 'a narrow bridge' beneath which 'Hoarse
waves . . . in eddying circles wheel.' (viii, 2. Cf. K 84.) And near
this water

the little path he long had trod
Is, as *by magic, vanish'd* from his eyes—
In vain *to find its trace the wanderer tries*—   K 92-4

* Which reappears in his Bk. iv.

until he finds, concealed by shrubbery, the opening to the winding path. It leads him through *a cavern's mouth* (cf. K 85) and

> *Thro'* the steep mountains *to a dell* profound,   K 73, 77
> *Sinks down* a hundred steps—wild *fairy* work, I   K 93
> ween.
>
> (OBERON VIII, 3)

In the next stanza Huon encounters the hermit, as Endymion does the aged priest in Book I.

It is revealing, and at times amusing, to watch the creative process of minute recollection and reproduction: to note how Keats' fountain vanishes 'fairy-quick' and his bewildered 'wanderer' (cf. *End.* II, 137) seeks it; while Huon's path (which is Endymion's in reversed direction, into instead of out from the sacred groves) vanishes as by magic and, bewildered, that 'wanderer' seeks it. Keats knew every feature of the hermitage and its peculiar environs and drew endless inspiration and guidance from *Oberon,* as the following passage further indicates.

II, 103-5, 115-25 (p. 133):

Out of *the fountain* that we saw above, a nymph arises who says to Endymion:

> *'Youth!*
> *Too long, alas, hast thou starv'd on the ruth,*
> *The bitterness of love:* too long indeed,
> Seeing thou art so gentle.'

And she speaks of her 'level lilies . . . My charming rod, my potent river spells' and of how she *'bubbled up To fainting creatures in a desert wild.'* She pities him, has been his guide ('I am but as a child'), and tells him: 'thou must wander far In other regions, past *the scanty bar To mortal steps'* before he can discover his *'love.'* This revealing phrase again links Endymion with the hermit.*

This fountain nymph of the strange words, powers, and 'charming rod' had herself wandered up the cliffs with Huon and undergone metamorphosis. And she was evidently subject to the daemon king.

---

* Cf. *End.* I, 359-61: 'mortal star . . . fragile bar That keeps us from our homes ethereal' where dwells the hermit's Love. (Cf. p. 117.)

For it was by Oberon (whose charming rod is a lily) that the lovers were punished 'on the desert strand' * with starvation and ruth and bitterness; Rezia,

> While *hunger*'s gnawing fang her heart devours:
> . . . pants—she *faints, sore* parch'd with burning heat!
>
> (vii, 49)

And when she has fainted, Huon 'half-mad, half-praying' pleads for water. The daemon king pities them, and Huon soon 'Casts on the fountain' his grateful eyes. For Keats that fountain became the nymph, as her words reveal.

II, 144-59 (p. 133):

The sequence, moreover, continues. After the fountain vanishes, 'The wanderer, Holding his forehead,' says:

> 'O what a *wretch* is he! and when 'tis his,
> *After long toil* and travelling, *to miss*
> The *kernel* of his hopes, how more than *vile:*
> Yet, for him *there's refreshment* even in toil;
> Another city doth he set about,
> Free from the smallest pebble-bead of doubt
> That *he will seize on* trickling honey-combs:
> *Alas, he finds them dry; and then he foams . . .*'

and so on till 'show *How quiet death is.*' The passage is localized on the desert shore by the nymph's remark: 'fainting creatures in a desert wild.' It is a symbolical rendering of Huon's desperate search for food, his discovery of the golden fruit after anxiously toiling part way up the cliffs, and that fruit's vileness—its heart or *kernel* bitter as gall and rotten through and through (*Oberon* vii, 53-4). Huon sheds 'bitter tears' and his lip *'foams'* while Rezia quietly awaits *death* and at last faints. It is soon thereafter that Oberon's fountain appears.

II, 211 ff. (p. 134):

Endymion's *descent into the earth* is suggestively marked by a sequence of incidents and allusions. No sooner has the fountain nymph

---

* *Oberon* vii, 38, two stanzas before the apostrophe to love.

vanished near the cavern's mouth (as Huon's path to the hermitage vanished in the cavern), than Endymion decides

> 'He ne'er is *crown'd*
> *With immortality,* who fears to follow
> Where airy voices lead: * so through the hollow,
> The silent mysteries of earth, descend!'

(Did Huon's path, which Endymion had been following to this point, have something to do with this? And did Huon's cavern recall Titania's descent into a cave?) Fifty lines later, after seeing myriad wonders, Endymion comes upon 'A quiver'd Dian.' And then, symbolically, the 'journey homeward to habitual self' seems 'crude and sore' or like a 'mad-pursuing of the fog-born elf'—that is, Shakespeare's Puck, probably conjured forth here (II, 277) by his master's more potent namesake. *Unhappy in that solitude,* Endymion feels exhausted by the *effort to understand the mysteries of 'dismal elements'* and yearns for *the loveliness of 'our green earth,'* to anoint his eyes 'with the heaven's light.' † And soon (II, 341-6) he sees leaves,

> And flowers, and wreaths, and ready myrtle crowns
> Up heaping through the slabs: refreshment drowns
> Itself, and strives its own delight to hide—
> Nor in one spot alone; the floral pride
> In a long *whispering birth enchanted grew.*

In connection with this sequence and the sequel, the 'still alarm' and 'sleepy music' and the identity of the 'heavenly benignant guide' who leads him to the bower of Adonis, the similar sequence in the hermitage canto of *Oberon* is noteworthy. For after the hermit's spiritualizing talks with the lovers, Rezia, expecting her child, observes *the rebirth of spring* and the 'motion, murmur, *universal life'* amid 'nature's temple.' ‡ Two stanzas later Wieland turns to (the *elemental love* story of) Titania and tells how in her grief for the loss of Oberon's love,

---

* As Huon is led repeatedly: here symbolic of divine inspiration.

† That is, the poet is exhausted by intellectual inquiry and yearns for divine beauty, his native domain, whose forms inundate his vision—as so often happened to Keats.

‡ VIII, 50-2. Cf. p. 332 above and Pan's realms.

Downward she rushes in this *dreary* grave,
To mourn her being, and beneath the *cave*

brood in despair (VIII, 60). After long *striving to understand* the state
of mind of the ruler of *the elements,* she *becomes weary* of the cave and

Lo! *at her wish,* as sink the rocks away,
A new Elysium opens on her sight.
(VIII, 64)

Thus, *by her enchantment,* the sacred groves (Endymion's homeland)
with their *trees and flowers sprang up,* in whose midst

Stood the lov'd *grotto,* her sequester'd throne:
Whence, from the grove, by *whispering* night-winds blown,
Soft notes seraphic flow'd . . .
(VIII, 65)

A glance at the previous page shows that this sequence closely resembles
the main outline of Book II of *Endymion,* which deals with 'elemental
passion.' That sequence may well have been the reason that Keats, following the plot pattern and theme of the hermit's and the lovers' spiritualization, now interpolated an appropriate Grecian tale of elemental
love: the bower of Adonis, symbolizing the rebirth of vegetation. It is
significant that the *Oberon* sequence continues to parallel Keats': in the
very next stanzas Rezia is guided fearfully to the bower by Titania-
Diana, where her child is born. And that scene colored the bower of
Adonis.

Endymion continues his 'fairy journey' until at length he hears aerial
music and feels *'still alarm.'* 'Through *winding alleys'* and *led by*
[Diana], *'a heavenly benignant guide'* (II, 377), he comes to where
'thick *myrtle* branches' brush against his head. There he sees *the bower*
'Full of light, *incense, tender minstrelsy'* in which *lies sleeping* the
beautiful youth Adonis. Keats' picture and his knowledge of the myth
have been traced to Ovid, Shakespeare, Spenser and Bion. But some
distinctive features were drawn in from Titania's 'enchanted grot' to
which in this same book Keats had already alluded.

For we saw Rezia beneath the thickening boughs observing the rebirth of nature. (Adonis = vegetation.) When shortly thereafter her

hour approaches, like Endymion she wanders through 'the incense' and the mazelike paths (cf. 'winding alleys') until suddenly she comes, led by the invisible Titania, to the *ivy-screened* entrance to a grot, from which at other times invisible hands push alarmed intruders away. Entering, she feels cutting pains shoot through her body. She reclines upon roses and moss and soon, her senses dissolved, sees this:

> It seems, that o'er her eyes *pale moon-beams* glide,*
> Gradual, in deep and deeper shadow dy'd,
> Till softly hush'd to *sleep,* oblivion stills her heart.
> And from within her a confusion gleams
> Of *lovely shapes;* some *o'er her* sweep, some roll'd,
> Each in the other *floating,* fold on fold;
> Mixture of wond'rous mood—and now it seems
> Before her knees three *lovely angels stand:*
> Clear to her gaze their mystic rites expand:
> And, lo! *a woman* veil'd in roseate ray,
> Holds to her lips, as dies her breath away,
> A wreath of *roses* fresh that *bud beneath her hand.*†

Earlier in this book, ii, 59, of *Endymion,* we saw 'a wild rose tree' from which Endymion took a bud which 'buds . . . beneath his sight' to become 'the little herald' (or child) that led to the one track. Keats had long since followed Rezia into Titania's bower. And now again he heard the 'tender minstrelsy' thus:

> For the last time her higher beating heart
> Thrills with a short and *softly-silenc'd pain*—
> The forms are fled away—she swoons again—
> And now, without remembrance of a smart,
> *Wakes* to *soft notes,* and seems afar to hear
> Their low-*lull'd* echoes dying from the ear . . .
>   (OBERON VIII, 73)

For the angelic spirits have vanished and only the 'elfine queen' is visible, *tenderly* clasping the new-born child. This haunting and charming scene, to which Mathew had first alluded, occurs at the end of the

---

* Classical scholar that he was, Wieland had Titania retain the visible marks of the moon goddess in her every appearance. Not concealed by Sotheby's translation, this doubtless was but another of the many reasons for Keats' fascination.

† *Oberon* viii, 71-2. Note the sequence continued from the previous page. The sequence parallels that of *Endymion*.

hermitage idyll. It was next in line in the long sequence of incidents and image-clusters, concerned with the theme of love's spiritualization, in Cantos vii and viii of *Oberon:* a sequence which, practically from beginning to end, provided hints and materials 'dissolved, diffused, dissipated' in the kindred *Endymion* pattern.

II, 377-441 (p. 134):

Thus in the scene of the bower or grot of Adonis we find the same mazelike paths, incense, 'tender minstrelsy,' 'ivy mesh,' suggestive 'lily stalks,' and the traditional cupids (who 'stood' like Rezia's angels), one of whom is here engaged in 'muffling to death the pathos' while another is 'distilling odorous dew' and yet another 'fluttering-wise Rain'd violets' upon the sleeping eyes of the youth: all this like Titania's *floating* spirits who *muffle* Rezia's *pains* with *roses.* Both sleepers awake and the spirits vanish. Endymion like Rezia is invited to 'recline upon these living flowers.' These are some of the elements which Keats clearly derived from *Oberon.* Their metamophosis is instructive. And I suspect, in the light of the self-same sequence, that Rezia's observation of 'universal life' and wandering into Titania's bower after the latter's tale of elemental love had been told, had something to do with suggesting Adonis' appearance in the second book of Endymion's spiritualizing experience, a book dealing with 'elemental passion.' Among other things, the music he hears is in accordance with the second stage of the hermit's spiritualization: the hearing of angelic harmonies in nature: aerial music which originates in Titania's bower.*

* The composite bower of Adonis appears to have been colored by a second grot in *Oberon:* that of the voluptuous queen of sense by whom Huon [and Glaucus] are tempted. The queen's bower appears amid the *'myrtle* grove' to which 'the wanderer' is lured, ostensibly to 'deck *the bow'r,* Where nature pour'd profuse *each varied flow'r.'* In this grot, from which invisible hands hold him as from Titania's, Huon sees that *'light* . . . *thro'* the *rosy bower* Glides from the moon . . .' The image of the moon alone must have been magnetic. Was it, shining through the bower, the reason Endymion, 'where thick myrtle branches' brushed his head, 'Over a bower . . . as the sunset peeps into a wood, So saw . . . panting light . . .'?

When Huon enters this *rosy* bower, he sees 'Where *deck'd with* heavenly *light* a Houri glows, And, *on a* yielding *bed* of soft repose, Displays her charms . . . in beauty's dazzling *pride'* (xii, 13-15). With this compare Keats' bower 'full of light' where 'on a silken couch of rosy pride' the beautiful youth lies, whose Apollonian curves rival those of the nymphomaniac queen of sense, Almansaris, who left her marks on Glaucus' queen of sense in *End.* iii.

III, 418 ff. (p. 137):

Keats' Glaucus, whose story is handled 'with absolute freedom,' *
evidently was meant to represent a poet ('I am a friend to love, to loves
of yore,' III, 300); a poet who had erred from the ladder of love ('Fool!
I began To feel distemper'd longings,' III, 374). And we must recall
that Glaucus, 'a lonely youth on desert isles,' loved 'to the very white
of truth' Scylla, who was his unrealizable ideal of love and beauty. In
his misery at the vainness of his pursuit of her, he decided to turn to
the enchantress Circe (sensual pleasure) for help.† And so, one day he
fell into a swoon.

> K 418   'When I awoke, 'twas in *a twilight bower;*
>   Just when *the light of morn,* with hum of bees,
> 420   *Stole through* its verdurous matting of fresh trees.
>   How sweet, and sweeter! for *I heard a lyre,*
> 422   *And over it a sighing voice expire.*
>   *It ceased*—I caught light *footsteps;* and anon
> 424   *The fairest face* that morn e'er look'd upon
>   Push'd through a screen of *roses.* Starry Jove!
> 426   *With tears, and smiles, and honey-words she wove*
>   *A net* whose thraldom was more bliss than all
> 428   The range of flower'd Elysium . . .'

Bliss recalls the hermit. Elysium and roses recall Titania's bower. Did
it flash through Keats' mind? In a moment Glaucus adds: 'She took
me like a child of suckling time, And cradled me in roses,' III, 456-7.

But there let us pause a moment and turn to *Oberon.*‡ Huon seeks
Rezia within the forbidden gardens, and one evening the lovely queen
(who repeatedly is termed 'the enchantress') comes upon him there,
the fairest youth her eyes had ever seen (cf. K 424). Huon's beauty and
coldness so pique her that she soon lures him into her gorgeous chambers, he believing her message to be from Rezia. Revolted by the sen-

---

* E. De Sélincourt, ed., *Poems,* 1936, p. 438.

† Note the overtones of Huon's story.

‡ After the hermit's death, the spiritualized lovers are separated. Rezia is abducted
by corsairs and Huon is left to die in the deep forest. Rescued at last by daemonic
intervention, *he is borne through the air in the arms of a spirit* (cf. *End.* I, 641 ff.
and 701: 'A disguis'd demon mission'd'). In Tunis he learns that his beloved,
immured in the harem, had been saved from the sea when the pirate ship was
destroyed by Titania's lightning bolt.

sual queen's wiles, his constancy remains unassailable; the enchantress descends from her throne, lays aside pomp, seats him beside her and hands him a goblet of wine. Then she takes a *lute,* and sings *sighing*ly of her passion for him, until, overcome, lute and voice *expire* (cf. K 421-2). Precisely as Glaucus says (cf. K 426), *with tears, and smiles, and honey words* of promise *she weaves her net*—but, in vain. Her frenzy at her failure spent, a few hours later 'at the *morning* hour' she enters her *'twilight'* and *'rosy bower.'* (*Oberon* XII, 12-14. Cf. K 418, 425.) Some of its features we have already seen in connection with that of Adonis.* Then she lures Huon past its leaf-*screened* entrance and doubtless hears his 'firm *footsteps'* as he approaches (cf. K 423). A moment later, she imprisons him in her smooth naked arms, against which he struggles.† But Huon has more than Glaucus' 'o'ersweeten'd soul.' His constancy to his ideal love never abandons him and he prefers to die by fire rather than to accept the unblessed throne the enchantress offers. Even the most casual collation of the purpose, incidents, imagery, and phraseology in the two temptations must reveal how the voluptuous *Oberon* episode has been interwoven with the Glaucus myth.

We know how in *Oberon* 'this fierce temptation went'; that Huon did *not* bow to this 'arbitrary queen of sense' (*End.* III, 461)—but that he remained steadfast to his ideal of love and beauty and later in the same Canto XII was borne back through the air over land and sea. (Cf. Keats' phrase 'o'er the billows rude' in *End.* III, 464—where it significantly occurs between the arbour temptation and the later scene in the haunted forest.) The lovers were borne over sea and land to Oberon's palace in the enchanted forest where, as we shall see, they are welcomed by the jubilant aerial spirits when their mission has been accomplished.

III, 467-578 (p. 137):

If we would catch even a fleeting glimpse of the creative process, it is important to bear in mind two things: first, that, in the same sequence as Glaucus', the bower temptation of Huon and his presence in the enchanted forest are parts of the pattern of spiritualization; and that

---

* Cf. note p. 341 this Appendix; and the streaming light and 'each varied flow'r' with K 420, 428.

† A patent link with Shakespeare's *Venus and Adonis.* Was it thus that the queen's bower came to leave its mark on that of Adonis in Book II?

both incidents occur, closely linked with the mission, in Canto xii. Second, that Huon (and Keats) had been in the same forest before. This is important, because the forest in Canto xii, where his mission terminates, explicitly recalls Huon's earlier wanderings in the forest in Canto ii and thus all his experiences at that time. And it is there, at the very outset of his mission, that Huon like Glaucus entered that same 'mazy forest' of fearsome enchantment. Keats knew this: for half a score pages, the streaming *Oberon* imagery appears in *Endymion,* now interfused with Greek myth of hoary antiquity, now quite untransmuted; now in clusters, and now disseminated. But all of it is from the haunted forest as it appeared in the opening cantos of Wieland's romantic tale.

First of all, this is what Keats saw in those opening cantos: 'It chanc'd *one morn'* that Huon in storm and *rain* found himself on (W 2) * a dim path that wound through a wood. *Stumbling,* sliding, groping, he is compelled to cut his way through bush and briar and (4) *descend* into 'wild glens' until 'on a steep ascent' he sees the circling *forest* (i, 13). *Night* falls, and still he *wanders* on:

W 6   The starless *gloom* of raven-feather'd night
       That wrapt the welkin round, the wood unknown,
  8   And, for the *first time heard,* the *thunder*ing tone
       Of lions, that th' accustom'd ear af*fright:*
 10   Tones, from the midnight *death*-like *silence round,*
       Fearfully echoing, on each side rebound,
 12   As on from rock to rock their *horrors* roll'd:
       These might have mov'd the stoutest warrior bold,
 14   And hearts unus'd to *fear* had *shudder'd* at the *sound.*

       So fares our knight: tho' none from woman sprung
 16   Had e'er beheld his cheek with *terror* pale;
       The *hideous roarings* that *his ears* assail
 18   Shake his stout heart: with sinews loose, unstrung,
       His arm and knee drop nerveless: 'gainst his will
 20   *Fear* stands *upon his brow* in *dew-drops chill* . . .
                                              (OBERON i, 15-16)

But Huon remembers his vow, and with drawn *falchion* wanders on through the fearsome black night.

* Throughout this Appendix, numbers appearing in paraphrased passages refer to elements from *Oberon.*

22 Not long his step the winding way pursued,
    When on his wistful gaze, so him beseems,
24 The light of *distant fire* delightful gleams.
    His cheek flash'd crimson as *the flame* he view'd.
26 *Half wild* with hope and *fear* he rush'd to find
    In these lone woods some glimpse of *human kind.*
28 And, ever and anon, at once the ray
    Flash'd on his sight, then sunk at once away,
30 While rose and *fell the path* as hill and *valley* wind.

    Sudden the way that *led deep* rocks among
32 *Sunk* in a cavern, from whose pit profound
    Sparkl'd *a* crackling *flame* . . .
                            (OBERON I, 17-18)

(W 34) Because it was fringed by bushes above, 'the mazes of the clefts between,' the flame shone *through* the *bushes.* It was reflected by the rocks (36) 'like a verdant fire,' to the wanderer's *amazement,* who stood motionless a moment 'amid th' *enchanted scene.*' With these vivid and detailed pictures let us now compare some of those in Glaucus' tale.

'*One morn* she left me sleeping,' he begins echoing Wieland's opening phrase. He sought for the enchantress, but she was gone. And so great was his disappointment that he sought 'the *forest* o'er.' But what did he see there?

'*Wandering about in* pine and cedar *gloom*	W 6
Damp awe assail'd me; for there '*gan to boom*	W 1, 8, 20
A sound of moan, an agony of *sound,*	W 14, 17
Sepulchral from the distance *all around.*	W 10
Then came a conquering earth-*thunder,* and rumbled	W 8
That fierce complain to *silence:* while I *stumbled*	W 10, 2
Down a precipitous path, as if impell'd.	W 4, 31
I came to *a dark valley.*—*Groanings* swell'd	W 29-30 *
Poisonous *about my ears,* and louder grew,	W 17
The nearer *I approach'd a flame*'s gaunt blue,	W 33
That glar'd before me through a thorny *brake.*	W 35
This fire, like the eye of gordian snake,	W 36
Bewitch'd me towards; *and I soon was near*	W 37
A sight too fearful for the feel of *fear:*	W 37, 20, 26
In thicket hid I curs'd the haggard *scene*—	W 37

* And W 41, below.

The banquet of my arms, my *arbour queen,*
Seated upon an uptorn forest root . . .'

           (END. III, 477-500)

with the hideously *transformed men* around her.

But breaking the spell, we find that in the last three lines Glaucus is no longer Huon wandering alone in rain and blackness, terrified by thunder and awful roarings, until he sees and hastens down the precipitous path to the green fire that bewitched him. Huon's lions have become a weird menagerie, and the shapes of Keats' men show that we are not even in the Homeric land of Circe. What, then, could have happened? For this is *not* the same arbour queen as before. The answer, I think, lurks in the *Faerie Queene,* whose title led to repeated associations in Keats' mind with *Oberon.* For by Spenser's Acrasia, of the sensual Bower of Bliss, Sir Guyon's chastity is tried as Sir Huon's is by the enchantress Almansaris. And Sir Guyon is told that 'These seeming beasts . . . *this* Enchauntresse hath transformed . . . *Whylome her louers.'* * The clue to Glaucus' experience lies in that conception—and in the enchanted forest of Oberon. Two enchantresses and the latter, I think, coalesced in Keats' mind.

For Huon and his new squire, as soon as their stories have been narrated, wander by sun and starlight, *'Three days* down Libanon's romantic height' amid the cedars.† And almost immediately before their course another 'gloomy forest lay' (II, 10). Although Huon is all for taking the shortest route, the old squire is not. Of *this* forest he says:

      'They speak no good of it—at least, 'tis said,
      That none who enter e'er return again!'

(Is not this true also of Circe's domain, the Circe of Homer?)

      'You smile, and deem, I see, my caution vain;
      Yet, trust me, Sir, beneath that haunted shade,
      A tiny wicked goblin holds his court.
      There foxes, harts, and *deer* alone resort,

---

* *F. Q.* II, xii, 85. Spenser and Wieland in part drew on the same source, 'Huon de Bordeaux.' Spenser's Sir Guyon or Chastity and allusions to Oberon in this Acrasia episode were the links that, as early as the '1815 Poems,' led to Keats' repeated association of Spenser and *Oberon.* And we shall see other links below.

† II, I, and cf. Keats' 'cedar gloom.'

Men, once as good as we—in form the same—
Heaven knows in what wild skin our human frame
Shall be ere dawn array'd to make the demon sport!'
(OBERON II, II)

Keats' apparently conventional 'foxes shy and antler'd deer' (*End.* III,
469) appeared on the outskirts of his haunted forest. But this ominous
thought, 'Men, once as good as we'? * And 'in *what* wild *skin* . . .
human frame Shall be . . . *array'd'?* Were these echoes of folklore and
that question 'what skin' now a hint to Keats? There is no doubt that
here, within the pattern of spiritualization, in the forest adjacent to
Huon-Glaucus' temptations by the [bower] queen of sense, there lurked
ready to Keats' hand this suggestion of shape-shifting which is one of
the daemon king's most characteristic powers. The sultana, sensual
queen and *enchantress* that she is, had no such powers. But evidently
her nature and function, of proving the wanderer's chastity, recalled
Spenser's queen of sense, who recalled the Greek Circe. I suspect that
these associations were inevitable because of the adjacence of the episode
of the sultana to the forest of Oberon, wherein his powers of shape-
shifting are revealed—powers which both the sensual Acrasia and Circe
possess.

Let us enter the forest and see.

W 37   Now as o'er all the veil of twilight hung,
        While slow they wind the haunted shades between,
   39   A *herd* of harts and hinds at once are seen,
        That in full course before their path-way sprung.
   41   Their ceaseless *groans,* like warnings, *strike the ear,*   K 490
        And their large eyes o'erflow with many a tear.
   43   (So Sherasmin beneath th' uncertain light
        Will fain remark) and, sure, the *piteous sight*
   45   Seems to proclaim, 'Oh, fly! haste, haste! *your fate draws*
        near!'
                                        (OBERON II, 14)

These groanings and this 'piteous sight' were yet another link with
the Circe story. Glaucus' fate, as well as Huon's, was 'drawing near'
even as the squire hinted. But Huon now is fearless; he

---

* Cf. Spenser, in the stanza already cited: 'These seeming beasts are men indeed.'

. . . springs at once among *the herd:*
W 47   *They vanish* in a wink *like* yielding *air* . . .

Aʌd Huon and the squire proceed as 'In sweet forgetfulness all stilly slept (W 48); Along the wood no nightly murmur crept, *All noiseless* . . .' This is one of the clusters drawn into *I Stood Tip-toe*, the earlier 'Endymion' * Keats had seen this passage once before: in connection with Endymion. And no wonder.

In midst the gloomy forest, the garrulous squire regales Huon with ghost and daemon lore. And incidentally he first reveals something of Oberon's eerie nature:

'True, known to all, when cocks at day-spring crow, †
W 49   Then *all the goblery* at noon of night
         Who creep in *darkness, demon, elf,* or *sprite,*
51   Soon as they hear his warning trumpet, *go,*
         As if a storm had blown them all away;
53   But the strange sprite that here delights to play
         His woodland pranks, unlike their race, methinks,
55   But like mere mortal, lives, and eats, and drinks,
         And open court maintains, and walks at open day!'
                                        (OBERON II, 22)

Circe does this too. And Keats wrote: Circe's herd of transformed men *'as by a whirlwind* writhen' at her bidding 'went through the air like' a huge snake 'and so vanished.' But the squire's 'strange sprite' now appears almost immediately—and after a picture of the moon, in which Keats was deeply interested still:

The moon full-orb'd now gain'd the etherial plain,
W 58   And as her beams thro' wavy branches play'd,
         The twinkling fairy-dance of light and shade
60   Confus'd their *wilder'd* eyes . . .

And while they gaz'd around in mute despair,
62   'Mid the *wild woods* a distant castle gleams
         As woven from the evening's rosy beams . . .
                                  (OBERON II, 25 and 27)

(W 64) And suddenly *the golden gates of the* fairy *palace burst open,* 'And forth a silver car drawn on by leopards' rolls. The wanderers

---

* Cf. 'sweetly they slept . . . and then there crept a little noiseless noise.'
† This line may have caused Keats to recall Milton's *L'Allegro*, echoes of which appear in *End.* III, 500, 505, 524 ('shapes,' 'shrieks,' ' 'mong rushes Stygian').

(66) fly the dwarf in an *agony of terror* pursued by '*A tempest*, wing'd with lightning, storm, and rain' which overtakes them and engulfs them in 'Darkness that hides the world.' It 'peals, cracks, blows, As if (69) the *uprooted* globe would split in twain,' but through it all they hear the gentle whisper 'of th' aërial form' (ii, 30).* And then he (71) blows his elf-horn and causes a procession of nuns and monks, who had been on a *pilgrimage* and among whom the wanderers have (73) sought refuge, to dance like *fauns* and *satyrs*. The squire, who had maligned Oberon and forced Huon to flee, also whirls madly (75) until the daemon king *waves his lily wand* and breaks the spell, and then hands him the goblet, whose *fairy wine* '*reanimates* his soul' (ii, 47). Of this phantasmagoria the scattered fragments were disseminated with fine abandon over a half dozen pages of the subsequent *Endymion* pattern.

End. iii, 518 ff.:

Glaucus sees not only the *enchanter* Oberon's transformed foxes and deer. He sees also Almansaris-Circe-Acrasia 'the arbour queen,' the 'queen of sense' and the 'fierce temptations' of her lover: a composite '*enchantress*.' He sees other 'shapes, wizard and brute' than Oberon's, but figures evidently evoked by the squire's timely midnight dissertation and pointed hint: 'what shape.' Glaucus to a considerable extent sees with the eyes of Huon:

'She *lifted up the charm:* appealing *groans*   W 75, 41
From their *poor* breasts went sueing to her *ear*
In vain; remorseless as an infant's bier
She whisk'd against their eyes the sooty oil.
Whereat was heard a noise of painful toil,
Increasing gradual to *a tempest* rage,   W 66
Shrieks, yells, and *groans* of torture-*pilgrimage;* †
Until their grieved bodies 'gan to bloat
And puff from the tail's end to stifled throat:
Then was appalling *silence:* then a sight   W 48
More wildering than all that hoarse affright;
For *the whole herd, as by a whirlwind* writhen,   W 46, 52

---

* This again is part of the cluster drawn into various poems of the Mathew period. (And cf. Keats' 'uptorn forest root.')

† That of the monks and, I think, Milton's 'shrieks and sights unholy.'

Went through the dismal *air like* one huge Python   W 51, 47
Antagonizing Boreas,—and *so vanish'd.*   W 47
Yet there was not a breath of air: she banish'd
These phantoms with a nod. Lo! from *the dark*   W 49
Came waggish *fauns,* and nymphs, and *satyrs* . . .'   W 73
                    (END. III, 518 ff.)

A careful comparison of this scene with the one Huon saw will
reveal how Oberon's transformed men, in the likeness of hinds and
harts, have (probably by virtue of the squire's provocative *'what* shape')
become yet more sinister. The herd that dissolves in air, the *'piteous*
groans,' the 'goblery' in *dark*ness have been retained along with the
pursuing *tempest* and the *pilgrims* dancing like *fauns* and *satyrs.* But
Oberon's powers of transforming sinful men have blended with the
powers exerted in the transformation of their lovers by Acrasia-Circe,
who has been modified further by Oberon's queen of sense.* And like
Oberon's deer, Keats' transformed elephant speaks with human voice.

Oberon's dreamlike enchanted forest, with its vision of sinful men
changed into the likenesses of beasts, provided the spark that released
the full creative impulse, and with it the imagery that till that moment
had slumbered in the depths of Keats' memory. But it is also evident
that Huon's earlier *experience of terror* in the first forest setting fused
repeatedly with his adventures in Oberon's wood. That is apparent from
the lines that Keats now wrote.

End. III, 556-70:

                    . . . truth had come
Naked and sabre-like against my heart.   W 21
I saw a fury whetting a *death*-dart;
And my slain spirit, overwrought with *fright,*   W 9
Fainted away *in that dark* lair of *night* . . .   W 6 ff.

It is suggestive that like Huon's so did Glaucus' adventures in the forest
begin 'one morn.' But Huon's *fright*ful adventures before he saw the
green flame occurred in the dark night, even as Glaucus here implies.

---

* Almansaris, let us remember, is the bower queen, tool in the trial of Huon's
spirituality, which precedes the accomplishment of his mission.

. . . *terrors manifold* divided me   W 16
A spoil amongst them. I prepar'd to *flee*
Into the dungeon core of that *wild wood:*   W 62
I fled *three days*—when lo! *before me stood*   W 66
Glaring *the angry witch.*

(Huon, we saw, journeys for three days to Oberon's 'wild woods'; and therein he flees until the wizard-enchanter stands before him.)

O Dis, even now,
A *clammy dew* is *beading on my brow,*   W 20
At mere remembering her pale laugh, and curse . . .

In the earlier forest, when Huon heard the reverberating echoes of thunder from all sides and the roaring of lions in the darkness, 'Fear stood upon his brow in dew-drops chill.' And again, Circe's curse could be no more revealing:

'So, *fairy*-thing, *it shall have lullabies*
Unheard of yet; and it shall still its cries
Upon some breast more *lily*-feminine . . .'
(END. III, 575 ff.)

We saw Oberon's potent lily wand; and Circe seems to know that the fairy music which provides Huon a 'delicate *lullaby*' is as yet unheard in *Oberon,* where it occurs before his vision of the 'woman like a goddess' who turns out to be his 'eastern queen.'

End. III, 668 ff.:

Probably, too, it was Oberon's daemonic *tempest* which evoked Shakespeare, for soon Prospero's scroll and the shipwreck appear in the picture. Yet the tempest was watched by Glaucus (III, 668) '*with many a* scalding *tear* and many a *groan,*' echoed, perhaps, from Wieland's transformed deer, driven away by a storm, with 'their ceaseless groans . . . with many a tear.' And the old man's hand having given up the wand and scroll, magic treasures (cf. Oberon's magic gifts after the tempest had abated), 'then 'gan *abate The storm*' and Glaucus is 'athirst to search the book' (III, 674 ff.) as the squire is for the gift goblet. A few lines later Glaucus reads Endymion the scroll concerning *the mission* to lay 'side by side' all 'lovers tempest-tost' (cf. Rezia and Huon on their way to the hermitage), and also concerning Endymion's being 'a *youth, by heavenly power loved and led.*' It is significant that it is also after the tempest that the heavenly power Oberon tells of his love for Huon since the latter's birth, and that having given him the fairy gifts Oberon *promises his aid in the achievement of Huon's mission* in Bagdad. This, yet another vital structural analogy, indicates that Keats had not forgotten the larger design.

III, 790-802 (p. 138):

There are a few more echoes. Endymion's kindred mission accomplished, 'all were *re-animated*' as was the squire by the *fairy wine.* Then strange 'noise of *harmony,* pulses and throes Of gladness *in the air*' are heard: 'Delicious symphonies' shed 'unseen *leaves* of sounds divine' as

> The two deliverers tasted a pure wine
> Of happiness, from *fairy*-press ooz'd out.

These are allusions to Oberon's leaf-like aerial music that provided Huon's lullaby, and to the fairy wine that had strayed thus far from the enchanted forest (above).

III, 803-10; 823; 850-7; 864-5; 891-2; 933-4:

The subsequent procession of the lovers into the iridescent (composite) palace of Neptune is clearly based upon the lovers' welcoming into the twilight-tinted, floating palace of Oberon in the enchanted forest. That palace stood in the forest twice visited by Huon: where (cf. Glaucus) he saw first the transformed men in the shapes of beasts and where later (cf. Endymion) he saw, at the reconciliation of the lovers, the elfin procession and ecstasy of the *aerial* spirits and their marriage melodies and dancing and crowning of the wanderer and his bride with garlands and wreaths (cf. Keats' '*dance, song,* and *garlanding*' and 'Love took *wing*'). It is clear that that final diaphanous vision of the ecstasy of spiritualized love evoked the triumphant conclusion of Book III of *Endymion,* when the mission, similar both in kind and effect, has been accomplished. (Cf. *Oberon* XII, 78 ff.)

III, 1024 (p. 138):

Endymion hears the airy voice of his heavenly mistress say: 'Immortal bliss for me too hast thou won.' The suggestion for this probably came from Titania's words to Rezia: 'Then shall your life, like ours, be pure delight' (x, 11). Much more significant are the words and appearance of the daemon king at the palace welcoming. With Titania by his side, he appears as a youth on whose face *'eternal beauty* smil'd'; and he says to the spiritualized lovers: 'Receive from friendly hands *the gift divine* . . . So never from your hearts shall *happiness* recede' (xii, 71-2). In connection with Endymion's quest for immortality, highest happiness, love, and beauty in the divine, this must have been one of the most fertile hints in all of *Oberon,* the pattern by which Keats was guided.

iv, 30-70 (p. 138):

As we saw, Wieland's apostrophe to love and allusions to Rezia's royal birth and sacrifice of an eastern throne for love, had been prefixed to the 'fainting creatures in a desert wild' episode (vii, 40) and assimilated into the first portion of Book ii of *Endymion.* It is also significant that in the sacred groves, of the spiritualizing visions, the wanderer Huon had confessed to the hermit all his history till that time. He had told the sage of how, shortly after his experiences in the enchanted forest, he had first seen his ideal of love and beauty in a prophetic dream by a marvelous stream: of how 'near him a woman like a goddess stands,' * who, after their impassioned caresses, was *cast into the swirling waters* in *a fearful storm.* Huon had told the hermit of his first meeting with the eastern princess, of how they had eloped from the palace and of the tempestuous aftermath which brought the lovers to the desert isle and then to the hermitage. Keats knew all this. And he knew that just before their strange elopement, when the daemon king emerges from the air before their eyes and bids Rezia ponder her fateful step, *the eastern maid had parted gladly from* her father's palace and *native land* beside *the paradisal banks of* the sacred river *Euphrates:*

> W 1   Wealth, glory, splendor, all an empty name:
>   *From these* it little seems at once *to part,*
> 3   So the enchanted *maid* her Huon keeps . . .
>   (OBERON v, 74)

And enchanted she had been ever since her first glimpse of him in a dream.

* iii, 58. Cf. Mathew's 'Lines.'

Shortly after his dream by the marvelous stream, she had dreamed that her hated wooer Babekan pursued her with his hounds, 'urg'd her, in form a *hind*,'* to flee in mortal *terror* down a mountain through a wild *wood*. When escape seemed impossible, a dwarf of wondrous beauty had appeared in a car drawn through the air by two young lions. In his hand he held a blossoming lily wand; and by his side sat a strange knight, beautiful as a young god or seraph, with whom at first sight she fell in love. The aerial car had descended; the dwarf had *touched her with his lily wand;* the hind's skin had fallen off and *her human shape* had been restored. At his urging, blushingly she had mounted the car, and seated between the dwarf and *her skyey lover* had ascended, until breathless she awoke.

Passing over the trip through the air, let us now turn to Book iv of Keats' romance, the book which concerns human love as a stage in the quest for fellowship with essence. Endymion to 'heaven's airy dome Was offering up a hecatomb of vows' when a woman's voice reached him thus:

> 'Ah, woe is me! that *I should fondly part*   W 2
> *From my dear native land!* Ah, foolish *maid!*
> Glad was the hour, when, with thee, myriads bade
> Adieu to *Ganges and* their *pleasant fields* . . .'
>   (END. IV, 30-3)

Here are a different sacred river and 'myriads'; but verbal echoes and the same departure as that of the wanderer Huon's eastern maid. Endymion hears the voice, and oddly bows his head through 'thorny-green entanglement Of under*wood . . . anxious* as *hind* towards her hidden fawn.' Keats recalled Rezia's wild wood, terror, hind's skin, for *'Is no one near to help me?'* the voice continues in the next line. And a few lines later Keats interpolates this:

> IV, 52   Thou, Carian lord, hadst better have been *tost*
>   *Into a whirlpool. Vanish into air,*
>   54   Warm mountaineer! for canst thou only bear
>   *A woman's sigh* alone and *in distress?*
>   56   See not her charms! Is *Phoebe* passionless?
>   Phoebe is fairer far—O gaze no more:—

* IV, 46 ff. (another link with Ovid's tale of Actæon, in which Titania is Diana).

58   Yet *if thou wilt behold all beauty's store,**
        Behold her panting in the forest grass!
60   Do not those *curls of glossy jet* surpass
        For tenderness the arms so idly lain
62   Amongst them? Feelest not a kindred pain,
        To see such *lovely eyes in swimming search*
64   *After some warm delight* . . .

And then the woman's voice resumes:

66   'O for Hermes' *wand,*
      To touch this flower *into human shape!* †
68   *That* woodland Hyacinthus *could escape*
        From his *green* prison, and here kneeling down
70   Call me *his queen* . . .'

and so she continues to speak of *love,* while he 'upon a bough . . . leant, wretched.' But there let us pause a moment.

Whatever other elements may have been interwoven, it is quite obvious that this entire exceptional complex is a tissue of reminiscences: of Huon's dream of his ideal of love and beauty—his 'eastern *queen*' and *'woman like a goddess'* ‡ whom he tried to follow when she was cast into the swirling water. With that dream were interwoven elements from Rezia's dreams: Oberon's wand that restores her shape and enables her to escape; and her second glimpse of Huon in the wooded palace gardens, when the night before her dreaded wedding revelry, she

W 5   . . . seems within the harem's *green* alcove
        Sunk in *warm* fancies of enchanting *love*—   K 64, 69 f.
  7   Sweet restless wishes, *sad*ly-pleasing fears,
        Now *heave her breast,* and dim *her eyes in tears,*   K 63
  9   While, *to the youth* ador'd, *her thoughts desponding*
        rove.

                                        (OBERON V, 2)

After her first vision, *'The shadow* flies, but from her heart again He never fades: the youth . . .' (IV, 49). But now she dreams that with (W 10) 'swift unquiet pace, She *searches* groves . . . lawns . . . bowers.' And sighing in her distress, 'oft mute she stops, oft starts with

* Cf. Huon's ideal.
† Cf. Rezia.
‡ Note the appearance of Phoebe, the goddess, in K 56.

pale delight If but a shadow wave,' until at last she sees her *shadowy lover* (W 12) from the skies, hides behind a tree, and the dream *vanishes.*

Aside from the same distressed and tearful search, it is significant that in an earlier draft Keats' despondent damsel engaged in 'fruitless search' and melts 'after some beauteous youth' (cf. W 9) precisely like Rezia. Keats also wrote 'Sweet shadow, be distinct awhile and stay.' * And Endymion sees his eastern maid in 'green covert' and 'thorny-green entanglement of underwood' in a setting like Rezia's. He even sees *'Her* gentle *bosom heave'* (cf. W 5, 8). But the shifting and elusive pictures crystallize yet more, so that there is no doubt as to the identity of Endymion's minutely similar maid.

IV, 99 ff.:

For he feels 'as one by beauty slain,' asks forgiveness for violating her *bower,* addresses her as 'young angel! fairest thief! Who stolen hast away the wings wherewith I was to top' the heavens:

> IV, 110   'Dear maid, sith
> *Thou art my executioner,* and I feel
> 112   *Loving* and *hatred, misery* and *weal,*
> *Will in a few short hours* be nothing to me,
> *And* all my story that *much passion slew me . . .'*

He asks her pity and envisages a storm:

> 120   'Scowl on, ye fates! until *the firmament*
> *Outblackens* Erebus, and the full-cavern'd *earth*
> 122   *Crumbles* into itself . . .'

If we recall the *Oberon* pattern, we need hardly ask with the eastern maid, 'Why must such desolation betide?' For Endymion is still alluding to that pattern: to the fearful daemonic storm that Oberon unleashes 'a few short hours' after Rezia's dream vision; the punitive storm that breaks when mortal loving begot divine hatred, and misery led to the hermitage and bliss; when much passion led Wieland's wanderer to be 'presumptuous against love, against the sky, against all elements'; and

---

* Cf. H. W. Garrod, ed., *P. W.,* 1939, p. 160: Keats' earlier 'fruitless search' (line 63) and 'after some beauteous youth' (line 72). Huon was a youth beautiful as a seraph, a god. (Cf. Keats' 'young angel,' line 108.)

his transgression was punished by the heavenly power almost with death. In that elemental storm, streams of fire pour from the *black* clouds; earth's axis *cracks,* and furious winds pile the sea to mountainous heights. Later in his romance Keats alludes to this storm again.* For it is Rezia who, because sympathy for Huon's suffering led to the consummation of their love, almost proved his executioner. She still is identical with Endymion's eastern 'queen' and 'guilt' and we have come to the famous Song of Sorrow.

It has long been thought that the 'Song of the Indian Maid represents a fusion in Keats' mind of two distinct stories—the medieval "Lay of Aristotle" and the Greek myth of Bacchus.' † To these, however, the story of Huon and Rezia must be added in the new light that *Oberon* sheds upon the sixth to ninth stanzas. For this is what Keats wrote:

> IV, 188   *'Beneath* my *palm trees, by the river side,*
>   I *sat a weeping:* what *enamour'd bride,*
>   190   Cheated by *shadowy wooer from the clouds,*
>   But *hides* and shrouds
>   *Beneath dark* palm *trees by a river side?'*

Skirting the vision of Bacchus and his revelers, we find also this picture:

> 209   *'Within his car, aloft, young* Bacchus stood,
>   Trifling his *ivy-dart,* in dancing mood,
>
>   ·   ·   ·
>
> 215   And near him rode Silenus on his ass,
>   Pelted with flowers as he on did pass
>   Tipsily quaffing . . .'

Now Keats had read of Rezia's vision of Huon 'beauteous as *a god'* aloft in Oberon's car with the dwarf and the lily wand. He had seen the bride of Babekan, enamored and weeping for her shadowy wooer from the clouds, the night before the dreaded revelry, in her second vision as she vainly sought him *beneath the dark trees* and then *hid* from him in the gardens *near a river's side.* (With this cf. K 188-92.)

* *Oberon* VII, 17-19. Cf. Keats' ' 'twould be a *guilt'* (*End.* IV, 134) and also IV, 652.
† Finney, op. cit. I, 277.

Yet how could the stream of images of Bacchus and his rout of revelers, of Ariadne possibly, but certainly memories of Titian and other painters: how could they possibly have been drawn into the design of *Endymion?* How and why were they drawn in? I think *Oberon* again provided the hooks and eyes, for the following reason. Besides the car and the suggestive 'beauteous as a god' in the eastern maid Rezia's vision, in an adjoining stanza Keats had seen this, as early as the Mathew period. Immediately after Huon's dream of the woman like a goddess, the fairy canopy vanished. And his vision of the 'eastern queen' was associated with this landscape:

> *'Where* high *Euphrates* winds its gentle tide,
> Onward they took their solitary way,
> *Beneath* o'ershadowing *palms* that dim the day.   K 188, 192
> Enchanting land! creation's fairest pride!
> Slowly they went . . .' *

In this *riverside* setting as Huon still dreams of his 'visionary *bride,'*

>   . . . the distance melts away—
> *On*ward *they hasten,* till the mid-day heat   K 216
> In shadowy groves compels them to retreat:

(These groves were a link with the shadowy ones of Rezia's vision. Cf. K 190.)

> There as th' *o'erflowing goblet thirst subdues,*   K 217
> And thrice *with nectar draught* their strength renews,

Huon's thirsty *companion,* his *old* squire who rides 'a *mule*-like thing,' repeatedly *drinks the fairy wine* (*Oberon* iv, 23). Now glance back at Keats' lines 188-216. Huon, beauteous 'as a god,' probably provided a hint. That hint, with the antics of his thirsty old companion on the mule, evidently stirred memories of Bacchus, to which the drunken revelry that Rezia fears may have further contributed. The eastern maid's two visions, the picture of the squire, and the myth coalesced. And so for a time Keats wandered from the pattern, in pursuit of other pictures.

The Bacchus episode is no more than a thread in the design of

---

* *Oberon* iv, 19. The next lines of this stanza left echoes in the opening lines of *Hyperion.* (Cf. p. 315.)

Endymion. And we have seen that up to and beyond that episode Keats had continued to identify his lovers, both wanderer and eastern queen and their meeting and visions and mossy cave and so forth, with Huon and Rezia. If anything, then *Oberon* with its vivid pictures of elements shared with Titian or others—the car aloft, the young god, the palms by the riverside, the thirsty old companion on his mule— must have evoked recollections of the Bacchus myth.* As Wieland's images coalesced with those pictures in Keats' mind, pictures of Bacchus in his car, the god brought with him a train of exotic associations which momentarily poured into the *Endymion* sequence. The legendary Bacchus, with the various minor features gleaned from Diodorus and Rabelais and Ovid, is actually an irrelevant adornment. In itself it had no intrinsic relation to the pattern or theme of *Endymion:* the gradations of happiness and quest of immortality and highest happiness by a 'youth, by heavenly power loved and led,' a youth who because of his love for the eastern 'queen' thinks himself disloyal to the heavenly power. That main theme takes us back to Huon and Rezia and *Endymion.*

IV, 320 ff. (p. 139):

Hardly has the Song of Sorrow come to an end than Keats resumes the theme of his fourth book, human love—conceived in terms of Wieland's wanderer and his 'woman like a goddess.' Endymion's sympathy leads him to love the eastern maid; he hears an airy voice say 'Woe! Woe to that Endymion' and as they

> Leant to each other trembling, and sat so
> *Waiting for some destruction*—when lo,
> Foot-feather'd Mercury appear'd sublime;

strikes the earth with *his* wand and causes 'diving *swans*' to appear and two *steeds,* on which the wanderer and his mortal love fly through the air. Before the Song of Sorrow Keats had alluded to the storm. Evidently this 'destruction' is what Huon and Rezia feared as Oberon

---

* Bacchus and Oberon's car coalesced again later, in the *Ode to a Nightingale,* as we shall see. Incidentally, the hounds that pursued Rezia probably recalled Actæon in Ovid. And from Ovid Keats seems to have derived the main outline of the Bacchus myth.

flies before their eyes, when their forbidden love has been consummated. For against that the heavenly power had warned them—after their flight from the palace and flight through the air in heavenly bliss because their dreams of love had come true. Echoes of that flight in the car drawn by 'four swans, for horses' (*Oberon* v, 80) now appear in *Endymion*.

iv, 367-70:

> There curl'd a purple mist around them; soon,
> It seem'd as when around the pale new moon
> Sad Zephyr droops the clouds like weeping willow:
> 'Twas Sleep slow journeying with head on pillow.

As Wieland's lovers journey through the air in the *misty* night, the terrified nurse *pillows* her *head* on the squire's shoulder and *sleeps* (*Oberon* v, 81-3). The lovers meanwhile feel 'Joys that in Paradise the blest await.' In Keats' parallel sequence, his lovers actually visit a pagan paradise. And thereafter, for good reason, they feel 'What horrors may discomfort thee and me. Ah, shouldst thou die from my heart treachery!' Endymion's 'Even when I feel as *true* as innocence' (iv, 474) and what follows show that Keats was still following the outline of the *Oberon* love story.

iv, 621-771 (p. 139):

After the Cave of Quietude and the interpolated hymn, of the 'voices sweet Warbling the while as if to lull and greet The wanderer in his path,' the lovers awake back on earth.* Endymion would live 'in love and peace among (Pan's) forest wildernesses,' feels he has loved an illusion, and says:

> 'O I have been
> *Presumptuous against love, against the sky,*
> *Against all elements,* against the tie
> Of mortals each to each . . .'

* Cf. *Oberon* xii, 74-5. Suggestions for the 'skyey mask, a pinion'd multitude . . . voices sweet warbling' may also have come from the hermit's experience of Titania's aerial music. (Cf. viii, 27.)

and elemental love. He has 'bent His appetite beyond his natural sphere' hence all but *'starv'd and died.'* He renounces all but human love, and says:

> 'Caverns lone, farewel!
> And *air of visions,* and *the monstrous swell*
> *Of visionary seas!* No, never more
> Shall *airy voices cheat me to the shore*
> *Of tangled wonder, breathless and aghast.*
> Adieu, my daintiest Dream! although so vast,
> My love is still for thee. *The hour may come*
> *When we shall meet in pure elysium.'*

And a moment later he speaks of dwelling in the mossy cave with his eastern maid. In all this his identity with Wieland's wanderer is obvious. Keats had come back to Canto VII of *Oberon:* the lovers' presumption against the king of the elements, his monstrous sea storm, the desolate shore, the bitter delusion of the golden fruit, Huon's reproaches to his airy guiding power (cf. 'cheat'), the starvation and punishment of the wanderer and the 'eastern queen' who almost died. Keats had returned to the scene assimilated into the first part of his Book II, and for all his close adherence to the *Oberon* pattern his larger purpose is clear.

IV, 669 ff.:

For 'Now,' Endymion asks,

K 670   'Where shall our dwelling be? *Under the brow*
           Of some steep mossy *hill,* where ivy dun
672   Would hide us up, although *spring leaves were none;*
        And where dark yew trees, as we rustle through,
674   Will drop their scarlet berry cups of dew?
        O thou wouldst joy to live in such a place;
676   Dusk for our loves, yet light enough to *grace*
        Those *gentle limbs on mossy bed reclin'd:*
678   For by one step the blue sky shouldst thou find,
        And by another, in *deep* dell *below,*
680   *See,* through the trees a little *river go*
        All in its mid-day *gold* and glimmering.
682   Honey from out the gnarled hive *I'll bring,*
        And *apples,* wan with sweetness, *gather thee . . .'*

And a few lines later we see also (Oberon's) *'rill, Thou haply mayst delight in,'* which Keats now fills with 'fairy fishes.' It is the same water —'and hark! at once a viewless rill' appeared—which Oberon sent when Rezia fainted: the fountain which the nymph had said arose for 'fainting creatures in a desert wild.' * The entire episode derives from *Oberon,* including Huon's vision from the mountainside of how 'The sun-beams streak the western wave with gold.' For it is under the brow of the steep crags that the lovers' cave is situated. And there too:

> . . . no leafy bow'rs a sheltering shade supply.   K 672
>
> . . .
>
> At last where opening rocks a cleft disclose,
> By Huon's searching eye *a cave* is seen:
> Faint, in his arms he bears *the eastern queen,*
> And *lays her* in its shade to cool repose:
> Then with hoar *moss,* and many a sunburnt reed,   K 677
> (Alas! how grateful in the hour of need)
> He strews *her bed* . . .
>
>   (OBERON VII, 39)

It is significant that early in Book IV Endymion's Indian maid is a 'Queen.' For the two eastern maids are still identical—a 'woman like a goddess' in the same mossy cave, with the same wanderer. And the very next stanza brings us to Wieland's apostrophe to love, which is so significant in connection with the thematic gradations of happiness: 'O love! thou only balm of every woe . . . What joys with thine compare, thou heaven below' (VII, 40). That apostrophe had already appeared in the first line of Keats' Book II.

But now we see that like Endymion's so does Huon's 'eastern queen' *joy to live in such a place.* For:

> Not golden halls by pomp imperial trod,
> Can boast a *grace* that like this savage grot   K 676
> Charms Rezia's eye! *and in this desert spot*
> *He to her bosom prest becomes a god!*

In the light of Endymion's impending apotheosis—through love of *his* 'woman like a goddess,' *his* eastern queen—apotheosis that occurs shortly

---

* *Oberon* VII, 58. Cf. *End.* II, 119.

after this mossy cave episode, that hint in its setting must have become electric for Keats. As for Rezia:

> The rugged flint on which *her limbs repose,*   K 677
> *Where* love with mould'ring *moss* the cavern strews,
> Seems richer than the pearl-embroider'd *bed,*
> And far more fragrant than fresh odors shed
> From *lily*'s perfum'd *breath,* or scent of vernal rose!

In the parallel passage Keats duly wrote: 'my river-lily! one human kiss! one sign of real breath' (IV, 664-5). And returning to Huon's gentle beloved, we find that:

>   . . . on this arid *strand,*   K 654 *
> This bleak, unknown, inhospitable land,
> Where mountains hurl'd on mountains frown around,
> *To soothe keen famine what can here be found,*   K 682
> Now gone the golden bowl, withdrawn the fairy hand?
>
> With swift unwearied foot the youthful knight
> Climbs up the rocks . . .
>   (OBERON VII, 41-3)

and after agonizing toil finds the golden fruit—Endymion finds honey, apples, and sorrel (K 683). With the golden fruit he returns to the mossy cave only to find its heart or kernel vile. That bitter disappointment causes the famished Rezia to faint, and the rill to appear—incidents which had already appeared in Keats' Book II.

But here in Book IV Keats was not losing sight of his design. In IV, 720-731 'His briar'd path to some tranquility' and 'the flutter of this heart had ceas'd' allude to Huon's path toward the hermitage and spirituality and to his earlier resolution to die in a cavern when Rezia's heart seems to have stopped. And soon (IV, 751-71) Endymion's eastern maid identifies herself and the pattern with finality: she says to the youth by heavenly power loved and led:

> *'I may not be thy love: I am forbidden—*
> Indeed I am—thwarted, affrighted, chidden,
> By things I trembled at, and gorgon *wrath.*
> Twice hast thou ask'd whither I went: henceforth

* 'shore of tangled wonder.'

Ask me no more! I may not utter it,
Nor may I be thy love. *We might commit*
Ourselves at once to vengeance; we might die;
We might embrace and die: voluptuous thought!
Enlarge not to *my hunger* . . .'

And thus too, like Huon through suffering and the hermit's influence, Endymion renounces physical love and says:

'A hermit young, I'll live in mossy cave,
Where thou alone shalt come to me, and lave
Thy spirit in the wonders I shall tell.'
(END. IV, 860-3)

There 'white Chastity shall sit.' And thus his apotheosis is at hand. He does not hear the aerial music of Cynthia, as the hermit did. But the eastern 'queen' undergoes her metamorphosis, the human love becomes divine, and as goddess she says:

' 'twas fit that from this mortal state
Thou shouldst, my love, by some unlook'd for change
Be spiritualiz'd.'
(END. IV, 991-3)

From beginning to end, for all the modifications, the action of Book IV follows the outline of Huon's love for the eastern queen, *the 'woman like a goddess.'* Whether or not that phrase was meaningful to other readers of *Oberon,* to Keats it was. And he knew, too, of Huon and Rezia's spiritualization. He knew that they, who like Endymion had been presumptuous against the heavenly power, have been changed; so that at the hermit's bier Huon asks Rezia if she feels: 'as if *a ray of light Fell on thy soul from yon celestial height? So never did I feel frail nature rais'd . . . To soar to highest deeds on heavenly wings* elate' (*Oberon* IX, 41). That is Endymion's attitude toward the heavenly moon. From beginning to end the themes, like the characters and incidents, closely correspond.

➽ APPENDIX IV ➽

(Addenda to *The Eve of St. Agnes*)

(p. 166):

Keats' use of 'old dames' in *St. Agnes* is revealing. In stanza v he says that Madeline, 'whose heart had *brooded* . . . On love, and wing'd . . . care,' had heard *'old dames'* many times tell of the rites. In stanza x he says that only *one 'old beldame'* showed the lover any mercy, and in stanza xi he writes: 'Ah, *happy chance!* the aged creature came, Shuffling along with ivory-headed wand.' It is she who says of the lover's venture: 'thou must hold water in a *witch*'s sieve, And be *liege-lord of all the Elves and Fays.'* In the next, stanza xv,

> K 1   Feebly she laugheth in the languid moon,
>   While Porphyro upon her face doth look,
>   3   Like puzzled urchin on an *aged crone*
>   Who keepeth clos'd a wond'rous riddle-book,
>   As spectacled she sits in chimney nook.
>   6   But soon his *eyes grew brilliant, when she told*
>   His lady's purpose; and he scarce could brook
>   8   Tears, at the thought *of those enchantments* cold
>   And Madeline asleep in lap of legends old.

The 'old dames,' 'beldame,' 'aged creature,' 'aged crone,' and Angela, who is evidently Madeline's nurse, appear to have been one and the same person, patterned after a similar agent in the plot of *Oberon*.

In that poem, the Prince of Lebanon's betrothed, whom Huon retrieves from the giant along with the talisman, is named Angela. But an old woman, a character whose function is almost exactly that of Keats' Angela and 'old dames,' appears in Cantos iv and v as the mother of Rezia's nurse. Hardly have Huon and his squire entered Bagdad than 'they *chance* . . . *to meet,* Propt on her crutch, a little *aged crone'* (iv, 36: cf. K st. xi and also K 3). She leads the way to her hut where Rezia's lover remains in hiding for a night, gives him 'Rich milk, and juicy peaches . . . And figs, now blackening' in her

365

garden near the Euphrates (iv, 38). Then the *'loquacious dame'* (cf. K st. v) tells the lover of the preparations for the revelry, and of Rezia's first dream of her *enchantment* and retransformation into human shape by Oberon's *wand* and of her shadowy lover descended from the sky, over whose haunting image 'she *broods'* (iv, 46-9: cf. K st. v, xi, xiv, and K 8). Upon the lover's retiring, the 'grandam' watches him for some time; and the next morning she is the *'happy* crone . . . hurry'd in' to Rezia's chamber where she *tells* the dreamer *over and over* again of Huon's coming (v, 14: cf. K st. v, xi). The same old woman, just before he ventures into the revelry, helps the lover don the disguise *Oberon* left for him in the hut, the night of Rezia's enchanted 'visions of delight.' And 'the grandam' cries: 'There's *witchery* in the scene' and is answered by the squire: 'Aye . . . 'tis he! the friendly sprite' (v, 27: cf. K st. xiv). This linking of lover's venture, Oberon, and witches is precisely that of Angela.

Sotheby's word 'grandam' and Wieland's conception seem to have evoked both Angela and the 'old dames,' all of whom are one and the same. She intercepts the lover, hides him, provides fruit; links the venture with the supernatural; tells the dreamer, whose *'sparkling eyes'* flash when she is told of her lover's coming, as do Porphyro's eyes when told of the other dreamer (cf. K 6). And the 'enchantments' Angela reveals to Porphyro are Oberon's enchanted 'visions of delight' seen in Rezia's sleep. Minutely Wieland's 'grandam' *is* Angela. And probably she led Keats' mind back to his own grandam, when he was a 'puzzled urchin,' waiting to hear—a fairy tale?

(p. 168):

In connection with *Endymion,* we saw how in Canto x, Huon was borne through the air from the hermitage, in the arms of an invisible missioned spirit of the air, to the harem gardens of Tunis. Put abed a few days in consequence of *a fever,* the result of his sufferings,* he hears at last that his lovely bride has been immured in the harem. And disguised as a gardener, he ventures again and again into the forbidden precincts outside the walls in a vain *attempt to catch sight of* Rezia. Thus

* It is curious that Keats wrote 'he had a fever late' (st. xii).

W 2   *Meantime* with grief the beauteous gard'ner dies—
       With unsuccessful toil, sev'n *tedious* days,
4   *Around the* harem's *wall the lover strays,*
       Where Rezia, sure, with equal misery *sighs.*—   K 66

             .   .   .

6   Not thro' a lattice had he seen his bride . . .   K 113 *
                  (OBERON XI, 32)

Where Rezia sighs? We saw her sighing in her chamber before the revelry in the other royal palace, before the entrance of Huon. Did Keats remember also?

Let us turn back to his interpolation of Porphyro's whereabouts, the interpolation paralleling Wieland's in Canto v:

K 74   . . . Meantime, across the moors,   W 2
       Had come young Porphyro, with heart *on fire*
76   *For* Madeline. *Beside the* portal doors,
       Buttress'd from moonlight, *stands he,* and implores   W 4
78   All saints to *give him sight of* Madeline,
       But for one moment in the *tedious* hours,
80   That he might gaze and worship all un*seen* . . .   W 6
               (EVE OF ST. AGNES, ix)

In the three next stanzas Porphyro ventures into 'those *chambers'* which, as he learns from Angela, held 'barbarian hordes,' as for Huon on his first entrance. Notwithstanding that similarity, Porphyro's situation and mood, and the motivation for his entrance are strikingly like Huon's on his second entrance. For both lovers at their mortal peril are spending 'tedious hours' outside the hostile walls, within which their ladies sigh; and both at first are seeking merely to catch sight of her. Huon's two entrances had blended for the first time in Keats' new pattern.

Huon's present situation is complicated by the fact that the 'liege-lord of all the Elves and Fays' had withdrawn his aid; and by the circumstance that a lovely queen (Glaucus' 'arbour queen') has been smitten by Huon. And *'Meanwhile* Almansaris, her soul *on fire' for* him (cf. K 75-6) has been scheming and dreaming as to how to lure him into the palace. Like Madeline

* The 'little moonlit room,' whither we shall follow Angela and Porphyro in a moment, is 'Pale, *lattic'd* . . .' (st. xiii).

she calls the *night*.
Kind fortune aids her *vision of delight,*
All obstacles removes . . .

(OBERON XI, 43)

This 'vision of delight' is the third appearance of Sotheby's haunting phrase, each time in a passage evidently magnetic for Keats. It so happened that the sultan—not Rezia's father, this time, but still a *sultan*—had arranged *a feast* in honour of Rezia, and he had thus unwittingly provided the opportunity to have Huon *furtively led into the chambers of the* regal *seer of 'visions of delight.'* (Is not this reminiscent of Porphyro's situation?) Unconsciously Huon himself, desperately trying to catch sight of his beloved, had removed the other obstacle for the queen. For, as he *grieves, the nurse* proposes a *stratagem* and says '*A sudden thought* now strikes me' (XI, 33)—namely, to send a message in the language of flowers into the harem. Accordingly Huon gathers lilies 'and myrtle *bloom*ing on the flow'ry spray, The *rose*, the jasmin, and the jonquil gay.' *

Turning back to *St. Agnes,* Angela (the nurse?) having told Porphyro that 'men will murder upon holy days' and he having *grieved* to think of Madeline 'asleep in lap of legends old' seeing her 'visions of delight,' Keats immediately echoes two phrases, saying:

> K 136   *Sudden a thought* came *like* a full-*blown rose,*
> *Flushing* his brow, and in his pained heart
> Made purple riot: then doth *he propose* †
> *A stratagem,* that makes the beldame start . . .
>
> (EVE OF ST. AGNES, xvi)

The stratagem being of course that Angela was

> K 163   . . . *to lead him,* in *close secrecy,*
> Even to Madeline's *chamber,* and there hide
> 165   Him in a closet . . .
>
> (st. xix)

At first the old nurse is shocked and Porphyro protests he will not harm his love and threatens to *seek out certain death*—'Awake, with horrid

---

* XI, 34. Stratagem, and 'blooming,' and 'rose' with the kindred overtones of lover's grief and joy are in adjacent stanzas.
† Cf. the nurse.

shout, my foemen's ears, And beard them, though they be more fang'd than wolves and bears' (st. xvii).

It is significant that immediately after the vain attempt to catch sight of the one lady, there is in both instances the same pattern of grief, nurse, 'a sudden thought' which turns into a stratagem linked with blooming roses and a threat of certain death. But the stratagem also eventuates in much the same way.

In *Oberon*, when the nurse's stratagem has been carried out, she flies back flushed,* and tells Huon:

> '*This* day my lord *beholds again his bride*:
> Beneath the *midnight* silence *softly move*,   K 163
> The door is open . . .
> Watch'd by the slave who waits thy steps *to guide* . . .'   K 163
>   (OBERON XI, 40)

And Huon's feelings concerning the stratagem are such that he says to the nurse (cf. Porphyro in st. xvii to the nurse): 'Ah! if I knew that *death with terrors* crown'd' would strike, 'yet not the less delight thy words had shed' (XI, 41). All this is in each instance connected with the stratagem to lead the lover secretly at midnight through the hostile castle to his beloved's chamber while revelry removes the obstacles. The complex moods of the lovers, the situation, setting, motivation, and actions are still substantially akin and in similar configuration. It was but the beginning of the coalescence, in Keats' mind, of Huon's two entrances.

(st. xxiv, p. 171):

In the light of the evidence (in *Endymion* and *Lamia* as well as in *St. Agnes*) that Keats knew the episode of the queen minutely, it is noteworthy that a luminous window appears in that episode of *Oberon*. While the queen still dreams of Huon (XI, 21), 'Whene'er *eve's glimmering* beams her steps allur'd, *Painting* the *windows streak'd* with many a ray . . .' she wanders restlessly about her chambers. That there was such a window is significant, since it may well have provided the impulse that set Keats to painting his.

It is also, if less, noteworthy that somewhat earlier, while he is still

---

* 'Her cheek warm-*glowing from* extatic *thought*,' XI, 39 (cf. K 136-7).

outside the walls within which his beloved sighs, Huon in the *fruit* orchard 'wreathes . . . curious *knots, and garlands* gay' of *flowers* (xi, 2). And immediately on entering the *splendid* chamber, when his guide has hurried away, Huon confronts the dazzling queen arrayed in pearls and gleaming *diamonds;* while soon thereafter he sees the *queen's* 'speaking *blushes'* and 'cheeks *deeper-dy'd'* (xi, 62).

Keats' window appears, only two stanzas after Porphyro's furtive entrance into the chamber, thus:

> A casement high and triple-arch'd there was,
> All garlanded with carven imag'ries
> Of fruits, and flowers, and bunches of knot-grass,
> And diamonded with panes of quaint device,
> Innumerable of stains and splendid dyes,
> As are the tiger-moth's deep-damask'd wings;
> And in the midst, 'mong thousand heraldries,
> And twilight saints, and dim emblazonings,
> A shielded scutcheon blush'd with blood of queens and kings.
>
> (EVE OF ST. AGNES, xxiv)

The location of this gorgeous window in the sequence parallel to the appearance of the resplendent queen, may harbor the reason for Keats' indulgence in his rich composite picture, to which various sources contributed. And it is likely that the queen's windows, even as her blushing and rank, had something to do with the coloring of the royal escutcheon in the less exalted baronial hall of Madeline's father.

(st. xxvi, p. 172):

Having told her dream to the nurse, who glances about the chamber to see where the lover is concealed, Rezia steps *out of bed*

> W 1 Veil'd in her night-robe, that with *wavy play*
> Roll'd like a *mist,* and scarce *conceal'd* her charms . . .

Then the 'happy crone is hurried in' and tells and retells of the lover's arrival, while the whisperers help the dreamer into the *rich attire* befitting her rank. Even in Sotheby's stilted rendering, Wieland's picture retains clear details. Thus

> W 4 . . . each clust'ring braid
> Of Rezia's *hair* by Fatma's skill display'd,

6   Beneath her finger winds in wavy play.
       'Mid ebon *locks* her fingers *intertwine*
8   *Pearls* that more bright than glist'ning dew-drops shine.
       Her ear-rings, necklace, seem one diamond stone . . .
                                    (OBERON V, 16)

Thus, if Rezia robes after her 'charmed soul mid visions of delight Wove in her waking hours anew the dream' and *she dreams awake in her bed,* Madeline *dis*robes just before her visions of delight 'where swart Paynims pray.'

That disrobing, appearing in the same pattern of a dream of love come true, is significant. For Porphyro, as if he were Huon actually concealed in the chamber, sees his beloved in part at least through Wieland's eyes:

> Anon his heart revives: her vespers done,
> Of all its *wreathed pearls* her *hair* she frees;   W 8
> *Un*clasps *her* warmed *jewels one by one;*
> Loosens her fragrant boddice; by degrees
> Her *rich attire* creeps rustling to her knees:
> Half-*hidden,* like a mermaid in *sea*-weed,   W 1-2
> Pensive awhile *she dreams awake,* and sees,
> In fancy, fair St. Agnes *in her bed* . . .
>   (EVE OF ST. AGNES, XXVI) *

Not only the wreathed pearls and enumerated jewels but also the hint for the 'half-hidden . . . mermaid in sea-weed' may have come from Rezia. 'Scarce concealed,' 'veil'd,' 'mist,' 'wavy play' all were hints, since mermaids play in the waves. Keats' disrobing scene, dreaming awake abed, and visions of delight are in reversed sequence but in the same pattern of a dream of love come true. The structural analogy is more significant than the details, some of which derived from elsewhere.† (See below for a variant of Keats' mermaid.)

(st. xxvi and xxxiii, p. 175):

In the chambers of the queen, the lover 'unwillingly betray'd, Feels nature melt in the voluptuous glow' but turns away from the *'siren*

---

* In one draft, Keats wrote 'she lays aside *her veil.*' Rezia's silver one appears at the revelry.

† Cf. also p. 310 f., notes 17 and 18.

show' (xi, 58) and thinks of his vow to the angelic Rezia. There may have been a hint for Madeline's 'deceived thing' in Huon's 'unwillingly betray'd.' But in his explicit thoughts of Rezia there was an inescapable link to facilitate her coalescence with the queen. That link was strong, since Huon dwells upon the image of Rezia, their first kiss, and his vow: dwells at length on all this in the very stanza where the regal seer of 'visions of delight' notes the change in his features and tries to arouse his love by taking up her lute and singing her ditty.

There is also a clue which hints that the extensive process of the fusion of the two seers of 'visions of delight' had begun earlier in Keats' mind. In the stanza of the disrobing (xxvi: see above) on which Keats worked feverishly and which he recast again and again, he wrote in a rejected version that Madeline appeared

> Half hidden like a *Syren* of the Sea
> And more melodious . . .

Mr. Ridley's comment on this is noteworthy. He says (op. cit. p. 156): 'There is no point in Madeline's being either more or less melodious than a Syren (unless [Keats] had for the moment intentions of *making her rather than Porphyro sing* . . .).' I suspect that Keats had just that intention, or even the intention of having both lovers sing, like the queen and Huon. I suspect that it was the siren-queen whose lute, lute-playing, and singing provoked that intention. For Madeline acquired more than one trait from that seer of 'visions of delight.'

❧ APPENDIX V ❧

(Addenda to *Lamia*)

(p. 196):

As a note to the last line of the romance Keats appended this:

'Philostratus, in his fourth book *de Vita Apollonii*, hath a memorable instance in this kind, which I may not omit, of one Menippus Lycius, a young man twenty-five years of age, that going betwixt Cenchreas and Corinth, met such *a phantasm* in the habit of a fair gentlewoman, which *taking him by the hand*, carried him home to *her house*, in the suburbs of Corinth, and told him she was a Phoenician by birth, and if he would tarry with her, *he should hear her sing and play*, and *drink such wine* as never any drank, and no man should molest him; but she, being *fair and lovely*, would live and die with him, that was fair and lovely to behold. The young man, a philosopher, otherwise staid and discreet, *able to moderate his passions*, though not this of love, tarried with her a while to his great content, and at last married her, to whose wedding, amongst other guests, came Apollonius; who, by some probable conjectures, found her out to be *a serpent, a lamia;* and that *all* her furniture was, like Tantalus' gold, described by Homer, no substance but mere *illusions*. When she saw herself descried, *she wept,* and desired Apollonius to be silent, but he would not be moved, and thereupon she, plate, house, and all that was in it, vanished in an instant: many thousands took notice of this fact, for it was done in the midst of Greece.'

Burton's 'Anatomy of Melancholy,' *Part* 3. *Sect.* 2. *Memb.* 1. *Subs.* 1.

In the light of the queen, the phrases I have italicized are noteworthy as links that must have facilitated the integration.

Lamia II, 34 ff. (p. 219):

Huon finds that he has been lured into the queen's magnificent chamber where *'gold* and lazuli the walls o'erlaid' as if all *Golconda* and Siam's 'rifled mines' had poured their *riches* there (XI, 47). And even as Lycius' 'spirit pass'd beyond its golden bourn,' he soon thinks of his ideal while the queen's sensuous joys are offered him. Realizing

that his ideal of love and beauty is by comparison of 'angel kind,' *
Huon becomes inattentive and thinks ever farther beyond the queen's
'empery of joys.' She, like Lamia 'ever watchful, penetrant,' shortly

> *his speaking features understands,*
> W 2　　*Reads his chang'd soul.*　　　　　　　K 34, 39

Seizing her lute, *she begins* (like Burton's lamia) to sing and *sigh.*
When her attempted embrace is frustrated and she hears Huon's firm
reply to her song, then

> Th' enchantress, *'gainst her will,*
> W 4　　*Feels his superior force*—tears wildly fill
> Her eye indignant . . .
> (OBERON XI, 59 and 65)

and she *dismisses* him. In other words, like Lamia, she 'saw this with
pain': her lack of power over the youth of whom she is enamored.

(p. 220):

With Lamia's reaction in mind (II, 34 ff.), let us glance at the sublimated texture of *The Eve of St. Agnes,* where

> There was *a painful change,* that nigh expell'd　　W 2
> The blisses of her dream so pure and deep
> At which fair Madeline *began to weep,*　　　　　W 4
> And *moan* forth witless words with many a *sigh* . . . W 3

In both *Oberon* and *St. Agnes* at this point there is: lute-playing (which
also ceases in *Lamia,* though somewhat later †); a painful change read
by the lady from the features of the silent lover; and sighing and weeping—besides much more, as we saw.‡ Consciously or not, Keats, evidently
led by the queen's 'vision of delight,' selected some elements from the
Oberon scene and rejected those which he felt unfitting. And the
imagination sublimated and transmuted what it assimilated.

Again, in the parallel 'love in a palace' patterns in *Oberon* and *Lamia*

---

* Note Lycius' 'heavenly progeny.'
† Cf. 'By faint degrees, *voice, lute, and pleasure ceased'* (II, 265).
‡ Cf. chap. IV, p. 178, *St. Agnes,* xxxiv. That stanza adjoins the delicate scene
of the consummation of Madeline and Porphyro's love and 'love's alarum'—the
'tempest fell' of the angry Oberon, who in Lamia's 'palace of sweet sin' hovers
threateningly above the chamber door.

there is a painful change when the youth 'mused beyond' the dazzling enchantress, whose penetration enables her in each case to read the change of mood from his features. Thereupon both Lamia and the enchantress-queen are pained and sigh. But it is noteworthy that Lamia also *moans* as does Madeline. For at this point, for some dozen consecutive lines, the imagery of *Lamia* is closer to that of the adjacent stanzas of Madeline's idealized romance than to that of the thwarted one of the queen. Keats' mind, perhaps drawn to the former by the lute-playing of the queen, proceeded for the moment to retrace his own earlier pattern.

Thus in *The Eve of St. Agnes,* st. xxxv, Madeline says: 'Oh *leave me* not in this eternal woe, For if thou diest, my Love, *I* know not *where* to go.' With this compare Lamia: 'You have deserted me;—where am I now? . . . you have dismiss'd me; and I go From your breast houseless . . ." (II, 42-4).

At this point in *Oberon* Huon is dismissed by the frustrated 'fair seducer' and leaves her palace in the first light of *morning.* Confronting the nurse of the stratagem, he accuses her of treachery until he realizes: 'Thou wert thyself *deceiv'd*—my evil *stars* prevail.' In *St. Agnes* we saw how after the consummation of love, Madeline, in contrast with the forsaken queen who curses the youth, says (st. xxxvii): 'I curse not . . . Though thou forsakest a deceived thing; A dove forlorn and lost . . .'

And the words of her lover in the next stanza are noteworthy: 'Say, may I be for aye thy vassal blest? Thy beauty's shield, *heart*-shap'd and *vermeil*-dyed? Ah, *silver* shrine . . .' For Lycius says to Lamia: 'My silver planet, both of eve and morn!' (cf. Huon). 'Why will you plead yourself so sad forlorn [cf. the dove] While I am striving how to fill my heart With deeper crimson.' (Than the earlier 'vermeil'? And was Keats striving to excel that dialogue?)

Lamia II, 62-4 (p. 220):

Cf. *Oberon* XII, 56, 60-1, 66: '*Throng on throng*' flocks to see the execution in the street, until 'with echoing *outcry loud*' the sultan and queen hasten up to intervene. But Huon blows the elf-horn. 'Dance! till ye weary *gasp, depriv'd of breath*—Huon permits himself this slight revenge alone,' he says to *his foes* who would burn him alive. A moment later, 'thro' the air the swan-wing'd chariot flew . . . lightly *touch'd the ground'* and the lovers 'mount *the car'* bound for the *bridal* pageant.

Lamia ii, 65 ff. (p. 221):

Shortly before the *Oberon* scene above, Rezia, tempted by the sultan, defends Huon by saying of the treacherous queen: '*A wily snake* Deceiv'd him and thyself' (xii, 49). And a few stanzas earlier, that queen, her crown on her head and in her gleaming robes, mysteriously appeared in Huon's prison in the night. *She takes his hand,* tells the youth, 'my life on thine depends,' and offers him the throne if he will but love her. (In other words, in the *Oberon* sequence the *proposal of a public marriage* is made by the temptress rather than by the youth Huon-Lycius.) And the queen hints the latter's conflict, saying '*wake to fame! Let glory to the world thy deeds proclaim!*' (In the parallel 'Love in a palace' pattern in *Lamia,* we hear the trumpets and Lycius' desire.*) But Huon, steadfast rather than 'perverse' like Lycius, refuses. And the 'wily wanton *tries* each subtle art, *To bend the spirit* of th' unconquer'd youth.' (Thus Lycius tries 'Perverse, with stronger fancy to reclaim her wild and timid nature to his aim'—which is that of the queen: cf. K 70-1.) The queen 'lures, now threatens, *falls his feet before,' beseeching him to change his purpose,* of rather dying at the stake than being inconstant to his vow. (Cf. K 66-8.) Huon remaining inflexible, the queen, now pale, now flushed, now smiling, now in tears, at first soft-voiced but now strident as she 'curses loud' in impotent fury, is in torment of 'madd'ning passion lost.' (*Oberon* xii, 32-7.)

That Keats derived many hints from this 'grievous torment' is obvious. Reminded perhaps by the last phrase he also drew upon the queen's earlier fit of maddening passion. Thus at the conclusion of Huon's first temptation, *when she hears his words* that nothing 'can wake . . . new desire,' then, like Lamia,

> th' enchantress, 'gainst her will,
> Feels his superior force—*tears wildly fill*
> Her eye . . .   K 66

And having dismissed the youth, she retires to her couch where her convulsed soul is bared:

* Cf. also the trumpet in *End.* i, 737.

Meanwhile Almansaris, her soul on fire,
Wild passion raging in her fiery breast,
Seeks on her couch assuasive rest: *
In vain—wild groans the demon of desire.
The strange adventure of the shameful night
Illusive all: a man thy beauty slight!   K 44-5
(OBERON XII, 1)

While the italicized phrase was another link, with Burton's 'all . . . illusions,' the queen's thought—'a man thy beauty slight'—is suggestive of Lamia's realization, in the parallel sequence, of her impotence with the youth she had lured into her palace. But now the queen's reactions reveal their effect upon those of Lycius:

These thoughts to maddening rage *her soul inflame:*
Death, tenfold death, shall expiate the offense!
How loath'd the monster that bewitch'd her sense!

(Lamia had bewitched the senses of Lycius, whose passion grows cruel.)

A dragon seems far lovelier to the dame.
Now pride and jealousy the wretch detest,
The *furi*ous fit now dies, *by love supprest—*   K 78, 72
Desire and vengeance swift as thought succeed:
Before her, *drop by drop,* the wretch *shall bleed!—*   K 75-6
Now, in her arms enchain'd, she dies upon his breast.
(OBERON XII, 2)

In other words, in her torment her passion grows cruel and bloodthirsty. And precisely like Lycius, despite her love she would delight in Huon's suffering or sorrow. Then her frenzy is somewhat soothed: woman again, she thinks of the youth she had lured into her palace as 'a hero, *god,* surpassing human birth' (cf. K 79), and of how 'Plain on *his brow*' (cf. K 77) nature had stamped his regal heritage. To such thoughts

Almansaris, in whose empassion'd blood
A sly seducer creeps, *her soul resigns,*
Follows where'er th' infernal fiend inclines,
And sinks *in willing slavery* self-*subdu'd.*   K 81-2

Like Lamia, who 'burnt . . . lov'd the tyranny, and all subdued,' the queen's soul was 'on fire' for the youth by whom she was subdued (*Oberon* XII, 3-7).

* Cf. Lamia.

A comparison of the imagery in its similar sequence makes clear enough, I think, that the lovely African queen (cf. Lamia regina) in her twofold schizophrenia of burning love and bloodthirsty hate and of pleading submission and demoniac fury has in Coleridge's phrase been 'dissolved, diffused, dissipated' in Keats' design. By transference and transfusion she has visibly colored the actions and moods both of her alluring counterpart Lamia in her kneeling, weeping, beseeching, burning, self-subdual, etc. and of Lycius in her thought of fame and glory, her attempt to 'bend the spirit,' and her frenzy of love and 'passion cruel grown' to the point of fierceness and bloodiness in 'self-despite.' The violent and complex *Oberon* scene with its rich overtones was assimilated into a new pattern and given a similar but much more subtle human motivation. The queen's actions and reactions provided hints for those of both Lamia and Lycius, so that 'fine was the mitigated fury' indeed. It is noteworthy too that in the refitted pattern of Keats' romance the queen's two wild fits of fury and their sequel have been dovetailed in reversed sequence, which otherwise still parallels that of *Oberon,* the 'tale from faery land.'

Lamia ii, 105 ff. (p. 222):

Hardly has Lamia been subdued and consented to the bridal than Lycius, 'whispering in midnight silence,' thinks of her as *'not mortal* but *of heavenly progeny'* as well as of regal 'dazzling frame.' She, however, artfully feigns sleep to avoid further questioning and to heighten the suspense as to her identity. The clues as to that lie in the *Oberon* pattern. For no sooner in its thronged streets have Huon and his bride seated themselves in Oberon's chariot than they are borne to the daemon king's palace. Some of its features, and elements of the bridal pageant, reappear in the parallel sequence of *Lamia.* For now Keats wrote:

> It was the custom then to bring away
> K 106   The bride from home at blushing *shut of day,*
> *Veil'd,* in a chariot, *heralded along*
> 108   *By strewn flowers,* torches, and *a marriage song,*
> With other pageants . . .

In this he was probably confirmed by the authority of Potter.* But the 'other pageants' in the pattern are suggestive of why he consulted Potter. In *Oberon,* prophetic of a later age, he had seen Huon and *his* bride flying through the air in *'the chariot.'* And 'where twilight sweeps Her *veil* of shapeless mists' they observe the moon mirrored in sleeping lakes, till suddenly,

> as if woven from the *rosy eve,*   K 106
> Radiant before their sight a floating palace springs.

In a moment the golden gates open and a score of immortal virgins 'float before their ravish'd sight'; and Huon leads his bride to the fairy palace

> 'mid *the songs* of that angelic band
> That, *rang'd before them,* glide in graceful row,
> And, as they step, their path *with roses strow.* †   K 108

That Keats derived hints from this scene and corroborated them in Potter is suggested by his use of elements in the description of Oberon's palace. Shortly, Keats describes Lamia's 'faery roof' and the 'noise of wings.'

Lamia II, 110-118 (p. 223):

Lamia, who like the mortal queen of the dazzling frame in *Oberon* lures the youth into her palace, is also 'penanced lady elf.' And in the bridal pageant of the fairy tale queen Titania reappears, her penance ended by the lovers' constancy. The composite nature of Keats' heroine is again shown by his next lines, in which the mortal and immortal queens—and features of their palaces—were almost visibly interwoven. Continuing, he wrote:

> K 110   With other pageants: but this fair unknown
>   Had not a friend. *So being left alone,*

---

* In John Potter's *Antiquities of Greece,* which Keats knew, Douglas Bush found such phrases as these: ' "The bride was usually conducted in a chariot from her father's house to her husband's in the evening . . . to conceal her blushes"; and again, "torches were carried before her . . . They were sometimes attended by singers and dancers . . ." ' ('Notes on Keats' Reading,' p. 786.)

† *Oberon* XII, 67-8, 74. And cf. the torches at the execution.

112   (Lycius was gone to summon all his kin)
         And knowing surely she could never win
114   His foolish heart from its mad *pomp*ousness,
         She set herself, high-thoughted, how to dress
116   The misery in fit magnificence.
         She did so, but 'tis doubtful how and whence
118   Came, and who were *her subtle servitors.*

Here Lamia, who reappears in a moment 'regal drest' beside 'an un-tasted feast,' is clearly the African queen. It was she who could never win Huon's heart *with* her

> pomp, which far outshines
> Each brilliant scene his eye had e'er survey'd.
> (OBERON XI, 47)

That enchantress could set herself to prepare the feast for Huon, and to enrich the magnificence of her chambers and dress, because her consort was preoccupied with Huon's bride, the enamored sultan's fair unknown guest (cf. K 110). It was this desertion which first made the queen wretched with hate and jealousy. But when she meets Huon, it also

> *Leaves* the sultana *free* and unconfin'd   K 111
> To pass her time and leisure as she can,
> And weave at liberty each secret plan,
> Where slaves at will start up to *serve her subtle* mind.
> (XI, 31)

The closely similar situation of the two enchantresses, deserted in 'Love in a palace,' can hardly be coincidence. The last line, of which Keats' 'her subtle servitors' is a clear echo, reveals the process by which the supernatural overtones in the palace of the mortal queen helped effect the fine fusion of natural and supernatural features in Lamia's composite palace.

Lamia II, 119-31:

Thus 'her subtle servitors' take us back to Oberon's palace of the immortals. For Keats next wrote:

> . . . her subtle servitors.
> About the halls, and to and *from the doors,*
> K 120   *There was a noise of wings,* till in short space
> The glowing banquet-room shone with wide-arched grace.

122   *A haunting music,* sole perhaps and lone
         Supportress of *the faery-roof,* made moan
124   Throughout, as fearful the whole charm might *fade.*

What had happened seems clear enough. Whether by the 'subtle servitors' or the *Oberon* sequence or both, Keats was reminded of the tenuous palace 'woven of the rosy eve' (cf. K 124), *from whose* golden *gate* 'float' the immortal virgins, the winged aerial spirits of Titania and Oberon. (Cf. K 119-20.) The daemon king and his 'bride in moonlight's modest ray' appear to welcome the mortal lovers before this diaphanous fairy roof, as the bridal pageant unfolds, accompanied throughout by 'the play of golden harps' and 'songs of that angelic band.' (Cf. K 122-4.) That Keats conceived of Lamia, the 'penanced lady elf' thought to be 'of heavenly progeny,' as of the 'angelic band,' is hinted by her possession of just such subtle servitors and 'viewless servants' and 'faery roof' as Titania's. It is not doubtful how and whence came the winged servitors, who are clearly aerial spirits found in Oberon's daemon-haunted palace.

What is more, in Lamia's palace

> K 125   Fresh carved cedar, *mimicking a glade*
>   Of palm and plantain, *met* from either side,
> 127   *High in the midst,* in honour of the bride.

And Oberon's palace appears thus:

>   Girt with a pleasant *grove,* sweet shades between,   K 125
> W 2   Where *arch*ing rose-*trees meet* in wavy play,
>   Appear'd the *palace* whose alluring ray
> 4   *Bright* thro' the wood's o'ershadowing foliage seen,
>   *Diffus'd* around its *wide*-resplendent *light.*   K 121
>   (OBERON XII, 69)

This is noteworthy because Lamia's faery palace contains the 'glowing banquet-room' that 'shone with wide-arched grace' while Oberon's fairy palace also glows and shines 'with wide-resplendent light' through the arching trees of the forest. Again, in Lamia's palace 'a glade' of trees 'met'; while 'arching . . . trees meet' to form a glade around Oberon's. That Keats derived hints from the abode of Oberon's daemons is even more unmistakable in the light of an earlier reading for line 129 of *Lamia.* Keats rejected that line probably because of rhyming difficulties. But in it he wrote:

... palm and plantain *met from either side*
High in the midst in honour of the bride: W 2
Two palms and two plantains and so on;
On either side *a forest* they . . .

Did he mean to convey 'resemble'? He never finished the line and
crossed it out. But his imagery of the arching trees reveals that he transferred outdoor features of Oberon's forest palace within doors in Lamia's,
that of the 'penanced lady elf.' Into her palace as into Oberon's mortals
soon enter.

The fusion of mortal and immortal, of natural and supernatural, is
further revealed by Keats' next lines in which a 'stream of lamps,' a
reminiscence from Mulciber's palace, illumines (Huon's) 'untasted feast'
with Lamia 'regal drest' beside it. She, moreover, 'mission'd her viewless
servants' and 'faded at self-will' like Titania. And after some further
description of the setting, the guests and Apollonius appear within 'That
royal porch.' *

The furniture appears to have been borrowed in considerable part
from the palace of the queen. Keats wrote

173   Of wealthy lustre was the banquet-room,
           Fill'd with pervading brilliance . . .

He mentions the heavy 'gold of cups and goblets' and tables loaded with
'a feast' and the 'silken couches,' all of which set the guests wondering

198   Whence all this mighty cost and blaze of wealth could spring.

The 'self-resplendent blaze' in the queen's magnificent chambers came
from 'Siam's and Golconda's rifled mines,' and the 'wanton luxury' and
pervading brilliance are just such as Lamia's. Huon's 'enchantress' also
offers him a golden cup and magnificent feast and rests upon her 'damask
couch.'

The queen, moreover, when the youth had been lured into her palace,
appeared first from behind the *splendid golden curtains* of 'airy texture'
with her beautiful slaves about her. And the effect having been calculated
beforehand, when the wine had been offered Huon, the lovely slaves
gyrate voluptuously in a dance

* Cf. *Lamia* II, 131 and 150 ff. with *Paradise Lost* I, 728-31. Also *P. L.* I, 710-12,
with *Oberon* and *Lamia* II, 122-3.

. . . of pow'r the dead to raise,
W 6   Or draw embodied spirits down to gaze.
(OBERON XI, 56)

The queen knew the effects of wine upon the appreciation of feminine
beauty, and she evidently reminded Keats. For he wrote of

                      the gorgeous dyes,
K 200   The space, the splendour of the draperies,
           The roof of awful richness, *nectar*ous cheer,
208   Beautiful slaves, and Lamia's self, appear,
           Now, *when* the wine has done its rosy deed,
210   And every *soul* from human trammels *freed,*   W 6
           No more so strange; for merry wine, sweet wine,
212   *Will make Elysian shades* not too fair, *too divine.*   W 5

Keats rejected the dance, but the supernatural and erotic overtones in the
queen's thought ring through his last line. And it is noteworthy that
Sotheby wrote that 'Not at the gayest feast the *heavens* behold' does
Hebe more seductively reach '*nectar*' to Hercules than the queen reaches
the wine to Huon (XI, 55). 'Lamia's self' is the queen: her slaves
with Hebe's help have become 'Elysian.' *

Lamia II, 217, 239 ff. (p. 223):

   It would seem that in *Lamia* elements from the palace of Oberon's
'angelic band' and from that of the enchantress-queen who 'follows . . .
the infernal fiend' were almost visibly interwoven with features of the
palace of Satan. Lamia's palace is clearly a composite of all three. Yet
Keats seems to have recalled another palace. With the legend guiding
him to a close, he wrote:

           The herd approach'd; each guest, with busy brain,
K 151   Arriving at the portal, gaz'd amain,
           And enter'd marveling.

If Milton's 'hasty multitude Admiring enter'd' recurred to his mind, he
had not forgotten that Huon entered the queen's golden bower marveling.† For the latter (K 208 above) reappears in a moment. And I think

---

* For 'the roof' (K 207) see *Paradise Lost* I, 717.
† *Oberon* XI, 47: 'He startles at the pomp.'

that, even as in the case of *The Eve of St. Agnes,* Huon's second entrance into a palace recalled and blended with his previous one. In *Lamia,* too, revelry, feast, bridal, guests, royal palace appear quite naturally to have recalled the feast in the palace of Rezia's royal father, where the bridal revelry, interrupted so strangely by the 'liege-lord of all the Elves and Fays,' had fed the springs of *St. Agnes* so copiously.

In *Lamia,* just before the 'splendid draperies' and 'beautiful slaves' indicate that we are in the queen's chambers, Keats wrote the magical lines:

> K 199 Soft went the music the soft air along,
>   While fluent Greek a vowel'd under*song*
> 201 Kept up among *the guests,* discoursing low
>   At first, for scarcely was the wine at flow;
> 203 But when the happy *vintage* touch'd their *brains,*
>   *Louder* they talk, and *louder come the strains*
> 205 Of *powerful instruments:*—the gorgeous dyes . . .

And therewith we are in the queen's palace. But in the earlier bridal-banquet scene in *Oberon* there were also guests and wine and powerful instruments, thus:

>   Already cymbals, drums, and fifes resound, K 205
> W 2 With *song* and string the festive palace clangs,
>   The sultan's head already heavy hangs,
> 4 While *vinous* vapors float his *brain* around: K 203
>   Already mirth in *freer* current flows . . .   K 204
>   (OBERON V, 34)

as Huon enters. The similar bridal revelry, instruments, 'vinous,' 'brain,' and 'freer' are significant.

For now 'with uplifted brow in wild amaze Th' admiring *guests* upon the stranger gaze.' Rezia, we know, remains *'tranced* with *fascinated eye'* as she 'still views her dreams [of love] and ever downward bends.' And that is exactly the situation of Madeline at the revelry in *St. Agnes.* Now, a scant dozen lines beyond his 'powerful instruments' Keats wrote in *Lamia:*

> K 217 *baskets* of *bright* osier'd *gold* were brought
>   High as the handles *heap'd,* to suit the thought
> 219 Of every guest . . .

Did he not also write in *St. Agnes* (st. xxxi) of how Porphyro 'these delicates . . . heap'd with glowing hand. On golden dishes and in baskets bright'? Two stanzas earlier in *St. Agnes* the 'boisterous, festive clarion, The kettle-drum and far-heard clarinet'—the powerful instruments—reappear in exactly the same sequence as in *Lamia*. (Cf. W 1.)

The slim thread we have been following is not illusory. Keats was again retracing his earlier steps in Canto v and *St. Agnes*. And since he was, was he interested in Wieland's slaying of the bridegroom at this bridal feast and the 'fascinated eye' and the appearance there of the guardian god of love and the vanishing of that daemon prince? Perhaps the *Lamia* sequence will throw some light upon that.

Immediately after the 'powerful instruments' (K 205) the African queen or 'Lamia's self' appears with the slaves, followed by the baskets (K 217). Then for a few lines Burton guides the shuttle until the famed attack on Apollonius obtrudes. But only until Lycius, who 'scarce saw in all the room another face . . . checking his *love trance*,' realizes that the intruder's *hypnotic eye* is affecting the 'alarmed beauty of the bride.' (Rezia's 'tranced with fascinated eye' shows once more that Keats recalled Canto v.) Then his outcry bringing no response from her whose hand had become *icy*,

> K 261   'Lamia!' he cried—and no soft-toned reply.
>   The many heard, and *the loud revelry*
> 263   Grew hush; the stately music no more breathes;
>   The myrtle sicken'd in a thousand wreaths.
> 265   By faint degrees, voice, lute, and pleasure ceased;
>   A deadly silence step by step increased,
> 267   Until it seem'd *a horrid presence there*,
>   And not a man but felt *the terror in his hair*.

The lute had not previously been mentioned. But it and the queen's voice and the dance of the beautiful slaves ceased suddenly in her palace where there were many wreaths. Did Keats' myrtle sicken as Huon did? But in the other palace, that of Rezia's 'visions of delight,' the revelry ceased for a more terrifying reason.

Lycius delivers his vain imprecation, as a climax terming the malevolent orbs of Apollonius: 'demon eyes.' Then at last, as Burton had told, the lovely enchantress reverts to traditional type and with a scream vanishes. But unlike Burton's hero, Keats' Lycius falls dead, the bridegroom at his own wedding feast.

In that revised conclusion and the bestowing of demon eyes upon Apollonius and in the sinister overtones above (K 267-8), the composite nature of *Lamia* once again is apparent, and there are clues further clarifying its machinery and Keats' intention. The love trance of Lycius and the boisterous music and drunken guests unmistakably reveal that he had recalled the wedding feast in *Oberon*. At that revelry, so vital in the genesis of *St. Agnes,* Keats had seen *the terror of the wedding guests caused by the visible slaying of the hated bridegroom.* The horrid presence (cf. K 267-8) of the blood-spurting torso before their very eyes affected the guests as if

> . . . the *dread* visage of Medusa fell
> Swift flashing on the sight . . .
> . . . when Perseus shakes the viper *hair.** K 268

Now traditionally Lamia had been a viper present at a wedding feast. And Wieland's use of that image in his scene of terror evidently haunted Keats' inner eye, led him to see 'a horrid presence there' and to feel 'the terror in his hair.' The *Oberon* scene probably helped bring about the death of Lycius. For Keats also seems to have remembered how

> The jocund blood that warmed each merry guest   † bar
> Suspends its *frozen* course,

when Rezia's suitor is slain. (Lamia's hand becomes icy.) And 'Like *ghosts*' they *shiver* from their seats. (Lycius sinks 'beside the aching ghost.') At that same fateful wedding feast where the bridegroom is slain, as Keats knew, the daemon king appears.† He is the Love who hovered above Lamia's chamber door and who had some causal connection with the ruination of love in a palace. 'For all this came a ruin.' His preternatural eyes are suggestively recalled by the 'demon eyes' of the malevolent Apollonius who, like Oberon, would not have the youth

---

* *Oberon* v, 37. Cf. 'Of all the Gods, whose *dreadful* images' (K 279) with this 'dread visage of Medusa . . . Perseus.' Did Keats change the mythical figures to gods, generalizing the hint?

† When Madeline in *St. Agnes* 'panted all akin to spirits of the air and visions wide.' Keats had used this scene before.

succumb to the sensual joys that seduce and destroy. Such was 'the moral' to which Keats alluded.

Oberon, Otho the Great, and *Lamia* (p. 227):

Bearing in mind the fact that we first see Lamia the 'gorgeous snake' in conjunction with the 'prosperous woods' and 'king Oberon's . . . sceptre,' let us turn to the forest in Canto II of *Oberon,* where the power of the sceptre or wand is revealed. On the outskirts of the enchanted forest, against which the superstitious squire had warned him, Huon had seen the herd of harts and hinds with large fair eyes that seemed to weep. (Cf. the eyes of Lamia in serpent's guise.) And the squire had explained that these beasts had been

> '*Men, once* as good as we—in *form* the same—
> Heaven knows in what wild skin our human frame
> Shall be ere dawn array'd to make the demon sport!'
> (OBERON II, II)

The author of *Endymion* had already taken hints for the denizens of Circe's wood from this. But in *Lamia* the 'gorgeous snake' says:

> 'I was a *woman,* let me have *once* more
> A woman's shape . . .
> Give me my woman's *form* . . .'

a . . the echoes are not illusory.

Now the squire, gratefully garrulous, it will be remembered, expatiated upon demon lore, if not quite accurately about Oberon. He told Huon this: Although '*demon, elf,* or sprite' generally flee at 'dayspring,'

> '. . . the strange sprite that here delights to play
> His woodland pranks, unlike their race, methinks,
> But *like mere mortal* lives, and eats, and drinks,
> And open court maintains, and walks at open day!'
> (II, 22)

(So too does Lamia, 'lady elf, demon's mistress,' when her woman's form has been restored and beneath her faery roof she commands her 'viewless servants' and 'subtle servitors' of the sound 'of wings.') But almost immediately after Huon learned all this, in the same enchanted forest as that of the bridal pageant he saw the floating fairy palace for

the first time and then the daemon king's self, who pursued the terrified
wanderers with a tempest, while

> . . . heard from time to time amid the storm,
> The *gentle whisper* of th' *aërial* form
> Breath'd forth a lovely tone . . .
>
> (II, 30)

(Above the forest when her woman's shape has been restored we hear
Lamia: 'in the air, her new voice luting soft.') A moment later, when
he confronts Huon, Oberon holds the lily wand or sceptre in his hand.
And 'lovely as he was, on all around Strange horror stole, for stern the
fairy frowned.' And forthwith certain hypocrites are constrained to
whirl in the mad dance.

But if the malevolent as well as the beneficent powers of the daemon
king were visible so early, he also told Huon at that meeting the equivalent of what Glaucus told Endymion, that he was 'a youth by *heavenly
power* loved and led'—who would retain Oberon's favor, as he had since
childhood, so long as his heart remained pure. And he added these
significant words:

>   '*Thy heart is pure, no baseness taints* thy blood—
> W 2   Thy ways are straight: where honor, duty call,
>   Thou ask'st not flesh and blood—no fears appal—
> 4   Thou in thyself confid'st when proofs assail:
>   So that my favor, knight, can never fail:
> 6   *On spotted souls* alone *my vengeful torments fall!*'
>
> (OBERON II, 40)

In other words, the squire notwithstanding, the grievous torments of
this daemon, however horrible, are not in sport but in divine earnest.
He is the 'guardian god' of love and purity whose vengeful torments
fall 'on spotted souls alone' and who can transform sinful men into
beasts and penance even his mistress-queen. In *Lamia,* let us remember,
he appears both as Love—who hovers threateningly above the inmates
of the palace, 'of sweet sin' and 'more grievous torment,' with whose
ruin he is somehow connected—and as Hermes who hears the mournful
voice in the sacred isle, and who transforms and conveys the penanced
one to that palace, where 'proofs assail' the youth Lycius.

This part of 'the moral' of the 'tale from faery land' illuminates *Lamia* further, it seems to me. And the powers of the daemon king, his punitive power over 'spotted souls' and powers of shape-shifting, throw a good deal of light upon Lamia's past. For she was 'a woman once'; she appears as 'gorgeous snake'—'some penanced lady elf, some demon's mistress'—who has obviously been penanced by transformation into a serpent; and she would have the god restore her human shape because she loves a youth. The penance of Lamia and its reason are related to Oberon's powers and curse. The mystery is quite dispelled by a scene in the work that Keats wrote synchronously with *Lamia,* namely, *Otho the Great.*

Although four acts of that play, designed as a pot-boiler, were written in collaboration with Charles Armitage Brown, we know from him that Keats ' "wrote the 5th act in accordance with his own views." ' * Some of those views, unmistakably evoked by Oberon's words in the enchanted forest, throw a clear light upon the channel in which Keats' mind was faring in this period when also *Lamia* was being composed. The reason why Lamia had been transformed is hinted clearly and startlingly, it seems to me, by Auranthe in Act v, scene ii, of *Otho the Great,* to which it is essential that we now turn for a moment.

In that pervasively Shakespearean tragedy, Prince Ludolph, reconciled with his father the Emperor, has at last been granted his dearest wish, the hand of Auranthe, sister of Conrad, Duke of Franconia. But hardly have the vows been exchanged than the impetuous prince discovers that Auranthe is *a wanton deceiver who had vowed falsely* and long been the *mistress* of Albert. (On the occasion of the banishment-in-penance of Titania, let us remember, Oberon had cursed just this sort of wanton whose vows and tears alike are false and whose evil passions are those of the 'bosom snake'—and the 'wily snake,' the African queen, of 'Love in a palace.') But Auranthe, threatened with exposure, on her wedding night flees into *the forest* after Albert, whom her satanic brother in treachery there mortally wounds at cost of his own life. Ludolph, informed of their flight, had pursued his faithless wife and her lover into the forest only to lose them. And he says:

* Cf. Brown's Memoir, Houghton-Crewe Collection, as cited in Finney, op. cit. II. 656.

'Escap'd—fled—*vanish'd melted into air*—
She's gone—I cannot catch her! no revenge!'
(OTHO THE GREAT V, i, 24-5)

Then suddenly he hears Auranthe shriek.* Discovering Albert dying,
he sees Auranthe rush in to her lover and embrace him, and thus discovers all: 'Ha! There! there!—He is the paramour!' Albert, long since
conscience-stricken, wishes death to be speedy, to release him from the
many 'horrors.' Ludolph, however, vents his wrath in phrases which,
through their irony, are incomparably enlightening. This is what he says:

'Auranthe! what can he mean?
What horrors? Is it not a joyous time?
Am I not married to a paragon
"Of personal beauty and un*tainted soul*"?   W 1
A blushing fair-eyed *purity!* A *sylph,*
Whose snowy timid *hand has* never *sin'd*
Beyond a flower pluck'd, mild as itself?
Albert, you do insult my bride—your *mistress*—
To talk of *horrors on our wedding-night!*'
(OTHO THE GREAT V, ii, 19-27)

(Oberon's words to Huon in the forest, and the overtones and the conclusion of Lamia's story.†)

Albert having vainly pleaded not guilty, Ludolph proceeds:

'Hear you, he pleads not guilty!
You are not? or, if so, what matters it?
You have escap'd me, *free as the* dusk *air,*
Hid *in the forest,* safe from *my revenge;*
I cannot catch you! You should laugh at me,
Poor cheated Ludolph! Make the forest *hiss*
With jeers at me! You tremble—faint at once,
You will come to again. O *cockatrice,* ‡
I have you! Whither wander *those fair eyes*
To entice the devil to your help, that he

* Cf. Lamia who vanishes, melts into air, disappears after her metamorphosis
(I, 165-6).
† The wedding night of horrors in Lamia's 'palace of *sweet sin.*' And she is a
'penanced lady elf, some demon's mistress' like the sinful 'sylph' and 'mistress'
Auranthe.
‡ Serpent.

> *May change you* to a spider, so to crawl
> Into some cranny to escape *my wrath?'*
> (v, ii, 29-40)

This imagery in a work written at the same time as *Lamia* and echoing phrases from it * sets in high relief the weird pattern of punitive transformation. Here, more transparent than when interfused in the legend frame of *Lamia,* is evidence of the *Oberon* impact: in these shifting precincts of the forest, the enchanted forest, the 'prosperous woods.' In this forest lurks the answer to the riddle of the transformed Lamia. For Auranthe (wanton, deceiver, faithless wife—like Oberon's accurst 'bosom snake' on whom 'vengeful torments fall') explicitly is a *tainted* soul who has *sinned.* And she too is likened first to a *sylph* 'free as the air' (like Titania-Lamia who is 'some penanced lady elf'), and then (like Lamia) to *a serpent* to be *transformed* by that other 'demon's self' Satan. And lest it escape us that Ludolph has spoken with the vengeful wrath of Oberon, the 'guardian god' of love; lest we overheard the echoes, as Albert groans and dies, the tormented bridegroom, who is himself soon to die, dispels the last shred of mystery as he says: 'There goes *a spotted soul!'*

The daemon king in the forest of the transformed men, whom he does not transform in sport, told Huon not only 'thy heart is *pure,* no baseness *taints* thy blood' (cf. Ludolph's ironic 'untainted soul,' 'fair-eyed purity'); but also that he possessed punitive power: 'On *spotted souls* alone my vengeful torments fall.' These torments include transformation. And the vengeful Ludolph echoes Oberon's very words. This once again reveals that during the weeks in which *Lamia* was also being composed Keats' thoughts were revolving upon 'the moral' and machinery of *Oberon.* The play shows that Keats was preoccupied with Oberon's powers of inflicting 'grievous torment' and transformation as penance for impurity and sensuality, and with his curse upon the sensual 'joys that seduce' and their high-priestess, the deceitful woman who is the 'bosom snake.'

Thus while in *Oberon* it is the 'wily snake' and African queen, in *Otho the Great* it is Auranthe, the wanton and 'cockatrice,' who is the embodiment of that curse. *Lamia,* on the other hand, is far more complex. The 'gorgeous snake' and 'regal drest' Lamia is closely related to

---

* Cf. 'melted into air,' 'eyes . . . so fair,' 'free as the air' etc., all in Part I of *Lamia.*

the African queen. But Ludolph's allusions—'a Sylph, whose . . . hand has . . . sin'd,' a 'cockatrice' whose 'fair eyes' would entice the demon prince Satan to 'change' her shape—this imagery coincides with the pattern of *Lamia*. It shows that Auranthe is also related to Keats' conception of Lamia, the penanced elf transformed into snake who persuades another daemon prince to change her shape. In her resemblance both to the queen and to Lamia, Auranthe corroborates this: the reason that Keats came to conceive of Lamia as penanced lies in Oberon's curse on the snake-like African queen, Lamia's human and regal prototype; and the nature of the penance lies in the serpent and lamia traditions and in Oberon's powers, of punitive transformation, over spotted souls.

Now the sin that evoked the curse upon the queen and Auranthe is clearly sexual and ethical. But the complexity of Lamia's nature—of her who is part sensual and mortal African queen and part pure and heavenly Titania, part 'real woman' and part symbol of a psychic power—this complexity makes the cause of Lamia's penance more difficult to understand. Sensuality is hinted in Keats' phrases 'sweet sin' and 'Love, jealous grown of so complete a pair,' in Oberon's words 'proofs assail' and curse upon 'joys that seduce,' and in the queen's 'bewitched . . . sense,' but that cause became perplexed in the course of the evolution of Lamia's composite nature. That her 'sweet sin' is against love is clear. But this 'love' is no longer sexual alone: it was conceived, I think, as in the 'pleasure thermometer' in *Endymion,* as the highest form or the Love divine, as a spiritual ideal against which also Glaucus of the 'serpent-skin of woe' had sinned. The sensuous but gentle Lamia would seem to have sinned against a love that is ideal, spiritual, and daemonic. The sexual and literal conception in *Otho* gave way before the spiritual and symbolic in *Lamia*. Its heroine, of 'heavenly progeny,' became the symbol evidently of sensuous beauty and sensations and intuition, which, if they sinned at all, sinned against reality in the eyes of reason and against a youth's ambitions of enduring fame in the eyes of a philosopher.

'Sweet sin' is a motif derived from 'the moral' of the 'tale from faery land' to which Keats so frankly alluded. But it is a motif lost in the larger design and in the manifold symbolism which enriched but beclouded *Lamia* the daemonic romance.

Echoes of *Undine* in *Lamia* (p. 236):

Keats spent the summer of 1819 at Shanklin and Winchester working on *Otho* and *Lamia* and had finished both by 5 September. After staying in the latter place from 13 August to 10 September, he returned to London to see Mr. Abbey in George's behalf and stayed from September eleventh to fifteenth. On the eleventh he met Woodhouse at Taylor and Hessey's and the next morning, Sunday the twelfth, he had breakfast with Woodhouse at the Temple. During their talk Keats must have spoken of *Undine*. For after returning to Winchester, he wrote to Woodhouse on the twenty-first:

'And *don't forget* to tell Reynolds of the fairy tale *Undine*. Ask him if he has read any of the American Brown's novels that Hazlitt speaks so much of—I have read one call'd *Wieland*—very powerful—something like Godwin. Between Schiller and Godwin. A domestic prototype of S[c]hiller's Armenian.' *

Among other things, this letter seems to reveal an interesting instance of association.

I suspect that Keats' mind went from *Undine* to Brockden Brown to Schiller by some such train of thought as this: fairy tale, Undine, water-spirit; subject to daemon king, Oberon, Wieland; (*Wieland*) the American novel like Godwin and (Wieland's contemporary) Schiller. Some such association must have been inevitable in the light of Keats' intense absorption in *Oberon* and its daemonology throughout 1819.

Besides its testimony as to Keats' familiarity with other works of German literature than *Oberon,* however, this letter is peculiarly pertinent in conjunction with *Lamia.* For Keats mentioned *Undine* (first translated in 1818) a very short time after finishing his own daemonic romance, whose genesis was so vitally linked with *Oberon.* And *Lamia* contains a considerable number of elements which appear to be reminiscences of *Undine,* particularly aspects of daemonology that supplement the lore Keats had long since found poetically embodied in *Oberon.*

We know that Wieland's Titania left many traces in *Lamia* and was vital to the genesis of Lamia's protean nature. But in *Oberon* the penanced elfin queen is rather a shadowy figure who stands out in no such relief and bold individuality as her awful consort. Consequently there

* *Letters*, p. 389. Italics mine.

are facets of Lamia's nature which may well be the result of the modification of Titania by the lesser daemon princess, the water-spirit Undine.*

Among others, the latter possesses these traits: She is *'dainty'* (p. 17), and *'wild* and untamed' (p. 28); yet (p. 52) *'timid* in spite of her wildness.' (Lycius bends Lamia's 'wild and timid nature to his aim.') And the knight's proposal of marriage finds Undine 'grave, thoughtful, gently trembling' (p. 59).

With respect to Lamia's 'sorrows soft and new' after her love for the mortal Lycius has been consummated, one is reminded of Undine's winning a soul and of her delineation of the nature of Paracelsian elemental spirits. Her explanation comes in the wake of her changed nature, which, originally wild, wilful, and childlike, becomes 'mild and *gentle* as an angel' after the wedding.

'Thou shouldst know, my beloved,' she tells her lover, 'that there exist in the elements beings not very unlike you men, and who yet seldom let themselves be seen by you. The wondrous *salamanders* glisten and sport in the flames; the rough malicious *gnomes* dwell deep in the earth; *the woods are haunted by spirits which are of the air;* while the *far*-spread race of water-spirits live in lakes and *streams* and brooks.'

After describing the crystal vaults and coral gardens and noble ruins in the home of her kindred, she tells of the innermost nature of elemental spirits:

'We have no souls; the element animates us; it *obeys us* as long as we live.'

(The words of Lycius to Lamia soon after meeting her are significant: 'To thy far wishes will thy streams obey.' *Lamia* 1, 262.) And Undine continues:

'It even scatters us as soon as we die; and we are gay, without care, as are nightingales and golden fish . . .'

(Did the latter comparison remind Keats of his own nymph and her fish in *Endymion,* whose colors he bestowed upon Lamia, the gorgeous

---

* All my references are to *Undine:* a Romance from the German of De La Motte Fouque. New York, Phinney, Blakeman and Mason, 1860. The phrases I have cited from this version, substantially reappear in the earliest translation accessible: Philadelphia, E. Littell, 1824. This edition, according to B. Q. Morgan (*A Bibliog. of Germ. Lit. in Engl. Transl.,* Madison, 1922, p. 114), is 'probably a reprint' of the first English edition of 1818.

snake, who seemed some 'penanced lady elf'?) And from personal experience, as it were, Undine explains:

'A soul can be obtained by one of our kind only by a union of deepest
love with one of your race.' It is thus that 'she *gained the sorrows* of those
gifted with souls' (p. 74).

There was yet another passage in *Undine* which must have fascinated
Keats. After the wedding, Sir Huldbrand is haunted by fearful thoughts
that he 'had married a fairy, or else a wicked mocking being of the
world of spirits.' And in the wedding night he is troubled by 'strange
fearful dreams of spectres who, grinning mysteriously, strove to disguise
themselves as fair women, and of fair *women* who suddenly appeared
with faces of serpents' (p. 67).
Did this have anything to do with Keats' writing:

> Her head was serpent, but ah, bitter-sweet!
> She had a woman's mouth with all its pearls complete?

Keats also wrote of Lamia's 'sorrows soft and new' and of the 'tender-
personed Lamia' and her 'soft-toned reply.' And he wrote that Philosophy
would 'empty the haunted air and gnomed mine' and spoke of 'Haunters
of cavern, lake, and waterfall' and Lamia's appearing to be 'a Naiad of
the rivers' or that 'greenest woods be thy domain.' And they are her
domain: the 'prosperous woods' linked with Oberon's sceptre, and 'a
forest' near the shore of Titania's sacred isle, where the penanced lady
elf first appears as serpent. I suspect that the hints as to the nature of
her domain were forthright in both instances: that Keats conceived of
his Lamia as part aerial and part water spirit.*
The echoes of *Undine* are many. And Keats' recommendation of that
fairy tale coincides with the composition period of *Lamia*. Thus in view
of all the evidence, it is likely, I think, that Lycius' suspicion that Lamia
is a 'Naiad of the rivers' is well founded. Keats' simultaneous reference
to *Undine* and Wieland may well be a clue as to how the charming
water spirit and her 'sorrows new' came to supplement Titania's and

---

* It is noteworthy, too, that in the composite *Song of Four Fairies* of April 1819,
the salamander appeared together with three other elemental spirits of earth, air,
and water, and an echo from the *Midsummer Night's Dream,* and the floating
palace in Wieland's enchanted forest—all commingled.

the queen's sorrows and the daemonology Keats learned from *Oberon*.*

In Burton, Lamia is still an evil phantasm whose essential form is that of a serpent. In Keats' romance, on the other hand, that is explicitly not so. Essentially a woman in form, even as Undine says, his Lamia is a being of quite another sort, whose beauty and charm, devotion and mild submissiveness—combining, as it were, the gentleness of Titania with the wildness and timidity of Undine—quite won Keats' sympathy. That is something the traditional lamia and the African queen alone could never have done. Therein, perhaps, lies another reason for his violent outbreak against Apollonius. That philosopher does 'empty the haunted air' and overlooks Lamia's gentle nature: he destroys the delicate composite which was the poet's dream.

* It is possible, too, that the death of Undine's mortal lover, the fickle Huldbrand, on his wedding night, helped suggest the death of Lycius.

❧ APPENDIX VI ❧

(The Overlapping Patterns)

Not only did Keats explore every canto of *Oberon;* he revisited most, while in some he wandered with more or less regularity. Below appear the *Oberon* cantos and his own poems, arranged chronologically, in which they left traces major or minor. The major ones and such as were vital to genesis appear in capitals. Cantos II, III, V, VIII, XI, and XII were evidently most provocative, while VIII (hermitage) bewitched him from first to last. The magnitude of the *Endymion* saturation stands out, and also the odd overlappings.

CANTO I: *Endymion* III

    II: *To Some Ladies,* 'Shell St.,' *I Stood, End.* III, *Otho, Lamia*

    III: *'SHELL STANZAS'* (Mathew's LINES), *Sonnet* V, *to Clarke, End.* III

    IV: *End.* IV, *Hyperion, St. Agnes*

    V: *End.* IV, 'Hush hush' [?], ST. AGNES, *La Belle Dame, Lamia, Cap and Bells*

    VI: *End.* IV, *St. Agnes, La Belle Dame, Lamia, Otho, Cap and Bells*

    VII: *The Poet, End.* I, II, IV, *St. Agnes, La Belle Dame, Lamia*

    VIII: *To Some Ladies* (Mathew's LINES), *Epistle to Mathew, To My Brother George, to Clarke, Sonnet* V, *Calidore,* SLEEP AND POETRY, *I Stood Tip-toe,* ENDYMION I, II, III, IV, *Mermaid Tavern, Bards of Passion, St. Agnes, La Belle Dame,* ODE TO PSYCHE, ODE ON A GRECIAN URN, *Ode to a Nightingale, Lamia, Fall of Hyperion*

    IX: *End.* IV, *Lamia*

    X: *End.* II, THE POET, *Ode on Indolence,* LAMIA

    XI: *End.* II, III, *St. Agnes,* LAMIA, *Cap and Bells*

    XII: *Epistle to Mathew, To My Brother George, End.* III, *Song of Four Fairies, La Belle Dame, Lamia,* CAP AND BELLS

Some of the overlappings, as we saw in connection with the evidence, were the result of synchronous composition. Many seem to have been caused by associations of ideas and pictures, as his mind momentarily retraced earlier paths. (The sinful consummation of love, for example, occurs in Canto vii and explains the three last poems' overlapping with the tale of Glaucus, as they did again in Cantos xi-xii, the temptation scene.) Some doubtless were fortuitous, though they emphasize what attracted Keats. But in general, chronology and affinities of theme seem to have been the most significant determinants in the pattern; these and the hermit in Canto viii, who dominates and transcends every other element in the romance. His presence and that of the penanced Titania and the childbirth scene in the elfin grot explain the roster of 19 poems that bear traces, four of them vital, of Canto viii.

But Keats also saw much in the enchanted forest where Oberon's powers are first revealed (Canto ii). And he profited notably from the curse (vi) and from the episode of the queen (xi-xii) and the iridescent scene of the return to the daemonic palace (Canto xii). How whole-heartedly he was drawn to the romance is indicated by his use of every Canto. And the endurance of his fascination is shown by his return to the same passages at the end of his career, which he had explored in the beginning.

Adams, John Quincy, *Oberon, a Poetical Romance* in Twelve Books. Trans. from the German of Wieland . . . by . . . Edited by A. B. Faust, N. Y., F. S. Crofts, 1940.

Beattie, William, *Life and Letters of Thomas Campbell* (3 vols.), London, Moxon, 1849.

Beyer, W. W., 'Coleridge, Wieland's *Oberon* and the *Ancient Mariner*,' *Review of English Studies*, London, vol. xv, No. 60 (Oct. 1939). 'Coleridge, Wieland's *Oberon* and the *Wanderings of Cain*,' ibid., vol. xvi, No. 63 (July 1940).

Biese, Alfred, *Deutsche Litteraturgeschichte*, Muenchen, Beck, 1907.

Blunden, Edmund, 'Keats' Friend Mathew,' in *English*, the Magazine of the English Association, London, 1936, vol. i.

Bruford, W. H., *Germany in the 18th Century:* the Social Background of the Literary Revival, Cambridge, At the University Press, 1935.

Bush, Douglas, 'Notes on Keats' Reading,' in *PMLA*, vol. i, No. 3 (Sept. 1935).

Carlyle, Thomas, *Life of Schiller*, 2nd ed., London, Chapman and Hall, 1845.

Clarke, Charles and Mary Cowden, *Recollections of Writers*, London, 1878.

Coleridge, H. N., *Specimens of the Table-Talk of the Late S. T. Coleridge*, London, John Murray, 1835.

Coleridge, S. T., *Biographia Literaria*, London, J. M. Dent, 1930.

Colles, H. C. (ed.). See Grove, Sir George.

Colvin, Sidney, *John Keats*, 3rd ed., London, Macmillan, 1920.

Colwell, W. A., 'The First English Translation of Wieland's *Oberon*,' in *MLN*, vol. xxii (1907).

De Stael-Holstein, Mme. the Baroness, *Germany*. Trans. from the French. In 3 vols., London, John Murray, 1813.

Drayton (Michael), *The Works of* . . . ed. by J. William Hebel, Oxford, Shakespeare Head Press, 1931.

Duentzer, Heinrich, *Erläuterungen zu Wielands Oberon*, 2nd ed., Leipzig, Ed. Wartig, 1880.

Eckermann, J. P., *Gespraeche mit Goethe,* Leipzig, Brockhaus, 1883.

Finney, Claude Lee, *The Evolution of Keats's Poetry* (2 vols.), Cambridge, Harvard University Press, 1936.

Fouque, De La Motte, *Undine:* a Romance from the German of . . . N. Y., Phinney, Blakeman and Mason, 1860.

Francke, Kuno, *A History of German Literature,* N. Y., Henry Holt and Co., 1931.

Genest, John, *Some Account of the English Stage from 1660 to 1830,* Bath, H. E. Carrington, 1832.

[Goethe, J. W. von], *Goethe Jahrbuch,* ix, Frankfurt, 1888.

Gooch, G. P., *Germany and the French Revolution,* N. Y., Longmans, Green and Co., 1920.

Greenwood, Alice D., 'English Prose in the xvth Century' in *Cambridge History of English Literature,* N. Y., Macmillan Co., 1939, vol. ii.

[Grove, Sir George], *Grove's Dictionary of Music and Musicians,* ed. by H. C. Colles (3rd ed.), London, Macmillan Co., 1929.

Gundolf, Friedrich, *Shakespeare und der deutsche Geist,* Berlin, Bondi, 1920.

Hazlitt, William, *The Spirit of the Age,* London, J. M. Dent, 1939.

Hettner, Heinrich, *Geschichte der deutschen Litteratur im 18. Jahrhundert,* Leipzig, Paul List, 1929.

Hewlett, Dorothy, *Adonais,* N. Y., Bobbs-Merrill Co., 1938.

Jaeck, E. G., *Mme de Staël and the Spread of German Literature,* London, Oxford University Press, 1915.

Keats, John, *The Letters of* . . . ed. by Maurice Buxton Forman, 2nd ed., with revisions etc., Humphrey Milford, Oxford University Press, 1935.

Poems, ed. by E. de Sélincourt (5th ed.), London, Methuen, 1936.

Poetical Works, ed. by H. W. Garrod, Oxford, Clarendon Press, 1939.

Klee, Gotthold, 'Wielands Leben und Werke' in *Wielands Werke,* (4 Bde.), Leipzig und Wien, Bibliographisches Institut, [1900?], vol. i.

Koch, Max, 'Christoph Martin Wieland' in *Allgemeine Deutsche Biographie,* Leipzig, 1897, vol. xlii.

Das Quellenverhaeltnis von Wielands Oberon, Marburg, 1880.

Latham, Minor, *The Elizabethan Fairies,* the Fairies of Folklore and the Fairies of Shakespeare, N. Y., Columbia University Press, 1930.

Lowell, Amy, *John Keats,* Boston and New York, Houghton Mifflin, 1929.

Lowes, John Livingston, *The Road to Xanadu*, Boston, Houghton Mifflin, 1930.

Meisnest, F. W., 'Wieland's Translation of Shakespeare' in *MLR*, vol. x, 1914.

Milton, John, *The Poetical Works of* . . . London, Oxford University Press, 1925.

Murry, John Middleton, *Studies in Keats*, New and Old, 2nd ed., London, Oxford University Press, 1939.

Keats and Shakespeare, London, Oxford University Press, 1935.

Nadler, Josef, *Litteraturgeschichte der deutschen Staemme und Landschaften*, 2nd ed., Regensburg, Jos. Habbel, 1924.

Nethercot, Arthur H., *The Road to Tryermaine*, Chicago, University Press, 1939.

Ridley, M. R., *Keats' Craftsmanship*, Oxford, Clarendon Press, 1933.

Robertson, J. G., *History of German Literature*, N. Y., Putnam, 1902.

'Shakespeare on the Continent' in *Cambridge History of English Literature*, 1929, vol. v.

Schroeder, F. W., *Wielands Agathon und die Anfaenge des modernen Bildungsromans*, Koenigsberg, 1904.

Shakespeare, William, *The Tragedies, Comedies, Historical Plays* . . . *of* . . . London, J. M. Dent, 1924 (3 vols.).

Shelley, Mary W., *Frankenstein*, London, J. M. Dent, 1941.

Sotheby, William, *Oberon, a Poem from the German of Wieland*. In Two Volumes, London, Cadell and Davies, 1798.

Spenser, Edmund, *The Poetical Works of* . . . London, Oxford University Press, 1937.

Stadler, Ernst, 'Wielands Shakespeare' in *Quellen und Forschungen zur Sprach- und Kulturgeschichte der Germanischen Völker*, No. 107, Strasburg, 1910.

Steinberger, Julius, *Bibliographie der Wieland Übersetzungen*, Göttingen, Selbstverlag, 1930.

Stockley, V., *German Literature as Known in England: 1750-1830*, London, Routledge, 1929.

Stokoe, F. W., *German Influence in the English Romantic Period*, Cambridge, At the University Press, 1926.

Thorpe, Clarence De Witt, *The Mind of John Keats*, N. Y., Oxford University Press, 1926.

Vaughan, C. E., *The Romantic Revolt*, N. Y., Charles Scribner's Sons, 1907.

White, Newman Ivey, *Shelley* (2 vols.), N. Y., Knopf, 1940.

Wiegler, Paul, *Geschichte der deutschen Litteratur,* Berlin, Ullstein, 1930.

Wieland, [C. M.], *Gesammelte Schriften,* Herausgegeben von der . . . Preussischen Akademie der Wissenschaften, Berlin, Weidmannsche Buchhandlung, 1935, Band xiii.

Werke, Leipzig, J. G. Göschen, 1828, vols. 50-53.

Zeiger, Theodor, *Beiträge zur Geschichte des Einflusses der neueren deutschen Litteratur auf die Englische,* Berlin, Duencker, 1901.

❧ INDEX ❧

Entries in capital letters are the titles of the principal works mentioned in the text.